Ideas Across Cultures

HARVARD EAST ASIAN MONOGRAPHS
150

IDEAS ACROSS CULTURES
Essays on Chinese Thought
in Honor of Benjamin I. Schwartz

edited by
PAUL A. COHEN
and MERLE GOLDMAN

Published by COUNCIL ON EAST ASIAN STUDIES, HARVARD UNI-
VERSITY and distributed by HARVARD UNIVERSITY PRESS, Cambridge (Massachusetts) and London   1990

The Council on East Asian Studies at Harvard University publishes a monograph series and, through the Fairbank Center for East Asian Research and the Reischauer Institute of Japanese Studies, administers research projects designed to further scholarly understanding of China, Japan, Korea, Vietnam, Inner Asia, and adjacent areas.

Library of Congress Cataloging-in-Publication Data

Ideas across cultures : essays on Chinese thought in honor of Benjamin
    I. Schwarz / edited by Paul A. Cohen and Merle Goldman.
        p. cm.
    Includes bibliographical references.
    ISBN 0-674-44225-3
    1. China—Intellectual life.   2. Schwartz, Benjamin Isadore.
I. Cohen, Paul A.   II. Goldman, Merle.
DS721.I34   1990
951—dc20   90-33239
                                                        CIP

To Benjamin Schwartz,
whose example of the engaged intellect—
rigorous and temperate, opinionated but undogmatic—
has been an inspiration to generations of scholars and students.

Contents

Contributors

David Arkush specializes in modern Chinese intellectual history at Indiana University. His works include *Fei Xiaotong and Sociology in Revolutionary China* (Council on East Asian Studies, Harvard University, 1981), and "Orthodoxy and Heterodoxy in Twentieth-Century Chinese Peasant Proverbs," in K. C. Liu, ed., *Orthodoxy in Late Imperial China* (University of California Press, 1990). Most recently, he is editor and translator, with Leo O. Lee, of *Land Without Ghosts; Chinese Impressions of America from the Mid-Nineteenth Century to the Present* (University of California Press, 1989).

Hao Chang is Professor of History at Ohio State University. His works in Chinese include *T'an Ssu-t'ung: An Intellectual Portrait* (Taibei: Linking Press, 1988) and *Essays on Our Times* (Taibei: Linking Press, 1989). In English, he is the author of *Liang Ch'i-ch'ao and Intellectual Transition in China (1890–1907)* (Harvard University Press, 1971) and *Chinese Intellectuals in Crisis, Search for Order and Meaning, 1890–1911* (University of California Press, 1989).

Paul A. Cohen is Edith Stix Wasserman Professor of Asian Studies and History, Wellesley College, and an Associate of the Fairbank Center for East Asian Research, Harvard University. He has written widely on nineteenth- and twentieth-century Chinese history and is currently at work on a study of myth, history, and experience as alternative constructions of the past, using the Boxer movement as his main case study. His most recent book is *Discovering History in China: American Historical Writing on the Recent Chinese Past* (Columbia University Press, 1984).

Merle Goldman, Professor of History at Boston University and an Associate of the Fairbank Center for East Asian Research, Harvard University, is the author of *Literary Dissent in Communist China* (Harvard University Press, 1967) and *China's Intellectuals: Advise and Dissent* (Harvard University Press, 1981). She is the editor of three books relating to Chinese intellectuals and is currently completing a book on China's democratic elite.

Germaine A. Hoston, a specialist in Chinese and Japanese politics, is Associate Professor of Political Science at The Johns Hopkins University. She has written *Marxism and the Crisis of Development in Prewar Japan* (Princeton University Press, 1986) and articles in numerous scholarly journals. Currently, she is completing a revision of her doctoral dissertation (Harvard 1981) to be published as *Marxism and the National Question in China and Japan* (Princeton University Press, forthcoming).

Jeffrey C. Kinkley is the author of *The Odyssey of Shen Congwen* (Stanford University Press, 1987), the translator of Hsiao Ch'ien's (Xiao Qian's) memoirs, *Traveller Without a Map* (London: Hutchinson, 1990), and editor of *After Mao: Chinese Literature and Society, 1978–1981* (Council on East Asian Studies, Harvard University, 1985). Currently he is studying Chinese detective stories and coediting, with Helmut Martin, a book of autobiographical essays by modern Chinese authors. He is Associate Professor of History at St. John's University in New York City.

Leo Ou-fan Lee is an expert on contemporary Chinese literature. He is Professor of East Asian Languages and Civilizations at the University of Chicago and Director of the Center for East Asian Studies. His books include *The Romantic Generation of Modern Chinese Writers* (Harvard University Press, 1973). He is especially interested in Lu Xun and has written a book, *Voices from the Zen House* (Indiana University Press, 1987), and edited a conference volume, *Lu Xun and His Legacy* (University of California Press, 1985).

Thomas A. Metzger is the author of *The Internal Organization of Ch'ing Bureaucracy: Legal, Normative, and Communication Aspects* (Harvard University Press, 1973) and *Escape from Predicament: Neo-Confucianism and China's Evolving Political Culture* (Columbia University Press, 1977). His current research is on ancient and twentieth-century Chinese intellectual history. He is Professor of Chinese History at the University of California, San Diego.

Andrew J. Nathan is Professor of Political Science at Columbia University. He is the author of *Chinese Democracy* (Knopf, 1985) and *China's Crisis* (Columbia University Press, 1990). He is also the co-author with R. Randle Edwards and Louis Henkin of *Human Rights in Contemporary China* (Columbia University Press, 1986).

Don C. Price, author of *Russia and the Roots of the Chinese Revolution* (Harvard University Press, 1974), is Professor of History at the University of California, Davis. Problems of biography and personal history and the relations between the traditional cultural legacy and modern political thought, with a particular focus on problems of liberalism and democracy, are his current research interests. He is presently working on a biography of Song Jiaoren.

Hoyt Cleveland Tillman, Professor of History at Arizona State University, has written *Utilitarian Confucianism: Ch'en Liang's Challenge to Chu Hsi* (Council on East Asian Studies, Harvard University, 1982). Currently, he is completing a book that explores the development of a sense of community among *Daoxue* Confucians in the twelfth century. He is also writing a monograph on the making of a hero, a study of Zhuge Liang in Chinese historical consciousness.

Don J. Wyatt is Assistant Professor of History at Middlebury College. His research interests include Chinese thought traditions of all premodern periods, with particular specialization in the early Song era. He has published in the *Harvard Journal of Asiatic Studies* and co-authored *Sung Dynasty Uses of the I Ching* (Princeton University Press, 1990). He is now completing an intellectual biography of the cosmologist Shao Yong.

Introduction

PAUL A. COHEN AND MERLE GOLDMAN

One of the central, in some ways most bewildering, ironies of human history is the frequency with which occurrences that are generally viewed negatively, such as wars, inadvertently give rise to consequences that confer substantial benefits upon society. Benjamin I. Schwartz, the man in whose honor this book has been assembled, graduated from Harvard College in 1938 with a magna in Romance Languages and Literatures and was headed for a career in high-school teaching. He actually did teach French for a while and earned an MA from Harvard's School of Education in 1940. But World War II intervened. Sent by the U.S. Army to language school to study Japanese, Schwartz spent the war years in Washington in the Intelligence Branch of the Signal Corps, helping to break Japanese codes. After the war, he took part in the American occupation of Japan until his discharge in 1946, whereupon he entered the Regional Studies East Asia MA program at Harvard. His main interests had by then shifted to China.

After earning his doctorate at Harvard in 1950, Schwartz taught there in the Government and History Departments until his retirement in the spring of 1987. During that span of almost four decades, through his teaching and writing, he became a major force in the field of Chinese studies, setting standards—above all in the area of intellectual history—that have been a guide and source of inspiration to students and scholars not only in the United States but worldwide. Schwartz's influence extends well beyond the China field; it has also cut across conventional disciplinary boundaries, touching political science, religion, philosophy, and literature, as well as history.

Although the range of learning at Benjamin Schwartz's disposal is vast—an omnivorous reader, he is also a polyglot with a working command of ten foreign languages—this learning is not conveyed as a fixed body of knowledge or set of truths. More in the Socratic or Confucian spirit, it takes the form of a relentless questioning of received wisdom, an abiding skepticism toward conventional formulations, an impatience with intellectual posturing, and a capacity to see complexity where others would simplify, while at the same time discerning what is fundamental in the complex. For Schwartz's students—not only those who studied with him formally but also those countless others who have spent time in his intellectual company—it is these qualities of the inquiring mind at work that have been the real inspiration, the true wisdom for which we are so much in his debt.

In a retrospective assessment of Schwartz's teaching style, Jerome Grieder of Brown University, a former student, writes of

> all the classroom lectures on Chinese politics, or intellectual history, where Ben would begin with a simple declarative statement which he would then spend forty-nine of his allotted fifty minutes qualifying; lectures that seemed to neophytes sometimes disconcertingly rambling—until one reread one's notes, months or years later, to discover how honestly, and subtly, and precisely Ben had suggested the enduring criteria of final judgment, even if he had reserved his own verdict. This was where I, at least, came to recognize the modest, reliable, and utterly humane genius of the man. Ben is *a profoundly memorable and great teacher*—not an easy role to portray historically, as Confucius and Mencius must know—but essential to a perception of the historical (and personal) significance of Ben Schwartz, the unforgettable phenomenon, the beloved and cherished participant in one's own quest for knowledge and understanding.

A man of paradoxes and odd juxtapositions, Benjamin Schwartz is not easily categorized as a scholar-thinker. Thus, profoundly interested in the world of ancient Chinese thought, he has also written on the rise of communism in China and on Sino-Soviet relations. Temperamentally unwilling to be confined by his professional involvement as a "China specialist," he has always engaged in the broader intellectual issues of his day, as evidenced by his public response to Allan Bloom's best-selling assault on American higher education[1] and his searching critique some years ago of Hannah Arendt's treatment of Jews and Judaism in her "religion of politics."[2] Although Schwartz's writings are of the highest seriousness, his personality has a playful and fun-loving side (as reflected in the occasionally irreverent little booklet entitled "The Schwartzian Analects," compiled by his students in celebration of his sixtieth birthday). A frequent and vigorous defender of the "area-studies" approach, with its implicit emphasis upon the defining importance of culture, Schwartz has consistently displayed faith in the existence of a world of common humanity transcending cultural boundaries. Most striking, the wielding of power (Mao Zedong), the search for its secrets (Yan Fu), and the moral and other issues pertaining to its proper use (Confucius, Mozi, Laozi, Han Feizi, and the Neo-Confucians) has been for him a subject of intense and abiding intellectual fascination. Yet, it would be hard to find someone less interested than Benjamin Schwartz in the trappings of personal power.

This brief introduction is not the place to survey the substantive contents of Benjamin Schwartz's work. Rather, we should like to identify several of the driving concerns or "orientations" (to borrow a favorite Schwartzian term) that have characterized his scholarly approach from the start and lent his writing—as Confucius said of his own thought in the *Analects*—an inner coherence transcending specific subject matters and cutting across apparent contradictions.

In a comment on the flyleaf of Schwartz's *The World of Thought in Ancient China*, the historian Ying-shih Yü compared his work to that of Isaiah Berlin: "Like Berlin, Schwartz is also 'against the current.' He takes nothing for granted and completely frees himself from what is called the 'tyranny of concept.'"[3] This spirit, above all the insistence upon taking "nothing for granted," flows, indeed, through all of Schwartz's work. In the very first pages of *In Search of Wealth and Power*, for example, he warns us against casually assuming, in our efforts to comprehend the encounter between the West and the "non-West," that the West, which we think we know so well, "is a known quantity," or, conversely, that the non-West, which we do not know nearly as well, can nonetheless be summed up by such "fashionable categories" as "pre-industrial society" or "traditional society."[4]

The problem in these instances does not lie in the use of the categories themselves—West, non-West, pre-industrial, traditional, and the like. Schwartz is no conceptual nihilist. Rather, the problem arises when we are insufficiently vigilant in our use of conceptual categories, and when, because they have become habitual, we have stopped actively thinking about these categories, they acquire in our minds an inappropriate—and therefore misleading—degree of precision and exactness. They become, as Schwartz himself puts it in the first chapter of his book on Yan Fu, "spuriously lucid."[5] Schwartz's instinctive reaction to such spurious lucidity is to unmask it by analyzing rigorously the presuppositions buried within the offending concepts and by plunging headlong into the empirical world these concepts claim to illuminate. Thus, he insists that "in dealing with the encounter between the West and any given non-Western society and culture, there can be no escape from the necessity of immersing ourselves as deeply as possible in the specificities of both worlds simultaneously. We are not dealing with a known and an unknown variable but with two vast, ever-changing, highly problematic areas of human experience."[6]

Dialogue, interaction, and the traversing of different worlds are, in fact, central to the Schwartzian "method." Sometimes, as in the Yan Fu book, the worlds mediated are literally worlds, as both author and subject move back and forth between China and the West, illuminating (albeit on different levels) first one, then the other world in the process. Often, the dialogue is established between scholar-thinkers: In his writing as well as his teaching Schwartz typically develops his own intellectual stance by commenting, sometimes critically, sometimes with approbation, upon the positions of others (Joseph Needham, Hannah Arendt, Herbert Fingarette, and Maurice Freedman, to name but a few).

Always, Schwartz insists upon the dialogic relationship between subject and object, ideas and contexts. Thus, in the Introduction to *Chinese Communism and the Rise of Mao,* he acknowledged "the transcendent importance of objective conditions,"[7] but at the same time he insisted upon the shaping importance of the ideological presuppositions of the leaders of China's Communist movement. Situations, he wrote, do not

> automatically create their own results. *The manner in which . . . tasks are met or not met* is determined quite as much by the ideas, intentions, and ambitions of those who finally assume the responsibility for meeting them, as by any other factor. The fact that in China the Communists, with their own peculiar presuppositions, have inherited the responsibility for meeting these tasks will, I think, be a factor of paramount importance in determining the shape of future objective situations.[8]

Schwartz readily acknowledges the role of context in the shaping of ideas: Yan Fu's reading of nineteenth-century Western thought, Mao Zedong's adaptation of Marxism-Leninism in the twentieth century, Confucius's ideas on politics and morality during the Spring and Autumn period—all were in some meaningful sense products of the objective circumstances of their respective eras. Yet the conscious concerns and preoccupations that these circumstances elicited were not mere reflections of culture, social structure, constellations of interests, or a Foucaultian discourse. They also, Schwartz asserts, had an autonomous existence of their own, enabling them, as ideas, to shape in turn the objective circumstances—the contexts—of their own and future epochs.

An analogous claim is ventured by Schwartz in the realm of historical interpretation. No believer in the possibility, or even (one suspects) desirability, of a completely detached reconstruction of the past, Schwartz believes that "the history of the past inevitably continues to be the history of the present."[9] Nonetheless he registers doubt with respect to the view, currently fashionable in some circles, that, "in all interpretation of texts, the texts are mere pretexts for the creative endeavors of the interpreter." Receptive to the possibility that texts may "impose definite outer constraints on the thought of their interpreters," Schwartz posits the existence of "a constant dialectical interaction between text and interpreter," requiring those who would gain insight (however modest and imprecise) into a text's original meaning to strive to learn as much as possible about the milieu within which the text first made its appearance.[10]

The possibility of acquiring some degree of genuine understanding of another cultural context, however, rests on the premise—Schwartz refers to it sometimes as a "hope," sometimes as a "faith"—that "lying below and beyond culture" there exists "a realm of the universally human."[11] This is not to deny the existence or importance of authentic cultural difference or of differences of historical context that are in part culturally conditioned. But the differences are as apt as not to be commensurable ones. Indeed, it is their very commensurability that, on the one hand, insures against the dead end of full-blown cultural relativism and, on the other, makes possible the comparative study of human thought.[12]

To take a conspicuous example from Schwartz's own writing, the cultural and historical context in which Yan Fu found himself in late-Qing China caused Yan to give a special reading to nineteenth-century Western social and political thought, linking social Darwinism and liberalism and identifying the Faustian-Promethean nature of Western civilization as key to the modern West's "enormous output of wealth and power."[13] "It would nevertheless be quite wrong," Schwartz insists, "to dispose of Yen [Yan] Fu's treatment of Western ideas as a distortion of modern Western thought in a non-Western mind."[14] The connections Yan Fu illuminated were not of his own invention. Social Darwinism and liberalism are also linked, although in a somewhat different way, in the writings of Herbert Spencer. The problems Yan grappled with, above all that of "the relation between the Faustian religion of the limitless pursuit of wealth and power and the achievement of social-political values,"[15] are by no means exclusively Chinese problems. They are problems that have perplexed and tormented intellectuals in other non-Western societies also. Moreover, they are problems that are far from having been solved in the West itself.

It is precisely these and other comparable problems—profound human predicaments, cutting across cultural boundaries both spatial and temporal, that remain in the late twentieth century as problematic as ever—that are Schwartz's central concern as a thinker and the primary object of his attentions as a scholar. From this perspective, the value of China as an object of study does not rest in any qualities of exotic uniqueness it may possess; nor, certainly, is it of value as the West's "other" in some absolute sense. Rather, China is valuable as an alternative repository of human experience, a vast laboratory (with its own distinctive furnishings) for the exploration of universal human dilemmas. The ultimate reason for studying China—or any other society/culture—is nothing less than to deepen and enrich our understanding of the human condition.

Given the nature of the "Schwartzian project," it is entirely fitting that the essays in this book, all by scholars who studied with Benjamin Schwartz, embrace an expanse of time stretching from the Zhou dynasty to the present and a range of subject matters that is equally inclusive: ancient and medieval Chinese thought, the fate of democracy in early Republican China, the development of aesthetic modernism in the 1920s and 1930s and its re-emergence in the post-Mao era, the emphasis on spiritual regeneration and cultural transformation in Chinese and Japanese Marxism, popular values in twentieth-century China, the larger issue of what part our own values should take in the study and assessment of other societies and cultures, and the equally broad issue of how we are to address substantively and methodologically the relationship between Chinese modernization and China's traditional culture.

Despite this heterogeniety and despite the fact that two of the contributors (Germaine Hoston and Andrew Nathan) are political scientists, three (David Arkush, Jeffrey Kinkley, and Leo Lee) in their writing bridge the disciplines of history and literature, and five (Hao Chang, Thomas Metzger, Don Price, Hoyt Tillman, and Don Wyatt) are historians with strong philosophical or intellectual-history interests, there is a definite coherence to the volume as a whole. Almost all the authors consciously address either aspects of Benjamin Schwartz's overall approach or specific themes dealt with in his work, in some instances suggesting modifications of Schwartzian conclusions. Not surprisingly, every one of the contributions is about ideas and takes ideas and their societal roles seriously. The essays have ambitious agendas. And most, either explicitly or implicitly, introduce a comparative dimension. Although understood and presented in the specific context of China, the issues raised in these comparative efforts exist in and are important to the world beyond China as well. Exploring them in both their Chinese and non-Chinese settings, therefore, carries the potential, characteristic of so much of Schwartz's own writing, to illuminate a broader canvas of human thought.

The first essay, by Hao Chang, challenges Schwartz's view of the time at which an "axial-age breakthrough" (the concept is Karl Jaspers's) took place in ancient Chinese thought. Insisting that such a breakthrough must involve a fundamental challenge to the central values and institutions of the previous civilization, Chang argues that this breakthrough did not take place in the early Zhou (as Schwartz has suggested) but, rather, several centuries later, during the time of Confucius. The "nobleman" concept of the *Analects* represented a radical new departure from the core cosmological myth of the pre-Zhou and early Zhou. As further developed—and "democratized"—by Mencius, it involved the capacity of every man, at least potentially, to communicate with Heaven—a capacity that during the early Zhou and before had been the exclusive prerogative of the Son of Heaven. Thus, a "rival order," an alternative locus of meaning and authority, centered initially on the model of Confucius himself, was established in the middle and late Zhou. The old cosmological myth, revolving about the Son of Heaven, was not, however, rejected. On the contrary, it was perpetuated and even elaborated. What distinguishes the axial-age breakthrough in China, therefore, is not so much a complete break with the earlier myth but the emergence of a tension between one tendency in Confucian thought that sharply contested this myth and another tendency that perpetuated it. This tension, Chang concludes, continued at the heart of the Confucian tradition throughout its later development.

The contributions by Don Wyatt and Hoyt Tillman, like that of Hao Chang, address issues pertaining to the Confucian tradition as a whole (and in Tillman's case the thought of the non-Confucian Mo Di as well). Their focal themes are, however, more specific in nature. Moreover, both authors pay considerable attention to the Neo-Confucian phases of Confucianism's development, another area of Schwartzian concern. Wyatt's essay explores the widely held view that traditional Chinese thought was "this-worldly" or mundane in its central orientation. While not contesting this view in its entirety, he urges that it be modified in two important respects. First, he insists that, insofar as "traditional Chinese thought" is taken to include Daoism and Buddhism as well as Confucianism, the claim of "this-worldliness" is far too sweeping. Second, he argues that, even in the case of Confucianism, a distinction must be drawn between the substantive thought of the Confucian heritage, which sometimes was not especially this-worldly, and the language used to convey this thought, which very often *was* this-worldly. Toward the end of his piece, Wyatt posits a number of differences between the Chinese and Western philosophical traditions and tries to account for the development within the former of a more broadly accessible mode of philosophical discourse.

A uniquely this-worldly challenge to thinkers in both China and the West has been and is the problem of how to reconcile individual self-interest (*si*) with the general interest (*gong*). For Yan Fu and his Western interpreter Schwartz, it would appear, the notion that the pursuit of individual interests might be conducive to the general good—that *si* need not, as Confucians typically argued, undermine *gong* but might actually support it—had its origins in modern Western thought. Hoyt Tillman, however, after an examination of the evolution of the "utilitarian problematique" in China, concludes that the ancient thinker Mo Di (as Schwartz himself analyzes him) and even more markedly the Song Confucian thinker Chen Liang arrived at comparable positions centuries before Yan Fu. Given the revival of interest in Chen's writings in Yan's day and the recent discovery of his influence on major Qing thinkers with whom Yan Fu was almost certainly familiar, Tillman believes it not unlikely that Chen exerted an impact (though indirect and unacknowledged) on Yan's own utilitarian thinking. He does not, however, rest his case on the establishment of such a link. His more fundamental concern is to bring the Chinese utilitarian tradition into sharper focus by showing how thinkers from three widely separated periods of Chinese history, when faced with comparable national crises, found utilitarian modes of thought compelling.

Although we have placed the next piece—by David Arkush—under "Literature and Culture," it is not easily typed. It is based on materials from the twentieth century, but there is nothing especially "twentieth century" about their contents. It is concerned with thought and values, but they are the thought and values of the unlettered and unschooled rather than of the highly educated. Finally, the literature Arkush explores—folk opera transcribed by scholars in 1929–1930 in Dingxian, Hebei—is rural, popular, and authorless. The contents of these folk operas were shaped by the ordinary Chinese who performed them from memory, and the moral universe of the North Chinese villagers who attended them, Arkush argues, was very likely influenced, in turn, by the operas. Examining the stories contained in these works, therefore, provides access to the values informing people's everyday lives. Arkush focuses in particular on moral conflicts within the family, the operation of moral obligations in society, and the ways in which the political and religious realms assisted in the preservation of the moral order. In his conclusion, he raises the intriguing notion that the operas may have given village communities a means of resisting, however subtly and indirectly, the cultural and ideological hegemony of the rural elite.

The next two pieces, by Leo Lee and Jeffrey Kinkley, are firmly in the twentieth century, not only chronologically, but in terms of the substantive issues they address. In contrast with Arkush, Lee and Kinkley deal with literature that is unabashedly urban in origin. Moreover, even in the case of a work like Zhang Xinxin's *Peking Man,* with its deliberate effort to record and convey the thoughts and feelings of ordinary people, it is "high culture," at least in authorial intent, if not in voice. Lee's interest is in the new form of consciousness that emerges among Chinese intellectuals around the time of the May Fourth Movement. He explores two facets of this consciousness: the modern conception of history that structured the most diverse doctrinal systems and philosophies of life of the 1920s and 1930s; and the modern aesthetic consciousness—"modernism"—that also developed during these decades among writers and creative artists. Lee's essay moves back and forth between the West and China. Whereas in the West aesthetic modernism represented a reaction against technological and economic modernity, as well as the modern, linear understanding of history, in China, Lee finds, the relationship between the two modes of modern consciousness has been, for a number of reasons, a good deal less antipathetic.

The revival of Chinese modernism in the 1980s, one aspect of the more general intellectual flowering of the post-Cultural Revolution years, is the central theme of Jeffrey Kinkley's essay. Zhang Xinxin, the young writer-journalist whose work Kinkley examines, is the quintessential modernist, taking political and social risks, experimenting restlessly with different media and literary forms, constantly in search of new cultural frontiers to traverse. Kinkley finds in Zhang an "expansiveness" akin to that of such turn-of-the century intellectuals as Yan Fu, Liang Qichao, Tan Sitong, and Zhang Binglin, whose importance in the pre-May Fourth transformation of Chinese values Benjamin Schwartz long ago recognized. Criticism of Zhang Xinxin for her aesthetic modernism (she was a prime target of the campaign against "spiritual pollution" in 1983–1984) suggests a belated emergence in China of the tension between modernity and modernism that Leo Lee observes in the nineteenth- and twentieth-century West but finds absent, or at least muted, in the China of the 1930s. Paradoxically, though, in post-Mao China it is "bourgeois" modernism that has been periodically assaulted by Communist modernizers, whereas in the West modernists typically have viewed themselves as the very antithesis of bourgeois, assailing a modern world that they believe to be bourgeois to its very core.

Although the next two essays are grouped together under the heading "Political Theory," the individual problems they address could not be more disparate. Germaine Hoston's wide-ranging, comparative exploration of the theme of spiritual regeneration and cultural transformation in Marxist thought concentrates on China and Japan, but points to a similar emphasis in the theoretical writings of Latin American and African Marxists. Much in the manner of Schwartz's treatment of Yan Fu, Hoston moves beyond the tendency to view this phenomenon merely as a series of "'practical' adaptations of a Western revolutionary theory to non-European contexts" and considers the possibility that non-Western Marxist perspectives may have an important theoretical contribution to make, filling apparent lacunae in original Marxism and supplementing "the 'partial' perspectives of a theory that reflected only the West European historical experience."

Don Price's essay begins with the question why Chinese political revolutions in the twentieth century failed to generate democratic outcomes. Taking the 1911 Revolution as his prime example, Price analyzes the constitutional debates of that era, with special attention to the political stands of Song Jiaoren and Zhang Shizhao, an admiring student of British parliamentary democracy. Although Song and Zhang, going beyond Yan Fu, appear to have valued constitutional arrangements not merely for the national strength they promised but also because both men were genuinely committed to government accountable to an electorate, their efforts ultimately failed. Price sees this failure as resulting not from any one factor (such as historical contingency or China's political culture) acting alone, but from a confluence of several different factors, all of which affected adversely the chances of democracy in the early Republic.

The final two chapters, although different from each other in almost every way, are alike in being concerned with methodological issues in cross-cultural discourse and in staking out clear and strong positions on how these issues may best be addressed. The central focus of Thomas Metzger's essay is the time-honored question of continuity and discontinuity between premodern and modern China. One of the problems that arises as soon as this question is posed is the descriptive one of determining whether China's traditional culture, in particular Confucianism, was supportive mainly of the interests of the group or of the individual. Another issue deals with the widely held belief that, when mainstream Chinese and Western intellectuals discuss culture, history, and modernization, they do so in essentially the same terms and share a common world of discourse. Metzger maintains that this is an illusion. The Chinese discourse on these issues is in his view highly distinctive, being marked by a deep-seated, often unconscious, tendency that he calls "optimistic this-worldiness." This tendency has in modern times been a major impediment to the realization of such goals as political pluralism. If these goals are to be attained, Chinese thinkers of all stamps, on the Mainland and Taiwan, must come to a clearer recognition of the distinctive character of their own discourse on modernization.

Andrew Nathan's concluding essay, like Don Price's piece, addresses the fate of democracy in China. Nathan's approach, however, unlike Price's, is prospective, concerned not with the failure of Chinese democracy in the past but with the possibility of its successful establishment at some point in the future. Although democracy's future in China is clearly a matter of great personal concern to Nathan, it is not his paramount interest here. He introduces this issue for illustrative purposes in order to probe the larger question of how historians and social scientists are to evaluate another culture. In engaging in such evaluation, ought we to apply values in which we ourselves believe (a position Nathan labels "evaluative universalism") or ought we to base our evaluation on values prevalent in the culture we are studying ("cultural relativism")? Nathan argues forcefully in favor of the former alternative and is convinced that this is the only basis for generating truly fruitful cross-cultural dialogue. Although Benjamin Schwartz would doubtless advance his own arguments for the achievement of this goal, the goal itself—the establishment of a "universal human discourse"[16]—has always been at the center of his life and work as a scholar.

Part One
Thought

ONE

Some Reflections on the Problems of the Axial-Age Breakthrough in Relation to Classical Confucianism

HAO CHANG

The recent publication of Benjamin Schwartz's *The World of Thought in Ancient China* reopens the issue of the axial-age breakthrough in ancient China.[1] In this essay, I intend to explore two specific problems: first, the dating of the onset of this breakthrough; second, the nature of the breakthrough as reflected in the development of classical Confucianism.

Schwartz takes the view that the axial-age breakthrough initially emerged in the early Zhou (that is, the twelfth or eleventh century B.C.) when the new belief in Heaven and Heaven's Mandate first arose:

> At its deepest level, the idea of Heaven's Mandate presents us with a clear apprehension of the gap between the human order as it ought to be and as it actually is. Here we find clear evidence of that religio-ethical transcendence— that critical spirit toward the anterior development of high civilization which seems to be the earmark of the axial age in all the high civilizations.[2]

If we accept Schwartz's broad definition of the axial-age breakthrough, we may agree with his dating of its initial emergence to the early Zhou. We must remember, however, that an awareness of the gap between the order as it ought to be and the order as it actually is exists to varying degrees in any culture beyond the primitive level. Certainly some sense of this gap and the critical consciousness accompanying it are already present in such archaic civilizations as ancient Mesopotamia or Egypt where no axial-age breakthrough ever took place.[3] Thus, in my view, what distinguishes the axial-age breakthrough is no mere sense of a gap but something more complex that I hope will become clearer later on in this essay. In this connection, suffice it to say that one necessary element in this "something more complex" is doubtless a sense of transcendence or critical consciousness of a radical nature that involves a direct or indirect challenge to the central values and institutions of the anterior civilization. That seems to be what happened in the other ancient-civilization areas where the axial-age breakthrough took place. Consequently, the crucial question is whether a heightened critical consciousness that opens up a radical gap "between the human order as it ought to be and as it actually is" had occurred with the emergence of the belief in the Mandate of Heaven in the early Zhou.

To answer this question it is necessary to begin with a brief examination of the "anterior development of high civilization," especially Shang thought. On the one hand, some scholars emphasize the continuity of Shang thought with the primitive religious culture of the Neolithic period. On the other, we are now told that some religio-moral concepts such as *tianming* and *de*, which used to be associated exclusively with the early Zhou, have been found on the oracle bones of the late Shang period. However complex and controversial the picture of Shang culture, one central characteristic is clear: the mythical participation of human society in the cosmic order as controlled by divine beings. The pervasive practice of divination by plastromancy, the centrality in Shang society of the worship of ancestral spirits and nature deities, and zoomorphic images as shown on the Shang bronzes seem to point to a picture of the human order as embedded in the divine-cosmic order, which reminds us of the cosmological myth that historians like Eric Voegelin found lying at the core of ancient Near Eastern and Egyptian civilizations.[4]

The focal point of this cosmological myth of archaic China is the role and function of the royal lineage as perceived by the Shang people. First, the king combined the roles of political leader and chief shaman. Further, with the help of his ancestral spirits, he served as the pivotal channel of communication with the divine-cosmic order, a kind of "omphalos" or sacral center, where Heaven and earth meet and divine being flows into society. Such is the cosmological kingship that stands at the center of the Shang political order.[5]

It is against the background of this Shang cosmological myth that we need to evaluate the significance of the early Zhou's belief in the Mandate of Heaven. In the Shang worship of Di or Shangdi, the relation between this high god and the royal ancestral spirits was often characterized by a vagueness and fluidity, suggesting that the two were, in the minds of Shang people, not clearly differentiated. By contrast, in the Zhou people's worship of Heaven, Heaven is conceived as clearly separate from the Zhou royal ancestral spirits.[6] In consequence, the concept of Heaven's Mandate carries a clear sense of transcendence not found in the Shang belief in Shangdi.

This new concept of transcendence involves a sense of gap between what Schwartz calls the order as it ought to be and as it actually is. The clearest indication of the gap is that the concept of *de* began to loom large in the early Zhou texts and bronze inscriptions. What did *de* mean? In the beginning it may have referred to a mana-like power. But, as it emerged in early Zhou literature, it had come to acquire some moral connotations associated with such concepts as *xiao* (filial piety) and *jing* (vigilance and piety). More important, in the course of the Western Zhou it had become identified with the code of *li*.[7]

As repeatedly pointed out by scholars, *li* probably originated as a code of religious rituals. But over time it also came to embrace rules governing social occasions. As a code of moral-ritual propriety, *li* aims to regulate the behaviors of upper-class people down to the smallest details. Further, it embodies prescriptive ethics oriented solely toward insuring outer behavioral compliance. There is little sense of interiority to this kind of ethics that would reflect the stirring of spiritual aspiration or inner guilt.

Did the code of *li* carry any critical spirit toward the central institutions of the anterior civilization? This critical spirit is certainly lacking insofar as the kinship institution and the ancestral cult still lie at the core of the *li* code. To discover whether there was a critical spirit toward the other major institution of the anterior order of Shang, the cosmological kingship, we must look at the political order as prescribed by the *li* code.

As Schwartz observes, the political order plays a crucial role in the Zhou civilization inasmuch as it believed that only the political order can bridge the gap between the order as it should be and the order as it is.[8] At the core of the Zhou political order is the institution of the Son of Heaven; and this institution is marked by both continuity and discontinuity with the cosmological kingship of the Shang. On the one hand, according to the doctrine of the Mandate of Heaven, the institution of the Son of Heaven is not bound up with the bloodline of the Zhou royal house; its occupancy is theoretically open to human competition on the basis of moral merit. To the extent that the doctrine of the Mandate of Heaven is integral to the institution of the Son of Heaven, it marks it off from the Shang institution of the cosmological kingship, which is tied together with the bloodline of the Shang royal house. However, in considering the institution of Son of Heaven, it is important to make the distinction between the institution and its human occupant. While its human occupant is variable, the institution itself is invariable and is still believed to be imbedded in the cosmic order. Whoever occupies the institutional role of Son of Heaven is still viewed as the sole linkage with Heaven as the controlling power in the cosmic order. Only he can mediate between the human order and the cosmic order and bridge the gap between the order as it is and the order as it should be. Therefore, the sense of transcendence and the critical spirit that attends the belief in the Mandate of Heaven turns out to be still predicated on and circumscribed by the institution of the cosmological kingship. The belief represents a new departure, but still within the cosmological myth, not outside it. In short, the Son of Heaven proves to be an institutional variant of rather than a break with the Shang cosmological kingship.

In view of the character of both the moral and the political order that followed the rise of the religious belief in Heaven's Mandate, I see no sense of a radical gap between the order as it should be and as it is, and by the same token I find it difficult to argue as Schwartz did for the inauguration of the axial-age breakthrough in the early Zhou culture.

As for placing the breakthrough in the late Zhou period, after 770 B.C., I certainly see some new developments pointing to a break with the cosmological myth as far as classical Confucianism is concerned.

But we must not lose sight of the fact that the break is accompanied by a continuity that classical Confucianism still maintains in some ways with the cosmological myth. When we take both continuity and discontinuity into account, we again see a picture of axial-age breakthrough more complex than Schwartz defines it on the basis of a gap between the order as it is and as it should be. Let me start with a brief examination of the *Analects* (fifth century B.C.), which expresses an ethic very different from the prescriptive ethic embodied in the code of *li*. Underlying this new ethic is a sense of estrangement based on the realization that the world had gone astray. As Confucius repeatedly observed and intimated in the *Analects*, the world is out of order (*tianxia wudao*).[9] To restore order to the world, a moral regeneration is required.

For Confucius, the beginning of this moral regeneration is for every person to be aware that he is faced with two modes of existence or two paths of life—the path of moral degeneration which he called the "small man" (*xiaoren*) and the path of moral elevation which he called the "noble man" (*junzi*).[10] The paramount challenge of life is to make the right choice and to pursue the path of the noble man.

To pursue this path compliance with the code of *li* is still essential but not enough. Beyond this outward compliance, a noble man must also embody in his life a host of virtues enjoined and expounded in the *Analects*. A close examination of these virtues and of the relation of some of them to *li* reveals a sense of moral interiority one does not find in the kind of ethic exhibited in the code of *li*. The presence of an awareness of the need for self-examination as reflected in such phrases as *nei zixing* or *neixing* (inner self-reflection) and *nei zisong* (inner self-accusation) explicitly attested to this sense of moral inwardness.[11] It is also implicit in Confucius's conception of a balance between "outer forms" (*wen*) and "inner substance" (*zhi*).[12] More important, in the *Analects* such core virtues as the cardinal trio of *zhi* (intelligence), *ren* (humanity), and *yong* (courage) as well as *yi* (righteousness), *xin* (trustworthiness), *zhong* (loyalty), and *shu* (reciprocity) are sometimes defined and elucidated on the assumption that an inner life exists.[13] Because of this dimension of interiority in the moral thought of the *Analects*, *dao* is no longer construed as something that transforms a person from out-

Chang

side. Rather it is something one can develop only through one's own self. As Confucius put it, it is "man who develops *dao* rather than *dao* that develops man."[14]

This sense of moral interiority must not be overemphasized to the neglect of the importance of outward compliance with *li*. But there is no question life emerges in the *Analects* as subject to two pulls: the outward pull of compliance with *li* and the inward pull of moral-spiritual striving. In other words, we find in the *Analects* a prescriptive ethic not alone but fused with an ethic oriented to inner motivational transformation and spiritual aspiration. We may call this new ethic a tensive ethic inasmuch as it embodies a moral-spiritual tension not found in the prescriptive ethic of *li*.

Apart from its moral-spiritual depth, the new ethic found in the *Analects* also exhibits a dynamism that contrasts sharply with the static character of the ethic of *li*. This can be seen nowhere more clearly than in the nature of such ultimate moral ideals as *ren* and *sheng* (sagehood) as defined in the *Analects*. It is well known that Confucius tended to give different answers to different persons each time he was asked for a definition of *ren*. In Confucius's numerous discourses on the concept, *ren* was variously identified with some of the specific moral virtues. But, when one takes into account these discourses as a whole, it is obvious that *ren* is also meant to be more than just the sum total of all these specific moral concepts.

As we probe deeper into Confucius's discussion of *ren*, we discover that its elusive quality is by no means accidental. On the one hand, Confucius says, "If I want *ren*, then I will have it."[15] On the other hand, *ren* is something that, along with *sheng*, even Confucius himself dares not claim to have fulfilled.[16] Moreover, Confucius considers *ren* as something indispensable to every moment of a noble man's life, no matter how hectic and stormy his life is at that moment.[17] Yet, meanwhile, *ren* is described as something so difficult to attain that only his best student, Yan Hui, can be said to have lived his life in accordance with the ideal enduringly.[18] Further, *ren* imposes such a heavy responsibility on a person that only death is allowed to stop the effort to achieve it.[19] Obviously, *ren* emerges in the *Analects* as something paradoxical which, while within the reach of everyone, takes such an effort to achieve that no one can claim to have completely fulfilled it for good. Given the elusive quality of *ren*, the tensive ethic of the *Analects* is never a structure of finite demands and injunctions similar to the ethic of *li*. It is perhaps best seen as an open-ended process which starts with concrete virtues and specific norms but can never be exhausted by them. It is indeed a path made up of infinite demands and challenges. The end of this path, call it *ren* or *sheng*, is something one can aspire to but can never lastingly attain.

With this inner depth and dynamism, the new tensive ethic symbolized by *ren* widens the gap between the order as it should be and as it is to a far greater extent than the gap opened up by the ethics of *li*. Thus the new ethic marked a radical departure from that of the early Zhou.

The radical quality of this departure is enhanced by another aspect of the new ethic of the *Analects:* the person of Confucius. In the *Analects*, the personality of Confucius stands as a living testimony to the moral-spiritual faith expressed therein. It serves as a kind of "concrete universal" for its moral ideals, thereby beginning a new development in classical thought toward a break with the idea of cosmological kingship.

Although Confucius was depicted in the *Analects* as usually silent about Heaven, a close examination of the text reveals that, on a number of occasions, Confucius made direct references to Heaven; and these references point not only to a profound piety toward Heaven but also a kind of "prophetic spirit" in Confucius who claimed to have a special relationship with Heaven. On one occasion, for example, when his life was put in jeopardy by someone called Huan Gui, Confucius was quoted as saying, "I am born with virtue from Heaven, what can Huan Gui do to me?"[20] On another occasion, referring to his rapport with the beyond, he made the remark, "Isn't it Heaven who really understands me?"[21] Such observations and others betray a strong sense of trust in and support from Heaven.

Equally important is the fact that Confucius was perceived by other people of his time to have been a person given a special mission by Heaven. In the *Analects*, he was sometimes believed to be "made a sage by Heaven" (*tian zong zhi jiang sheng*) in order to provide a model for others;[22] sometimes he was believed to be "the wooden tongue of a bell" (*muduo*) sent down by Heaven to warn people about their misbehaviors.[23]

Further, in the eyes of his students, he had a stature comparable to that of the ancient sage-kings.[24] In short, Confucius comes through in the *Analects* as the paradigmatic "noble man" who enjoys a privileged rapport with Heaven usually claimed only for the Son of Heaven. Consequently, classical Confucianism sees the "noble man" as a center of meaning and authority apart from the Son of Heaven. Thus, unlike the doctrine of the Mandate of Heaven which, as pointed out above, is a new development within the cosmological myth, this trend is a new departure outside it.

The *Analects'* radical departures from the moral and political thought of the early Zhou become even more pronounced in Mencius's thought, resulting in a heightened critical spirit. Part of this critical spirit grew out of Mencius's relentless application of the ideals of the *Analects'* new ethics to a critique of the political order. For Mencius, the title of king (*wang*) can be assumed only by someone whom he called a "man of humanity" (*renzhe*), someone who has fulfilled the moral ideals of *ren* and *yi* in his life.[25] A ruler who does not meet this moral requirement is by definition not a ruler and thus can be removed. In short, tyrannicide is morally justified.[26]

More important is the critical spirit that springs from a world view that lies at the core of Mencius's thought (fourth century B.C.). This world view generalizes Confucius's personal experience of a special linkage with Heaven and is nowhere more clearly seen than in Mencius's emphasis on the primacy of the mind-heart (*xin*). On the one hand, the mind-heart is seen as the repository of innate moral senses; on the other, it is deemed a sensorium of transcendence because the innate moral senses are believed to be an endowment from Heaven. Inasmuch as every person has a mind-heart, everyone has an inner linkage with Heaven.[27]

Mencius's conception of inner linkage with Heaven is accompanied by a dualistic conception of self. As Mencius observed, every human individual has two "bodies" (*ti*): the higher body, which he called either "noble body" (*guiti*) or "great body" (*dati*), and the lower body, which he called either base body (*jianti*) or small body (*xiaoti*).[28] If one allows the higher body to take possession of one's self, then one will become what Mencius called a "great man" (*daren*), the noble man.[29] If one allows the lower body to take possession of one's self, then one will become a "small man."[30] Whether the "higher self" or the "lower self" is in control turns solely on the cultivation of mind-heart (*yangxin*). For, through the cultivation of mind-heart, one can make manifest the innate moral senses as the essence of the human self and is thereby able to "know Heaven" (*zhi tian*) and to "serve Heaven" (*shi tian*).[31] Thus, outside of the Son of Heaven, not just Confucius but everyone has the potential of communicating with Heaven and of becoming a sort of cosmic agent.

Once one becomes a cosmic agent, he wears the title of *tianmin* (heavenly citizen) or *tianli* (heavenly official).[32] He is honored not because he has worldly wealth and power but because he has acquired a "heavenly honor" (*tianjue*)[33] through moral cultivation and thus enjoys a "heavenly stature" (*tianwei*), "heavenly rank" (*tianci*), and "heavenly stipend" (*tianlu*).[34] Thus, in Mencius's thought there emerged a concept of an order based on the model of Confucius rivaling the existing order based on the Son of Heaven. This dualistic concept of order was epitomized in such dichotomies as virtue (*de*) vs. political rank (*wei*) and spiritual way (*dao*) vs. political authority (*shi*), which cropped up in the text of *Mencius*.[35] The development toward a break with the notion of cosmological kingship became even more accentuated than in the *Analects*.

In *Xunzi* (third century B.C.), one sees a parallel development, albeit expressed in a different form. Admittedly, there is some basic inconsistency in Xunzi's world view. On the one hand, he emphasized the "separation between Heaven and man" (*tian ren zhi fen*). For him, Heaven has its own rhythm and runs its own course without regard for human affairs. Consequently, he took exception to Mencius's idea of "knowing Heaven."[36] Yet, the tendency to conceive of man and his moral actualization in cosmic terms still bulks large. Nevertheless, both aspects of Xunzi's world view, however inconsistent with each other, were at odds with the thrust of the cosmological myth.

Xunzi's emphasis on the "separation between Heaven and man" helps to account for his explanation of the formation of the socio-political order in terms of its social function rather than its supposed supernatural origins. Indeed, the very formation of a human group is ascribed to the necessity of human beings to band together for survival and fend off the rest of the animal kingdom.[37] The same social utilitarianism also characterized Xunzi's view of the origin of political institutions. He looked upon the institution of rulership (*jun*) as something indispensable to bringing people together to form an integrated social order.[38] Kingship (*wang*) was also sometimes defined as the person capable of inspiring people's trust and "drawing them toward him" on the basis of his moral authority.[39]

Against the background of the cosmological myth, the social utilitarianism in Xunzi's thinking implies a "decosmicization" and desacralization of the political order. However, alongside the social utilitarianism in his thinking was a tendency toward moral actualization in cosmic terms. For Xunzi, as for Mencius, the key to moral actualization is the cultivation of mind-heart (*yangxin*) seen as the vital center of the human self.

Xunzi's approach to this cultivation of mind-heart is again characterized by some incongruity. On the one hand, there is his well-known "objective," "intellectualistic" approach centered on the idea of learning by way of the mind-heart from the external normative order of *li*.[40] On the other hand, the text of *Xunzi* also featured a sort of inward approach built around the idea of sincerity (*cheng*) viewed as an inner disposition of mind-heart.[41] According to one key passage of the text, if one could hold fast to the virtues of *ren* and *yi* with the sincerity of the mind-heart, then one could accomplish the transformation of character and thus fulfill what he calls the "heavenly virtue" (*tiande*).[42] The thrust and tone of this part of *Xunzi* sounds almost exactly like *Mencius*.

Whatever approach one employs, as long as one carries out moral transformation through the cultivation of the mind-heart, one becomes a noble man. Having become a noble man, one is transformed into a cosmic agent. That is, through cultivating his mind-heart, a noble man not only aligns himself with the cosmic rhythm and lives in tune with Heaven; he can also "complete" Heaven's course and serve as an instrument of *dao* in the human world.[43] This idea of the noble man as a cosmic complement to Heaven runs parallel to Mencius's definition of the noble man as a "citizen of Heaven" (*tianmin*) or an "official of Heaven" (*tianli*). Playing the role of cosmic agent, Xunzi's noble man embodies a critical spirit that sometimes goes even farther than Mencius's. As

Xunzi observed, "The noble man follows the *dao* rather than the ruler . . . and he follows the ideals of righteousness rather than the father."[44] This is virtually a total negation of the cosmological myth, which one does not find in Mencius. Although Mencius put moral ideal higher than ruler as the source of political authority, he never unequivocally put it higher than father as the symbol of family authority.

The idea of noble man as a cosmic agent and thereby also an alternative center of meaning and authority apart from the Son of Heaven was given a more systematic expression in the two chapters in *Li ji* (third or second century, B.C.–Records of rites), namely *Daxue* (Great learning) and *Zhongyong* (Doctrine of the mean). *Li ji* was a Confucian classic which probably didn't get written down until the early Han. But it is safe to assume that the ideal expressed in the book already flourished in the late Warring States period.[45]

Zhongyong takes as its point of departure the idea of the interiorization of Heaven's Mandate already implied in Mencius. It thus opens with the statements: "The Mandate of Heaven constitutes nature. The articulation of nature makes for the Way. The cultivation of the Way brings about the edification of the world."[46] This clearly implies that the noble man, having received Heaven's Mandate as his nature, becomes the source of truth and meaning. Not surprisingly, Confucius now appears in *Zhongyong*, as he also does in *Mencius*, as the paradigmatic noble man, the sage who is "matched with Heaven" (*pei tian*) and thereby put on the same pedestal with the founding sage-kings of the Zhou dynasty.[47] The noble man now clearly represents a rival source of order vis-à-vis the cosmological kingship.

Equally important, both *Zhongyong* and *Daxue* hold that the key to political order is the moral-spiritual cultivation of the self which boils down to the transformation of the mind-heart. This is a culmination of the idea already adumbrated in Confucius, Mencius, and Xunzi—that the political order becomes solely the function of a transcendentally grounded mind-heart rather than something that must be aligned externally with such rhythms of the cosmos as celestial revolutions and vegetative cycles. Thus emerges a cardinal faith of classical Confucianism: Political order is the human personality writ large.

The concept of political order in classical Confucianism, therefore, is quite different from the concept of order that underlies the early Zhou's notion of the Mandate of Heaven. In the early Zhou, the Son of Heaven is seen as the only linkage with Heaven as the center of the sacred beyond, whereas, in classical Confucianism, the noble man, as epitomized in the paradigmatic personality of Confucius, is seen as a separate and independent channel of communication with Heaven. Thus one may speak of a dualistic conception of order in classical Confucianism: a community of moral-spiritual agents versus the existing sociopolitical order centered on the cosmological kingship.

Further, the nature of the linkage in the two cases is also different. In the case of the early Zhou's concept of Son of Heaven, as pointed out above, the human occupant of the institutional role is determined on the basis of moral qualities. But the institutional role itself is seen as imbedded in the cosmic order. Thus, the human order and the cosmic order are still linked up together in an *external* and *substantial* way. In this form of linkage between the two orders, the Son of Heaven plays the role of a cosmological linchpin which depends as much on his performance of ritual duties as on his moral merits to keep the human order aligned with the cosmic rhythm. By contrast, the linkage between Heaven and the human world in the case of the noble man is essentially inward in nature. Because of the interiorization of the Mandate of Heaven in classical Confucianism, the mind-heart is seen as the fulcrum of the linkage between Heaven and man. Thus, the two different conceptions of order are accompanied by two divergent versions of the world view based on the idea of the unity of Heaven and man. While the cosmological kingship of early Zhou is premised on a world view based on the idea of an *external, substantial* unity of the cosmic and human orders, the dualistic idea of order envisaged by classical Confucianism is bound up with the world view based on the idea of an *essential* and *internal* unity of Heaven and man. Because of these departures from early Zhou thought regarding the conception of political order and world-view, there is a strain in classical Confucianism toward a break with the cosmological myth.

This discontinuity with the cosmological myth, however, must not be taken as the whole picture of classical Confucianism's relation with early Zhou thought. For, significantly, side by side with the two chapters, "Daxue" and "Zhongyong" in *Li ji,* there are other chapters such as "Wangzhi" (The kingly institution) and "Yueling" (monthly ordinances) where the idea of cosmological kingship is not only preserved intact but also elaborately fleshed out.[48] This is seen more clearly in the "Yueling" chapter, which revolves around a list of ritual duties to be performed by Son of Heaven and his entourage in the so-called Hall of Light (Mingtang) during each of the twelve months of the year. The rituals and the arrangements of rooms in the Hall of Light are spelled out in the framework of the correlative cosmology. The ritual activities of the king in every month of the year, such as the room he occupies in the Hall of Light, the color of the clothes he wears, the food he eats, and so forth, are carefully correlated with various natural phenomena, such as the growth of animal and vegetable life and the movements of the sun and constellations.[49] In short, the Son of Heaven, in performing his role, must align and attune himself in the most detailed way with the rhythms of the cosmos. Here is the idea of cosmological kingship presented most elaborately. To be sure, the "Yueling" chapter of the *Li ji* was probably written in the early years of the Former Han, but, since similar ideas were found in such texts as *Guanzi, Lüshi chunqiu, Chunqiu fanlu, Huainanzi,* and *Bai hutong,* one may presume that these ideas were widely circulated from the late Warring States period to the early Han.

The ideal of cosmological kingship presented in "Yueling" points to the continuity of axial-age thought with the archaic thought of the late Shang and the early Zhou. True, the elaborate and systematic correlative cosmology so prominent in "Yueling" was nowhere to be found in the earlier period. But some of the cosmological symbolisms that constitute the correlative cosmology already had roots in archaic thought. For one thing, the cult of the "gods" of the five directions (*wufang di*) was found in the oracle-bone inscriptions. This seems to be the predecessor of the emphasis on the five directions (the four cardinal directions and the center) in "Yueling."[50] The primacy of the north-south axis that guides the construction of the Hall of Light can be traced back to Shang culture and even earlier.[51] The *ganzhi* symbolism, which also constitutes an element in the cosmological symbolism of "Yueling" appeared too in the Shang culture.[52] The dualistic yin-yang symbolisms, which did not have a place in "Yueling" but figured prominently in such related literature as Dong Zhongshu's *Chunqiu fanlu,* can be dated back to the early Zhou when the cosmological myth crystallized in the form found in the doctrine of the Mandate of Heaven.[53] More important, the notion that the central institutions of society such as kingship and family are imbedded in the cosmic order was as integral to the archaic cosmological myth as to the cosmological myth of "Yueling." This notion seems to have persisted from the Western Zhou into the Eastern Zhou period as seen in a number of statements in the *Zuo Commentary,* which present the whole institutional order embodied in the code of *li* as imbedded in the cosmic order.[54]

Despite the presence of strands of thought indicating a break with the cosmological myth as discussed above, some traces of the myth can be found even in the major texts of classical Confucianism. A close examination of the *Analects* shows that Confucius by and large accepted all the traditional rituals and cults. Once he was quoted as saying that anyone who grasped the meaning of the imperial sacrifice to the ancestors would have no difficulty in running the empire.[55] Since the royal cults of Heaven and ancestor worship lay at the core of the traditional ritual order, one may assume that the idea of the cosmological myth still had some hold on Confucius's thought.

The same can be said of Mencius who, for example, believed the Hall of Light to be a component of what he called "kingly government" (*wangzheng*).[56] The Hall of Light was the central institution celebrated in "Yueling" to symbolize the idea of cosmological kingship. Xunzi, also, spoke of the hierarchy of human society as coeval with Heaven and earth and viewed the principle of superordination and subordination as something "ordained by Heaven" (*tian shu*). All these instances suggest that the cosmological kingship couched in the framework of the correlative cosmology in "Yueling" is an outgrowth and elaboration of an uninterrupted line of thought stretching back to the cosmological myth of Shang.

Thus, in classical Confucianism one sees not only an intellectual trend toward a break with the cosmological myth but also continuity with it. In this aspect of late-Zhou thought a radical gap emerged between the order as it should be and as it is. But accompanying this radical gap was a counter-tendency to contain and constrict it. From this vantage point, what distinguishes the axial-age breakthrough is perhaps not so much a clear-cut break with the cosmological myth as a tension between a challenge to the cosmological myth and an elaboration of the myth. This tension was not present in early-Zhou thought but persisted at the heart of the Confucian tradition from its inception on.

TWO

A Language of Continuity in Confucian Thought

DON J. WYATT

A number of Sinological scholars and interested observers have commented on what has long been perceived as the "this-worldly" orientation of traditional Chinese thought, often as distinguished from the assumed "other-worldly" orientation of Western thought. Despite its prevalence, this perception of Chinese thought has solicited little critical examination. To be sure, more than a few scholars have touched on this issue in a cursory fashion. Fung Yu-lan, Ch'u Chai, Angus Graham, and others have all mentioned the apparent "this-worldly" quality of Chinese thought in various contexts.[1] Nevertheless, the questions of whether a "this-worldly" approach to knowledge is actually a staple of Chinese thought and whether it is pervasive elicit deeper investigation, if only because of the persistence of "this-worldliness" as an operational "given" among many present-day historians and because of the overwhelming influence that its truth would seem to exert on the shaping of our overall perceptions of Chinese culture.

What scholars like Fung, Chai, and Graham seem to have had in mind in describing Chinese thought as "this-worldly" is a philosophical orientation that concentrates foremost on human-centered affairs within the known limited context of our condition as mortal beings. However, based on this definition of "this-worldliness," it is clear that much of the reason these scholars have designated Chinese thought as "this-worldly" is actually the result of an interesting conflation of terms. Even in speaking of Chinese thought, as a whole, as "this-worldly," what most scholars have really been implicitly referring to is Confucian thought. Although the terms *Chinese* and *Confucian* will not be used coterminously in this essay, readers must bear in mind that many attributes frequently and loosely said to be constituents of Chinese thought broadly are more properly the province of this specific school.

Confucianism has, of course, long been recognized as representing the dominant line of traditional Chinese intellectualism, greatly overshadowing the main alternatives of Daoism and Buddhism throughout much of China's traditional history. Moreover, the primacy Confucian thought has historically given to what is seen as the extreme practical side of almost exclusively human existence has encouraged its categorization as "this-worldly." It is not surprising, therefore, that the orientation of Confucianism has emerged as representative of the entire body of Chinese thought in the minds of numerous scholars.

Still, even as it can be taken as representing the major stream of Chinese thinking, calling Confucianism exclusively "this-worldly" is not much more helpful than offering the same appraisal of Chinese thought in general. Without evidence, the designation seems simplistic, dismissive. To suggest that Confucianism, as a philosophical school, is incapable of addressing issues of metaphysical importance is to reduce its range of comprehensiveness, to diminish its capacity for effectively attending to the full life experiences of its adherents.

Nevertheless, the persistence of the notion of inherent "this-worldliness" warrants an inquiry into its premises. It is logical to start by first considering that medium through which any form of thought is most immediately expressed—Confucian language, which, especially in its argumentative mode, has greatly influenced the characterization of the school as "this-worldly." Confucianism is widely acknowledged to have numerous conventions of language that can be described as "earthy" or "earth-bound." However, we must be cautious in assuming that the use of such language conventions in themselves confines the parameters of Confucian discourse strictly to the "this-worldly" realm. The level of abstraction achieved by Confucian thinkers in their discussions of substantive concepts is sufficient evidence that their deliberations transcended "this-worldly" boundaries, despite the language used. In this essay, I shall try to illustrate that most authors are almost invariably extending characteristics drawn from Confucian language to Chinese thought when they refer to the latter as categorically "this-worldly." More important, I hope to prove that, even if Confucian thought is to be perceived as "this-worldly," this designation points specifically to a persistent trait underlying its language conventions (how ideas are presented and framed) and not at all to some kind of built-in limitation to the Confucian capacity for conceptualization, which in fact stands on a par with Western classical tradition.

What follows is an investigation of Confucian philosophical "this-worldliness," with the understanding that the orientation exhibited by Confucianism has been largely assumed to exemplify Chinese thought in general. This will involve two perennial aspects of Chinese thought generally but of Confucian thought in particular. First, the method of argument by analogy will be considered. Analogy has been chosen because it perhaps best embodies characteristics suggestive of a this-worldly ethos. Among these characteristics are universality of application, immediacy of apprehension, and functional simplicity. Analogy, as an argumentative device, is especially expressive of the Chinese affinity with this world.

The principle of analogy, by design, allows almost any concept to become an analogue for another concept or set of concepts, so the possibilities for analogical pairings are always virtually infinite. Consequently, a second theme—*xing* or nature—will also be examined and used to restrict the parameters of inquiry still further. *Xing* is one of a handful of terms that serves as the focus of inquiry not only during the Warring States period (ca. 450–220 B.C.) but significantly beyond it; it also figures preponderantly in the discourse of much later Chinese thought. Therefore, within Chinese thought spanning several epochs, *xing* is not simply one pedestrian concept that can be arbitrarily chosen from among many. *Xing* can be seen as a metaphysical concept of indomitable importance throughout all the fertile eras of Chinese thought because it encapsulates all human motivation, aspiration, and potential.

The Language of Confucianism

The starting point for the idea of Chinese thought as "this-worldly" is undoubtedly the strongly empiricist (knowledge acquired through experience) outlook of traditional Chinese thought. All the diverse early schools, either directly or indirectly, concerned themselves with governance and group ethics.[2] The early philosophers, whether engaged in the observation of nature or (more typically) of the motivations behind human behavior, based their ideas on the experience of the real world and made them applicable to that world. More often than not, the true testing ground for their ideas was society itself: The feasibility of a plan for government, for instance, depended on its capacity for being put into practice. Traditional thinkers first concentrated on direct apprehension of knowledge through the sensory experience of the concrete (and largely) social world and only then turned their attention toward more metaphysical questions. This predilection for "this-worldly" experience is evident even in the most metaphysically mature works of early Chinese philosophical literature, such as the *Zhongyong* or *Doctrine of the Mean* (third or second century B.C.). Despite its relatively late composition and its primary emphasis on man's relationship with Heaven, the *Zhongyong* states, for example: "Only the man who places himself in the midst of worldly affairs is capable of transforming other men."[3] Thus, the longstanding appreciation Chinese thinkers have held for tangible everyday experience has, as much as any other factor, greatly shaped the prevailing image of the entire Chinese philosophical tradition as preoccupied with this-worldly concerns. In the appropriate words of Frederick Mote, "The Chinese world view kept man's attention on life here and now and made Chinese thinkers responsible for ordaining the forms and patterns of that life."[4]

However true the contention of a this-worldly Chinese philosophical ethos may be, China's different philosophical schools must be seen as committed to this ethos in varying degrees. More than any other school of traditional thought, Confucianism is associated with the this-worldly nature of existence. It has historically demonstrated a decisive preference for societal engagement over abstract investigation of the inanimate universe. In contrast to the concern with life after death characteristic of so many other early belief systems in China and elsewhere, Confucianism has mostly focused on the everyday functioning of man in his present world.

The this-worldly grounding of Confucianism is also discernible in the language it characteristically used. Among all the early schools, Confucianism stands alone in its emphatic faith in man's perfectibility through the use of correct language. For the earliest Confucians, language itself became a vehicle of morality. One way in which the moral function of language in Confucian thought differs from that of the West has been pointed out by Chad Hansen: "While in early Western philosophy, there is a kind of assumption that the primary role of language is in describing the world and communicating ideas or beliefs about the world, Confucianism assumes that the primary function of language is the instilling of moral attitudes which affect choice and action. Language should be manipulated because one can thereby control and influence action through manipulation of moral attitudes."[5] Hansen's assertion is vividly borne out in the *Lunyu* or the *Analects* when Confucius (551–479 B.C.) exclaims: "How remarkable that a group of men can meet all day long, engage in trivial displays of intelligence, and never once make mention of the term *righteousness* (*yi*)!"[6] Beginning with the founder, Confucianism regarded the espousal and inculcation of moral values as the principal function of language.

Concomitantly, Confucianism eschews language of amoral content. Historically, Confucians have limited the range of subject matter suitable for truly moral discussion. This is seen in the *Analects,* in which it is stated that Confucius never spoke about "miraculous events, feats of strength, civil disorder, or spiritual beings."[7] Excluding these categories, Confucians sought to achieve moral ends through language that restricted the content of appropriate discourse. These aberrant categories represent the exception rather than the rule of everyday life; two of them—miraculous events and spiritual beings—are thought to be beyond the normal range of sense apprehension and therefore impossible to confirm. With respect to its choice of language, Confucian thought gives preference to commonplace, verifiable entities over abstract, elusive ones.

Confucian language also manifests this-worldly stylistic conventions.

As Donald Munro states in his *The Concept of Man in Early China,* "Confucian writings . . . are generally prosaic, straightforward, and commonsensical."[8] They are frequently placed in contradistinction to Daoist writings in order to underscore their distinctiveness in this respect. Daoist writing, again according to Munro, "excels at the use of parables, allegories, and anecdotes that suggest an idea rather than explicitly stating it."[9] Laozi and Zhuangzi, for example, advise us to be wary of the inadequate capacity of language for describing the *dao* or the Absolute and then proceed to present us with either elliptical or intricately paradoxical justifications for this caveat. In contrast to the mystical embellishment so often prominent in *Zhuangzi,* the writings of the Confucians are plain-spoken, deliberate, and confident in the capacity of ordinary language to express profound truths. Confucius of the *Analects* remarked simply that "it will suffice that the language one uses gets the point across."[10]

Whereas the image content of Daoist language seems calculated to evoke insights through references to the strange and fantastic, Confucian language attempts to engender the beginnings of a moral consciousness precisely by avoiding references to the unusual or bizarre. Shadowy ghosts, imaginative beasts, and subtle abstractions wander freely through the Daoist literary landscape. Confucius's successor Xunzi (ca. 340–ca. 245 B.C.) does at one point refer to "pools of dragons" when discussing the merits of education.[11] Still, nothing in the writings of the classical Confucian philosophers compares with Zhuangzi's immense roc-bird Peng, which uses its unfathomable wingspread of several thousand *li* to soar upward from the sea en route to the Southern Darkness.[12] The moral resolve implicit in the Confucian approach to language does not accommodate such extraordinary imagery, viewed as untoward and distracting from moral progress. Undeniably, philosophical Daoist language also employs its own definitive set of realistic symbolic imagery, such as the infant, the uncarved block, the valley, water, the wheel, and a host of subsidiary images. Zhuangzi even said that "the true sage abandons the light that dazzles and takes refuge in the common and the ordinary."[13] Nevertheless, in *Zhuangzi* as well as *Laozi,* these ostensibly ordinary images are appreciated predominantly for their value as abstractions and coexist with a set of fabulous imagery—like the Invisible, the

River Lord, the mythical one-legged *kui,* and so forth—that cannot be found anywhere in Confucian literature.

Thus, even within their shared empiricist context, Confucianism is linguistically distinct from such schools as Daoism, Yang Zhu, and, to a certain extent, early Mohism (inasmuch as the Mohists explicitly posited a belief in an active, willful, and quasi-anthropomorphic Heaven). Whereas Confucian thought is "sensationalist" philosophically because it assumes that perceptions of the ordinary senses convey an accurate depiction of what is real, it is clearly "anti-sensationalist" in the literary sense. The Confucians held all manner of fanciful language to be non-purposeful and potentially immoral, an evaluation that would seem to signify more than mere stylistic scruples.

Clear distinctions in usage are evident in the linguistic conventions of China's ancient schools; such contrasts as between Confucian language, with its almost exclusively familiar imagery and deliberately placid voice, and the ethereal, overawing, and sometimes jolting language of philosophical Daoism have led some Sinological scholars to theorize on the demarcating function of language within thought generally. Pierre Do-Dinh, for example, in contrasting the Chinese and the Indo-European linguistic traditions, has written that, even if differences in language do not prove that every body of thought is reducible to its language, such differences at least support the idea that "many forms of thought, or what we take to be such, are merely forms of language, that properly speaking they are without content, that they are auto-productions of the language."[14] Do-Dinh's rather radical assessment clearly indicates the extreme to which some scholars perceive the content of thought to be dictated by language, that inasmuch as it can be said to have content at all, thought is entirely language-bound. Speaking with more reserve and specifically of Chinese thought, the late Sinologist E. R. Hughes also noted the role of language as a controller and shaper of thought. In emphasizing the conditioning function of language in Chinese thought, Hughes stated that: "R. G. Collingwood described philosophy as 'thought of the second degree, thought about thought.' The distinctively Chinese epistemological reply to that would be to say, 'Yes, more or less, but we do not know what your thinking is until it is expressed in language.'"[15] Thus, it would seem that Chinese

thinkers have long recognized language as the chief influence on philosophical discourse, and consequently, in the Chinese context, much of
the practice of philosophy has historically been essentially the critiquing of language.

CONFUCIAN ARGUMENTATION

If we are to accept the contention of a this-worldly ethos in Confucian
thought as valid, then this ethos must necessarily be reflected in the argumentation of the school. Munro states that Confucian thinkers typically employ one of three types of argumentation: the rhetorical "chain
argument," argument by appeal to antiquity, and argument by analogy.[16] One of the most famous examples of the use of the chain argument in the *Analects* concerns the correct use of language as dictated by
the crucial doctrine of *zhengming* or the "rectification of names." The
argument proceeds in part as follows, with Confucius responding to his
incredulous disciple Zilu:

> You, how boorish you are, indeed! When a gentleman is ignorant of some-
> thing, he should offer no opinion. If terms are not correct, then what is said
> will not accord with what is intended. If what is said does not accord with
> what is intended, affairs will not achieve success. If affairs do not achieve suc-
> cess, rites and music will not flourish. If rites and music do not flourish,
> punishments will not fit the crimes. If punishments do not fit the crimes, the
> common people will not know where to put hand or foot. Thus, when the
> gentleman specifies a term, it is sure to be usable in speech and when he
> speaks of anything, it is sure to be practicable. The thing about the gentleman
> is that he is never careless where speech is concerned.[17]

Despite the intricate step-by-step development of this argument, its linkage is not really logical.[18] Still, this sort of chain reasoning represents a
highly stylized and characteristic Confucian form of argument.

The Confucian attempt at philosophical persuasion based on the
appeal to antiquity is by far the most frequently used type of argument,
its appearances in Confucian literature so common that they warrant little comment. Confucius's persistent references to paragons of virtue like
the Duke of Zhou and other exemplars are inspired by the desire to cite
precedents in the revered past for present-day actions. They are a direct

outgrowth of the historical-minded leanings of Confucian thinking. The formulation of this type of argument can be quite complex because it demands detailed historical knowledge on the part of the formulator. The special insight we can gain from the argument appealing to antiquity, however, is the extent to which Confucians view the past as adumbrating the present and the future. Consequently, when a disciple once asked if the circumstances of those who will govern ten generations in the future can be known, Confucius responded:

> The Yin built upon the rites of the Xia and what it added and discarded can be known. The Zhou built upon the rites of the Yin and what it added and discarded can be known. Should there be an heir to the Zhou, even a hundred generations from now, its conduct can be known.[19]

In addition to these forms of argumentation, Confucians also used analogy. More than chain argument or appeal to antiquity, analogy is a constituent feature of the thought of all past and present cultures, the form that seems most readily to lend itself to the expression of a this-worldly viewpoint. Analogy as a tool of thought exists in every culture before the development toward formal logic, because analogical arguments have a kind of universal accessibility that appeals perhaps as much to untrained minds as to the philosophically sophisticated.[20] Still, to say that analogy exists *prior to* logic risks being somewhat misleading. As Angus Graham has correctly observed, stating that analogy exists prior to logic should not mean going to the extreme of implying that "on the borders of logic there is a loose form called argument from analogy."[21] Rather, as Graham further states, it means that "all thinking starts from a spontaneous discrimination of the like and the unlike, and tendency to group the similar in categories and expect similar consequences from similar conditions."[22] Understood in this light, analogizing can be construed as perhaps representing the first step toward philosophizing.

Moreover, the seemingly timeless and cross-cultural incidence of analogical reasoning has been frequently and convincingly noted. J. David Bolter, speaking of ancient Greece, remarks that "analogies from contemporary crafts were common in poetry and philosophy. This should not surprise us, for the spindle and the potter's wheel were as much a part of a philosopher's formative experience as the famed colors of the Aegean, the rugged mountains, or the inquisitiveness and garrulity of the Greek people."[23] Similarly, on both the high and popular cultural levels, analogy is a perennial fixture in Chinese thought. In the particular case of Confucian argumentation, analogy is simply a more immediate alternative than either chain argument or argument from antiquity. It frees both the erudite Chinese philosopher and the Chinese common man from the quasi-logical demands of chain argument and from the sometimes tedious historical data and obscure allusions required to construct the argument appealing to antiquity.

One way of explaining the prevalence of analogical arguments in Confucian thought may be that they tend to function as methodological "tethers"—grounding devices that direct one's attention away from undue other-worldly speculation toward a preoccupation with the more conventional concerns rooted in the observable world of normal experience. This would seem particularly true in the case of the early Confucian school. Confucius, as noted earlier, expressly called for the rejection of inquiry into matters outside the purely knowable and practicable, such as the supernatural. Still, to suggest that analogies of essentially identical content could not be used to the opposite effect—to engender a sense of first concern with the other-worldly—would of course be erroneous. We shall in fact see that analogies of identical or at least very similar content within the same Confucian tradition were also used to achieve precisely the opposite result. They could be used rather to point to certain inherently other-worldly dimensions of Confucian thinking, such as speculation on the most metaphysical aspects of human nature.

ARGUMENT BY ANALOGY AND THE CONCEPT OF HUMAN NATURE

Let us now see how philosophers of the classical and later Confucian (Neo-Confucian) tradition used this-worldly analogical arguments to promote their individual interpretations of the central and evolving concept of *xing* or human nature or, simply, nature. Benjamin Schwartz, in his *The World of Thought in Ancient China*, describes how the term *xing* eventually became pivotal in the emerging debates within Confucianism at the same time that it also figured significantly in the discussions of other schools.[24] In this way, *xing* eventually became part of what Schwartz calls a common discourse—a shared vocabulary of a broad spectrum of modes of thought. Schwartz urges going beyond purely philological evidence in the investigation of ideas. He states that "the history of an idea may be more than the history of the term with which the idea ultimately comes to be identified."[25] This is singularly relevant when examining the earliest instances of Confucian deliberation on *xing*.

The term appears in the *Analects* on only two occasions, and it is not at any time presented in an analogical context. The first involves Confucius's disciple Zigong's remarking that "one can get to hear about Confucius's accomplishments but not about his views on human nature and the Way of Heaven."[26] The second is Confucius's own often-quoted statement that all men are "similar by nature but they diverge through practice."[27] In many respects, the first statement is more revealing than the second because, by not listing it among Confucius's accomplishments, Zigong at least offers the assessment that a well-formulated conception of *xing* may have been something Confucius was still struggling to develop.

The absence of explicit analogical references to *xing* does not preclude the possibility that Confucius made analogical references—however oblique—to life situations that deal with human nature. As the scholars Shu-hsien Liu and Antonio Cua have pointed out, Confucius never felt any apparent compulsion to give rigorous definitions of his key moral concepts, such as *ren, yi* or *li*.[28] Possibly because he already presupposed a rudimentary working knowledge of these concepts in his constituency, he typically illustrated his moral directives through concrete situations which provide ample evidence of the this-worldliness underlying Confucian thought. Many of these situations present case studies of Confucius grappling with some notion that undeniably approximates a concept of human nature as seen, for example, in the following passage in the *Analects:*

> Zai Yu was in bed in the daytime. Confucius said, "A piece of rotten wood cannot be carved and a dried-up dung wall cannot be troweled. What is the use of condemning Yu?" He then added, "I once assumed that a man's actions would always conform with his words. Now, having heard a man's words, I go

on to inspect his deeds. It is because of Yu that I have changed in this respect."[29]

At first glance, this passage appears merely to be commenting, albeit in a singularly negative way, on a major character flaw—laziness—of a particular disciple. It is worth noting that Zai Yu (also known as Zai Wo) was criticized by the Master more frequently than any other disciple.[30] When viewed in such a light, the passage seems to offer little more than supplementary biographical information on Confucius's dealings with one of his followers. This passage, especially as revealed by Confucius's concluding statement, however, represents more than a simple character judgment; it may reveal a process of empirical induction—a philosophical extrapolation from the particular to the general, from Zai Yu the disciple to men in general. In this extrapolation, Confucius is plausibly imparting views on something larger than a single undesirable behavioral trait of one individual. He may well be expressing opinions that are a nascent part of his vision of man *qua* man.

That Confucius could be probing toward some emergent conception of human nature may be immanent in the statement: "What is the use of condemning Yu?" On the one hand, this could mean no more than that Zai Yu is an incorrigible individual with no capacity for reforming. On the other, however, this statement may well suggest that Confucius regards Zai Yu's laziness as a mark of the nature of man in the abstract. In other words, Confucius could possibly perceive this kind of behavior on the part of a specific disciple as altogether in accord with widespread natural impulses that can neither be altered nor fully controlled.

The analogical structure and content of the above passage may foreshadow a concept of human nature. The stark comparisons involving Zai Yu, rotten wood, and a dried-up dung wall are earthy, familiar, powerful. The potency of these analogies is perhaps nowhere better described than in the commentary of Wang Chong (A.D. 27–100) who, more than five centuries later, expressed a sharp and lengthy critique of the appropriateness of Confucius's analogies. Wang stated:

> Being in bed in the daytime is a small transgression. But rotten wood and dried-up dung are things in such a decayed state that they can never be reclaimed and therefore constitute grave evils. If a trivial infraction becomes

punishable on the same level as a major crime, then how can people be expected to yield to punishment? If his nature (*xing*) was so bad as to be compared with rotten wood and dried-up dung, then Zai Wo should neither have been admitted into the school of Confucius nor ranked within one of the four classes of disciples. In the event, however, that his nature was actually good, then Confucius judged him too severely.[31]

Wang Chong's criticism of this analogical argumentation provides two illuminating insights. First, it shows the force and immediacy of Confucius's analogies in the mind of a much later thinker. Despite his distance in time and philosophical milieu from the classical Confucian school, Wang Chong was not able to ignore the enduring vitality of the school's argumentation. He did not object to Confucius's analogical method or line of argument but rather to his use of imagery that was overly severe and therefore not suited to the context. Second, and no less important, Wang clearly recognized this concrete episode as an implicit Confucian discussion of human nature; he even voiced the possibility that Confucius may have acknowledged the existence of a bad or evil nature. Of course, his hypothesis of an evil nature as a constituent of earliest Confucian thought could be an instance of historical hindsight or personal projection, or even a combination of these two processes. Wang Chong could either have been imputing to Confucius a concept of human nature not widely held until much later, or misrepresenting his own personalized idea of a bad *xing* as the idea of Confucius, or both. Still, Wang's overall critique of Confucius's original analogical argument stemmed from an interpretation of Confucius as seriously engaged in the deliberation on human nature—a subject on which he is reputed to have explicitly said next to nothing. Moreover, Wang Chong's offhand intimation that Confucius may have accepted the existence of an evil nature warrants a reconsideration of Confucius's supposed neutrality on the issue of human nature.

Mencius (ca. 390–ca. 305 B.C.), Confucius's most significant successor, was the first to articulate extensively the Confucian concept of *xing*. He is justifiably credited with establishing the conceptual precedent that human nature is originally and uniquely good. His positive interpretation of *xing* is the one that has prevailed within much of the later Confucian tradition and, in many ways, continues to shape the broadest outlines of even the most current trends in Chinese thought.

Mencius is also by far the most celebrated Confucian utilizer of analogical argumentation. A substantial number of literary and philosophical studies have indicated Mencius's preeminence in this respect.[32] The discussions on Mencius's use of analogy have generally been inspired by the desire of Western scholars to isolate apparent structural similarities between Chinese and Western philosophical discourse. In one of the earliest studies of its kind, I. A. Richards noted that, while differences do exist, certain analogical passages in Mencius seem "nearest to the forms of discourse familiar to us in Western thinking."[33] Hansen, in his *Language and Logic in Ancient China,* has echoed this sentiment in a more reticent manner by remarking that "some famous Mencian 'analogies' are muffed attempts at formal arguments."[34] Graham, probably the most unprejudiced and therefore generous contemporary investigator of Mencian analogy, argues that the use of analogy in Mencius displays both a developmental coherence and an internal logic.[35]

Analogy in the thought of Mencius is intimately connected with human nature. The most famous examples—those that begin the sixth book or "Gaozi" chapter of the work with his name—all center upon the discussion of *xing.* Even those who would maintain that the association between human nature and analogy in the *Analects* is at best indirect and indistinct must admit to the prominence of this convention in the *Mencius.* The subject of the analogical sequence that begins the sixth book is what exactly constitutes human nature. However, as Schwartz astutely surmises ultimately, "what is at stake is wholly the question of the source of morality."[36]

Mencius's particular understanding of *xing* is worth noting. *Xing* is a concept with a long evolution, but there is little evidence before Mencius's time that it connoted anything more than what Schwartz has called "an innate tendency toward growth or development in a given, predetermined direction."[37] The idea of a uniquely human *xing* distinct from the *xing* of other organisms is not strongly emphasized in this conception. However, by the early Warring States period, the concept of *xing* had already begun to evolve; two significant developments mark this change. First, despite the recognition of the uniqueness of any given *xing* to its species, the *xing* of man emerges as the preeminent focus of Confucian interest.[38] Second, the use of *xing* acquires a highly moralistic cast.[39] Confucian thinkers began to engage themselves almost exclusively with the investigation of the two qualities they felt made the *xing* of man distinct and elevated above all other *xing*—a mind with the capacity to know and choose between right and wrong and intrinsic social proclivities.[40] Thus, by Mencius's time, the concept of "nature" in Confucian thought had come to mean expressly "human nature." This conception of *xing*, which conforms well with the this-worldly priorities of the Confucian school, is the one Mencius inherited and tried assiduously to promote.

The first four of the series of Mencian analogies were actually initiated by Mencius's antagonist Gaozi, a thinker of indeterminate though perhaps rival Confucian philosophical persuasion.[41] In the first two analogies, Gaozi likened the nature of man to a succession of mundane naturalistic objects that Mencius rejected. When told, in the first instance, that human nature is like the *qi* willow but that instilling righteousness (*yi*) in human beings is like making willow cups and bowls, Mencius objected on the grounds that external pressures resulting in forcible mutilation are not required to make man moral. When Gaozi next suggested that human nature is like swirling water that shows no preference for eastward or westward (that is, good or bad) direction, Mencius countered that human nature always seeks the good just as water naturally seeks the lowest level, unless deflected.

The Mencian analogies climaxed with the third of the exchanges between Gaozi and Mencius, the most interesting of the analogies in that it diverges from the formula established in the two previous cases:

> Gaozi said, "That which is inborn is what is meant by 'nature.'"
> "Is that," said Mencius, "the same as 'white is what is meant by white'?"
> "Yes."
> "Is the whiteness of white feathers and the whiteness of white snow the same as the whiteness of white jade?"
> "Yes."
> "In that case, is the nature of a hound the same as the nature of an ox and the nature of an ox the same as the nature of a man?"[42]

Although Gaozi once again began the argument, Mencius immediately seized the initiative by means of a flawed analogy. In fact, in this dialogue it becomes clear how scant Mencius's appreciation for logic could really be. His description of "white" as what is meant by "white" was completely tautological,[43] providing the argument with no new information for furthering his thesis. Although the statement that "white" is what is meant by "white" was true simply by virtue of its component terms, it did not provide the argument (as Mencius assumed it did) with a workable definition for his subsequent idea of "whiteness." Therefore, despite what would seem to be a true conclusion, the *logic* of Mencius's argument—the procedural relationship between his premises and his conclusion—is not valid.

Nevertheless, even this realization should not prevent us from appreciating Mencius's analogical explication of *xing* for other reasons. This Mencian analogy, particularly in its last section, recalls the same kind of inductive extrapolation as in the example of Zai Yu in the *Analects*. In the above analogical exchange, however, Mencius was intent on leading Gaozi into the pitfalls of affirming an unsound inductive conclusion that even Gaozi himself could not accept. Mencius sought to undermine the idea of man's commonality with all other living things and advance the idea that human nature is unique. To Mencius, this uniqueness was absolutely crucial. In contrast to the natures of other animals, dominated by the impulses and appetites of sense gratification, the *xing* of man could be directed toward the achievement of moral ends.

Mencius objected to Gaozi's claim that human nature is that which is inborn if that inborn quantity can only be taken to mean the drive to satisfy such functions as the hunger for food and sex (the *xing* identifications which incidentally opened the fourth and final exchange with Gaozi). He did not deny that such attributes as the drives for food and sex are inborn, and he evidently did not oppose the contention that man shares these attributes in common with other animals. But, as Schwartz has rhetorically asked, "Why must one assume that only shared attributes are inborn?"[44] Indeed, Mencius made it his personal responsibility to highlight those inborn attributes of differentiation—the discriminating mind and social inclinations—that have their provenance only in the nature of man. Man's nature is categorically distinct from those of lesser animals in its emulation of Heaven because of this special endowment he has received from Heaven.[45] Thus, Mencius's debate with Gaozi tells us a great deal about how the human *xing* came to be perceived in early Confucian thought. Through his analogical argumentation, Mencius informs us of the unique primacy of the human *xing*.

The foregoing Mencian analogy, like its companion analogies and the one from *Lunyu* already considered, also reveals the this-worldly quality of its image content. Schwartz remarks that this specific analogical dialogue confronts us with "objects which we would all agree are as different from each other as one can imagine."[46] On a strictly physical or bio-physiological level, this is certainly true. If viewed, however, from the perspective of the this-worldly ethos thought to pervade Chinese thinking, all the objects in this or any other of the Mencian analogies are essentially of the most conventional kind, presented in the unspectacular style dictated by Confucian moral restraint. In the above dialogue, there are a number of commonplace images—feathers, snow, jade, a dog, an ox, a man. Within this given series of Mencian analogies, a plethora of similarly commonplace images are analogues and sub-analogues for human nature. The human *xing* is variously likened to a specific kind of willow tree and swirling water. Other, lesser images supplement these more primary ones—cups, bowls, and, later, a horse, roasted meat, wine, drinking water. All these images share the distinction of being neither grandiose, fanciful, nor obscure. Rather, they are life-sized, real, and easily comprehended. Moreover, they are described in language that is unremarkable and even sedate in tone and diction. Thus, despite its reputation as a stylistic advancement over the *Analects*,[47] the content of the analogies in the *Mencius* perpetuates the this-worldly orientation present in the earlier work.

ARGUMENTATION BY ANALOGY IN LATER CHINESE THOUGHT

The importance of argumentation grounded in the this-worldly did not end with the classical period of Chinese thought. We shall see below that this-worldly argument was vital to later Chinese thought as well. Once again, the Confucianists seem to have been leaders in perpetuating this orientation.

The concept of human nature—framed in this-worldly terms—was at the forefront of the speculations of the Song Neo-Confucians. Their discussions were probably every bit as vigorous as those that occurred during the classical era. Much of the extension of the concern with human nature into Neo-Confucian thought, like so many other intellectual bridges between earlier and later Confucian thinking, is due to Buddhism. In fact, Buddhism rekindled Song Confucian interest in the concept of human nature. Carsun Chang has pointed out how such tenets as the *Tathagatha* womb, which continually houses the essence of Tathagathahood, served to support the view, first espoused by Mencius, that the *xing* is innately endowed with some kind of moral standard.[48] The Song perpetuation of discussion on human nature was also furthered by such Tang dynasty formative Neo-Confucianists as Li Ao (774–836), whose limited written output is almost exclusively on the subject of *xing* and its recovery.[49] Yet, his later reputation as an ardent Confucian notwithstanding, Li Ao was much influenced by Buddhism and interjected much Buddhist interpretation into his consideration of human nature.

The weighty impact of Buddhist doctrine on the Neo-Confucian deliberation on human nature did not, however, stifle or subsume the discussion's independent development. The branch of Neo-Confucian thought initiated by Cheng Yi (1033–1107) made significant progress in a direction probably less indebted to Buddhism than to a concentrated scrutiny of the accumulated musings of the Confucian past. In the extant dialogues between Cheng Yi and his students, much energy is spent on Confucius's and Mencius's statements on *xing*. Cheng Yi utilized all the argumentational techniques customary within the Confucian tradition, as seen in his response to one of his followers' inquiries about Confucius's description of all men as nearly alike by nature:

> "Men are similar by nature but they diverge through practice." But if nature is unitary, what is the point of saying 'men are similar'?"
>
> Cheng Yi said: "This is only to speak of material nature. It is as in the familiar sayings 'quick by nature,' 'slow by nature,' and the like. How can nature itself be slow or quick? The term *nature* implied by Confucius's statement means 'that which is inborn.'"[50]

Another query about *xing* is marked by the following response, which makes full use of the argument type that appeals to antiquity:

> Someone asked: "If man's nature is originally immaculate, why does it become obscured?"
>
> Cheng Yi said: "This must be looked into to be understood. Mencius's saying that man's nature is good is correct, even though neither Xunzi nor Yang

Xiong [53 B.C.–A.D. 18] [who both came after Mencius] understood human nature. It was Mencius alone among all the early Confucians who could explain human nature. There is nothing about nature that is not good and it is instead one's aptitude (*cai*) [for carrying things out] that accounts for evil. Nature is really principle (*li*), and principle, for the sage-emperors Yao and Shun on down to the basest man, is one."[51]

Cheng Yi ultimately decided that *xing* should be equated with *li* (principle), the key concept for which his thought is best remembered. Interestingly, this equation of human nature and principle displays a certain formal affinity with the theories put forth by Gaozi, in that both men were attempting to define *xing* in terms of concepts. In two successive instances in the Mencian analogies already discussed, Gaozi argued that human nature is that which is inborn and that it is one's craving for food and sex. In this sense, Cheng Yi, like Gaozi, was positing a conceptual framework for understanding *xing*. Despite his highly probable substantive objections to Gaozi's contentions, Cheng Yi's equation of human nature and principle here was close in form to Gaozi's identifications because we see both men laboring to tell us what *xing* is in contrast to Mencius's efforts in the foregoing analogies to tell us what it is not.[52]

Cheng Yi's thoughts on human nature can be subsumed into a broader matrix of continuity on the basis of how they are expressed. In conformity with the tactics of those who preceded him, Cheng Yi made resourceful use of this-worldly analogies to drive home his most insistent points on the subject:

Nature comes from Heaven and aptitude comes from material force (*qi*). If material force is pure, then one's aptitude will be pure and, if material force is clouded, one's aptitude will also be clouded. This situation can be likened to wood. Whether a piece of wood is crooked or straight is owing to nature. But as for whether it is fit for making a main-beam, or a cross-beam, or a house's assorted rafters depends on the capacity (*cai*) of the wood. The aptitude of a man or the capacity of a thing may be good or evil but nature cannot be anything but good.[53]

And again:

Someone asked whether the emotions of happiness and anger arise from the nature.

Cheng Yi responded: "This is indeed the case because only after one possesses consciousness does one have a nature. Upon possessing nature, one then is capable of emotions. Without a nature, how can one even have emotions?"

It was also asked how it is possible for happiness and anger to rise from outside of the person possessing them.

Cheng Yi replied: "It is not that they arise from outside. Their expression is external but it itself issues forth from within the person."

Someone then asked if the nature's having the emotions of happiness and anger is like water having waves.

Cheng Yi affirmed: "One's being placidly calm is akin to the nature of mirroring water. But if this reflective water encounters sand or rocks or some other sort of uneven embankment, it then develops into rapids. Or if a wind happens to blow over it, then it develops crashing waves and billows that swell toward the heavens. But how do these manifestations constitute the *nature* of water?

"Human nature is comprised only of the Four Beginnings (*ren, yi, li,* and *zhi*). Yet, how is it that there are so many occurrences in the world that are not themselves good? Without water, how can there be waves? Without nature, how can there be emotions?"[54]

The this-worldly language anchoring these analogies not only links Cheng Yi's argumentation with that of Mencius and Gaozi but also solidly locates his discourse on *xing* within the greater tradition of Confucian thought. However, what is even more important is Cheng's recognition that the ordinary language that stocks his analogies can be used to raise and elucidate central concepts, like *xing,* and some supportive concepts such as material force (*qi*), capacity (*cai*), and the Four Beginnings (*siduan*), that are far larger and more elevated than the language used to discuss them. In these instances and elsewhere, like Confucius and Mencius before him, Cheng Yi seems to acknowledge tacitly that the this-worldly language that typifies Confucian analogies is fully expressive of even the most profound dimensions of thought.

The Confucian-minded thinkers who followed in Cheng Yi's wake continued to exhibit a general penchant and facility for this-worldly argumentation, and a conceptual model for their interpretation of *xing* finally reached fruition in the protean thought of Zhu Xi (1130–1200). As the most widely recognized synthesizer of Song Neo-Confucianism generally, Zhu Xi was also the clarifier of numerous inchoate intellectual tendencies of the period. The assumptions underlying Zhu Xi's approach to human nature, as with so many of his ideas, largely represent a rational continuation of Cheng Yi's thoughts on the matter. With regard to *xing*, Zhu Xi introduced his own ideas as well as ideas from other prominent Confucianists of the Song era and earlier which have since been interpreted as being Zhu's own.

Human nature, for both Cheng Yi and Zhu Xi, can be equated with *li* (principle). Zhu Xi, for his part, construed *li* to be the locus of man's intelligence as well as his moral makeup. Yet, despite its role as a primary and dictating concept for him, *li* did not seem to function as autonomously as for Cheng Yi. Instead, *li* worked more consistently with a rich complement of additional concepts. This tendency for *li* to be more dynamically integrated into Zhu Xi's thought results in a somewhat more complex view of *xing* because the two concepts were seen not only as wholly equivalent but also as embracing all life forms. In the above passages, Cheng Yi discussed human nature in connection with concepts like *li*, *cai*, and *qi*.[55] Below is a representative illustration of how Zhu Xi dealt with this same issue:

Someone asked: "If it is the case that material force and raw matter (*zhi*) have varying degrees of impurity, then doesn't the nature that Heaven bestows upon man also vary in its degree of perfection and imperfection?"

Zhu Xi said: "Human nature is not perfect or imperfect. It can be spoken of like the light of the sun or moon. If their rays shine on dewy ground, then one can see them in all of their brilliance. But if their rays shine through to the floor of a thatch-roofed hut, then there is diffraction—places where light shines through to the ground and places where it does not. Whenever there is impurity, it is material force that is impure. Therefore, penetrating through its obstruction is like [the process of] light shining through to the floor of a thatch-roofed hut.

"When obstruction occurs in the case of man, there is a principle that can penetrate it. Even in the case of animals, there is this [same unobstructed] nature [that humans have]. But animals are restricted by their physical forms. Animals are born with material force containing an extremely dense level of blockage and there are places where no principle can penetrate through it. Even the cases of the benevolence (*ren*) of the tiger and wolf, the sacrificial spirit (*ji*) of the wild dog and otter, and the righteousness (*yi*) of the bee and ant are ones in which there has been only a small amount of penetration, comparable to the penetration of a single shaft of light entering a crack. In the case of the great apes, there is greater penetration because their forms so resemble man. Thus, it is fitting that they are the most intelligent of all other living things. It is simply that they are not able to speak, that's all."[56]

In this passage, Zhu Xi used a panoply of interlocking conceptual relationships in his argument. Initially, he set out to answer a question about human nature, but the ensuing explanation explicated numerous other concepts to such an extent that he ended up saying essentially as much about the mechanics of the pivotal concepts *li* and *qi* as he did about *xing*.

Zhu Xi's explanation of his conception of *xing* bears a close kinship to its earliest and perhaps pre-Confucian interpretation. According to Schwartz, this interpretation may well have meant little more than the predilection of any organism for growth in a fixed direction.[57] In the case of human beings, this probably meant foremost "the tendency to live out one's own life in health, in the absence of anxiety, and in the moderate satisfaction of one's sensual desires."[58] The real evidence of Zhu Xi's success in recapturing what might be the original perspective on *xing*, however, comes forth in his opinion on the natures of animals. According to Zhu, animal nature is not radically different from our own in kind. It is neither perfect nor imperfect and remains, at all times, clear and unimpeded. It is rather always the *qi* of men, animals, and presumably all other things that blocks clarity.

Zhu Xi's discussion of *xing* was an elaborate construction built with this-worldly analogies. Taken as a whole, the above passage is actually a composite of a skillful succession of graphic analogies. Zhu's questioner set the process in motion by suggesting an analogous relationship between material force and raw matter, on the one hand, and Heaven-bestowed (human) nature, on the other hand. Zhu Xi responded by likening principle (and, by implication, nature) to the light rays of the sun and moon and comparing material force to a thatch-roofed hut, which, depending on its possessor, can vary in how much light it admits. Zhu concluded his argument by assigning a series of human-based conceptual virtues (*ren*, *ji*, and *yi*) to specific sets of recognizable animals that he believed, however approximately, were apt analogues for humans in their performance of instinctively programmed behavior.

As in the case of Cheng Yi, the occasions on which Zhu Xi utilized this-worldly analogies in argument were numerous. Again in connection with the discussion of *xing*, the following record of a disciple appears:

> We continued to examine fairly the various explanations of nature available.
>
> Master Zhu said: "In discussing it, one must first of all recognize what kind of a thing nature is. As for Master Cheng's equation of nature with principle, this is the most correct explanation. Now we must certainly speak of nature in terms of principle. After all, nature is still without form and is really only a principle of conduct (*daoli*). Among humans, nature is benevolence, righteousness, ritual, and wisdom. What kinds of shapes do these four have? They too are only this principle of conduct.
>
> "If one possesses this principle of conduct, one can carry out many affairs. It enables one to feel natural compassion and yet shame for one's own misdeeds; it enables one to be respectful of right and wrong. This principle of conduct can be spoken of in the same way that we speak of the nature of medicine—in terms of its nature being cold or hot. Medicine itself also [like the Four Beginnings] cannot be spoken of as having these properties. Rather, these properties only apply to the after-effects of taking the medicine. Yet, if it makes us feel cold or hot, then we speak of this as being the nature of the medicine. But it is really only like benevolence, righteousness, ritual, and wisdom."[59]

Here, through the similarly this-worldly device of medicine, Zhu Xi offered parallel confirmation of Cheng Yi's earlier argument that the nature of water is not its manifestations any more than the nature of medicine is its after-effects.

At still another juncture, Zhu Xi returned to the use of human-animal analogies to readdress the limitations of animal nature while at the same time emphasizing *xing* as the most important factor guiding and regulating the conduct of all living things—human and otherwise. Interestingly, this particular passage ends on a fervent ecological note:

> Within one body, there are five viscera and six bowels. On the outside, there are ears, eyes, a mouth, a nose, and four limbs. These are things that all people have. Benevolence, righteousness, ritual, and wisdom preserve these things and one's senses of natural compassion, shame over misconduct, and respect for right and wrong all spring forth from these sources. All humankind is so endowed and, in completing the five bonds of father-son, elder brother-younger brother, husband-wife, friend-friend, and sovereign-subject, no one is without these essentials.

This is also true of other living things, but they are restricted by form and by material force and incapable of change. But they also have a fragment [of humanity] and we only need to observe them to see that they too have the relationship of father-son. When there is male and female among them, then there is husband and wife. When there is large and small, then there is elder and younger brother. This leads to other comparable categories. Every species that collects in groups has the friendship bond and, if it also has members with superior minds, then it has the bond of sovereign-subject. This is simply because all creatures ultimately are originally the products of Heaven and Earth and, holding this basis in common, the great bulk of living things very much resemble the sages and worthies in their coming forth to comfort and oversee the myriad things.

Each thing is directed according to its nature. It is like [the development of] insects and grasses and trees. There has yet to be a time when they have departed from their natures. If you want to gather them according to the seasons and use them according to their times, then you must permit them to flourish in springtime by not subjecting them to untimely deaths, overturning their nests, or killing them in the womb. The grasses and trees confined themselves to mountain forests only after they were decimated by man. Only after the fear of man had entered along the marsh bridges did the otter sacrifice his fish. Only after the fields were cordoned off for the hunting of game did the wild dog forego his meals of small beasts. That which causes each of the myriad things to assume its place is nothing more than the situation of first recognizing that everything is originally brought forth by Heaven and Earth.[60]

In all of the above examples, as elsewhere, Zhu Xi's analogies are indeed arguments of multiple dimensions. This-worldly analogies permitted Zhu Xi to render densely complicated arguments in such a fashion that they became direct, forceful, and immediately appealing. Despite its subtlety, Zhu's discussion of human nature, by virtue of its overt analogical structure, selective image content, and ordinary language, projects a strong worldly flavor. Each constituent image within the several analogies within the several arguments is of incontestable accessibility. Zhu Xi fully achieved what Munro speaks of as the definitive utilitarian purpose of metaphor and analogy. Munro states that, although any given theory may not describe its own internal structural linkage, the use of analogies can provide new information that "can enrich the theory, making it more plausible by tightening its obvious connection to something mundane."[61] Much like Cheng Yi, Zhu Xi seems to have been quite cognizant of the capacity of analogy as a useful device for distilling more palatable conceptual products. Moreover, as illustrated in the last example, by using ordinary bodily, relational, and animal imagery, Zhu avoided any possibility of arriving at an arcane language of philosophical abstraction. The ordinary language of his argument points to and clarifies ideas of substantive, indeed other-worldly, significance. Therefore, among China's Song-period Confucians as well as those of the classical era, the intrinsic value of analogy, perhaps because it tends to dictate the use of ordinary language in philosophical discourse, was seen as obvious and unquestionable.

CONCLUSION

I have tried to discuss the idea of Chinese philosophical "this-worldliness" by elucidating the connection between a method of argument (analogy) and a concept of perennial discussion (*xing*) within Confucianism. Argument in this-worldly terms is inseparably connected with Chinese thought in the minds of numerous observers. Thus, one of the original questions set forth was whether a this-worldly approach to knowledge is actually a staple of Chinese thought. From the foregoing analysis of philosophical "this-worldliness" within both early and later Confucianism, we have seen that there is much evidence to support this association.

In this assessment, we have found that the varied Confucian heritage occupies a unique place within the large body of Chinese thought. Confucianism, more than any other school, is consistently taken to exemplify traditional China's core cultural values. Consequently, Chinese as well as Western historians of Chinese thought have cited the consistently practical-minded and this-worldly quality of Confucian argumentation as one of the school's enduring contributions to rational humanistic thinking in China. As much as any other single factor, the appreciation for sober, no-nonsense, "down-to-earth," and ordinary language in argument has come to stand for what we consider to be the Confucian approach to thought and outlook on life.[62]

Yet, a larger question is whether the preponderantly this-worldly approach of Chinese thought to knowledge means that it is itself essentially restricted to deliberation on the this-worldly. Our examination of analogy as a Confucian convention of argumentation has revealed that this-worldly means are not necessarily limited to this-worldly ends. Indeed, the most frequent topics of Confucian analogical arguments—as demonstrated by the case of *xing*—could hardly be more categorically other-worldly, that is, abstract and sublime in their implications. Schwartz is among the scholars who, in observing the levels of abstraction at which these speculations on human nature took place, has especially noted the metaphysical (even transcendental) quality of *xing* as a concept. He states that later Confucian thinkers believed that it was precisely this inner realm of the *xing* that connected man to the outer realm, that "bound man to the cosmos as a whole."[63] In this view, Confucians, like Zhu Xi, were clearly of the opinion that it was man's *xing* that most intimately linked him with the greater universe, serving as a vital connective bridge between the inner and outer, or this-worldly and other-worldly, realms of existence. Thus, at least with respect to the ends they sought to achieve through their arguments, Confucian thinkers must be consistently seen as having perceived *xing* as a profoundly expansive concept. Viewed in this light, the perception of Chinese thought as intrinsically confined to deliberation on this-worldly concerns would seem thoroughly undermined.

All the foregoing discussion leaves one final issue outstanding. Having established that there may well be a predilection in the main current of Chinese thought for this-worldly approaches to knowledge does not explain why it should be so. In other words, why have this-worldly methods of argument (for example, analogy) prevailed as the chief means of inquiring into even the most abstruse subjects in the Chinese intellectual heritage? Is there any single factor or set of factors that helps to account for the retention and persistence of this tendency over time?

One plausible way of resolving this lingering issue involves a reconsideration of the moral imperative underlying the use of language in Confucian thought. As stated earlier, Confucians felt that language, rather than being primarily descriptive as in the classical Western tradition, should affect conduct directly, by inculcating proper attitudes. Such a perception of language is therefore not so much immediately concerned with shaping how its users think as how they act. Proper actions were in fact seen as a verifying prelude to correct thought and, as we might expect, the language produced by this prescription would naturally seek first to conform more to the demands of the broad social and interactive world than to the private needs of the individual.

Such a language took on a heightened sense of importance among its users because its right or wrong usage directly impacted on one's actions in relation to others, a fact of life in traditional China that cannot be overemphasized. Confucian language thus took on a status beyond a tool of neutral expression. Its correct or incorrect use necessarily displayed one's degree of acculturation as an individual within a larger group-centered matrix of Confucian relationships and a still larger Chinese (but not altogether Confucian) social order. Language usage became deeply emblematic of one's social worth. Therefore, for the Confucianists particularly, the incorrect use of language indicated much more than the misuse of a term or a breach of syntax. It revealed a fundamental failure in cultural adaptation.

These conditions of social restraint attached to Confucian language must surely have been exacerbated by the fact that, while scholarship has always been highly prized, actual literacy has never been universal in China. Consequently, for Confucian learning and its values to be successfully disseminated as a body of thought, it was clearly important that the conventions of Confucian language be more than simply intelligible and shared; it was also important that they be as accessible as possible, even to the commonest of people. Of these features, accessibility becomes the key for understanding the remarkable continuity of Confucian this-worldly methods of argumentation. These methods, of which analogy is the most representative, even today remain indicative of how the tactics as well as the fruits of philosophical discourse were seen as potentially available to everyone. In short, the Confucian view of language can be seen as fully conforming with the Confucian view of man and its ideal that any man has the potentiality for becoming a sage.

In addition to its insights on the inescapable nature of Confucian language, the recognition of the potential sageliness of every man in China suggests some intriguing differences in the relationships of the Confucian and the classical Western philosopher to their respective audiences.

It is fair to say that, in China, the role of the philosopher never became as specialized or professionalized as in ancient Greek society. Consequently, the interests and concerns of the Confucian philosopher and his lay audience remained more intimate. In Greece, especially from about the fourth century B.C. onward, the occupation of the philosopher became increasingly specialized, with the assumptions shared between him and his audience becoming increasingly fewer. This development, in turn, led to the division of the whole science of argument into two distinct branches—the philosopher's logic and the politician's rhetoric.[64] By contrast, in China, and much owing to Confucianism, the division between the role of philosopher and politician never became so distinct, and the strong demand that philosophers should be able to convey their ideas to an audience much wider than simply other philosophers remained intact. The Confucian philosopher and politician, usually fused in one and the same individual, was never afforded the alternative of societal disengagement that became available to his Western philosopher counterpart. It was the Confucian expectation that thinkers should not stand aloof from society and that they be as capable of addressing the social needs as the intellectual needs of humanity. Confucian language, even to this day, reflects this expectation.

There is also perhaps an institutional reason why the Confucian philosopher's role and, consequently, his language never became as specialized as in early Greek civilization. In China's later imperial history, owing to the mostly Confucian-inspired civil-service-examination system, the number of shared philosophical assumptions between the philosopher and his audience actually increased. This must have been particularly true after the imposition of what was effectively an examination orthodoxy in the form of the thought of Zhu Xi after about 1300. This orthodoxy created a situation in which most of the men in the society strove to master the same linguistic tools needed for excelling through the theoretically meritocratic channels of the examinations. The uniform nature of this corpus of linguistic tools, best symbolized by the restriction of legitimate scholarship to the Confucian classics and only Zhu Xi's commentaries on them, can hardly be emphasized enough. The fact that this uniform corpus was studied by virtually everyone who studied at all doubtlessly encouraged a kind of language consensus. This consensus, though highly technical, was not intentionally exclusive; rather, like the Confucian ethical vision it fostered, it was intended to be embraced by the whole society. In the minds of the proponents of the examination system (implicitly the bulk of the population), to adopt a mode of communication outside the pale of examination scholasticism, deliberately detached from one of the most familiar rites of passage of male life, must have eventually come to seem unnatural. Therefore, the requirement that there not be an unbridgeable gulf between the crafted statements of the philosopher and folksy aphorisms of the common people had a firm institutional basis in China. Within the framework of the examination system, all men were regarded as potential philosophers (defined in Confucian terms as individuals whose love of wisdom is staked primarily in the knowledge and mastery of worldly affairs); the retention of numerous this-worldly elements in the language of Confucianism may be partially due to this fact.

Thus, in the end, the idea of an intrinsic and underlying "this-worldliness" in Confucian thought is closely bound to the longstanding recognition of *homo aequalis* in China, that is, the consensus assumption of a natural equality among men.[65] This assumption helps to explain why, despite the overt appreciation for structured hierarchical relationships in Confucian thinking, it is still difficult to make the case for a class-bound structure in Confucian language. Whereas Confucian society was sharply demarcated between the elite and the underclasses, there was no corresponding demarcation in Confucian language, the durability of which has historically rested in its capacity to appeal to and be used by all sectors of its constituent society. Without this capacity, the identification of Confucianism with the thought and associated values of Chinese traditional culture generally could never have become so complete as it has. For this reason, the idea that there is a pervasive this-worldly ethos that flavors and colors the entire rubric of what we understand to be Chinese thought has little meaning apart from an informed awareness of the largely Confucian language that has been assumed to express it.

THREE

Yan Fu's Utilitarianism in Chinese Perspective

HOYT CLEVELAND TILLMAN

Writing *In Search of Wealth and Power*, Benjamin Schwartz portrayed Yan Fu (1853–1921) as wrestling with utilitarianism and other Western social philosophies for answers to China's problems.[1] As explicated by Schwartz, Yan Fu perceived British utilitarianism through a framework of social Darwinism; for instance, Yan was not sensitive to the misgivings some utilitarians had (because of their welfare ethic) about the implications of social Darwinism. Fascinated with Herbert Spencer's message that competition among individuals striving for their own interests released energy that contributed to collective goals of the nation, Yan Fu valued the struggle for individual interests, which he contrasted to traditional Chinese views.

Schwartz's emphasis on Western influences upon Yan Fu meshed smoothly with the dominant temper of China historians in America during the 1950s and 1960s, a period dominated by the theme of China's response to the West and the premise of a break with tradition. Even in that context, by the early 1960s Schwartz demonstrated an appreciation for the complexity of Chinese tradition, and had turned aside from the more holistic approaches to tradition and modernity then prevalent. For instance, he argued that Yan Fu's attraction to Daoism was more than an emotional, traditionalistic attachment; hence, Schwartz had already come to a more nuanced view than

Levenson's choice between emotional attachments to and totalistic rejec-
tions of tradition.[2] It was the *Realpolitik* legacy of the Legalists that
Schwartz saw as an influence upon Yan's enhancement of state wealth
and power in translations of Western thought. Thus, Schwartz did not
ignore endogenous influences upon Yan's decisions regarding which
Western texts had most relevance to China's problems. Still, the thrust
of Schwartz's thesis centered on exogenous influences from the West.

During the quarter century since the publication of Schwartz's study
of Yan Fu, increasing attention has been given to interpreting fundamental values and issues in the context of China's own tradition(s) and history. In light of recent scholarship, how might we develop the
endogenous side of Schwartz's presentation of Yan Fu's intellectual
framework?

One route has already been explored by Mizoguchi Yūzō, who takes
an exclusively endogenous approach to underscore continuity from traditional thinkers to modern ones like Yan Fu. Tracing the traditional
roots of the modern problem of the general, or public, interest (*gong*)
versus individual self-interest (*si*), Mizoguchi draws attention to developments in late imperial China toward a naturalistic notion of principle
and a sense of individualism. However, his basic line of inquiry is
focused on what went wrong in modern China to thwart the evolution
of such important concepts as private interest and individualism. Mizoguchi focuses on mainline Confucians (such as Zhu Xi, 1130–1200) who
identified self-interest with selfish desires; hence, self-interest stood in
rigid contrast to ethical values ascribed to a true, but hidden, moral
nature within people. Buddhists also denied legitimacy to individual
desires and self-interests and regarded these interests and desires as an illusion; moreover, Daoists had concerns about individualized interests and
desires running counter to the *dao* in nature. It was such Buddhistic and
Daoistic notions that Yan Fu and other transitional thinkers borrowed
to reinforce Confucian biases against self-interest. Hence, the general
interest fell short of including the protection of individual interests and
rights. According to Mizoguchi's survey, Chinese Marxism has been the
logical conclusion of the social and intellectual evolution of the concept
of *gong* in imperial China: In spite of evolving egalitarian implications,
the notion of the general interest limited sympathy for individual

interests so that the idea of personal liberty has remained weak in relation to state power.[3] Although Mizoguchi has sketched in some of the
endogenous background for modern thinkers, he has not wrestled with
the exogenous influences from the West that had been presented by
Schwartz; moreover, he has ignored what was a significant, albeit frequently overlooked, component of the endogenous tradition.

It is to this missing link in the tradition that I turn to enhance the
endogenous component of Schwartz's picture of Yan Fu. Chen Liang's
(1143–1194) thinking about individual and public interest was grounded
in a far more positive view of individual desires and interests than that
held by his contemporary Zhu Xi. The question of whether or not Yan
Fu was influenced by Chen is a difficult one to answer, for, even if Yan
felt affinity with him, there was no compelling reason for him to cite
this twelfth-century utilitarian thinker. Drawing attention to minor
strains of Confucian thinking, like Chen's, as having prefigured some of
his own utilitarian ideas would not have furthered his polemics. In his
pleas for, and defense of, change, he brought to the fore what he
regarded as the negative legacy of mainline or orthodox Confucians. As
the cornerstone of state orthodoxy in late imperial China, Zhu Xi
loomed larger on Yan's horizons—either as an ubiquitous influence
(according to Mizoguchi) or as a symbol of the Confucian traditionalism against which Yan fought (according to Schwartz). In either case,
both of these more recent interpreters of Yan Fu apparently judge him
to have had more than a pedestrian knowledge of Confucianism; hence,
I am perhaps not wrong in positing that he was sufficiently schooled in
Confucianism to have been at least somewhat familiar with some of
Chen Liang's writings. Zhu Xi's debate with Chen, conducted through
their correspondence, was among the more famous expositions of his
thought, and some excerpts from Chen's letters to Zhu often traveled,
or were read along, with Zhu's letters. Problems of restoring the country after the Opium War and the Taiping Rebellion sparked a revival of
interest in Chen's writings as evidenced in the publication of two editions of his collected works during Yan's teens in addition to one
printed four years before his birth.[4] Furthermore, Chinese scholars in
our own day have credited Chen Liang with having had an influence
upon major seventeenth- and eighteenth-century Confucians (such as

Gu Yanwu, Yan Yuan, Li Gang, and Dai Zhen) who directly affected the immediate intellectual context for Yan Fu's ideas. Such studies are available for those who wish to trace threads of influence, and I have discussed elsewhere the issue of Chen's influence upon thinkers in late imperial China.[5]

My purpose here is not to pursue the question of Chen Liang's individual influence, but, following Schwartz's penchant for observing elements of continuity in problematique from one context to another, to bring into focus an endogenous tradition of utilitarian ideas. Instead of looking, as Schwartz does, to the Legalists for the native side of Yan Fu's penchant for searching for wealth and power and his affinity for Western utilitarian ideas, I shall highlight elements of a Chinese utilitarian tradition. Rather than ignoring Schwartz's findings (as Mizoguchi did), I shall build upon Schwartz's recent book on ancient China, in which he enriches the discussion of utilitarian thought by interjecting questions arising from studies of Western utilitarianism into an analysis of Mo Di (circa 480–390 B.C.). In *The World of Thought in Ancient China*, Schwartz discusses the thought of Mo Di in terms of John Rawls's points about conflicts between general and particular interests in Western utilitarianism.[6] According to Schwartz's earlier work, Yan Fu's utilitarianism was essentially Western; yet this later book presents Mo Di as having set forth ideas that laid the foundation for a Chinese tradition regarding utility and social benefits as criteria for value. Needless to say, European and Chinese contexts influenced the evolution of these utilitarian traditions in different ways, but Schwartz has been able to use questions about one tradition to shed light upon the other.

Similarly focused upon the utilitarian problematique in different historical contexts, viewing Chen Liang between Mo Di and Yan Fu will, I hope to show, suggest some of the complexity and direction of the evolution of utilitarian thought in China. Exploring some of Chen Liang's writings will demonstrate that there are several significant parallels to positions Yan Fu adopted centuries later. Whether or not Chen Liang actually conditioned Yan Fu's understanding of Western utilitarianism, juxtaposing them should expand our understanding of one component of a Chinese tradition behind his thought. Striving toward this primary goal involves both some adjustment of Schwartz's earlier picture of Yan

Fu and application of his questions concerning Mo Di's utilitarian notions in classical antiquity to Chen Liang's ideas in the twelfth century.

These three thinkers from widely separated periods in Chinese history have some common orientations. Yan Fu's judgment—that the state's wealth and power were more urgent and immediate than individual interests and liberty—arose out of a context comparable to Mo Di's and Chen Liang's. All three were obsessed with their government's inability to unify the country and protect the people from foreign encroachments. That sense of overwhelming crisis necessitated the subjection of individual interests to the national interest; moreover, such crises apparently facilitated their assumption of an identity between individual interests and the general interest. Nationalism was another major factor in Yan's thought, and I have elsewhere explicated Chen's nationalistic notions as being comparable to concepts of the *Volk* or national community prevalent in Central and Eastern Europe during the nineteenth century.[7] Even when the national interest was not in jeopardy, however, Chen and Yan evaluated individual self-interest in a far more positive light than mainline Confucians allowed. Since the inner logic of ideas does not function independently of society and polity, similarities in these three utilitarians' initial conditions hold promise for facilitating reflections about aspects of China's "utilitarian tradition."

SCHWARTZ'S UTILITARIAN PROBLEMATIQUE IN ANCIENT CHINA

The "state of nature" which Mo Di envisioned in the beginning was a state of self-regarding individuals in all-out conflict with one another. Such conflict pitted one group against another and one person against another, even within a group, because each sought particular and immediate advantage. Out of this chaos arose some "men of worth" who realized that a ruler could establish order, so the most wise and able was selected to be the sovereign ruler. The role of the ruler was to focus or enforce the attention of the people upon the general interest as the ultimate interest of each person. The ruler and the men of worth had also been self-regarding individuals, but they understood that their individual interests were served only when "the greatest happiness of the greatest number" was achieved. Dispensing wealth and status as rewards and inflicting punishments were necessary because people persisted in being actuated by self-love.

To counter this self-regarding tendency, Mo Di preached "universal love" which Schwartz glossed as "universal fairness or sense of equity" and as "an impartial reasoned concern for all men as ends in themselves."[8] To buttress this reasoned concern, the Mohists developed logic and dialectic disputation to demonstrate that such concern was instrumental in building and maintaining social order. Likewise, appeals to Heaven (*tian*) as a deity (who dealt impartially with the people and wanted them to deal in the same manner with one another) were instrumental means to achieving social order, rather than a genuine religious faith based upon love or reverence for the deity. Able neither to prove that Heaven could deliver immediate rewards and punishments nor to convince rulers to forgo immediate gains for long-term utilitarian goals, Mohists as a group soon declined.

While providing this overview of Mohism, Schwartz borrows two of John Rawls's observations about Western utilitarians to set up the discussion on Mo Di's utilitarian ideas. First, Rawls notes that utilitarians focus on the satisfaction of those desires associated with a person's "agreeable feelings" (a concept arising out of Jeremy Bentham's pleasure principle).[9]

In point of fact, Mo Di's ideal person appeared to have had different motives. Mo Di's worthy man was so committed to action for the common good that he was "sure to rid himself of pleasure, anger, joy, sadness, and love, but to employ *jen* [*ren*, benevolence or humaneness] and righteousness [*yi*, what is right, fair or just]."[10] Although he did mention the need to attract men of worth into government service with appropriate wealth and status, Mo Di assumed that worthy men would be able to transcend their own self-regarding feelings because of their superior intelligence. Through their reasoning about universal love and the example of Heaven's impartiality toward all, they perceived that all people should be regarded as ends in themselves; hence, they understood that the good of all would be served only by submitting to the general interest. Such individuals cultivated those virtuous dispositions required to be totally committed to the general interest and purged themselves of all other emotions that might distract them from their task. Mo Di believed that a correct disposition of the will would follow quite unproblematically from right knowing. In Mo Di's own case, he worked without any anticipation of reward from people or Heaven; moreover, he was not deterred by ill health or the failure of Heaven to reward his endeavors with success.

Although Mo Di's dedication may strike us as highly admirable, Schwartz points out that the philosopher's statements and personal example did not resolve the mystery about why one would be motivated to sacrifice for the common good. Being detached from individual "feelings," Mo Di's motivation remained a mystery because:

> No matter how convincingly the "altruistic" utilitarian may argue that in the end all human beings will reap the tangible benefits of the moral individual's behavior, it can never be demonstrated that he himself as a concrete living individual will reap any of these tangible benefits.[11]

In the context of discussing the Mohist metaphor of the craftsman's standard, Schwartz observes that to Mo Di the standard was Heaven itself as a conscious, willing being:

> There is nothing like taking Heaven as one's "standard." Heaven's actions are all-encompassing and unselfish . . . Thus the sage-kings took Heaven as their standard and their actions were effective.[12]

Although Schwartz does not make the linkage explicit, this metaphor would suggest that Mo Di's motive for sacrificing personal feelings for the pursuit of the general interest was implicitly grounded in the standard set by Heaven itself.

Second, Rawls notes that modern Western utilitarians have had to resort to an unaccountable or extraneous principle of universal moral sentiments as a mediating force between individual interests and the general interest. Their conception of justice is not really stable "unless sympathy and benevolence can be widely and intensely cultivated."[13] Likewise, Mo Di's notion of universal love was needed to weld individual interests and the general interest together. But, since Mo Di did not base his ethics upon inner springs of morality, how could such love flow from the utilitarian discourse on interest in itself? Without teaching the people to love one another, how could Mo Di hope to convince them to sacrifice their immediate particular interests for the sake of some distant and abstract interest of the whole society?

Mencius (between 390 and 305 B.C.) perceived this difficulty in Mo Di's assumption that the pursuit of interests leads to the elevation of the general interest over particular interests. Analyzing the logic of Mencius's critique of a Mohist's plan to convince two rulers—through an appeal to their sense of interest—to halt their warfare, Schwartz portrays the utilitarian predicament:

> Mencius's reply seems to be that so long as human attention is focused wholly on presumed "utilitarian" results—on the outcomes which are supposed to eventuate from given courses of action—the nature of the satisfactions achieved (security, wealth, power, or honor) are such that persons will tend to desire these outcomes for themselves here and now. The argument that the particular interests of individuals or particular groups will be served when the general interest "of the greatest number" is served is in fact not true for any given individual here and now. Hence, to the extent that the mind is fixed on goods such as security, wealth, ambition, or honor, the pursuit of the general interest will constantly disintegrate into the pursuit of particular interests. The message will simply pervade society that action should be predicated on considerations of interest, and particular individuals and groups will never be convinced that the satisfaction of their immediate concrete desires will be served by the satisfaction of long-term interest.[14]

Hence, according to Schwartz's interpretation of Mencius, the Mohists erred in assuming that the choice was between selfishness of individual pursuits and commitment to justice for the whole. The proper distinction should be whether the *motives* were fixed upon interests *or* upon benevolence and what is right.

Instead of resorting to an appeal to moral sentiments about impartiality, Mencius began from virtues rooted in the feelings. He claimed that the only way to achieve and preserve the general welfare was to cultivate the inner capacity of people to do what was right without regard for the consequences. In other words, Confucian virtues of benevolence and righteousness had to be treated as ends in themselves; moreover, individuals had to be regarded as having an inner capacity for acting in accordance with what was humane and right. The inner capacity of people— their human nature—became a basic issue. To Mencius, before the utilitarian calculus became engaged, the individual responded from inner virtues. In working for the general welfare, one resolutely willed to do the right thing and to nourish one's mind by reducing one's desires.[15]

THE UTILITARIAN PROBLEMATIQUE IN CHEN LIANG (1143–1194)

Among those who inherited and developed the utilitarian problematique of ancient China, none, perhaps, has more significance than Chen Liang. The question of the general interest and individual interests was the linchpin of his thinking on state and society. As he himself claimed, "What I've studied all my life are the two concepts called public (*gong*) and private (*si*)."[16] Elsewhere, I have characterized Chen's philosophy as a Confucian utilitarianism in direct challenge to the ethical philosophy of Zhu Xi.[17] Here, I would like to relate some specific aspects of Chen's thought to the utilitarian problematique explored by Schwartz in *The World of Thought in Ancient China*.

First, how would we relate Chen Liang to John Rawls's observation that utilitarians focus upon the satisfaction of people's agreeable feelings? When Chen Liang discussed human nature and desires, he emphasized the innateness and naturalness of desires for pleasures and rewards. In an essay on human nature, he quoted Mencius: "The way the mouth is disposed toward tastes, the eyes toward colors, the ear toward sounds, the nose toward smells, and the four limbs toward ease is human nature, yet therein also lies the Decree [from Heaven]."[18] Mencius had proceeded to add that, because these feelings were "decreed" as part of the larger natural order beyond the human, one should distinguish them from human nature in itself which was to be defined essentially in reference to the four basic Confucian virtues. Building upon this Mencian distinction, Zhu Xi posited both a physical nature and an ethical nature.

Chen, however, did not quote the second part of Mencius's statement about the Confucian virtues; moreover, he did not distinguish between physical and ethical natures. Chen reduced human nature to the natural human desires. As he remarked, everyone desires what enriches and brings esteem, as well as fears what impoverishes and demeans.[19] In his debate with Zhu Xi, Chen argued that desires were so natural that, as soon as people were born, they had such desires; even the sage kings of the golden age of early antiquity could not expunge such desires, which were inherent in the human mind.[20] On a more philosophical level, the *dao* itself was none other than the proper order of these feelings: "Is the *dao* anything else? It is nothing but the feelings of pleasure, anger, sorrow, joy, love, and hate attaining their appropriate expression."[21] Hence, in contrast to Mo Di, who called for leaders to rid themselves of emotions and desires for pleasure, Chen was not so hostile to the expression of such natural, universal feelings. There was nothing wrong, for example, with a ruler's indulging natural desires for sex and material things as long as the needs of the people for these same pleasures were met.[22]

In addition to such statements approving the satisfaction of desires basic to individual feelings, Chen Liang's life differs from Mo Di's in a way that permits addressing the question of motives for action. Chen Liang studied for decades to pass the civil-service examinations until he finally succeeded and attained his goal of an important government post. In contrast to Mo Di, who labored without any expectation of reward or any disappointment because of lack of success, Chen constantly complained of unfulfilled ambitions that drove him to extremes of emotion and frequent despondency.[23] Indulging his emotions, Chen's motivation differed not only from Mo Di's detachment from individual feelings but also from the quest for sagehood of his Confucian contemporaries. In short, Chen Liang appears more in line with modern Western utilitarians in his embrace of the need for all to satisfy pleasures arising from the feelings.

The more fundamental question remains: Why would one be motivated to sacrifice individual interests to the general interest? Following Schwartz's example in the case of Mo Di, we shall begin addressing this question with Rawls's second observation about utilitarians. Rawls notes that modern Western utilitarians had to introduce an unaccountable principle of moral sentiments, such as sympathy and benevolence, to be the mediating force between individual interests and the general interest. In a similar manner, Mo Di expounded the ideal of universal love; furthermore, Song Confucians advocated personal cultivation of benevolence. Hence, from the perspective of both his utilitarian and Confucian backgrounds, Chen Liang could be expected to emphasize benevolence as the bonding agent between individual interests and the general interest. But Chen did not give prominence to this virtue. Furthermore, he wrote so little about self-cultivation that, by the standards of the day, one could say that he ignored the subject. For a time, from his twenties into his mid-thirties, Chen had followed the advice of his teachers and friends to study those classics that emphasized personal cultivation; however, he later despaired of such efforts to change himself and did not emphasize self-cultivation in the way of contemporaries like Zhu Xi.[24]

Many Song Confucians approached Mo Di's notion of universal love when they followed Zhang Zai's (1020–1077) idealistic proclamation, "All people are my brothers and sisters, and all things are my companions."[25] In spite of this universalized sentiment, Song Confucians continued to uphold Confucian patterns of learning to love others through the medium of the family; hence, their proclamation still differed from Mo Di's. Of more specific concern here is Chen Liang's interpretation of Zhang's statement. He followed Cheng Yi (1033–1107) in using the concept that "principle is one, but its manifestations are many" to highlight the Confucian character of Zhang's proclamation. Chen explained "manifestations" (*fen*) as actual status distinctions within society; hence, the passage signified "the actuality of extending principle and preserving what is right and just."[26]

Chen Liang elsewhere made more explicit the linkage implicit here between social distinctions and what was just. He stated: "I have heard that there are two *dao* in the world: one is *fen* and the other is *yi*. . . . When *yi* prevails, then *fen* is established."[27] *Fen* meant both social roles and one's allotment or share. In other words, he was asserting that, when what was just or right prevailed, proper social distinctions would be firmly established. Such roles were not arbitrary because they were manifestations of *dao;* hence, conflicts between particular interests of individuals following their own desires and the general interest of society could be reconciled. If roles were grounded in what was just, Chen further suggested that one could stay within one's allotted role. Contention was unavoidable because of natural desire, but the antisocial consequences could still be avoided. He reasoned:

> When people are born, they cannot avoid having desires; when there are
> desires, there is certain to be contention. If the self is content with its own *fen*
> (share or allotted role), there will be no insatiable feelings toward others.[28]

Like human nature, one's *fen* was an endowment to each individual, but
Chen also emphasized its social connotations. The assumption here was
in accord with Confucian belief that the objects of desire were limited
in supply so restraints had to be internalized to insure that everyone
shared and received what was appropriate to his/her social status and
contribution.

On other occasions, Chen offered additional advice on preventing
natural desires and contention from becoming a problem for the general
welfare. After drawing attention to the feelings associated with our
senses, he commented in his essay on human nature: "Since these instinctive feelings come from human nature, they are what all people share;
since they yield to the Decree [of Heaven], there must be some way to
regulate them, but they cannot be suppressed."[29] Regarding how to regulate without suppressing the feelings and desires, he advised people to
heed the rules of their superior, and urged the superior to regulate the
people only in accord with the likes and dislikes inherent in their
natures. People who followed the models for society were to be
rewarded, but violators were to be punished. Instead of engaging individual whims and regarding regulations as products of one's own decisions,
those in superior positions should realize that rites and the system of
rewards and punishments were grounded in Heaven and human nature.

Other passages utilized the idea that rites were natural or grounded
in the larger order of Heaven. In his essay on the *Record of Rituals* (*Li
ji*), Chen claimed that the rites were actually patterns or rules of Heaven
(*tianze*). Conceding that the text itself was a compilation of polite manners among Confucians over the centuries down to the Han dynasty, he
still claimed that, if we practiced such ritual decorum, we would know
that the rites were also grounded in our own hearts and minds.[30] The
claim that the rites were also inherent in people's hearts and minds
could be interpreted as an appeal to moral sentiments for bonding
between general and individual interests. If so, there still appears to be
considerable difference between this innateness of a sense of ritual decorum and more emotive, encompassing sentiments, such as benevolence

or love. In the case of the rites, as with social roles and what was just, Chen primarily asserted that the grounding of social order for the general welfare was part of the higher order of Heaven or *dao*. This assertion is close to Schwartz's reading of Mo Di's universal love as "universal fairness or sense of equity." Rather than moral sentiments in general, Chen Liang based his appeal more specifically on a sense of fairness or justness. Furthermore, the role of Heaven as a model for impartial treatment of others also entered Chen's writings as it had Mo Di's. In an essay on the *Spring and Autumn Annals* (*Chun qiu*), he argued that Heaven was at the center of the classic because all rewards and punishments were mandated by Heaven. In reading the text, one could comprehend Heaven's *dao* only by having the perspective of "the public interest of the realm" rather than individual interests.[31]

The impartiality of Heaven as a ground for the general interest, however, did not negate Chen's concern for individual interests. Significantly, in another passage citing the impartial nature of Heaven, Chen declared: "If the public-mindedness in the rotation of the heavens and individual interests are mutually valued, the general interest and individual interests become one."[32] Both the general interest and individual interests should be valued so the general interest would encompass legitimate individual interests. The general interest and individual interests should ultimately be in harmony instead of being regarded as antagonistic opposites.

Such reasoning suggests certain idealistic assumptions. But Chen also had a practical sense of balance among conflicting interests. For instance, he chided Zhu Xi for suggesting the implementation of an idealistic well-field model from antiquity for land organization: "If situations were comparable [between antiquity and the present] and people could mutually benefit, even the people of today [different though they might be from the ancients] could cooperate with you, even without a compact."[33] Particularly noteworthy here is Chen's criterion of the people's mutual benefit as the basis for working together for the general welfare. If the people could mutually benefit, bonding would be adequate for cooperation, even without institutionalization through a compact.

If people did not voluntarily associate with one another for the mutual interest, the state could enforce the general welfare. Implicit in Chen's argumentation is the assumption that knowledge will affect action, but he appears to be more cognizant (than Mo Di) that an appeal to proper understanding alone was inadequate to elicit action. As already noted, Chen assumed a positive role for rewards and punishments utilized to encourage people to conform to social models. He went further in giving laws a crucial function in the internalization of attitudes supportive of the general interest:

> The human mind is mostly self-centered, but laws and regulations can be used to make it public-minded. This is why the prevailing trend in the world is inevitably moving toward laws and institutions . . . Laws and regulations are the public-minded or commonweal principle.[34]

One might say laws and institutions were a *Realpolitik* bonding between individual and general interests, but Chen apparently envisioned a Confucian function for laws (much like the rites) in transforming individual attitudes.

Such confidence in laws and institutions is striking, especially in contrast to Zhu Xi's emphasis upon self-cultivation and philosophical principles to change character. Chen also vividly portrayed this confidence in other passages:

> If laws and institutions were not correct, the principles for human society would not be established; if these principles were not established, the virtues of benevolence, what is right, propriety, and wisdom would have nothing upon which to rest; if these virtues had nothing upon which to rest, the function of the sages would cease.[35]

His order of priority here ranked laws and institutions as the foundation of Confucian virtues and the actions of the sages. Thus, he placed first what most moralistic Confucians ranked last among these three.

Chen Liang's ascription of a positive role to law in directing people toward the general interest did not weaken some of his Confucian assumptions about the limitations of laws and regulations. Elaborating upon Confucius's objections to laws, Chen claimed that stringent laws and regulations would restrict the actions of benevolent leaders but fail to bind ruthless people who, in their craftiness, could always find some way to thwart the intent of the law. But Chen proceeded to sanction the economic interests of individual households and to urge the government to accept limitations upon its role in restraining the interests of households. Acquiring enough land to be a small-to-middling landlord, he on occasion wrote to defend the interests of wealthy landowners against government interference.[36]

Joining together Chen's comments—about the positive and negative functions of law—would lend concrete substance to his statements that conflicting individual and general interests could be unified or brought into some kind of harmonious balance. The law should be used to transform people's self-regarding mentality into public-consciousness. Yet, the state should not be too aggressive in making and implementing laws. On the one hand, in defending the economic interests of households, he demonstrated sensitivity about the state's asserting the general interest. On the other hand, in commenting upon a land-reform proposal, he focused upon the need to ensure that the proposal would not have any negative impact upon military recruitment.[37] This emphasis on the strength of the military was of course linked to Chen's famous obsession with expelling the Jurchen conquerors and liberating North China.

It was this concern for the war effort that should, Chen felt, overshadow all individual interests. Writing his second letter to Zhu Xi, Chen complained that many of the literati and officials of the day failed to realize the urgency of defeating the Jurchen. The Song dynasty's mandate as well as the welfare of the whole realm was threatened as long as the Jurchen maintained their hold over the North. Chen lamented that, even at such extremity when everyone was in the same boat confronting the same storm, each person was busy making calculations for only his own life.[38]

Perhaps Chen Liang would have utilized this imagery of mutual peril and the common good if challenged to reply to Mencius's critique of the Mohist view of conflicting interests, so aptly capsulized as a utilitarian predicament by Schwartz. In his use of the metaphor of being on a boat facing a storm to represent being overwhelmed by foreign military and cultural encroachments, the necessity of regarding the general interest as one's individual interest appeared self-evident. Still, very much like Mencius, Zhu Xi did not concede that Chen's case was self-evident;

rather his responses included Mencian objections to Chen's utilitarian ethics.

In his letters to Zhu Xi as well as in his other writings, Chen Liang had other grounds for defending utilitarianism. Chen sought to unify results and utility with benevolence and rightness in such a way that utilitarian symbols would be sanctioned by Confucian ethical values. Such transcendence of traditional Confucian polarities also informed his reconciliation of individual interests and the general interest. Desires, which drove individual interests, arose from human nature and should not be suppressed. Rites, with which the desires were regulated for the general welfare, were grounded in the order of Heaven; furthermore, the impartiality of Heaven demonstrated its orientation toward the general welfare. For people to yield to one another according to ritual decorum and to hold their own interests and desires within reasonable limits, it was crucial for a sense of what was right and fair to prevail. Because of his views on land and other policy issues, as well as his perception of human desires and self-interests as natural, the mediation and balance of individual interests with the general interest was probably a more central concern for Chen Liang than transforming individual interests into the general interest. The exception to this priority was his obsession with expelling the foreign Jurchens and restoring Song control in North China. In the instance of foreign encroachment, the interest of the country superseded individual interest.

The Problematique in Schwartz's Yan Fu

Yan Fu's translations interjected Western ideas into the Chinese discourse on *gong* and *si*. In his translations of various Western works into Chinese, Yan Fu sought to identify for his readers the secrets of Western wealth and power so that China might utilize the most efficient means to modernization. Based upon his readings of major European thinkers and his personal observations in England, Yan Fu was impressed with the enormous cultural drive or energy leading to *collective* strength, an energy Schwartz labeled "Faustian" and "Promethean."[39] Seemingly almost beyond belief from a traditional Chinese perspective, an ethic of economic individualism, Yan Fu argued, could serve the collective interest. The British example proved to him that liberalism with its sense of individual rights and public justice contributed to the wealth and power of the state.

According to Yan Fu, England's economic expansion resulted from individual energy functioning in an environment of liberty grounded in law. England managed to release the energy of self-interested individuals and yet harness such energy toward national goals because individuals realized how intertwined were their individual and collective goals. Widespread Christian notions of God watching over the behavior of individuals served as a major check on anti-social tendencies.

Based upon this perception of the public spirit active in England, Yan Fu criticized Confucian ethics and views of law. Confucians had inadvertently encouraged narrow selfishness of immediate groups, like family or clan, at the expense of the whole state or society. Focusing upon particularistic relations (with other members of intermediate groups) slighted the development of public spirit. Confucians had little sense of an identity between individual and national interests. Nevertheless, Yan Fu recommended the use of filial piety to cultivate discipline among the masses as a kind of substitute for Christian piety, which enabled ordinary people in the West "to face death without regard for self-interest."[40] Furthermore, justice in China depended upon the judge as a person more than on an impersonal system of universal law. With such limited function of law, every area of culture was dominated by rules of ritual decorum. In accord with their focus on rites rather than laws, Chinese cultural elites did little to develop public spirit. Yan Fu depicted the contrast between cultures of laws and rites: In England, people were free from interference in matters that involved their own private affairs, but bound by duty to be concerned about affairs of the whole society. In China, affairs of society were the exclusive domain of officials, but others could interfere with their own individual affairs. Hence, people tended to concentrate upon defending their narrow interests and took no thought of the general interest of society.[41]

Yan Fu learned from Herbert Spencer that unleashing individual energies in competition was the most effective means for building national wealth and power. Spencer has also made a sharp distinction between his "egoism" or "energy of faculty" and what he regarded as the passive hedonism of the Benthamite utilitarians. In accepting this distinction, Yan Fu praised Spencer's "egoism" as motivated by an enlightened sense of self-interest because the energy of individual competition contributed toward collective goals. Schwartz has analyzed Yan Fu's point:

> Here we find the nexus of libertarianism, classical economic ideas and Darwinist imagery which constitutes the liberalism of Spencer. Yen Fu derives from him the profound conviction that the energies which ultimately account for the wealth and power of the social organisms of the West are energies latent in the individual; that *these energies are powered*, as it were, *by the drive of enlightened self-interest;* and that *liberty*, equality, and democracy provide the environment *within which this enlightened self-interest manifests itself—* within which human . . . potentialities are realized.[42] (emphasis mine)

In contrast to the West, where emphasis was placed upon preserving the self, traditional Chinese values emphasized restraining the self through ritual decorum in order to treat others properly. Hence, in Yan Fu's estimation, the West enhanced the power of society by encouraging the expression of individual energies, whereas China achieved its goal of harmony only by diminishing the energies of all. In the modern West, evolutionary struggle was permitted, but, in traditional China, struggle was deliberately inhibited in favor of social harmony.

In addition to the "egoistic" energies of Spencer's industrial entrepreneur, Adam Smith's writings on economic development explained the positive role of self-interest. Although Smith was famous for his emphasis on economic individualism, he and other utilitarians did not pit the interest of the individual against society's; enlightened self-interest and the general interest were seen as complementary. The greatest good or happiness for the greatest number of people remained for him, as for Bentham, an ultimate concern. Moreover, Smith's notion of an "invisible hand" governing economic activity was founded upon his faith in a pre-established harmony between the interest of enlightened individuals and that of society. Attempting to persuade Confucians with biases against regarding as moral the individual pursuit of material gain or self-interest, Yan Fu noted that Smith did not reduce his ethic to economic self-interest, but rather understood that morality arose from the human feeling of sympathy. Although Yan tended to regard Spencer's egoism as the primary source of morality and Smith's feeling of sympathy as derivative, such Western writers provided grounds for regarding self-interest and righteousness (what is right) as complementary rather than antagonistic opposites:

> Ever since the emergence of the theory of evolution it has become as clear as a burning flame that without righteousness there can be no utility and without the Way no profit, and it was the economists who anticipated this insight. Smith always maintained that, while the world is full of shallow men and ignorant men, there are no "mean men" (*hsiao jen*). The "mean man" presumably sees only his own interest. However, if we assume that he discerns his long-term, real interests, how does he differ in his behavior from the virtuous man? . . . The process of evolution does not treat the self-interest of the short-sighted and ignorant as true self-interest and does not treat narrowly abnegating self-righteousness or extravagant and excessive "righteousness" as true "righteousness."[43]

In Yan's argument, all traditional cultures had regarded self-interest as evil and had established moral philosophies upon negations of assertive energies among individuals, but, after the breakthrough provided by thinkers in the modern West, China could also embrace a positive view of self-interest as contributing to the general interest.

In translating Smith's *Wealth of Nations,* Yan Fu transmuted all references to the general interest or nation or society into language referring to the state's interests. The relative emphasis between public and individual interests was altered in translation. Whereas Smith's priority was the economic welfare of individuals as members of society, Yan placed the wealth and power of the state above individuals' economic welfare. Yan Fu's preoccupation with state power likewise distorted Spencer's dedication to individual liberty as an intrinsic value in itself: Yan's nationalism valued indidivual liberty primarily as a means to strengthen the Chinese nation. John Stuart Mill's defense of individual liberty as an end in itself (and as a means to the fullest development of individual personality) became in Yan's hand an exposition of liberty as a means to cultivate everyone's virtue and intellect to serve the needs of the state.[44]

While translating Montesquieu's *Spirit of the Laws,* Yan discovered the distinction between democracy and individual liberty; he realized that the freedom of the nation-state and the freedom of the individual were not necessarily complementary. Judging the freedom of the Chinese nation to be more urgent than the liberty of the individual, he assigned liberty to a second order of priority. Later, during the course of World War I, his faith in British liberalism as the path to modernization was shaken, and he became more open to authoritarianism because he was surprised that for several years Germany fought so successfully against Britain and other democratic nations. Overall, liberty was to him more a means than an end, and also a means more for the nation than for the individual. Hence, although he consistently championed enlightened self-interest and the rule of law, liberty and democracy gave way to shorter routes to China's modernization.[45]

CONCLUSION

In his polemics for change, Yan Fu appears to have overlooked Chinese precursors for his faith in enlightened self-interest and thus provided a basis for Schwartz's exogenous-based interpretation. Against the backdrop of traditional society in which personal material gain and self-interest were portrayed in a negative light, Schwartz's Yan Fu credited modern Westerners with the insight that utility and righteousness, as well as the *dao* and profit, were integrally related. But our research demonstrates that Chen Liang did indeed argue that such concepts as utility and rightness, and profit and the *dao*, were intertwined.

Chen Liang redefined Confucian polarities so as to extend to utility and self-interest the ethical sanction of what was right and proper. Equating human nature with human feelings, Chen sanctioned appropriate expressions of the emotions; furthermore, even his advice to regulate the feelings with rites did not call for renunciation or suppression of the self or private interests. Chen advocated valuing both the general interest and individual interests. If people mutually benefited, they could cooperate in society. Although he expected people to sacrifice in order to restore the dynasty's control of North China, he also advised the government against assertive interference with the economic welfare of private households. Interests had to be held in balance. The rites and laws that sustained that balance had to be in accord with what was right, as well as with human nature and the larger order of Nature or Heaven.

Having interposed Chen Liang between ancient Chinese utilitarian thought and Yan Fu's intellectual encounter with the West, we are able to perceive a degree of continuity in the Chinese utilitarian problematique. For instance, whereas Mo Di was indifferent to satisfying the desires associated with agreeable feelings, Chen made specific arguments about the legitimacy of proper expressions of the feelings and rejected efforts to suppress the emotions. Unlike Mo Di and Western utilitarians, who resorted to an unaccountable principle of moral sentiments to bind individual and general interests together, Chen Liang made little comparable use of the similar concept of benevolence or humaneness and the practice of self-cultivation. Given the centrality of this concept and practice among Confucians of his day, one wonders if he had less need to make explicit appeals to such moral sentiments because in large part they were taken more as a given than in either ancient China or the modern world.

Yet, it was other Confucian virtues—particularly a sense of what was right or just, along with loyalty to the country—upon which Chen primarily drew to support his utilitarian ethic. As a Confucian, he did not share Mo Di's hostility to family-oriented concerns; furthermore, he regarded ritual decorum as the principal means for cultivating an enlightened view of interests. In spite of Yan's criticism of much of the application of rites in traditional China, he advocated filial piety as a means to nurture discipline and sacrifice for the common good; hence, as for Chen, rites properly served to bridge private and public interests. Chen also emphasized the importance of laws and regulations in channeling self-regarding thinking into civic-mindedness. Laws and rites should, in Chen's view as well as in Yan's, be primarily aimed at affecting civic virtue and action rather than personal conduct and private affairs. Chen's multi-faceted discourse on interests might well be seen as an attempt to answer Mencius's classic critique against an ethic founded upon efforts to resolve conflicting interests. Ironically, Yan Fu's and Chen Liang's laments about Chinese routinely pursuing narrow and short-sighted interests demonstrated the dangers, about which Mencius had warned, of emphasizing interests as the basis for judgment. Neither Yan nor Chen, however, would have conceded that interests were necessarily so short-sighted. The challenge was to enlighten individual interests about the general interest. From such examples, we could plot several directional vectors from Mo Di to Yan Fu in which Chen would be intermediate, but much closer to the positions Yan Fu articulated. In short, beyond the mere continuity of polarities (such as interest or rightness, self-interest or public interest, laws or personal administrators), Yan Fu can be seen as being in a "tradition" which had already appeared long before in China and was generally oriented in directions similar to the ones he took with borrowed Western ideas.

Although pointing to commonalities between Yan Fu and a Chinese utilitarian tradition has perhaps qualified Schwartz's picture regarding endogenous intellectual strains, we have at the same time implicitly extended one point of further support to the core of his thesis. According to Schwartz, it was Yan Fu's fascination with the "Faustian" energy of the West that significantly defined his perception of utilitarianism. Convinced that individual energies released in competition and struggle had strengthened collective goals in the modern West, Yan Fu nationalistically embraced a credo that economic individualism served the wealth and power of China as a nation-state. In essence, Yan Fu's attention to Faustian energy precipitously enhanced the self-interest and liberty of the individual, but augmented the power of the state even more. Personal interest and liberty were perceived by Yan in instrumental terms—as means to national economic and political ends. Although Chen was nationalistic and had been willing to sacrifice personal interest in a war to liberate China from foreign invasion, he had not regarded private economic interest as a means to the country's ends. Yan Fu's lens of social Darwinism did so, and thus altered the perception of utilitarian priorities and values.

Part Two
Literature and Culture

FOUR

The Moral World of Hebei Village Opera

DAVID ARKUSH

Compared to the ideas of the great thinkers who populate Benjamin Schwartz's *World of Thought in Ancient China,* the world of thought of ordinary Chinese is much less accessible to us. Still, as Schwartz himself has pointed out, this world is not totally closed off, at least for recent times. Folkoric materials—tales, songs, proverbs, plays, and the like, mostly brief, imaginative rather than discursive—while not offering sustained reflection on great questions of humanity, society, and the cosmos of the sort that Schwartz discusses, tell us much about the ideas of the people whose culture they preserve. I should like to look at some of the moral concepts of North Chinese villagers before the Communist Revolution as revealed in a collection of folk operas. This is not the sort of inquiry Benjamin Schwartz would undertake, but it is not, I believe, altogether alien to his concerns.

I want to limit consideration here to one cohesive body of material. In the late 1920s, Li Jinghan and Zhang Shiwen, modern-minded sociologists working with Y. C. James Yen's Mass Education Movement in Dingxian in central Hebei province, arranged to have traditional folk operas which were still being performed there written down in order to preserve them before they died out. These operas, confusingly called in Chinese *yangge* or "rice-planting songs," transmitted only orally up to then, were published in 1933 under the title *Dingxian yangge xuan.*[1]

This collection has been surprisingly little studied in the half century since, though as historical material it is useful and revealing in a number of ways. It is fairly large: about 50 plays, 1,000 pages, half a million words. It is relatively unedited; sexually offensive language has not been excised, for instance, unlike things published in China since 1949. Its provenance, unlike, unfortunately, that of most Chinese folk materials, is well documented. We can situate these cultural productions exactly; we know where they were performed, in villages and market towns, and we know who performed them: amateur or semi-professional peasant actors playing for avid rural audiences.

This avidity makes plausible the notion that we can learn from operas about the shared ideas of the community that watched them. We have ample anecdotal testimony about the importance of operas for Chinese villagers and about how eagerly they were watched by all. *Yangge* plays, which were put on in most villages in Dingxian, were the "favorite entertainment of peasants, male and female, young and old," we are told. People would miss no opportunity to see them at New Year's, other festivals, and temple fairs; at other times they sang songs from them. These entertainments provided a rare opportunity for women to leave the home, and female relatives from other villages were invited to come for several days to see them. It seems likely that the operas not only influenced but were influenced by ordinary people—that they were shaped to a significant degree by local players and in response to audience demands. The Dingxian actors were farmers, largely illiterate, who used no scripts; the 1920s collectors had them recite the plays from memory.[2]

Perhaps the reason this material has been so neglected is that, in spite of its apparent simplicity, transparency, and accessibility, it is not easy to interpret. One cannot read directly from the simple surface discourse of folk material the conscious or unconscious feelings of the audience. It is not at all obvious why people watched these operas, what they found in them, what they took away from them, and consequently what they tell us of people's mental life. My assumption is that they found something more in drama in addition to simple entertainment, diversion, and escape from the humdrum tedium and harshness of everyday life. One of the reasons drama was so compelling may be that it also allowed people to play, in a safely distanced way, with attractive but dangerous ideas and desires: sexual impulses, moral doubts, subversive fantasies, matters that were upsetting or threatening for the community.[3] The Dingxian operas, I believe, were a way of exploring collectively troubling moral questions. In particular, they gave disguised expression to a chafing at the authority of elders in the family, a dissatisfaction with the dominant ethic of filial piety, a resentment against the rich, and a yearning for and faith in a source of moral authority outside local society.

FAMILY: FILIAL PIETY AND INTERGENERATIONAL CONFLICT

Compared to high operas, which often feature inspirational stories of virtuous behavior, the Dingxian operas have considerably less Confucian moralizing. In particular, they pay surprisingly scant attention to the central Confucian virtue of filial piety, or *xiao,* meaning basically obedience and respect to parents and ancestors, including, in the case of a married woman, her husband's parents and ancestors. No opera in the collection is centrally devoted to dramatizing and glorifying this virtue (an apparent exception, *Guo Ju mai zi*, will be discussed later), and only infrequently is *xiao* spoken of with admiration or exemplified by an admirable character.[4]

The few plays depicting approval of filial piety can be quickly summarized. In a murder story, *Longbao si jiangxiang* (Worship at the Longbao Temple), a daughter kills herself in order to provide a head and thereby, for legal reasons, help her father who has been wrongly imprisoned for murder; the wise Judge Bao is not fooled by the substitute head but he is won over by her supreme demonstration of filial virtue and has the father released; but there is much more to this complex crime drama. *Bian lü* (Turned into a donkey), about a rebellious daughter-in-law whose good husband is filial toward his aged mother, is a comic farce. In the Dingxian version of *Bai she zhuan* (The White Snake), the White Snake is in the end released from her imprisonment under Thunder Peak Pagoda when her grown son comes to pray to her at the site; but filial piety is far from an important theme in this story of the love of an immortal for a mortal. More ambiguous is *An'er song mi* (An'er brings rice), in which a wronged wife who has been driven out of the house by her cruel in-laws and has taken refuge in a nunnery is visited by her small son. His behavior, bringing her rice, is admirable, of course, as is that of the woman, who, refusing to speak ill of her in-laws, dutifully asks after them and instructs her son to be obedient and respectful to his evil grandmother. But the main discourse of the play would seem to develop a condemnation of family tyranny.

In fact, the oppression of the young by the old and the abuse of family authority are much more prominent elements in Dingxian operas than filial piety. The many plays that dramatize conflict between generations, in which the old are often villainous and the young good and appealing, make an issue of filial piety and, at least implicitly, question the legitimacy of such authorities and the value of obedience to them. These operas of intergenerational conflict deserve to be considered at some length.

Strife between mother-in-law and daughter-in-law is probably the most frequent and obvious generational stress point. In *Si quan* (Four exhortations), a 19-year-old wife, visiting her natal family for a few days, weeps despondently when the time comes to return to her husband's home. Her mother-in-law and sister-in-law mistreat her so cruelly, she says, that she would rather die than go back to them. *Banbudao qingke* (Tumbler invites a guest) shows a mother-in-law who refuses to let her daughter-in-law visit her home village for a temple fair; there is work to be done, she says, and furthermore she herself has not once gone to her natal home in all the years since she was married (in the end the less hardhearted father-in-law permits the visit). In *Jinniu si* (At the Jinniu Temple), a mother and father both dream their married daughter has jumped down a dry well and killed herself because of cruel treatment from her mother-in-law. The mother goes to visit her daughter and, finding the mistreatment confirmed (but not the suicide), gets into a verbal and physical fight with the mother-in-law.

In three operas, the mother-in-law, unable to abide her son's wife, goes so far as to order him to divorce her. *Xiaogu xian* (The good sister-in-law) shows a mother-in-law who, consumed with groundless hatred for her daughter-in-law, beats her and orders the son to divorce her, relenting finally only after her own good-hearted daughter, who sides with the innocent daughter-in-law, threatens suicide. Similarly, the mother-in-law in *Jiang Shichuang xiuqi* (Jiang Shichuang divorces his wife) suspects her daughter-in-law of stealing and putting a curse on her so that she will die and the younger woman come to power. The mother-in-law orders her son to divorce his wife; he obeys, reluctantly and tearfully, while at the same time trying to get relatives to persuade his mother to change her mind. The wife, rejecting suicide because of her infant son, takes refuge in a Buddhist nunnery. We have already noted *An'er song mi,* about just such a divorced daughter-in-law who, having been driven out of the family by her mother-in-law, is living in a nunnery where her young son visits her. In all these plays, the filial obedience of the husband to his mother's unreasonable demands for divorce is presented as obligatory and inevitable, not praiseworthy or admirable; he appears more a weakling than a moral hero.

Other sorts of intergenerational family oppression are also depicted. in *Shuang hong da shangfen,*[5] a wife, no longer young, is unhappily pressured by her in-laws to remarry after a wicked uncle has falsely led her to believe her husband is dead. *Gao Wenju zuo huating* (Gao Wenju sits in the courtyard) presents a husband who, after taking top honors in the civil-service examinations, is forced into another marriage by a high official's family. This powerful family then forges a letter of divorce to the original wife, who falls into poverty, sells herself as a servant, and by chance is bought by the official's family, who maltreat her. In *Dinglang xun fu* (Dinglang seeks out his father), where the conflict is, at least indirectly, again between the original wife (in this case represented by her son) and the high-ranking family of a second wife, the problem is not so much that the high-ranking family is evil but that the husband is fearful of offending them by recognizing his son by the first wife. In *Luo qun ji* (The gauze skirt), children are oppressed by a second wife: a brother and sister are turned out by a cruel stepmother (a concubine) while their father is away.

Operas of a rather different sort, those about romance or engagement, also frequently involve conflict between young people and the older generation. A young man and woman, generally about 18 years old, face opposition or obstacles raised by her parents, by a matchmaker, or by an older husband. The sympathy of the audience is clearly directed toward the young lovers and against their elders. Even when

such intergenerational conflict is not explicit, plays celebrating romantic love, it might be argued, are in themselves a challenge to patriarchal
domination, which demands that individuals subordinate their personal desires to the interests of the family and the orders of their elders.
So, too, is sexual libertarianism, of which there is a good bit in these
folk operas. Cases of minor and major sexual licentiousness, risqué
banter, adulterous assignations, and the like are presented without apparent censure—something that made the authorities sometimes attempt to
suppress local opera.

Let us concentrate here on examples where conflict between generations is more or less explicit. In several operas, the betrothal of an attractive young couple is broken or threatened by the fiancée's parents, often
for reasons of greed. In *Liu Yulan shang miao* (Liu Yulan goes to the temple), the engagement is broken when the woman's parents are offered a
better match, with a rich official, a widower and much older. The
young woman, who would rather marry her original fiancé even
though he is poor, berates the new matchmaker, attempts suicide, and
is harshly treated by her stepmother. In the end she runs off with the
original fiancé, presumably to a life of poverty, though she also has
plans to accuse her wrongdoers in court. *Yang Ershe hua yuan* (Yang
Ershe begs for alms) presents an engaged couple, both children of
officials, who become separated when his parents die; he becomes impoverished, and her father breaks the engagement. In the end, she gives
him money in the hope that he can hire a tutor, pass the exams, and go
to court to win her back. A poor scholar in *Yang Fulu tou qin* (Yang
Fulu seeks refuge with his in-laws) has been robbed of the engagement
tokens and is turned away by his fiancée's family. He tries to hang himself in their garden, is cut down, and tells his story to the fiancée, who
gives him money with which he will be able to bring a lawsuit against
her parents.

Feelings of discontent with arranged marriages, a basic exercise of
parental authority in rural society, can be found in other plays about
young lovers. In *Da niao* (The downed bird), a young man and woman
meet, fall in love, and carry out their own "wedding" ceremony, after
which he makes her promise to tell her parents nothing of all this. The
opposition in *Lan qiao hui* (Rendezvous at Blue Bridge) is the older

husband—53 and extremely ugly—of a beautiful 18-year-old girl. She encounters a handsome young man and they vow to meet in the middle of the night, presumably with the audience's approval. Dissatisfaction with matches made by parents and matchmakers (who act as parents' agents, perhaps deflecting some of the young people's resentment from the parents) is evident in *Jie nü diaoxiao* (Borrowing a daughter to send to a funeral), where an unscrupulous matchmaker has been bribed by the wealthy family of an ugly girl to make a good match for her. In *Jin-niu si*, the poor daughter-in-law's troubles stem from the fact that her father arranged her marriage after he had had a little too much to drink at the market. Similarly, the daughter-in-law in *Si quan* complains that everything was the matchmaker's fault.

What is most interesting in all this is not the idea that there are social stresses within a patriarchal family system, arranged marriages, and viri-local residence in a family of strangers for young wives, but that community sympathy was so clearly expected to be with the young and not the family authorities. That the audience would side with the power-less, women, and the young, and against family authority is an interpre-tation demanded by the perfect faithfulness of the young lovers, the greedy tyranny of the family, the pure blamelessness of the daughters-in-law, and the unreasonable cruelty of the mothers-in-law. Even the one exception—*Bian lü*, in which a daughter-in-law who beats her mother-in-law brutally with a stick is punished in the end by being turned into a donkey—derives its humor from the idea that the opposite, an oppres-sive mother-in-law, is the norm.

To be sure, these operas are not advocating rebellion against family authority. Some resistance or at least escape—young people making their own love matches or running away together—is depicted in operas about love and broken engagements, but there is something of an air of unreality about these solutions, which seem harmless fantasies in the make-believe context of the theater rather than principled opposition. The general attitude, especially in the mother-in-law and daughter-in-law plays, is not resistance, but acceptance, albeit grudgingly, of family authority. We have already noted in several divorce plays its being taken for granted that a husband will obey his mother's command to divorce his wife. The principle of submitting to domestic tyranny is made explicit in *Si quan*, where a sympathetic brother, hearing how his sister is mistreated, exhorts her not to commit suicide but to endure in the certainty that by accepting the system one will eventually come to power:

> Your mother-in-law is over 60 and cannot live another 60 years. Your sister-in-law is 18 or 19 and will be married off within a few years. Wait for those who will die to die and those who will marry to marry, leaving you to eat and drink. The narrow path of many years will be trod into a wide road, the ditch become a great river, the willow shoot grow into an old tree, and the daughter-in-law of many years will become a mother-in-law. (p. 711)

Still, it is suggestive that there is so little talk of filial piety as a moral virtue; that the husbands who obey their mothers' orders to divorce their wives, for instance, are shown more as weaklings than moral heroes. James Scott has argued that, in considering peasants' relationship with the ideas and values of the ruling elites, we should distinguish compliance from acceptance as legitimate. That members of subordinate classes find open defiance too risky and give verbal assent to the dominant elite does not mean that they really accept elite values and ideology.[6] In these plays, too, we should expect resistance to dominant values to be muted and keep in mind that indications of resigned acceptance of the necessity of obeying parents are weak evidence for true popular acceptance of filial piety as a value.

That one of the basic patterns of conflict in the Dingxian plays is generational, between sympathetic young adults and their tyrannical elders, suggests at the very least considerable ambivalence about filiality. If we are right in thinking dramas were a way of exposing troubling or threatening matters, then the prominence of the theme of family tyranny indicates that the moral ambiguities and contradictions in the duty of filial piety were troubling in the minds of Dingxian villagers. Of course, it might be claimed that it was only *abuses* of power that were felt to be objectionable and not the principle of *xiao* itself. Yet, this issue runs so deeply through so many operas that people must have found it a troubling moral problem; it seems more than just a matter of not living up to the ideal. Filial piety demands obedience to people in certain positions, and so to raise the possibility of unworthy authority is to raise doubts about the legitimacy of this very demand for obedience. The issue of family tyranny involves concern over the ethical rationality of *xiao.*

SOCIETY: CONSTANCY IN OBLIGATIONS AND RESENTMENT TOWARD THE RICH

An alternative and more egalitarian sort of moral value is suggested by the recurring emphasis on ethical constancy, maintaining obligations in spite of changed circumstances. This constancy is in opposition to *xiao* in that it is sometimes appealed to as a counter to parental authority. The obligations tend, unlike filial duty, to be based on voluntary agreements rather than hierarchical position within the family, and to be horizontal, in the sense of being between equals, rather than vertical. Though they sometimes occur between family members, these obligations can apply equally beyond the family.

The frequent giving of tokens in the Dingxian operas manifests such a concern for constancy and for obligations to be recognized far into the future. In *Lan qiao hui,* for instance, after the handsome student and beautiful (but married) young woman vow to meet in the night, they exchange tokens. In *Yang Ershe hua yuan,* the young man encounters difficulty when he loses his betrothal token, but eventually meets up with his fiancée, with whom he makes plans aimed at having him recognized as her intended husband. They conclude by exchanging tokens. "If in the future you have this gold hairpin," the woman says, "I will accept your poverty even if you become a beggar. If you don't have it, I won't recognize you (*renbuqing*) even as a courtier driving horses" (p. 33); and he makes a similar pledge to her. There is an almost identical passage in *Yang Fulu tou qin* (p. 204), which also has the comic parallel of a maid trying to give the man a shoe as her token to him. In *Luo qun ji,* the brother and sister who have been turned out of the house by their cruel concubine stepmother are subsequently forced to part, at which point he takes as a token a piece of her skirt, the skirt of the title. In *Erhuan ji* (The earrings), after the gambling husband has sold his wife, she gives him an earring as a token, saying that as long as he keeps this they will be able to be reunited. In the end, she returns to him and finds he has gambled away everything else but kept the earring. It matches hers and they recognize each other as husband and wife.

The tokens are symbols of social obligations—to give one is a pledge to recognize an obligation—and their prominence in the plays indicates the importance attached to recognizing such obligations. This concern is also evident in plays with crucial scenes about recognizing people; recognizing a person means recognizing one's obligations to that person. Both *Shuang hong da shangfen* and *Gao Wenju zuo huating*, for instance, center on husbands and wives who, separated for years, gradually come, in dramatic scenes at the heart of the plays, to recognize and accept each other. In *Dinglang xun fu*, which is about a son's seeking his father who had remarried into another family, the issue is whether the father will recognize his son—not literally, for the father had left before he was born and has never seen this child, but in the sense of acknowledging him as a son, that is to say, recognizing his paternal obligations to him; again, tokens play a part in the resolution.

This concern over constancy in recognizing obligations is not only, at least sometimes, an alternative moral principle to obedience to family authority, but also often seems to contain an element of resentment against the wealthy and concern about the corrosive effect of money and differences in wealth on the performance of duties to others, what we might think of as the problem of moral decay in an increasingly commercialized society with considerable social mobility.

It is frequently the rich who refuse to recognize their obligations to the poor. In the plays about broken engagements, the threat that the obligation will not be met generally arises from a change in the financial status of one of the parties: the (good, young, handsome) fiancé or his family have become poor, and often the (bad, old, ugly) rival is rich (*Liu Yulan shang miao, Yang Ershe hua yuan*). In *Shuang suo gui* (The two locked chests), breaking off an engagement when the other side becomes impoverished is explicitly condemned as "despising the poor and loving the rich" (*xian qiong ai fu*, p. 101). In *Xiao huayuan* (A small garden), we see a counter example: the admirable fidelity of a woman who does not reject her fiancé when he appears to her in rags pretending to have become a beggar.[7]

So, too, in the exchange of tokens it is sometimes made clear that the threat to the relationship is from changed social circumstances. When the young lovers exchange tokens in *Lan qiao hui*, the woman says, "As long as you have this [hair ornament], I'll not despise you even if you have become a beggar," and the man replies that he will accept her even as a kitchen slave if she has kept the token from him. Similar language is found in *Yang Ershe hua yuan*, quoted above, and *Yang Fulu tou qin*.

Money and borrowing are pervasive concerns, and the resentment of poor against rich is sometimes expressed. Twice we hear that "a poor man's talk is considered shameless, while a wealthy man's farts are crisp and sweet" (pp. 794, 853), and elsewhere someone pleads:

> Don't laugh at poor people wearing ragged clothes. Everyone dreams of riches and children, but wealth and honor are gifts of Heaven. (p. 673)

In *Erhuan ji*, an impoverished man during a famine sells his wife to a fabulously wealthy old landowner. The poor man is not at all blameless and the rich one is really rather kindhearted; yet her escape from the latter and return home is a happy ending. Another mild victory of poor over rich takes place in *Jie nü diaoxiao*, where the rich family of an ugly daughter, having bribed the matchmaker to make a match for her, find they have to send her to attend a funeral at her fiancé's house. They borrow a pretty substitute from poor neighbors who are indebted to them, but the trick is discovered, and the fiancé ends up marrying the poor girl. There is a comic scene in *Shuang suo gui* in which a rich miser complains he has only 10 *qing* of land and is not responsible for a poor relative, arguing with him over a grain loan while wanting to forget the 45 days of work building his house the other had done for him (pp. 85ff.).

Social mobility, particularly downward mobility, is a recurrent fact of life in the world of these operas. We are always meeting people like the beggar who was of rich family but squandered his inheritance on food, drink, and pleasures (*Yang Wen taofan* [Yang Wen becomes a beggar]); or the pottery repairman who had once owned land and a house (*Ju gang* [A pottery repairman]). Gambling in particular is said to be the ruin of many. The man forced to sell his wife in *Erhuan ji* had once been wealthy but lost everything through compulsive gambling. The poor woman trying to persuade a better-off neighbor to lend her some jewelry in *Jie didi* (Borrowing a hair ornament) had been born to wealth but married a gambler who pawned her jewelry and even his own clothes. *Wang Xiao'er ganjiao* (Wang Xiao'er the donkey boy) shows us a donkey boy who had come originally from a rich family but had gambled everything away; and similar declines have been suffered by characters in *Ding deng* (Holding a lamp on the head), *Yang fulu tou qin, Jie dang* (To borrow and pawn) and *Guanwang miao* (At the Guanwang Temple).

Upward mobility occurs, too, though generally in a wildly unrealistic way, such as winning top honors in the capital examinations.[8] Like downward mobility, upward mobility is sometimes shown as creating strains on personal obligations. In two plays, a husband has remarried into a rich and powerful family (in one case after winning top honors in the examinations), and the play is largely about whether he will recognize his humbler original wife or family (*Gao Wenju zuo huating, Dinglang xun fu*). This sense of constant social mobility, that today's wealthy were yesterday's poor and that today's poor were yesterday's wealthy, is of course a consoling thought for the poor. Especially if the rich owe their position to little more than luck (or "Heaven"), then they are no better than we are—indeed they are frequently not as good.

Resentment against the rich and concern about the strains placed on moral relationships by social mobility are found even in the Dingxian opera dramatizing a didactic story about filial piety. *Guo Ju mai zi* (Guo Ju buries his son) is the ancient story from the "Twenty-four exemplars of filial piety" (*Ershisi xiao*) about a model son willing to kill his child so that the family could have enough food to feed his aged mother. At the last moment, however (like Abraham about to sacrifice Isaac), this paragon of virtue is spared by divine intervention. In the Dingxian opera, as Guo and his wife are about to kill their child in order to save the grandmother, the audience sees a god of wealth bury 18 pieces of silver and gold for them to find and use to support the mother.

This, then, is an opera which should be expected to promote Confucian *xiao,* but our folk version is less concerned with filial piety than with the conflict of rich and poor. Much of the Dingxian play involves Guo's attempt to borrow from his maternal uncle, who, though well-to-do, heartlessly refuses to lend any more, even in order to keep his own sister (the grandmother) alive; indeed he even beats Guo, who is weakened with hunger. When the grandmother hears of this she says:

> I think of the years when we were rich and your family was poor. You borrowed gold and silver from us Guos then. But now that you are rich and our family is poor, you don't consider my Guo Ju as half a person. You are said to have rice to feed your fowls and dogs, but you don't consider old me a relative at all. (p. 273; cf. pp. 269–270.)

Near the end, as Guo Ju and his wife are walking away from the village to where they plan to bury their infant son, their talk is not about his mother or about his duties to his mother or even about the child; rather they complain about how the wealthy look down on them because of their poverty, and they muse that the rich won't be rich forever, that the poor still have will, and so on. Thus the ending—finding the gold—has more than a hint of supernatural support and vindication of the poor against the rich.

RELIGIOUS SANCTIONS

The matter of supernatural support brings us to Max Weber's argument that it is possible to escape patriarchal domination only by means of a religion that makes ethical demands. Only a religion grounded in a "supramundane God who raised ethical demands" would be "in tension with the irrationalities of the world" and could "oppose the world with rational, ethical imperatives." "The great achievement of ethical religions, above all of the ethical and asceticist sects of Protestantism, was to shatter the fetters of the sib."[9] This raises the interesting question of to what extent Chinese folk religion had an ethical content and thus gave people leverage with which to oppose family authority.

There is evidence in the plays of gods thought of as basically magical and not ethical, spirits to be manipulated, by magic, rituals, or promises—spirits who do not make ethical demands on people. We frequently see people vowing to carry out a religious deed in exchange for some divine benefit, uttering such prayers as "Buddha, if you grant my request, I will donate oil [for temple lamps] four seasons every year"

(p. 449) or "Gods of the Three Stars, if you get me and my son out of this prison I will build a temple with images of you in it" (p. 321), or promising to worship at the god's temple if certain demons are exorcised (p. 949). One such exchange seems astonishingly lopsided: A man vows to restore a temple and make an image of the god if he is made emperor (p. 212). Such deal-making with the gods does not suggest they are a moral source that could challenge social convention.

There are other indications in the Dingxian plays, however, that folk religion did have an ethical content—that the gods do make demands concerning people's behavior. That Heaven or the gods reward the good is asserted from time to time: For instance, we are told in two different plays, once by the bodhisattva Guanyin herself, that only vegetarians and the good get to Heaven.[10] Supernatural enforcement of moral laws may also be suggested by the proverb, which appears in two operas: "You won't have to fear ghosts knocking on your door in the middle of the night if you've done nothing to give yourself a guilty conscience [*kuixin*]."[11]

More significant, in a number of plays, we see deities intervening in the world to rectify wrongs, punish the wicked, or reward the good. A prince about to be killed by his parents is saved by a god in one opera (*Da niao*, p. 35), and in another the South Sea goddess (Nanhai laomu, that is the bodhisattva Guanyin) has restored to life a man who had been murdered by a villain (*Yang Ershe hua yuan*, p. 25). Elsewhere an immortal (*da xian*) helps a boy find his father, and, in the same play, Heaven saves an innocent man from death (*Dinglang xun fu*, p. 339). We can find Buddha ordering a local god (*tudi*) to look after the chastity of a virtuous wife (*Longbao si jiangxiang*), and, in a complicated war story, the Jade Emperor rectifies all in the end and makes the aggrieved family deities in a temple (*Fan tang*). Threat of supernatural punishment is used to make someone pay a debt (*Shuang suo gui*, p. 84).

We also see people making vows before the gods on the order of "May the gods split me in two with lightning if I am not telling the truth" (p. 76). These may be found in numerous places (for example, pp. 32, 300, 900–901). Not only are such religiously sanctioned vows frequent; there is every indication that they were regarded seriously. In one play, a person's oath to Heaven to keep a secret gives the other person the confidence to tell the secret (p. 550). In another, a vow taken by a man and a woman in a temple not to commit sexual impropriety on pain of divine punishment restrains them later while they are on a journey, staying together in an inn and greatly tempted (*Bai cao po.* By contrast, the evil monk in *Longbao si jiangxiang* is ready enough to swear falsely; p. 452). Two operas show supernatural punishment for breaking a vow, where there are really other moral issues involved. In *Zhuang Zhou shan fen* (Zhuangzi and fanning a grave), the Daoist philosopher's discovery of his wife's fickleness is all part of a plan by Guanyin to bring him Buddhist enlightenment by breaking his attachment to her. At the end of the play, the fickle wife is killed by supernatural forces because she had sworn to be faithful to her husband after his death. In *Bian lü*, too, a daughter-in-law who maltreats her mother-in-law is changed into a donkey because she had taken on oath not to do such things.[12]

Let me quote from a scene from the opera *Wang Mingyue xiuqi* (Wang Mingyue divorces his wife). Wang Mingyue is a good man who, with his good wife, offers wine to various gods and gives money to the poor and needy and for the repair of roads, bridges, and temples. But, because his wife is childless after many years of marriage, he reluctantly comes to the decision that he must divorce her—sadly for he is a kind man and she has been good to him. The scene then shifts to Heaven where the Jade Emperor is receiving reports and giving orders to subordinates (in the manner of a Chinese official or of the emperor). Looking over the records of good and evil, this supreme deity sings:

> I look up and observe that in Shandong there are gangs of demons and bandits. In my Golden Palace I proclaim "Listen, Green Dragon. You are to go to Shandong and in the middle of the night extirpate all of them."
>
> I look up and observe that in Shanxi a wicked man named Wang Xiao'er is committing evil and not good, reviling his parents and cursing his neighbors. White Tiger, you go to Shanxi and cut him down at noon.
>
> I look up and observe that in Hubei the common people are suffering because it has not rained for three years. Li Changgeng, go to Hubei and make a third of an inch of rain fall at noon.
>
> My ears are hot, my eyes jumpy, and my mind uneasy. I raise my head again and see that in the Luoyang area of Henan there is a man called Wang Mingyue who repairs bridges and roads and builds temples. Such a virtuous person deserves nine sons; yet I see he is without an heir. In my Dragon

Palace I blow a magical breath and tell Songzi Niangniang [a deity who sends children], "A golden boy and a golden girl are being given you, whom you are ordered to send Mingyue's family in Luoyang." I flick the sleeves of my robe and descend from my dragon throne. (p. 575)

This does not sound much like the "wild and irrational" deities who "can do anything" which Weber thought would make "ethical rationality . . . out of the question."[13] Rather, it would seem that gods who are conceived in such a way as we have just seen are indeed exercising ethical demands. But there is a further question. Are these ethical demands in tension with the world? Or is no more being demanded than what Weber called a "pious conformism with the fixed order of secular powers"?[14] In other words, are the gods really supramundane or were they thought of as basically part of the worldly order and thus unable to make demands to transcend it?

Here we come to the well-known similarity in Chinese popular thought of heavenly and earthly bureaucracies; that Chinese tend to think of gods in terms reminiscent of government officials—what Schwartz called the "bureaucratic metaphor"—has often been noted,[15] and would seem to suggest that gods are conceived as really part of the social order and not a challenge to it. In support of this similarity, it is interesting to note in the Dingxian plays scenes of heavenly bureaucracy,[16] of a local god worrying about what his superior will say,[17] or of someone threatening to commit suicide and make an accusation in the underworld, which is depicted as a court of law.[18]

More interesting, gods are like officials in that both function in operas to rectify justice and restore the moral balance in the universe.[19] Sometimes a good though low-ranking magistrate may render justice;[20] elsewhere it takes a higher official like the wise Judge Bao to solve a murder.[21] In some plays, it is just taken for granted at the end that, for instance, justice will result when the widow of a murdered man is finally able to get a letter to her father, who is a high-ranking government official;[22] or that the emperor will punish an evil high official if he is informed about him.[23]

Indeed, the importance of law and law courts—in spite of frequent depiction of corrupt officials—and the readiness of people to turn to law to rectify wrongs in these plays are remarkable. Officials often appear as evil, corrupt, or incompetent, and in one play it is said that "a law court is worse than a stove," because people get so burned by the judicial system (*Dinglang xun fu,* p. 329: an innocent man has been framed for murder by an evil official who went so far as to kill a servant girl as part of the setup, and then bribed a judge to convict him). Nonetheless, there is a remarkably frequent tendency to look to lawsuits for recourse, even in rather minor matters. That one party to an engagement can bring suit if the other enters another engagement is made explicit in *Liu Yulan shang miao,* and mentioned also in *Yang Ershe hua yuan* and *Yang Fulu tou qin;* and an actual courtroom scene with judgment in such a case forms the conclusion of *Shuang suo gui.* In that play, too, when the wife flees, her father and her husband sue each other over the matter (p. 94). The possibility of family affairs getting into court also appears in *Shuang hong da shangfen* (p. 464), where a widow wants to make a legal accusation against her in-laws for trying to make her remarry, and also against her husband for leaving her in such a vulnerable situation. In *Jie nü diaoxiao,* after two peasant women get into a fistfight, the loser threatens to go to the law (p. 700), though this may be partly a joke. In *Da niao,* we see a woman threaten to take to court a man who entered her garden; but he says she would be disgraced, and calls her bluff (p. 38). (It is interesting to note also the frequent resort to written legal instruments. Apart from engagement contracts, we find a written marriage contract [specifying dates, presents, and so on] in *Shuang suo gui* [pp. 60–61], and written declarations of divorce [*xiu shu*] mentioned in no less than four operas.)[24]

A similarity of functions of supernatural and governmental forces is underlined by instances in which both act together to right wrongs. In a play in which river bandits have killed an official and carried off his wife, three years later the wife's brother, a high censorate official in disguise making a secret investigation, discovers the crime and has them killed with help from the god of Taishan.[25] Another opera shows Guanyin descending to earth and taking on human form to help the good hero, who is about to commit suicide; he subsequently determines instead to take his grievance to court for resolution.[26]

Yet, I would argue that maybe it is really officials who are like gods, intervening in the world from outside to correct the irrationalities in the world. The crux of this distinction is whether or not they are always affirming the social order and particularly patriarchal domination. As Schwartz has written, "The application of the bureaucratic metaphor to the numinous world did not *necessarily* lead to the view that the divine bureaucracy would invariably support its human counterpart."[27] Here I think it is significant that sometimes officials and gods and the general moral thrust of the operas are really *against* family authoritarianism. Let me illustrate with an extended summary of the plot of the rather amusing *Shuang suo gui.*

This opera is about a girl whose fiancé has become impoverished, and whose father consequently breaks off the engagement (by the ruse of announcing that she has died and staging a mock funeral). He quickly has her engaged to another man, but she still wants to marry the original fiancé; and, while her parents are out, she lets him into her bedroom. The parents return unexpectedly, and she hides him in her chest. But, before he can get away, she and the chest (which contains her dowry) are carried off to the house of the new fiancé for the wedding. There that man's sister opens the chest, discovers the original fiancé inside, recognizes him as someone she had previously been attracted to, and takes him off to *her* bedroom where he ends up in *her* chest. The two women then get together and decide that they *both* want to marry him, and the three of them carry out a sort of do-it-yourself wedding ceremony and run away together. They are subsequently apprehended by the authorities (on the father's instigation) and taken to court. But the magistrate—and here we see what sort of values are thought of as being promoted by officials (who act much like gods, I am arguing)—fines the father for breaking the original engagement, fines the second fiancé for trying to marry a woman who was already engaged, and turns the money over to the two women who go off with their new husband presumably to live as a happy threesome ever after.

Such an imaginary official, siding with rebellious young lovers against the authority of the father, seems very unreal. He is resolving the plot the way gods do in many folk operas (as a deus ex machina, if you will), and he is upholding a moral principle—recognizing a contractual obligation (a betrothal) in spite of changed financial circumstances of one of the parties—that is in opposition, quite clearly here, to the high Confucian value of obedience to parents.

Although peasants in Dingxian, like people everywhere, went to the theater for entertainment, excitement, and escape from the monotony of everyday labor and deprivation, the operas they liked to watch were not just escapist fantasies, but contained elements of moral discourse. Through these operas, villagers were able to explore their potentially subversive chafing at abuse of power in the family and the doubts raised by such domestic tyranny about the legitimacy of family authority and the ethic of obedience. Plays also expressed people's resentment against the rich and the appealing idea of fidelity in recognizing personal obligations without regard to financial consequences. Finally, they embodied people's desire to believe that morality is deeply embedded in the cosmos—a very ancient Chinese idea—that evil is punished and good rewarded, if necessary through the intervention of outside forces, sometimes gods and sometimes officials, acting in rather similar ways.

Much of this suggests that folk opera was in village communities a kind of "weapon of the weak," one of James Scott's "everyday forms of peasant resistance." That is to say that cultural and ideological hegemony in rural North China was not complete, that the moral categories and values of the ruling elites did not totally dominate the thinking of subordinate classes. The Dingxian plays indicate that, in a vague and not very explicit way—but of course it is necessary to disguise subversive ideas—people were able to penetrate and demystify the prevailing ideology of filial piety, raise questions about its justness, articulate alternative social values, question the morality and authority of village elites, and find in imagined religious and political forms extra-societal moral leverage against the existing order. I am overstating, to be sure. We have but hints of all this in these folk operas, which were surely always more entertainment than political discourse. Yet the hints are there, and they suggest that these folk operas were in some ways a means of expressing, in suitably muted form, mildly subversive ideas.

THE 48 DINGXIAN OPERAS (WITH PP. IN LI & ZHANG, 1933)

An'er song mi (An'er brings rice ["A Filial Son" in Gamble 1970]), 258–267

Bai cao po (The white grass slope), 207–222

FIVE

In Search of Modernity: Some Reflections on a New Mode of Consciousness in Twentieth-Century Chinese History and Literature

LEO OU-FAN LEE

In twentieth-century Western literature and the arts, the terms stemming from the word *modern—modernity, modernism, post-modernism—*have so dominated creative imagination and critical thinking as to become themselves paradigmatic "traditions." In China, such terms have remained on the margins of intellectual discourse as amorphous metaphors with confusing, often flippant, connotations through most of this century. In recent years, however, the word *modern* has suddenly come into intellectual fashion in post-Mao China, in part because it is semantically linked with the word *modernization,* which has been further canonized in the official "Four Modernizations." In contemporary Chinese literature, the word *modernism* (*xiandai zhuyi*) has been a subject of heated debate (as it was in Taiwan in the 1970s) and a catch-all phrase comprising various new artistic trends derived from a resurgent craze for Western literature among the post-Mao generation of young writers and critics: "obscure poetry," "stream-of-consciousness" fiction, Marxist-humanist arguments about "alienation," experiments in "black humor" and "magic realism" (à la Garcia Marquez), and the "searching-for-the-roots" movement. To this may now be added the discussions on "post-modernism" which seems to have captured the attention of avant-gardist elements on the intellectual scenes on both sides of the Taiwan Straits.[1]

It would be convenient to dismiss all such talk of Chinese "modernism" and "post-modernism" as irrelevant echoes of a new Western craze. It is also tempting—an approach one should resist—to consider such literary and artistic manifestations merely "superstructural" products of a modernizing society (Taiwan) or ideological by-products of new government policy (PRC). I should like to argue, however, that the roots of these recent "modernisms" can be traced to a new mode of historical consciousness developed since the turn of the century. This new historical consciousness, based on a new conception of time and human progress, has tended to dominate the general outlooks of Chinese intellectuals of different political persuasions; it has also served to inspire new forms of literary creation that have come to be known, since the Literary Revolution of 1917, as New Literature. However, as I shall argue in the second part of this paper, the new literary sensibilities are not coequal with but ultimately subordinate to the new historical consciousness. In contrast to its European counterparts, modern Chinese literature has been so intertwined with history that the artistic stances of modern Chinese literature are not adverse to historical modernity.

HISTORICAL CONSCIOUSNESS

What is so "modern" about modern Chinese history and literature? Is it still meaningful to follow the May Fourth iconoclasts and speak of a distinctly modern Chinese outlook or mentality that marks a clear ideological break from that of "tradition"? Much, of course, has been said about the iconoclastic side of the conspicuous anti-traditional ideology of the May Fourth intellectual revolution. But in what ways did the May Fourth generation, and their predecessors, attempt to define their difference from the past and articulate a new range of sensibilities which they would consider "modern"?

In the popular May Fourth parlance, to be "modern" means above all to be "new" (*xin*), to be consciously opposed to the "old" (*jiu*). The proliferation of journal titles and terms composed of the word *new* was striking. From Liang Qichao's "New People" ("Xinmin") and Chen Duxiu's "New Youth" ("Xin qingnian") to such prevalent compounds as "New Tide" ("Xinchao"), "New Literature and Art" ("Xin wenyi"),

"New Life" ("Xin shenghuo"), "New Society" ("Xin shehui"), and "New Epoch" ("Xin shidai"). This intellectual posture of newness does not by itself represent anything new, for in traditional China there were indeed recurrent debates between "new" and "old"—or between "moderns" and "ancients"—in matters related to scholarly texts as well as government policy. What makes for the qualitative difference in the May Fourth formulation lies rather in its implicit equation of newness with a new temporal continuum from the present to the future. In other words, the notion and value of "newness" are defined in a context of unilinear time and a unilinear sense of history that is characteristically untraditional and Western. The most eloquent manifestation of this new historical consciousness was the notion of "epoch" (*shidai*)—the heightened awareness that China had entered into a "new epoch" of world history which rendered its destiny no longer separate but an integral part of mankind. Thus, we find in this new historical outlook an emphasis on, even a mystical apotheosis of, the moment "now" as the pivotal point marking a rupture with the past and forming a progressive continuum toward a glorious future.

The general contour of this new temporal orientation is by now well known—so well known, in fact, that it is taken for granted by most scholars and remains little studied. Yet it obviously has a consequential bearing on understanding the issues of China's "modernity."

In a pioneering paper on "Chinese Intellectuals' Notion of 'Epoch' in the Post-May Fourth Era," Lung-kee Sun traces the first signs of this "advent of modernity" in the late Qing Self-Strengthening Movement: Xue Fucheng, for instance, assessed his own time as marking the end of China's isolation and the "dawn of an epoch of association among nations."[2] Both Xue and Wang Tao considered these changes as irreversible, regardless of human wishes. By 1895, Kang Youwei and Yan Fu had fully embraced this unilinear thinking about time and history coupled with "an almost mystical faith in progress."[3] As pointed out by several recent studies, this conception of history represents a drastic departure from the traditional cyclical view, a view shaped by the alternation of the "Five Elements" and the Confucian notions of dynastic cycle and "Yi zhi yi luan"—a period of order, then one of chaos.[4] Kang's famous three-stage theory of the ages of "decay and chaos," "rising peace," and "universal peace," though based in part on the *Gongyang* and *Liyun* texts of his New Text Confucianism, is altogether a forward-looking, prophetic vision of history moving in a "unilinear, irreversible process of evolutionary development." This view, according to Hao Chang, is less indebted to these ancient Chinese texts, whose seemingly linear view is nevertheless "couched within a larger cyclical framework" than to "the Western view of history, which is a process of unilinear development in both its secular and religious guises."[5] For this essentially Western scheme, Kang was indeed influenced by Yan Fu as well as by some of the publications of Christian missionaries, such as Timothy Richard and Young Allen.[6] Yan Fu stated categorically in 1895:

> The greatest and most irreconcilable difference between Chinese and Western thinking is that the Chinese love the past and neglect the present, while the Westerners strive in the present to surpass the past. The Chinese believe that to revolve from order to disorder, from ascension to decline, is the natural way of heaven and of human affairs. The Westerners believe, as the ultimate principle of all learning and government, in the infinite, daily progress, in advance that will not sink into decline, in order that will not revert to disorder.[7]

Insofar as the primary sources for this unilinear view are Western-derived, the translations and writings of Yan Fu occupied a place of seminal significance—in particular, his introduction of what has come to be known as Social Darwinism. It is commonly assumed that the Darwinian and Spencerian principles of "natural selection" and "survival of the fittest" lent themselves not only to a nationalistic imperative for China to strive for survival but to increased emphasis on human progress as a key component of this new vision of history.

It must be borne in mind that Darwin was *not* the first scientist to observe the phenomenon of biological evolution in the animal species: Lamarck preceded him and had a direct impact on Herbert Spencer. In fact the term *evolution* had been in circulation for half a century before Darwin's *The Origin of Species* first appeared in 1859. As Stephen Toulmin has pointed out, it is one of the small ironies in the Western tradition of Darwinism that "the term 'evolution' plays very little part in all of Darwin's own writing: It is not used, for instance, in the first edition of *The Origin of Species*. The connection between Darwin's theory of 'natural selection' and traditional arguments about 'organic evolution' was made explicit only subsequently."[8] Furthermore, in Darwin's own writing, "natural selection" does not necessarily imply the valorization of "survival of the fittest." Darwin "was interested only in finding a general explanation for the organic changes that in fact occur, not in demonstrating that the March of Evolution takes place always Onwards and Upwards."[9]

The indiscriminate application of Darwin's "science" to the other realms has resulted in blurring "the crucial differences between organic species and human races, nations, or classes" and led to a "conception of Evolution as Cosmic Progress—revealing a universal and irreversible direction of historical development in the natural and human worlds."[10] This confusion in nineteenth-century Western thought between evolution as a biological or zoological theory and evolutionism as a doctrine of historical and cosmic progress gave Darwinism a much broader meaning and appeal in modern European thought. Yan Fu, through his effective interpretations of Spencer and Huxley, further popularized this confusion in his own country.

It can be argued that Yan Fu's interpretation purposefully hinges on such a confusion. In his 1895 essay on the "Origins of Power" ("Yuanqiang"), he briefly describes Darwin's theory only to demonstrate its relevance to the human world because "human beings are but a species of animals." He then applauds Herbert Spencer for having developed a grand system that comprised all and for having used the evolutionary theory to "explicate affairs of human ethics and government."[11] It was precisely in establishing such an analogy between the animal and human realms that Yan was able to decry the deterministic implications of Darwin's theory. Without human intervention, the Darwinian idea of progress could only lead to scientific fatalism determined by such "objective" elements as heredity and environment which "replaced conscious, logical choice as the main determinants of human action."[12] Yan Fu's reading of Social Darwinism thus represents a reversal of this fatalistic tendency (which was also observable in nineteenth-century European thought) by asserting the central importance of human volition in both individual and collective forms. Benjamin Schwartz, in his classic study of Yan Fu, has specifically pointed to Yan Fu's interest in "the

Faustian-Promethean exaltation of energy and power both over non-human nature and within human society." As he comments: "What interests Yen Fu is not so much the Darwinian account of biological evolution qua science, even though science is a cherished value. It is precisely the stress on the values of struggle—assertive energy, the emphasis on the actualization of potentialities within a competitive situation."[13]

Yan Fu's reading of Social Darwinism, in Schwartz's analysis, has basically leaned toward "the stream of social-political idealism" in its concern with "the nature of relations among men within the larger macroscopic structures of political and social life and with the shaping of those structures to promote these social-ethical ends."[14] Subsequent Chinese writings, all influenced by Yan, tended to expand the scope of his view. On the one hand, evolutionism had entered the May Fourth ideological discourse as a central component through the writings of Chen Duxiu, Lu Xun, and others. In Chen's famous plea to youth, he incorporated a great deal of Social Darwinian rhetoric and considered "progressivism" to be one of the five cardinal characteristics of New Youth. In another well-known article lauding "The French and Modern Civilization," he included evolutionism as one of the three major French contributions and paid special tribute to Lamarck. Before he was converted to Marxism, Chen had become a true believer in historical progress. The imprint of this new outlook is clearly seen in Chen's proclamation of a "twentieth-century consciousness" in an essay called "The Year 1916":

> The epoch in which you are living, what epoch is this? It is the beginning of the sixteenth year of the twentieth century. The changes of the world are evolutionary, different from month to month, year to year. The shining history is unfolding faster and faster . . . To live in the present world, you must raise your head and proudly call yourself a person of the twentieth century; you must create a new civilization of the twentieth century and not confine yourself to following that of the nineteenth. For the evolution of human civilization is replacing the old with the new, like a river flowing on, an arrow flying away, constantly continuing and constantly changing.[15]

This positive conception of the new epoch represents a clear affirmation of a new historical consciousness that focuses on the present as a dynamic flow of progressive change—a temporal scheme of the succession of centuries, instead of dynasties, that includes China in the mainstream of world history. Interestingly, exactly seventy years later (1986) in post-Mao Beijing, the idea of "twentieth-century consciousness" was once again hoisted by three young Beida leaders as the guiding concept of their massive project to rewrite the history of modern Chinese literature, as they attempt to bring Chinese literature to reenter the world.[16]

As the word *evolution* or *jinhua* (literally "progressive transformation") became part of the modern Chinese vocabulary, replacing the less frequently used *yanhua* or *tianyan* (as used in Yan Fu's translation of Huxley's *Evolution and Ethics*), more scholarly or semi-scholarly writings on evolution also became available, which both gave a fuller history of the Darwinian strains than Yan Fu had done and extended the concept of evolution, in fact, to philosophical discussions of "cosmic progress." Although the rich literature on this subject awaits more in-depth study, my preliminary research has revealed that not only did some of the most renowned thinkers—Zhang Dongsun, Zhang Junmai (Carsun Chang), Li Shicen among them—write extensively about evolution; general treatises, popular pamphlets, scholarly texts, and translations were also published in the 1920s and 1930s. As in the case of some general literary histories about Western literature and literary theories, as Bonnie McDougall has discovered,[17] most of these general philosophical writings are based, in part or in whole, on a number of Western books mostly in English, such as:

Thilly, *History of Philosophy*
Perry, *Philosophy of Recent Past*
———, *Present Philosophical Tendencies*
Elliot, *Modern Science and Materialism*
Joad, *Introduction to Modern Philosophy*
Marvin, *History of European Philosophy*
Külpe, *The Philosophy of Present [sic] in Germany*[18]

All of these presumably included chapters on evolution. A translation of Walter Libby's *Introduction to Contemporary Civilization* had a first chapter titled "The Idea of Progress." There was also a 100-page pamphlet on "Evolution and Eugenics" ("Jinhua lun yu shanzhong xue") coauthored by Chen Changheng and Zhou Jianren (Lu Xun's third brother) in the popular series "Dongfang wenku" published by *Dongfang zazhi* (Eastern miscellany) of the Commercial Press.[19]

An understanding of the general intellectual contours of the post-May Fourth discourse can be gained by examining how the ideas of evolution and progress are treated in these semi-scholarly and semi-popular works. In a sense, these texts may be regarded as part of the matrix of "ideological production" which brings about a modern historical consciousness. A number of examples given below will serve to demonstrate that Darwinian evolution was not only closely related to progressivism in the Chinese discourse but also to the ethical and "cosmic" tendencies which became increasingly pronounced.

In the pamphlet on "Evolution and Eugenics," the first two chapters are devoted to "The Reality of Evolution" and "Evolutionary Thought after Darwin." In his discussion, the author, Chen Changheng, has divided evolution into two categories: "Natural Evolution" and "Human Evolution or Progress"; the latter is further divided into "Acquired or Traditional Progress" and "Racial or Eugenic Progress" (titles originally in English).[20] Obviously tilting toward the significance of human evolution, the author states that even the process of natural evolution has been "increasingly directed by human beings" and that the general principle is "to create such an environment so that the fittest shall be the best and the best shall be the fittest therein." (originally in English)[21] Most interesting is the section "The Will to Progress and the Future of Evolution," in which the author reveals his ethical intention by showing fervently how human beings can "cause truth to become a factor to be fulfilled." "Truth" is here defined as "natural scientific," "social scientific," and "spiritual reality." In less than precise language (again in English), the author utters thoughts reminiscent of Yan Fu: "To help and enable the individual to recognize his or her highest standard of life, and thereby to enlarge his or her spiritual self"; "to unite and strengthen the social or common will of all the individuals so that the individual will may become a part of the common will."[22] One is also reminded of Hu Shi's famous discussion of the individual "small self" (*xiaowo*) and the collective "big self" (*dawo*). The former, having a will and a dynamism of its own, must ultimately become part of the latter in order to realize its full potential and meaning in life.

On a more scholarly plane, we find the same kind of concerns discussed in more rigorous philosophical terms and broader intellectual scope. A collection of Li Shicen's learned articles, first published in 1924, begins with an essay on "New Tendencies in Recent Philosophy," focusing on the pragmatism of William James and the intuitionism of Henri Bergson. Subsequent chapters deal with Nietzsche, Bergson, Eucken as well as Dewey and Russell. Li's Nietzsche chapter is especially revealing, as it makes extensive comparisons between Nietzsche's concepts of the superman and the Eternal Return and the Darwinian notion of evolution.

But the European thinker who seems closest to Li's sensibilities is Henri Bergson, as Bergson is also to Zhang Dongsun and Carsun Chang, who styled himself a disciple of Bergson.[23] Interestingly, not much scholarly attention has been devoted to the Chinese reception of Bergson, partly because Bergson has been long out of fashion in both Europe and China and partly because his "philosophic" ideas about intuition, *"durée,"* and *"élan vital"* are rather mystical and hard to grasp. But in his day, from the 1890s to the 1910s, Bergson was extremely popular and ranked with Durkheim as the main thinker of early twentieth-century France. After the publication of his *Creative Evolution* in 1907, "Bergson's lectures became major events. Tourists and society ladies flocked to them, as to one of the sights of the capital!"[24] Bergson was equally well known among early twentieth-century Chinese intellectuals; his reputation was equal to that of Bertrand Russell. Since Russell had severely criticized Bergson, the philosopher Zhang Dongsun rose to Bergson's defense and wrote a critique of Russell's critique of Bergson.[25] Zhang's interest was, expectedly, in Bergson's *l'Evolution creatrice,* which he translated into classical Chinese. In a lengthy chapter of his book, *Xin zhexue luncong* (Discussions on new philosophy), first published in 1928, Zhang considered Bergson's contribution to the theory of evolution to be truly "creative," surpassing the work of Spencer. In Zhang's view, Spencer's theory of "evolution" consists only of "consolidation or dispersion of matter and energy" and fails to rise beyond the natural level; it could only be called "strictly speaking, change (*bianhua*) and not progressive transformation (*jinhua*)."[26] But Zhang also realized that Bergson's creative formulations might be too mystical. Thus he introduced another variation, the "layered" evolutionary theory of "Emergent Evolution" developed by Conway Lloyd Morgan, S. Alexander, and others that combined matter, life, and spirit in a three-tier structure.

Li Shicen lauded Bergson as a "second Kant" and a "second Aristotle."[27] He considered the theories of the French idealist philosopher as basically compatible with James's, because both aim at constructing a dynamic "philosophy of life" that represents the ultimate of humanity, the former from a psychological and the latter from a behavioral standpoint.[28] Like Zhang Dongsun, he praised the "creative" ideal of Bergson, which he equated with freedom, and considered Bergson's differentiation between the organic and the inorganic (or animate or inanimate) as ushering in a "new dawn of philosophy." The crucial characteristic of the "organic" lay in its capacity for evolutionary growth. At the same time, however, Li saw the *durée* or organic growth as the surface phenomenon which was a "phantom" representation of the genuine *durée* of the "flow of life" which constituted "cosmic reality."[29] In Li's opinion, Darwin's evolutionary theory, though path-breaking, was still too causal and mechanical to reveal the truth of evolution. In comparison, Bergson was more profound.

Li's following remarks are worth quoting, not for their correctness of interpretation, but for exemplifying a continuing tendency among Chinese intellectuals to establish a cosmology of dynamic progress by extending the ethical and humanistic dimensions of evolution:

> In Darwin's explanation of evolution, he traces past origins and gauges the future from the present. Bergson considers evolution to be an endless continuing flow from past origins to the present and future. His so-called origin is nothing less than the vital impulse of life [Li's equivalent of *élan vital*], and this impulse is hidden in our consciousness to stimulate and encourage ourselves to incline toward creative paths constantly. Darwin's evolutionary theory emphasizes above all the term *fitting* in that the primary purpose of the duration of life is to fit into external environment. Bergson, however, considers *fitting* to be no more than illustrating the tortuous and unsteady path of evolution; it definitely does not point to or give us the direction of the path ... Only the primal force of evolution, that is the so-called impulse of life, can shoulder such a heavy responsibility. This impulse of life is also the spiritual reality that fills the universe. It possesses a powerful and special capacity for the creation of life.[30]

Li saw the path of evolution as a process of ceaseless struggle in which this life force gradually triumphs over matter. When it met with resistance, "it could not but divide itself in order to cope, thus splintering itself into myriad races and numerous individuals."[31] In a similar vein, Li discussed Nietzsche's concept of the "will to power" and deemed it compatible with Bergson's: Nietzsche's "superman" is a symbol of human evolution, a "signpost on the path of the progress of life—evolution—but not the ultimate goal.[32]

It is not difficult, without going into the dubious depths of Bergson's thought, to understand the source of his attraction to these Chinese thinkers. In the words of H. Stuart Hughes, it is "a kind of majestic biological fantasy"[33] built upon some forced analogies with Darwin's theory which, however, easily lent itself to spiritual reinterpretations. It fits nicely into a familiar framework of Chinese cosmological thinking which focuses on the "metaphysical" qualities of the "*qi*"—from Mencius's famous notion of "*haoran zhi qi*" to the varieties of "*qi*" in Neo-Confucianism—that seems transformed into a more vital "impulse of life." Moreover, the need for a new "philosophy of life" (*rensheng guan*) in a period of intellectual and spiritual confusion following the May Fourth Movement was obviously felt as expressed in the famous debate on "science and the philosophy of life." Understandably, Chinese Bergsonians found themselves in the philosophy-of-life camp. Zhang Dongsun and Carsun Chang did not oppose the value of science per se, but rather, as Zhang Dongsun summarized, the "spurious" claim made by Ding Wenjiang, Hu Shi, and Wu Zhihui that science possessed an omnipotence as knowledge. In a way, the effort of Zhang Dongsun and Li Shicen to establish a new philosophy of life paralleled that of Bergson's: "to define the nature of subjective existence as opposed to the schematic order that the natural sciences had imposed on the external world."[34] They found in Bergson a way of transcending natural science without lapsing totally into Chinese traditionalism as their critics charged.

Like Yan Fu's reading of Social Darwinism, their reformulations of Bergson are equally imbued with a high degree of human volition. They seemed as much taken with a view of linear progress as the Chinese Darwinists. The meaning of history or life was seen in a temporal scheme anchored in the present and oriented toward the future; the past as an externalized object for emulation was rejected by both Darwinists and Bergsonians. Thus, the impact of Bergson on Chinese intellectuals can be viewed in light of the Chinese reception of Darwin: A form of evolutionary progressivism was so deeply ingrained in their consciousness that it helped to solidify a new consciousness of time as a unilinear forward-moving flow from the past through the present to the future. It remained for the Chinese Marxists to give history a definable purpose by investing this progress of time with another new meaning.

Another piece of clear evidence of the stirrings of this new mode of historical consciousness was the effusive usage of the word *shidai* (epoch). As documented by Lung-kee Sun, the term—perhaps of Japanese origin—was first introduced in the decade before the founding of the Republic, and, by around 1927, it had become a catchword, especially among radical intellectuals. Of its various usages when first introduced, "*shidai*'s most important connotation came to be 'the present time' or 'our time,' always with the implication that it is a time of breathlessly rapid changes and incessant innovation."[35] The present epoch was, almost by definition, a "new" era radically different from all past periods, bringing "new tides" which could not be resisted. This sentiment was expressed eloquently in Luo Jialun's manifesto for the *Xinchao* or "New Tide" magazine. Accordingly, an individual living in this new epoch must seek to comprehend it: "Know your *shidai*" became a clarion-call. The words of the radical poet (later Trotskyite) Wang Duqing were typical: "Know your *shidai*! Your *shidai*—that is the present developmental stage of society you are living in—foreordains what you should do, and where to start."[36] Thus, the new consciousness of time also carried with it an imperative of timing: One would "lag far behind" the time if one were not vigilant; therefore, one should continually move forward with time and even "push it forward." For some young writers, the battle between the old and the new easily took on a radical imperative: "The old writers, lagging behind *shidai*, are in no position to shoulder the responsibility of expressing *shidai*'s life. This responsibility can fall only upon the shoulders of new writers, because the latter have a genuine feel for the life of the *shidai*!"[37]

This familiar configuration of concerns tended to produce a new personality type that Thomas Metzger has aptly called "the zealously ideological, heroic self." To varying degrees, this "heroic self" was not only basic to leftist radicalism and Maoism but also to modern revivals of Confucianism and the Sun Yat-sen—Chiang Kai-shek ideology of the Guomindang. Metzger gives six characteristics to this new vision: "First, the self is armed with a doctrinal system that explains the laws of the cosmos and history and fixes the goal of life. Second, one is filled with a fiery, selfless determination to 'struggle' for this goal. Third, thus determined, one is with 'the people' or with the people's 'real' desires . . . Fourth, in this struggle, perceived historical tendencies constitute a 'tide' filled with 'power' and moving irresistibly toward ego's goal. Fifth, in this light, the key problem is fusing ego's heroic spirit with this power-ful historical tide" by "*translating* an inner vision into the outer world," and finally, this heroic type, whether on the currently winning or los-ing side, "habitually expressed great optimism about the imminent change for the better in world affairs."[38] Of these six characteristics, one might add, at least four concern themselves with the new consciousness of history treated above. It was only with the awareness that China had entered a new epoch and was going through an epoch-making transfor-mation that a new "philosophy of life" based on energy and optimism was possible. The social-political contents of the various "doctrinal sys-tems" or philosophies of life did indeed vary a great deal, as Metzger has pointed out, but still a common "structure" or mode of thinking existed among modern Chinese intellectuals.

On the more popular level, this new consciousness had infused the urban world of commercial consumption and set a glamorous foreign-flavored lifestyle favored by bourgeois urbanites and writers. Shanghai, with its large and prosperous foreign concessions, became the center of this "modern" universe. As its chic Chinese transliteration indicates, the term *modeng* meant to be *à la mode,* to acquire a fashionable veneer and taste. The adjective *romantic,* which I used in my early book, *The Romantic Generation of Modern Chinese Writers,* to characterize this new urban literary temper in the post-May Fourth era,[39] does not do full justice to either the urban milieu in which such a temper was pro-duced or the temporal frame in which it was manifested. The treaty-port city, particularly Shanghai, constituted a "spatialization" of "modernity"—a configuration of space which crystallized the present moment, a self-contained world cut off and set apart from the traditionalism of the surrounding countryside. The journey of the progressive writers from the countryside to the city took on the added meaning of a temporal journey from a point of traditional past to arrival at the modern present.

Although advancing in time and joining the twentieth century in spirit, modern Chinese intellectuals during the 1920s and 1930s were not entirely comfortable with the concomitant problem of spatial change—not only in terms of the urban-rural split but also with regard to the greater realization that, with the twentieth century, China had become "one nation among many." In this regard, the vulgar Darwinian phrase "survival of the fittest" came as much to haunt as to elevate their spirits, because either the jungle image of competition in the raw (hence the domination of physical prowess) or the ideological canvas of imperialism (military and political power) posed a direct external threat. This shared sense of threat and anxiety, as is well known, lay at the core of their fervent nationalism.

Thus, "modernity" in China was loosely defined as a mode of consciousness of time and history as unilinear progress, moving in a continuous "stream" or "tide" from the past to the present; it also contained the valorized notion of the present as a new "epoch," not only unprecedented and qualitatively different from previous eras but better, which leads prophetically to a purposeful future. The influence of Darwinian strains of evolutionary thought in China led to the emergence of this new perception. Its dynamism was manifested especially among May Fourth and post-May Fourth Chinese intellectuals in an outlook of the ego's active fusion with the forward tide of history.

LITERATURE

It is not surprising, in view of the close interaction between modern Chinese thought and literature, that, on the literary scene of the 1920s and 1930s, the terms *shidai* and *xiandai* (with connotations of both modern and contemporary) were prevalent and used almost interchangeably. So, too, were such related phrases as *shidai xing* ("epoch" quality or the nature of the present era), *shidai gan* (sense of the epoch or temper of the age), *chaoliu* (tide or current) and *sichao* (currents of thought) or *wenyi sichao* (currents of literary thought). Some of these terms came from the introduction or partial translations of the works of Taine (time, environment, temper of an age), Georg Brandes (who wrote, among other books, *Main Currents of 19th-Century Literature*), Kuriyagawa Hakuson, and others. Titles of novels, stories, and literary journals often carried the words *shidai* or *xiandai*. For instance, one of the most fashionable literary figures in the Shanghai literary world, Ye Lingfeng, wrote a long popular novel, *Shidai guniang* (A girl of the times), worked as editor in the Xiandai Shuju (modern or contemporary bookstore), and edited a journal titled *Xiandai xiaoshuo* (Modern fiction).

Inevitably, two ideas began to take hold: the view, first raised by Hu Shi, that each epoch had its own literature; and the slogan adopted by many writers that "literature must reflect its own time." Both ideas obviously were derived from an acute time-consciousness which inclined toward the present moment. Lung-kee Sun has indicated that in Hu Shi's own textual scholarship the word *shidai* was used in a neutral sense (and it did not figure prominently in Dewey's thought), but it soon took on a "contemporary" meaning as "modern era."[40] By the end of the 1920s, both this modern-oriented notion of *shidai* and the idea that "literature must reflect its own time" had entered the "revolutionary" vocabulary of the radical writers on the leftist front, although the concept did not originate with Marx and perhaps owed more to Belinsky.

The infusion of these ideas into literary discourse has had profound consequences. The close connection between New Literature and the new consciousness of time and history created a Chinese matrix of literary modernism that diverged significantly from the fundamental tenets of European Modernism. The intellectual issues involved are extremely complex, since, as is well known, the mercurial nature of Modernism in the West has been "an ever-renewed cause for debates and discoveries."[41] However, despite divergencies of opinion there is at least agreement among Western scholars that Modernism does or did exist (depending on one's periodization between Modernism and Post-Modernism) and that, moreover, the term covers a wide range of historically related movements from roughly 1890 to 1930: Impressionism, Post-Impressionism, Expressionism, Cubism, Futurism, Symbolism, Imagism, Vorticism, Dadaism, Surrealism.[42] Most scholars also agree

that "one of the defining features of this Modernism has been the breaking down of traditional frontiers in matters of literary and cultural
concern."[43] Thus, there is at least a superficial ground for comparison
with the Chinese May Fourth Movement.

My earlier formulations of the emergence of a new sense of time
among Chinese intellectuals since the late Qing, and especially during
the May Fourth period, bear some striking resemblances to the post-
Renaissance view in the West. As Matei Calinescu, a leading scholar of
Western Modernism, has aptly described it: "Modernity was conceived
of as a time of emergence from darkness, a time of awakening and 'rena-
scence,' heralding a luminous future." "Man was therefore to participate
consciously in the creation of the future: A high premium was put on
being with one's time and not against it, and on becoming an agent of
change in an incessantly dynamic world."[44] The "modern" outlook of
May Fourth intellectuals also evinced some strong traces of what Calinescu calls the "bourgeois idea of modernity," which may be regarded
as a direct descendant of the post-Renaissance view buttressed by ideas
of Enlightenment and the development of the Industrial Revolution:
"the doctrine of progress, the confidence in the beneficial possibilities of
science and technology, the concern with time . . . the cult of reason,
and the ideal of freedom defined within the framework of an abstract
humanism, but also the orientation toward pragmatism and the cult of
action and success."[45]

However, as Calinescu argues, at some point during the first half of
the nineteenth century "an irreversible split occurred between modernity as a stage in the history of Western civilization—a product of scientific and technological progress, of the industrial revolution, of the
sweeping economic and social changes brought about by capitalism—
and modernity as an aesthetic concept."[46] The gap widened in the
course of the century, and the relations between the two modernities
became "irreducibly hostile." The modernity as aesthetic or cultural
concept, ever since its beginnings in Romanticism, had inclined toward
radical anti-bourgeois attitudes. "What defines cultural modernity is its
outright rejection of bourgeois modernity, its consuming negative
passion."[47] Its negativity lay in its profound disillusionment with the
positive notions of reason and progress, which in its process of "embour-

geoisement" had turned into "vulgar utilitarianism" and "the philistinism of middle-class hypocrisy."

Thus, the various movements associated with Modernism, all derived from this aesthetic modernity, point to an artistic stance that subverts realism and humanism, the two cardinal tenets of nineteenth-century historical modernity. It is also "anti-historical" in the sense that this modern sensibility "tends to see history or human life not as a sequence, or history not as an evolving logic; art and the urgent now strike obliquely across. Modernist works frequently tend to be ordered, then, not on the sequence of historical time or the evolving sequence of character, from history to story, as in realism and naturalism; they tend to work spatially or through layers of consciousness, working towards a logic of metaphor or form."[48]

If one looks at the Chinese literary scene at the time when these variants of Modernism reached a height in Europe, shortly after World War I, about the same time as the May Fourth Movement, it is obvious that the Chinese counterpart differed. To be sure, some vague notions of aesthetic modernism also found their way into certain literary journals. The phrase "art for art's sake" was consciously adopted by the early Creationists, albeit given a more positive and dynamic twist to the original meaning of Gautier's notion of *l'art pour l'art*. Ever since the mid-1920s, Baudelaire became in fact one of the most frequently translated French authors in China. What may be termed the post-romanticist tendency for the *artiste* to define a subjective realm of imagination as both a more private and more profound "reality" can also be found in the works—and artistic poses—of some Chinese writers in the early 1920s: not only the more famous Yu Dafu, but also the lesser known Feng Naichao, Lin Ruji, Yu Gengyu, and Fang Weide, even Lu Xun.

The crucial point of difference, however, is that these Chinese writers did *not* choose (nor did they feel the necessity) to separate the two domains of historical and aesthetic modernity in their pursuit of a modern mode of consciousness and modern forms of literature. There was *no* discernible split; on the contrary, humanism and realism continued to hold sway. The majority of writers, perhaps buoyed by their new historical consciousness, were eager to create realistic narratives that incorporated the unilinear sequence of historical time or the evolving sequence of character. The gingerly attempts of a few "romantic" or "neo-romantic" authors mentioned above to give some symbolic shape to the undulating "waves" of the private psyche were also made within the conscious framework of the modern "tides" of history.

Looking at the Chinese literary imagination from a European perspective, one can state the most obvious: The new consciousness of history—or more specifically, of the new mode of evolutionary thinking about time and history—had penetrated into Chinese discourses of literature as well. Bonnie McDougall's research on the early introduction of Western literary theories into China has revealed that Chinese writers relied heavily on a number of English textbooks of literary history that adopted an evolutionary scheme of progressive stages: from Classicism, Romanticism, Realism, Naturalism, to "Neo-Romanticism."[49] Influenced by the concept of evolution, Chinese writers and critics (from Liang Qichao, Chen Duxiu, Hu Shi to Mao Dun) came out in favor of realism and naturalism. Mao Dun, for instance, although fully aware of some of the avant-gardist trends in Europe which had moved beyond realism—particularly Symbolism, Expressionism, and Futurism (which he discussed in learned essays)[50]—stopped short of embracing these *"avant"* trends. In an announcement published in the *Xiaoshuo yuebao* in 1920, Mao Dun stated that contemporary Chinese literature had developed only to the point between classicism and romanticism, and in this "order of evolution" Chinese literature could not "leap to the sky in one step." Despite his considered effort to separate aesthetic concerns from the temporal, he nevertheless concluded that Western works of realism and naturalism must be introduced first for emulation.[51]

Why did modern Chinese writers embrace this Western type of modernity without developing any hostile attitude toward it in their conceptions of art and literature? Perhaps it would help, to answer this central question, to put both sides—the West and China—in their historical contexts. One reason, it might be argued, why the two modernities became "irreducibly hostile" in the West starting in the first half of the nineteenth century is that the first kind of modernity, as epitomized in the industrial revolution, was actually taking place, giving Western writers and artists something very real—and from their vantage point very negative—to react against. More specifically, the benefits and the evils of the industrial civilization were fully manifested in the urban middle class, with its taste of philistine vulgarity due to the accumulation of money. In China, however, in the 1920s and 1930s, modernity was more largely an unrealized idea than a tangible reality. Insofar as Chinese intellectuals experienced the "modern world" as an objective reality, it was in the guise of the modernity of *other* societies (the countries of Europe and America, and to some extent Japan). Since this modernity was introduced into China in the form of (or at least in close conjunction with) imperialism, the Chinese felt that they, too, had to have it in order to arrest imperialism's impact. Chinese intellectuals and creative artists, in other words, did not have the luxury enjoyed by their Western counterparts of adopting a hostile stance toward modernity.

On a deeper level, it may be noted that one of the central intellectual "fountainheads" of Western Modernism—a theory that radically altered the way in which Western artists and writers envision reality—did not have the same effect in China. Despite its early introduction in China in 1913,[52] the theory of Freud, unlike that of Darwin and Bergson, failed to make profound inroads into Chinese literary thinking and practice. To be sure, there were again some isolated examples of Freudian influence, such as Lu Xun's prose poetry collection *Yecao* (Wild grass) and some early crude stories written by Guo Moruo, both employing dream devices. But with a few notable exceptions (to be discussed later) most modern Chinese writers did not embrace the Freudian insight of the unconscious as a deeper structure of reality, as they later embraced, quite fervently, the Marxist concepts of social class and historical materialism as objective and "scientific" laws governing the outer reality. This apparent lack of separation between the two realms of the conscious and the unconscious perhaps reflects a holistic frame of thinking derived from the largely holistic tradition of Chinese philosophy,[53] a conception that sees the world as a "whole" in which boundaries between external and internal reality are intentionally or unintentionally blurred. More specifically, it can also be argued that the external demands of the era—unceasing social and political turmoils—were such that modern Chinese writers turned their obsessions outward: they could ill afford to indulge in introspective psychoanalysis. Consequently, the most notable tendency of Western Modernistic literature—the purposeful break with external reality and the incessant probing of the inner, fragmented psyche through a comparably fragmented system of language (hence the technique of "stream-of-consciousness")—did not really catch on among Chinese writers, in spite of their fairly up-to-date knowledge of such new Western samples. Again the case of Bergson, discussed above, provides another source of contrast.

In a perceptive book, *The Matrix of Modernism,* Sanford Schwartz has demonstrated the impact of the ideas of Bergson, Bradley, Nietzsche, and William James on two modern masters, Ezra Pound and T. S. Eliot. Specifically, Bergson's theory of "real duration"—the notion that real time constitutes an unbroken immanent flux that can only be grasped intuitively—serves to anticipate the stream-of-consciousness novel, because, through a skillful usage of language, such a "bold novelist" may be able to reveal, beneath the surface of everyday awareness (in Bergson's words from *Time and Free Will*), "a fundamental absurdity," "an infinite permeation of a thousand different impressions which have already ceased to exist the instant they are named. We commend him for having known us better than we knew ourselves."[54] Interestingly, while Chinese thinkers like Li Shicen and Zhang Dongsun apparently had no trouble incorporating the mystical and metaphysical side of Bergson, few creative writers had drawn much inspiration from Bergson. Again, knowledge about Bergson's possible link with Freud was widely known through Lu Xun's translation of Kuriyagawa Hakuson's book, *The Symbols of Repression* (*Kumon no shōchō*), which sees Bergson's élan vital as infusing Freud's concept of repressed libido, thus forming the basis of artistic creativity. But few writers were visibly influenced. The only notable product inspired by this combined "theory" was some of the pieces in Lu Xun's *Wild Grass* and a half-aborted mythic tale, "Mending Heaven."[55]

If we look further into literary sources of Western Modernism in addition to Bergson and Freud, we would be amazed to find that almost the entire gallery of major writers associated with various strains of European Modernism—from Baudelaire, Verlaine, Rimbaud, Wilde, Beardsley, Schnitzler, to Yeats, Joyce, Eliot, Hemingway, Faulkner, Amy Lowell, W. H. Auden, and Gertrude Stein—were known in China since the late 1920s, chiefly through a number of literary journals, all published in Shanghai. This special urban milieu, with its foreign concessions, provided a window for recent literary trends in the international arena. It was in this setting that some Chinese writers began to read about these Modernist authors in some of the well-known Western literary journals they were able to find, or even subscribe to, in a few Shanghai foreign bookstores: *Vanity Fair, Harper's, The Dial, The Bookman, Living Age* in English and *Lettre Francais* and *Le Monde* in French.[56] Some of the articles from these foreign journals were translated, together with photographs or cartoons, which the trend-conscious Chinese writers reproduced in their own journals: Shi Zhicun's *Xiandai,* Ye Lingfeng's *Wenyi huabao* (Literary pictorial), Shao Xunmei's *Jinwu yuekan* (Golden house monthly, modeled consciously after the celebrated *Yellow Book* in England).

This body of information remains little explored by Chinese scholars, who until recently considered it "decadent," hence immoral and not in tune with the ethical-progressive "temper" of the period as contained in the dominant tenet of realism. On the other hand, if one examines closely the artistic stances of these men and their journals, it is not surprising that they were groping toward a certain "modern aesthetic" that they would like to articulate in opposition to the theory and practice of realism as propagated by the leaders of the May Fourth Movement. In a sense, they may be considered China's pioneer literary modernists, whose literary opinions bore a certain affinity to the Western counterparts they promoted, though their creative work did not entirely reach the artistic frontiers of the Western avant-garde. Because this literary phenomenon, though isolated in Shanghai, remains so little known, it deserves a preliminary discussion.

The literary journal *Xiandai zazhi* (1932–1936) may be considered a leader in this enterprise. The journal's foreign title was originally in French—*les Contemporains*—which obviously signifies the editors' French education (both Shi Zhicun and Dai Wangshu, the journal's reigning poet, graduated from the Catholic Aurora University in Shanghai) and self-image: They wished to be "contemporaries" with their European counterparts. The literary tastes of these two men reveal a fascinating contrast. Dai Wangshu has been widely acknowledged to be a premier symbolist poet who did not really emulate Baudelaire but rather drew inspiration from the works of the French "later Symbolists"—Paul Verlaine, Francis Jammes, Paul Fort, Remy de Gourmont—as well as such Spanish writers as Lorca, Unamuno, and Azorin. The imprint of these writers on Dai's own experiments was a body of "soft-colored" poetry reminiscent of French Impressionist painting (in sharp contrast to the hard-edged and more "obscure" works by Li Jinfa). In comparison, Shi Zhicun's foreign tastes may be considered more "exotic" and daring. His favorite writers were Edgar Allan Poe, Marquis de Sade, Havelock Ellis, Amy Lowell, Freud, Joyce, and particularly the Austrian *fin-de-siècle* writer Arthur Schnitzler. In his earlier years as a college student, Shi was also much taken by early Soviet literature: he must have been one of the few Chinese writers who chose to see such Soviet writers as Alexander Blok and Mayakovsky not in political terms (as spokesmen for the revolution) but as members of an international "avant-garde." Interestingly, this stance of artistic radicalism did not meet with approval from his friends in the League of Left-Wing Writers who put pressure on him to return his experimental writings to a realistic mode.

The considerable corpus of Shi's fiction reflects a Janus-faced duality: Some of his stories were written in a simple realistic mode, but others were daringly "fantastic"; in fact, he was consciously experimenting with the erotic and the grotesque in such works as "The General's Head" ("Jiangiun de tou") and "Shi Xiu," a rewriting of a well-known incident from the traditional novel *The Water Margin* in a Sadist vein. In addition, with his reading interest in such authors as Poe, Barbey d'Aurevilly, James Frazer, Andrew Lang, Fiona McLeod, and Le Fanu, Shi had developed a penchant for the bizarre and the supernatural—not only about dreams and hallucinations, but also about sado-masochism, dandyism, fetishism, sorcery, witchcraft, necromancy, black magic, and Celtic myths. This medley of strange materials was put to good use in a dozen "fantastic" stories set in present Shanghai. He would have developed a subgenre, a kind of urban Gothic romance of repressed and not so repressed eroticism, if he had not been so hard-pressed by his leftist colleagues to give up this "bewitched journey" of literary experimentation.

What makes Shi's fiction so unusual is precisely that it was done against the current ideological grain of realism in both form and content.

He would place a story in a seemingly realistic setting—a railway station, a movie theater, a familiar street—with generally life-sized characters. But this frame of verisimilitude is nothing more than a fragile backdrop for the playing out of a psychological and fantastic drama. The action takes place beneath the surface of the characters' quotidian lifestyle, without much explanation of motive or intention in the plot: things—ordinary and extraordinary—simply happen to characters and trigger an inner turmoil of abnormal proportions, and the possible causes and consequences are often left dangling at story's end. In short, Shi Zhicun has constructed, however crudely, a narrative of implausibility that challenges and defies common sense. The final effect is to turn the realistic apparatus upside down—to the extent of suggesting that the clues to the fiction's "truth" lie beneath the surface, hidden in the murky layers of the characters' psyche. It betrays an obvious Freudian inclination, in pointing to irrational and subconscious forces beyond the ego's control. Unfortunately, Shi stopped such experiments abruptly with an abject postscript written in 1933 admitting that his efforts had been "futile," without achieving "any good effect."

Unlike the fate of his own fiction, Shi's championship of a modern mode of poetry in his journal achieved better results. Together with his friend Dai Wangshu, he endeavored to bring about a new style of poetry with the following features: (1) rhymelessness; (2) irregular lines and stanzas; (3) the use of archaic words and foreign idioms; and (4) a poetic meaning not easily understood at first reading. This style proved initially troublesome to some readers of the *Xiandai* magazine who considered it "hard to understand," hence "enigmatic" (a historical precedent for the same argument against the so-called "obscure poetry" in post-Mao China half a century later!). In an editorial comment titled "Again Concerning the Poetry in This Journal" (*Xiandai* 4.1:6), Shi issued what amounts to another manifesto:

> The poems published in *Xiandai* are poetry, pure modern poetry. They express the sentiments felt by modern people amidst the experiences of their modern lives who use modern phrases and idioms to construct a modern poetic form . . . (They) are largely rhymeless, and their lines are not neatly metrical, but they all possess rather fine texture, they represent the form of modern poetry, they are poetry.[57]

At first glance, the statement reads no different from Hu Shi's espousal of the living vernacular, *baihua*. As we read on, however, it becomes clear that the modern "sentiments" Shi Zhicun had in mind are a far cry from Hu Shi's sentimentality as exemplified in his early "experiments" collection (*Changshi ji*). In fact, Shi openly criticized the "neat rhyming patterns" of Hu's new-style traditional poetry written in the vernacular. What Shi Zhicun evidently had in mind is the free verse form (vers libre) to which he became attracted through his translations of Yeats, Amy Lowell, and Ezra Pound. In raising the issue of poetic "texture," Shi has also shifted the focus of discussion from "external" formalistic restrictions to the internal form of poetry itself. For what is "texture"—a term Shi supplied in both English and Chinese (*jili*)—if it does not refer to the matter of poetic language itself? In conceiving poetry as essentially poetic language, Shi is indeed not far off from the central tenet of Western modernist poetry. As Eliot did in his long poem "The Wasteland," Shi realized that "archaic words" and "foreign idioms" can be made to serve a modern poet's new vision.

What, then, constitutes the experience Shi would call "modern" which the new poetry is supposed to express? In the same manifesto he proceeds to describe a modern lifestyle with a distinctly urban imprint:

> The so-called modern life takes on all kinds of special forms: the harbors crowded with big steamers, the factories with roaring noises, the subterranean mines, the dance halls ringing with jazz music, the department stores in skyscrapers, planes engaged in air battles, race courses with big space . . . Even natural landscapes are different from what used to be. The emotions that this kind of life have aroused in our poets—can they be the same as those which the poets of former ages had evoked in their lives?[58]

As this extravagant mosaic reveals, what marks the present from the past is the vitality of the city—a landscape of capitalism brought about by sweeping economic and technological changes that held enormous appeal to Shi Zhicun and his friends, Liu Na'ou and Mu Shiying, who attempted with varying degrees of success to depict the rhythm and noise of such an urban landscape in their fiction. If Liu and Mu, lesser known now because of their "decadence," sang unstinting panegyrics of this modern style of urban life (Mu even went so far as to recapture the atmosphere of a dance hall with a language that swirls in circles, much like a waltz!), the avowed Marxist Mao Dun harbored deep-seated ambivalence in his masterful novel *Midnight:* Shanghai in 1930 (the setting of this "Romance of China") is depicted as an obvious microcosm of the emergent world of urban capitalism fraught with greed and vice; it is at the same time a city of tremendous energy generated by electricity, speed, and commotion—enough to shock an old "fossil" from the countryside to immediate death!

As Mao Dun's novel fully illustrates, Shanghai in the 1930s was a veritable island of tangible modernity and also a bastion of foreign imperialist presence. Given this conjunction, it was no wonder that most Chinese writers who resided there developed, like Mao Dun, an ambivalence toward this largest treaty port: They fully enjoyed—and indeed marveled at—the modern conveniences and material comforts Shanghai's concessions provided. At the same time, they also regarded the city a center of capitalist exploitation and debauchery.

Raymond Williams has described the history of English literature as a transition in setting from the pastoral "knowable communities" of the countryside to the "city of light and darkness."[59] If the city had indeed become the only possible habitat and artistic universe for all European Modernists, one can never cease to be amazed that the same urban transformation did *not* exactly take place in modern Chinese literature, despite the literary efforts of Shi Zhicun and his friends. For all its dynamism and allure, the modern city of Shanghai paled in moral and ideological significance against the massive countryside, the rural world that most Chinese writers affirmed as the genuine reality which their realistic writing must aspire to reproduce or recapture. The urban style of Chinese modernism in prose and poetry remained, as it were, in isolated splendor for about two decades (from the mid-1920s to the mid-1940s) and thereafter declined, to be overtaken by the triumphant power of the countryside, the Communist Revolution. The predominantly rural modes of social realism and socialist realism held sway in China for more than half a century. It was only after 1976, with the death of Mao and the downfall of the Gang of Four, that the city reemerged as the central place for a younger generation of radical-modernists; since 1985, some young poets and critics in Shanghai—Wu Liang, Zhang Xiaobo, and others—have begun to develop a new "urban consciousness" (*chengshi yishi*), a purposeful reaction against the country-side.

This rapid survey of the urban-rural interaction in modern Chinese literature suggests that the European experience of artistic modernism was not fully duplicated in China, although some measure of urban-based and Western-inspired avant-gardist experimentation was achieved. Marxist scholars would perhaps attribute this to the economic fact that early twentieth-century China had not reached the stages of "high capitalism" and "late capitalism" which presumably provide the infrastructure for high modernism and post-modernism. I have tried to argue that it was, ironically, historical modernity—the new mode of temporal consciousness that privileges and valorizes the present—together with its optimistic vision that does not allow for a full-fledged disillusioned reaction against it in the form of artistic modernism. If one brings in the case of Soviet Russia, the comparison is further complicated by the phenomenon of Russian futurists and constructivists who believed, also optimistically, in the capacity of modern art to express the infinite potentialities of the future world—a modernist stance which did not take root in China. Nor was modernity seen as so threatening to the native human essence that, as the Japanese thinker Takeuchi Yoshimi argued, it must be "overcome." Even such a rural nativist as Shen Congwen had stopped short of advocating total resistance to what he considered to be the inevitable tide of modernization.

What distinguishes some writers from the zealously heroic intellectuals (and revolutionary romantics) described earlier lies perhaps in a certain degree of ambiguity in the former's self-image. On the one hand, these writers shared the grand historical vision of the intellectual zealots in the public arena. On the other hand, however, they differed from the zealously ideological type in their lack of a sustained optimism due to certain private doubts and waverings about the "present."

Lu Xun, the foremost modern Chinese writer in terms of public renown, also exemplifies this ambiguity in the most anguished way. His entire outlook, it can be argued, hinged on an unresolved tension between his unequivocal support of all the enlightened "modern" causes of the May Fourth Movement and the incessant pessimism that haunted his private psyche with regard to the ultimate meaning of life. Thus, he openly voiced his belief in evolutionism while at the same time refusing to fuse his self with the onward positive tide of history: He would lose himself, as the recurring image of the shadow in his prose poetry suggests, in a dark void of the present. It is this type of uncertainty that provides the inner resources for a more subjective mode of aesthetic expression. In this sense, Lu Xun may be considered a great "modernist" in a unique way: Unlike most of his contemporary "modernists," who were either heroic zealots or tender-hearted humanists, Lu Xun has made a creative paradox out of the double meaning of modernity.

SIX

The Cultural Choices of Zhang Xinxin, a Young Writer of the 1980s

JEFFREY C. KINKLEY

Benjamin Schwartz reshaped the field of modern Chinese intellectual history by showing that the "real transformers of values and the bearers of new ideas from the West" were of "the generation that reached its intellectual maturity in the last decade of the nineteenth century and the first decade of the twentieth century."[1] That was to say, Kang Youwei, Yan Fu, Liang Qichao, Tan Sitong, Zhang Binglin, and Wang Guowei redirected Chinese thought even before the more iconoclastic May Fourth generation took the stage in the 1920s. In the years since Schwartz took up that theme, Western literary scholars have sought the origins of modern Chinese fiction in the late Qing. Schwartz's and Fairbank's students have meanwhile emphasized the growth of a medium whose Chinese origin, even as a transplant from the West, indisputably belongs to the late Qing—modern journalism.[2]

Though Yan Fu was the focus of Schwartz's own research in the field, Liang Qichao looms largest in the work of his students. Liang spanned, and truly linked, the fields of politics, journalism, and literature. He was, foremost, a political reformer, essayist, and publisher, the constitutionalist who unwittingly made China ripe for revolution. He also began the "elevation" of fiction—vernacular fiction—to the important (if utilitarian) role of reforming politics and social values; this largely still defines its status in China today. Liang Qichao's semi-vernacular prose even presaged the literary revolution of the 1920s. Such expansiveness (something a little different from Joseph Levenson's "cosmopolitanism," which implies a transcendence of nationalism) must be part of what attracted Schwartz to Kang, Liang, Yan, et al. as "the breakthrough generation."[3] They were, in fact, nationalists all; Wang Guowei committed suicide for his sovereign. Yet, his act reminds us that, far from having thrown off the claims of tradition to preserve "any old" national essence that might preserve the "race," Wang's generation's innermost values were rooted in tradition. These nationalists were thus more confident than many of their successors, Schwartz has pointed out, about discarding *elements* of tradition in the course of assimilating aspects of Western thought. They refused to commit themselves wholly either to a Chinese Essence or to Western Culture. Similarly, Schwartz himself, in critiquing modern times, faults neither rootless cosmopolitanism nor nativism so much as "provincialism within modernity": as when "the philosophy departments of England and America dispense linguistic philosophy, while the philosophy departments of France dispense existentialism, phenomenology, and Marxism, and their respective students have little to say to each other." His thinkers of the 1890s were bolder and more creative than that. They were in communication with most of the globe, even "subject peoples" like the Indians.[4]

A similar expansiveness attracts many of us now to another breakthrough cohort of innovators and creators in the 1980s: those who brought about China's surprising intellectual revival in the wake of the cultural-desert years of Maoism. The group includes thinkers, writers, and journalists, too, for the redoubtable journalist Liu Binyan now enjoys much of Liang Qichao's moral prestige, though not his organizational influence.[5] Accepted by the creative writers as one of their own (and elected a vice-chairman of the Chinese Writers' Association by them in 1985), Liu Binyan the journalist is in the mid-1980s quite possibly China's most famous "writer." His most fervent admirers would probably call him one of China's greatest reformers, too, though that would point to his integrity more than his creativity. In general, the more creative segment of the outward-looking 1980s writers is the generation of men and women in their twenties and thirties. It is they who are looking for cultural frontiers, while the middle-aged, including Liu

Binyan, are prone to consider experiments with modes of expression as mere games.[6] Zhang Xinxin (b. 1953), the writer-journalist who is the subject of this essay, reads and admires Liu the Just, but she is more of a free-thinker in cultural matters—a modernist by any definition, even after discounting the exaggerated accounts of her modernism by crusading Chinese anti-modernists. Yet, she is worried by China's loss of its tradition, too. Her point of departure is not, of course, immersion in traditional learning, as it was for the 1890s generation. Zhang Xinxin is playing catch-up after the bleak Cultural Revolution era of her teens. On the other hand, like a traditional Chinese, she has been educated at home, by books.

Zhang Xinxin's era is a time when Marxist ideology seems to have reached an extreme point in the process of "decomposition," which Schwartz already spoke of in 1951, referring to deviations that began as early as the time of Lenin.[7] Elemental nationalism may be one of the ideological beneficiaries of that decay. China is hypersensitive about its image abroad; its writers want more than anything else to win a Nobel Prize for literature; and students, even workers, have rioted against Japanese influence in the economy. Thus the slogans presently raised up against the intellectual expansiveness that Benjamin Schwartz cherishes are reminiscent of those current a century ago. Counterposed to the expression of uncomfortable truths, exploration of new forms, and writing for pure entertainment, are the state's unassailable principles of patriotism, promotion of Chinese forms over "spiritually polluting" Western ones (which echoes older commitments to "national essence" and Mao's "national forms"), and insistence that literature be edifying.

In the minds of some of her countrymen, Zhang Xinxin's writing has clashed with all three of those principles. Her supposed sins against the first two caused her to become a major target of the campaign against "spiritual pollution" of late 1983–early 1984. As Helmut Martin and Carolyn Wakeman first pointed out, that forced Zhang Xinxin at least to reconsider her commitment to subjective fictional social commentary and "Westernized" technique.[8] She abandoned her avant-garde fiction in 1984, undertaking, in succession, a detective novel, an extended subjective account of a trip to rural Shandong, and a journalistic oral-history novel. When the political fog cleared, she went on to explore history, film, and television.

Her new works transgressed against the third principle, that literature must be edifying. Friends who liked "the old Zhang Xinxin" were upset to see her change, while cultural conservatives ("leftists") remained concerned about the continuities in her career. One of them was her continued popularity among young adults. Yet Zhang Xinxin's forays into journalism, popular fiction, and the mass media may indeed be interpreted as new expressions of her modernism. Her reportage is not the sacred Party-directed journalism that held sway in the Maoist years and was reborn at the turn of the 1980s, in a less orthodox form, by enlightened Marxist crusaders such as Liu Binyan. Zhang Xinxin is influenced by the "journalistic tape-recorded novel" pioneered by Studs Terkel and Oscar Lewis—if she is not treading a path closer to that of Capote, Mailer, and Doctorow, who have mixed journalism and the novel for more complex intellectual and literary effects.[9]

Have her setbacks, then, made Zhang Xinxin inwardly as iconoclastic as the May Fourth generation? Many creative people of her generation, such as the "misty" or "obscure" poets affiliated with the 1979–1980 journal *Today*, feel the shame, anger, and sense of betrayal by older generations that was prevalent during the 1920s.[10] Yet, Zhang Xinxin seems more amused than shocked by China's remnants of "feudalism." To her, they are part of eternal human nature—not necessarily a congenital disease peculiar to the Chinese. Her cultural detachment is again reminiscent of the earlier times that excite Benjamin Schwartz: the era before May Fourth, when Chinese intellectuals thought nothing of combining fiction with journalism, high literature with the popular novel, and modern Western thought with themes from the Chinese tradition. Therefore this essay will interpret Zhang Xinxin's recent creativity not as a process of sloughing off West for East, modernism for journalism, or the elite for the masses, but as part of an eclectic, ever-broadening search for new material and new perspectives.

ZHANG XINXIN'S EARLY DEVELOPMENT AS A MODERNIST

As Leo Ou-fan Lee's chapter points out, not only was much of the West's modernist canon known in China before the Communist Revolution; China had its own fledgling modernist movement as early as the

1930s. To the Shanghai modernists Lee analyzes may be added Peking writers such as Fei Ming, Bian Zhilin, and at times even Shen Congwen and Xiao Qian (in *Meng zhi gu* or *Valley of dream*). But so fully was China purged of each and every aspect of modernism after 1949 that there seems no harm in reducing the complex movement to its constituents for our comparative purposes here, particularly since there is no consensus even in the West as to how the many elements fit together.

In subject matter, we refer to a modernist emphasis on the non-rational, the psychological, and the self-referential; in technique, to fractured narrative, stream-of-consciousness, "obscure" symbolism, idioglossia, and so forth; in philosophy, to a cult of the anti-traditional; and, in ethos, to one or another form of "modernist consciousness." That which intellectual historians trace back to the nineteenth century is a consciousness informed by Nietzsche, Darwin, Marx, and Freud, or a "bourgeois idea of modernity" (Calinescu, cited by Lee in his chapter) that celebrates science and reason. It culminates in the "other modernity," which rejects the reason and science, reveling instead in anomie, dislocations of time, perception, and values. Such disorientation may reflect social developments, as Marxists claim. On the other hand, the shift from James to Jameson may be less a matter of world view than of "mere technique," if one accepts Jameson's own view that language and the psyche, "including the great modernist theme of temporality," are "semi-autonomous" worlds of play for the artist (Lee, citing Jameson).[11] Zhang Xinxin's "consciousness" is naturally hard to grasp and often misconstrued by her foes, but her techniques link her to the international modernist movement quite concretely.

Having a high military cadre and writer for her father, Zhang Xinxin was able to read voraciously and unrestrictedly at home during her childhood. In third or fourth grade (c. 1961–1962), she was already perusing translations of pre-Revolutionary Russian and Soviet fiction. Browsing in China's many literary magazines, she found herself attracted to the relatively daring "poisonous weeds" now republished under the title *Chongfang de xianhua,* or *Fragrant Flowers Reblooming.* Soon she was tackling *Water Margin, The Romance of the Three Kingdoms, The Dream of the Red Chamber,* and so forth. Since her family hid its books during the Cultural Revolution instead of burning them, Zhang Xinxin, confined to home by illness through most of the 1970s, continued perusing everything from the Brontës to the Zhou philosophers and Han historians. She tried to acquire the high-school and college education that the Cultural Revolution denied her. But her contact with the international avant-garde came only in the post-Mao era. Leo Lee's modernists of the 1930s and the international writers they had introduced were already long forgotten in China.[12]

Zhang Xinxin published as early as 1976 and even penned some little stories in childhood.[13] Creative writing, in a sense her first calling, became only a "sideline" for her in the 1980s; her main profession is directing the Peking People's Art Theater. This position lets her examine, adapt, and stage new dramatic works without undue pressure to produce copy or otherwise fulfill the role of a "professional writer." Being a director has provided her with special insights into characterization and audience response, and opened up windows on the avant-garde drama, as is apparent in her works about young theater people. Trained at the Central Drama Academy, 1979–1983, Zhang herself has experience as an actress. Although Freud was reprinted in China only in 1985, she was able to learn many of the concepts of Western psychology from works by Brecht and Stanislavsky in the curriculum.[14]

Another formative experience in Zhang Xinxin's outlook on life was her 1969 rustication in the Great Northern Wilderness,[15] where the anomalies of the age led her to "see through" many innocent and not so innocent false fronts of contemporary life. Then she joined the army, worked as a nurse, married an artist who loved her only for her residence permit, and got divorced. Of the assets needed for ongoing self-education, Zhang Xinxin lacks only knowledge of foreign languages.

Zhang Xinxin came to prominence with her 1981 novella "Zai tong-yi dipingxianshang" (On the same horizon), a tale about a young woman disillusioned by her marriage, which many of Zhang's readers have assumed to be autobiographical. The narrative style of the piece is complex and "plotless" by Chinese standards of the times—full of flashbacks, shifting points of view, and "stream-of-consciousness." More prominent to its readers, though, was the sense of estrangement and lack of clear bearings it seemed to communicate. In fact it could be understood within a well-defined, though newly established, category of "young people's writing," as a work of youth alienation, indeed feminist youth alienation. Zhang's ideological "negativism" was self-evidently wrong to the society-affirming and philosophically positivist Marxists, with no need for subtle analysis of her literary style.[16]

Her alienated consciousness did show affinities with modernism. Moreover, by 1983 Zhang Xinxin was modernist not just in spirit but in technique. After the shrill criticisms of "obscure" poetry in 1981, she must have realized that cultural conservatives found new technique offensive just because it was difficult, regardless of the work's content or spirit, but she forged ahead anyway. Of particular interest are the stories she set within the acting profession.

"Juchang xiaoguo" (Theatrical effects; January 1983) explores role-playing and the relationship between art and life.[17] Its action is mostly refracted through the consciousness of one protagonist, a young actor fresh out of drama school. He has difficulty adapting to his first job, because nothing in the real world of pleasing an audience is quite like what he was led to expect in the academy. He finds himself in a lead role, responsible for pleasing not only general audiences but two old cadres who will decide whether or not his troupe can go on tour. He wants to perform well in another role, too. Having fallen in love with a young actress, he wants to impress her, personally and professionally. At times he daydreams about playing lovers' parts with her—Romeo to her Juliet. Unfortunately, his best role heretofore has been that of Molière's miser, Harpagon.

The story is modernist in several respects. It is mostly narrated in mixed direct and indirect interior monologue, with abrupt, unexplained, occasionally difficult, changes in mood and narrative mode. It probes the young man's psyche, alternating between evidently unconscious and conscious thoughts, some of which are lines from plays that keep flitting through his mind. Less tangible recurring Proustian sensations also enter his consciousness. Finally, the story is framed by paradoxical opening and ending passages, wherein the actor with great difficulty tries on a mask, both literally and figuratively. This frame implies that the body of the story is a memory or fantasy, or perhaps the main plot was "acting," whereas the putting on of a mask is real.

Some of the language is obscure, because of unstated sentence subjects. The following passage, describing the young man's experience of the joy of acting, illustrates the complexity and ambiguity of Zhang's prose:

> It was like being a horse just unbridled, freed from drawing its wagon. First it took short, faltering steps, then began to frolic, whinny, and finally gallop off in a frenzy. A fear of getting lost faintly flashed through his mind. That was left over from habit. Listen to the laughter below. How many diaphragms and bellies must there be, quivering up and down, obedient to your will. Keep laughing. Laugh again. No longer was his heart a horse, but rather a head-strong wind, picking up dust and whipping it up violently into a swirl. Laugh, laugh again. Amid the whistling wind and dust, his heart yelled out at him. So this is what acting is all about. Let yourself go. Laugh. Swirl. From up on high he looked down, far, far below at his sacred temple of art. So tiny. Oh, drama school, you poor fool. Four years of notebooks—what possible use? Rip them up, page by page, tear them into little tiny pieces, let them float away, trample them underfoot. He did a headstand on them, blew his nose on them, rolled across and urinated on them.[18]

"Theatrical Effects" has comic moments, too. It satirizes propaganda plays about the one-child policy, and ridicules the whole 1983 drama world, which was then suddenly becoming commercialized. Here we see the young man having a look around when he first comes to town:

> Just then they were busy putting snakes on display in this provincial capital. Three modern drama troupes—a provincial one, one belonging to the municipality, and a third from an outside city—were competing to see who could best perform *The Strange Case of the Beautiful She-Snake*. The rival billboard ads were each more marvelous than the next, but they had one thing in common. Though the male role, the good guy, was the lead, the Mata Hari was painted bigger and more alluring. The poster for the non-local troupe added: Kissing Right on Stage.[19]

There are also comic characters: the ancient cadres, the actor-protagonist (who acts foolish in front of the woman he loves and is caught by a policeman reciting lines from *The Miser* to a tree trunk), and, above all, a troupe director who twists the "sacred" drama-school concept of "theatrical effect" (said to be from Stanislavsky) until it means just getting audience laughs by any gimmick available. It is disillusioning—enough to make one wonder if life isn't indeed just play-acting.

Thus, for all her "interior" interest in psychology and the meaning of life, Zhang Xinxin remained concerned with reforming society and even criticized certain aspects of the reforms. A more striking example of that is her "Fengkuang de junzilan" (Orchid madness). This, too, is a story criticizing commercialism. To pin a label on it, it is a criticism of sideline economic activities going out of control. Hence the work was terribly out of phase with government policy when Zhang wrote it, in July 1983, though she is not, of course, a Maoist or conservative advocate of central state planning. She describes a whole city going crazy in its zest to grow and sell for profit a rare variety of flower that prospers particularly well in the local climate. Everybody wants in on the action:

> Young people awaiting employment pushed cartload after cartload of the *junzi* orchids. The flowers were reserved-looking, but the passion with which they were hawked had overtones of incitement. Other peddlers, of about the same age and dress but looking somewhat more indolent, were young workers on leave from various units. Their bosses couldn't stand them, so they'd launched them onto the market to compete with the unemployed. Soldiers were selling the flowers, too. The ones with baggy pants and two-pocket jackets were fighting men on official duty—noncombat duty, that is. They looked as serious and conscientious when taking your money as when they were on parade. The prices of the orchids varied—50, 100, 1,000, maybe 2,000. Depended on quality. Of course the choicest items didn't change hands right out there in the open.[20]

Professionals, even doctors, desert their real work to make big profits. So far, this is conventional satire, but then the tale turns into Zhang Xinxin's most obviously modernist piece. In what she admits is a variation on Ionesco's play *Rhinoceros,*[21] her rapacious townspeople turn into *junzi* orchids themselves. The hero, a last hold-out from commercialization as he watches his friends and neighbors succumb, is next in line to be transformed. The metamorphoses finally turn out to be just a dream—if the harder commercial "reality" was not the dream.

This journey into the Absurd (and perhaps the Butterfly Dream of Zhuangzi) is based on actual social dilemmas of Zhang Xinxin's times—on a story she heard from a friend, about how people in China's Northeast truly were caught up in a frenzy growing and selling *junzi* orchids (the seemingly satiric name, "Confucian gentleman" or "self-cultivationist" orchid, is the actual name of the flower). No one turned into a flower, but some did commit murder to acquire them, and cadres were corrupted too, a facet even Zhang Xinxin did not mention. "Orchid Madness" is thus a news story transformed into avant-garde fiction. The press did take notice of the commercial fad, and Zhang's own piece begins with a quasi-documentary touch, by quoting from a public notice and citing media reports.[22]

ZHANG XINXIN AND THE MIXING OF GENRES

During the campaign against "spiritual pollution" of 1983–1984, free-thinking young people's anomie came under attack again, as in 1979, when Democracy Wall was closed down, and 1981–1982, when older poets attacked younger ones for writing "obscurely." This time the syndrome of a so-called "school of modernism" (*xiandaipai*) was criticized and mined for other related unhealthy authors and tendencies. Zhang Xinxin was criticized for the disillusioned thinking of her early youthful characters, for some of her criticisms of society, and for her modernist outlook. Some critics attributed nearly all her "shortcomings" to influence from the Western "school of modernism."

Zhang Xinxin was denied a job and even her drama-school diploma for a year; her stories were literally seized off the printing presses.[23] She was of course very depressed, and may even have taken some of the criticisms to heart. For as her professional life collapsed in 1984 and she felt a comedown after completing her then unpublishable detective novel, she began to worry that her imagination was "deteriorating." Thereupon, she says, she and her new collaborator, Sang Ye (b. 1955, male, a journalist previously published in the Hong Kong and overseas Chinese press), began working on their Studs Terkel-influenced book of oral history reportage, *Beijingren: Yi bai ge putong ren de zishu*, or *Peking Man: A Hundred Ordinary People Tell Their Story* (the title, characteristically, has a whiff of history and of satire, for "Peking Man" refers not to the Pekingese but to the Chinese people, that is, *all* descendants of the *Homo erectus* who lived near Zhoukoudian).[24]

In 1984, Zhang Xinxin also wrote *Hui lao jia* (Back home), a subjective nonfiction account of her trip to her father's ancestral village. The piece has much in common with reportage, though Zhang prefers to think of it as an extended essay, while her editor, Wang Meng (then of *People's Literature*), wanted to publish it under the category of fiction.[25] Zhang Xinxin was clearly headed in the direction of nonfiction, even journalism. Yet, this direction is less of a departure from her earlier practice than it might seem. Despite her modernist techniques, Zhang's fiction had long adhered to real life, from her seemingly autobiographical early works, to modernist pieces like "Theatrical Effects," which remain autobiographical in a more abstract sense and contain satire of current events, to the Absurdist story "Orchid Madness," which is explicitly topical. Above all, Zhang was aware that documentary material and quasi-journalistic technique had been absorbed into modernist fiction itself. Intent on trying out new things, Zhang Xinxin was willing to ignore boundaries between genres and traditions.

Feng pian lian (Envelope, postcard, block-of-four) exemplifies that last tendency.[26] It is a "serious," indeed a modernist detective novel, with more than a hint of oral tradition and journalism, too—a step toward *Peking Man*. Although the occasion is simply the theft of a rare postage stamp, the novel enters the realm of the extraordinary from the start. Its title is written not in Chinese, nor in any language, but in unfamiliar postal symbols. We must take the author's word for it that they mean "envelope," "postcard," and "block-of-four."[27] The missing stamp is fantastic, too. It is "The Great Train Robbery Issue," said to date from 1923, when a gang of highwaymen (*tufei*) hijacked a train in Shandong and held its foreign and Chinese passengers for ransom. To communicate with the outside world, the hostages posted letters with homemade postage stamps, some allegedly reading "Bandit Post." Zhang Xinxin's story names real historical figures, such as Carl Crow, and the train robbery did occur, though Zhang's sources included interviews with people who merely lived near the scene of the crime—or in the area where it was still talked about. In fact, the story about the stamp is fictitious. The ironical Zhang Xinxin has used history to have some fun with her credulous readers.[28]

In the West, the combination of the "low" detective formula with "high," even metaphysical subject matter (as by Jorge Luis Borges and Umberto Eco) awaited the advent of modernism. The combination of

high and low is equally modern in China, although there was some precedent for it in the intellectually fluid era of Lin Shu and Liang Qichao.
Serious Chinese writers of the twentieth century have generally dis-
dained popular genres, from the advent of "Mandarin Duck and Butterfly" romances until the present day, when sensational and allegedly
lurid literature is swept from street corners in police crackdowns. Some
Chinese detective fiction, now sanctioned under the new label of "legal-
system literature" (part of it published by the Ministry of Public Security), contains comfortably "Chinese" heroics reminiscent of the heroic
socialist realist fiction in Mao's era.[29] Zhang Xinxin, however, characteristically borrows more often from the Western formula. *Envelope* has no
heroic detectives or detestable villains. Instead, it creates a typically
"Anglo-American" gallery of equally guilty-looking, "interesting" suspects. The novel mentions Agatha Christie and Edgar Allen Poe and, at
one point, gathers all the suspects into one room. There is a chase,
which might seem to desert the old classical formula for the heroics of
the "tough-guy" American whodunit or the socialist "legal-system"
genre, except that the pursuer is not a tough guy or brave policeman,
but a little girl. Zhang's plot is particularly Westernized in that all of her
detectives are amateurs, not police. Startlingly, the characters even admit
that they fear the police.

How *Envelope, Postcard, Block-of-Four* fits into Zhang Xinxin's own
creative history is ambiguous. She says she wrote it in a fit of passion
and euphoria, though when she completed the first draft, on 1 June
1984, she was still locked out of both the writing and dramatic professions. (I gather that she may have started the manuscript in 1983, before
the outer disasters struck;[30] because of them, neither *Envelope* nor
Peking Man could be published in China until 1985.) Despite being criticized for "wasting" her talent, Zhang immensely enjoyed writing *Envelope.*[31] At this time in her life she wanted not only to "learn from the
masses," as was commanded of her in the "spiritual pollution" campaign, but to *communicate* stories to them.[32] Detective fiction was popular enough to suit that goal. In the same spirit, Zhang would try
documentary journalism, and even the mass media. Popular genres
extended the "broadcasting range" of her fiction almost as television
extended the audience for her work in drama. She recalled a statement

by Beckett to the effect that, if people understood his plays, the works were failures.[33] That was not her style. It was not that she no longer valued the many-layered meanings inherent in "difficulty"; she also wanted to reach audiences. Like the actor in "Theatrical Effects," sometimes she really enjoyed moving them—even making them laugh.

In fact, Zhang Xinxin had not forsaken her social concerns or her experimentation. At the very least, *Envelope* is a comedy of manners in the Anglo-American tradition, creating a world of detail, clues, and local color dense enough to attract the aficionado who reads whodunits to "learn how the world works." Notable are Zhang's social dioramas of a stamp exchange, and a corner where retired people meet. These set pieces showcase her satiric abilities, for, as in "Orchid Madness," every other sentence contains a metaphor with a comic or ironic bite. Her senior citizens rattle on endlessly, repeating themselves and talking such nonsense as to make one feel embarrassed for them. The largest tracts of "information" are *Envelope's* thumbnail essays on philatelic history, mini-lectures on anomalies that render stamps valuable, and pointed observations about classes of collectors. Zhang Xinxin dispenses so much knowledge that she may be fairly accused of having overdone it, as in the old Chinese scholarly novels that C. T. Hsia feels were vehicles for the display of erudition.[34] Stamp collecting is not really exotic in China, but clearly it seems so to Zhang Xinxin.

Zhang's characters are finely drawn. *Envelope* details the lives, personalities, and driving ambitions of all the suspects, not just the means and motives they possess for stealing a precious stamp. Unfortunately all this character development, while giving *Envelope* excellences beyond the formula, attenuates its sine qua non—suspense.

Modernistic technique provides the other "serious" element. *Envelope* is related in unconnected cinematic segments; much of the logic of the plot is left to be filled in by the reader. We see a suspect walking down the street to the stamp market, looking over his shoulder. Cut. A little girl and a market guard are chasing another man. Cut. We're in the man's apartment, which is crammed to the rafters with expensive consumer goods. "How much do you want?" he asks, evidently offering to pay hush money. Cut. Now he's in another locale, asking again, "How much do you want? No, I don't have the stamp. I wanted to buy it from *you.*" Cut. Old people are reminiscing. A suspect tries to get a retired railway worker to tell about the stamp. But the stamp he describes is completely different from the one that other people think they know about. Cut. The reader must put the pieces together—must deduce not only who done it, but what has been done.

Because of the lack of an authoritative voice, there is confusion as to whether the stamp ever existed. At that, the plot becomes metaphysical and the quest Absurd. The international philatelic community itself has two different versions of how the stamps came into being, and what they look like. One version says that Carl Crow and a friend printed bilingual stamps, of which two survive in the hands of a Japanese collector. Yet the local Chinese stamp-collecting club has printed up facsimiles "for the enjoyment of its members" of a completely different Great Train Robbery Stamp. People complicate the situation by selling these counterfeits. But was the original real?

Ultimately the story focuses on an old man who claims to have been a hostage in the robbery and manufactured the only true Great Train Robbery Stamp, with a dragon cut from stationery. That is yet a third idea of the stamp; the man possesses it until it is stolen by his "Anhui housemaid," who is so ignorant that she steals and mutilates all his stamps to make a little picture gallery for herself. She sends the dragon on the one-of-a-kind stamp home, for use as an embroidery design. (Since *Peking Man* takes equally unkind cuts at its most famous character, a proud and ignorant mink farmer whom Zhang Xinxin has tagged the "Wanyuanhu taitai" or "Mistress Ten-Thousandaire," critics have not illogically concluded that Zhang is among the many Chinese intellectuals who feel no particular closeness to China's peasants.)[35] But it may be that the maid was planted in the old stamp collector's household by the fellow who recommended her—the one with the expensive lifestyle. We do not know. The old man himself may have made up his story about having been held hostage. Anyone could fabricate a homemade stamp and put "1923" on it.

Socially speaking, the subject is stamp collecting, not as a thing in itself like bell changing in a Dorothy Sayers novel, but as a metaphor for human obsession. A lot of people come to covet the old man's dragon stamp for its monetary value. That is social exposure of greed. But

Envelope is far more a twentieth-century satire than a nineteenth-century one (to speak in Western terms). Some characters come to want the stamp more than the money, just because everyone else wants it; they have caught the fever. Near the end, Zhang zooms in on a crowd scene. Hundreds of people have lined up to buy a new issue without knowing anything about it. We learn this by reading the text of a story filed by a *New York Times* reporter. He wants the outside world to know: The Chinese are going crazy over little pieces of paper. Like "Orchid Madness," *Envelope, Postcard, Block-of-Four* is about collective insanity.

And journalism? Besides the cameo reference just mentioned, we have seen that the fantastic plot of *Envelope* is partly based on a real news story from half a century ago. There may even be a link to *Peking Man*, for there are certain resemblances between some characters in the two works. Zhang Xinxin began interviewing people for *Peking Man* in early 1984 (the final draft of *Envelope* was written only in 1985), and some of the 100 subjects in *Peking Man* were her old acquaintances. Perhaps Zhang Xinxin reused some of her characters, if only unconsciously.[36]

PEKING MAN

Excerpts of *Peking Man* were first published in China in January 1985. It was a sensation: a masterpiece in a new format rationed equally among five of China's most prestigious literary journals and appearing in their premier 1985 issues, with the result that it dominated literary talk at the beginning of the New Year. *Peking Man* also marked the breaking of silence by an author who was all the more popular for having been persecuted for a year. Having been printed in America first, it even had a "special-unexpurgated-foreign-issue" cachet, as if it were being brought home only now that China, in the course of her liberalization, was sophisticated enough to tolerate its message. Within a year the work had spawned imitations.

The outstanding appeal of the work for ordinary readers must be its double challenge to China's hidebound literary and journalistic formalism. *Peking Man* penetrates the orthodoxy of officially approved thought with stark truthfulness, and shatters the structural formalism of socialist realism with the apparent randomness and open-endedness of its many conversations. There is no false idealism among the characters, no sanitization of the environment, no prettification of the language or final outcome, as in most Chinese fiction. Far less is there the political journalese, "positive" generalizing, and didacticism of reportage. The subject is as popular as a dime-novel murder: human lives, coping with both the Cultural Revolution and the confusing reforms of the present. Yet one oral history leads only to another, not to any lesson. For once, the reader really cannot foresee what will happen next. Even so, each life is, in its own way, a variation on each Chinese reader's own experience.

Zhang Xinxin and Sang Ye's "new" cinéma-vérité style itself creates an illusion of unprecedented lack of censorship. The reader unexpectedly overhears people react to the recorder. Near the end of an interview with one particularly unsavory character—and halfway through the book—one is shocked to learn that he has been revealing himself without even knowing he is being formally interviewed. He asks Zhang and Sang not to write what he has said (p. 396). Did they betray him? Fear of exposure to the authorities is one of those universal conditions that anyone can appreciate.

Although Zhang's and Sang's role was precisely one of "censorship," their characters enter taboo areas. Several joke about heads of Party and state. A theoretician of Marxism-Leninism confides that the Party is too rotten to be rectified and says that, in a true poll, few people would profess belief in Communism (pp. 259-260). A young man is asked point-blank if he believes in it; he tells Zhang and Sang that most writers other than Liu Binyan are liars, maybe including them (pp. 203-204). A factory salesman from Zhuoxian brags about bribing buyers. A border resident confesses that her husband crossed the Soviet border on a lark. A peasant woman explains how to break the one-child law. A United-Front official, angry about Taiwanese boatmen's smuggling, admits that he must appease them without appearing to be doing it for political reasons, even though he is. Several characters are bad role models, even unpleasant during the interview. Yet the authors could defend their selected interviewees as instructive and atypical people who did after all exist. Thus they include a former prostitute, the brother of a Qing emperor, a Taiwan fisherman who blew into Fujian during a storm, and two people who have experienced the correctional system.

The daring of *Peking Man* as journalism is partly due to its conception as a work for the American Chinese market. Says Wang Yu, the New York Chinatown editor who urged Zhang and Sang to undertake *Peking Man* and agreed to publish it, if they had been writing for the Chinese, their "psychology would have been completely different." They would have felt more inhibited. Even in New York they published under unknown pen names. Their earliest interviews were with famous people, including several friends and acquaintances in the theater and arts world.[37]

At the suggestion of Zhang's collaborator, the book was to be a Chinese version of Studs Terkel's *American Dreams*.[38] *Peking Man*, however, is more open-ended than the American original. Whereas Terkel's book has a theme—the American dream, as myth, motivation, and reality, *Peking Man* does not revolve around so particular a national ideal or self-conception—not even around any single period or social experience. Some characters tell how the Cultural Revolution or another past era shaped their lives; some focus on their dreams and disillusionments in the new age of reform; others talk about an occupation, a particular obstacle in Chinese society they have faced, or an activity they were engaged in when they caught the interviewers' attention (cycling, *qigong* exercises, etc.). A few characters are simply record-holders or oddities, such as the two beautiful women in the book; perhaps they were selected because *American Dreams* opens with a former Miss U.S.A. After *Peking Man* enjoyed its first Chinese exposure, in January 1985, it became open-ended in the fullest sense of the word, for Zhang and Sang continued their interviewing, allowing characters to comment on earlier segments of the book they had read (p. 309). *Peking Man* thus came to present itself as an ongoing poll of public opinion.

Studs Terkel's books, which ironically were inspired partly by Jan Myrdal's classic 1962 interviews of Chinese, are well-sifted collections of artfully condensed oral histories.[39] Proceeding from tape recordings of his interviews with hundreds of people, Terkel selects and creates "highly processed" oral-history transcripts. The degree of his alteration is never made explicit. It must be considerable, because the deponents' state-

ments are quite articulate, though reassuringly idiomatic. Terkel admits
that he is looking for elegance of expression: the "poets" among the people (his phrase, not Mao's), and "the phrase that explodes."[40] Probably
he deletes sentences, even paragraphs, simply because their ore contains
little metal. Still more unorthodox is Terkel's deletion of his questions
and comments from the text, turning dialogue into monologue. One
result is that the creativity and aggressiveness of the interviewer, in
broaching new topics, drawing comparisons, and so forth, are trans-
ferred to the interviewee. Like any producer of a manuscript, Terkel
must also decide how to order the interviews he keeps. In this there is
juxtapositional irony, as when one character appears to comment on
another. Otherwise, Terkel expresses himself only through the indirect
and veiled control he exercises as questioner. One might be able to guess
that Terkel is skeptical, liberal, and populist, from his focus on myths
such as "the American dream" and his choice of witnesses, but otherwise his views are concealed.

Hence oral historians have not criticized Terkel for having a hidden
agenda, but on the formal grounds of having heavy-handedly manipulated his transcripts and disguised his method to boot. One academic
maligned this amateur, results-oriented approach as "Terkelism."[41] Yet,
Terkel only takes to extreme the considerable "processing" of deponents'
words that oral-history technique allows. Professional oral historians do
not alter bad grammar or idiosyncratic idiom (nor does Terkel—they
add color to his books), but they freely censor false sentence starts, stut-
tering, pausers ("ah," "er, er"), and even repetition, so that the
deponent's "voice" may be more clearly heard.[42] Terkel's subtle and pervasive editing, caused by his quest for eloquence, moves oral history
into the realm of art, with all its refinement and authorial subjectivity.
And yet, American journalists, under the influence of the interpretation-
oriented New Journalism, have faulted Terkel for presenting mere "raw
materials"—a charge that has also been hurled at *Peking Man* by Chinese
creative writers.[43] In both cases, the issue between author and critics
might well be the absence of a clear attitude toward the material in the
oral-history novel rather than its absence of "artistic" processing.

Peking Man takes "Terkelism" one big step further, moving the genre
fully into the literature category. Like its model, *Peking Man* presents the

words of 100 people, distilled from over 300 interviews. Zhang and Sang delete their own questions and comments even more fully than Terkel does in his books. Moreover, Zhang Xinxin (who is generally considered the major author) typically did not refer to tapes or even notes as she wrote. She reproduced her deponents' stories from memory, freely editing, selecting, and even reordering the topics of discourse.[44] So the words and opinions in *Peking Man*'s depositions are authentic, but the conversations as we see them are invented. *Peking Man* is nonfiction, and possibly still within the bounds of oral history, but it could also be considered creative writing by Zhang Xinxin—with a little help from her friends, old and new. Its freshness must come partly from Zhang Xinxin's own talent with words.

Rather than try to classify *Peking Man* in relation to journalism, fiction, and history, let us distinguish between methods that convey information, historical voices, and more abstract appreciations of character. Workaday journalists and historians alike dig for information, asking questions over and over in order to ferret out and confirm the facts (Zhang Xinxin admits to having cross-examined people on occasion, but she has edited out the evidence of it.) No elegant transcript emerges from such labors. The taped record will be overwhelmed by repetition and evidence of the interviewer's strategy. The voice of the historian or journalist may even dominate the dialogue.

The oral historian, however, wants not his deponents' knowledge, but their voices: their styles of thought and expression, in the context of their individual worlds of experience. To this end, the interviewer works to get the speaker to produce a narrative. Grilling for information would spoil the narrative and hide the self-motivating voice; heavy editing, on the other hand, would falsify it. Attacked by regular historians for sacrificing "hard" facts in the pursuit of "soft" art, the oral historian counters by saying that voices are as illuminating as facts.

The creative writer moves one step farther from raw material, sculpting an impression of his or her subject. The result of this tertiary interpretive activity is a character sketch—or a piece of analytical New Journalism. The raw materials are both hard data and the character's own voice, but they are abstracted and transformed by the synthetic powers of the writer. The character sketch actually predates the novel in

Western (English and French) literary history; in its original seventeenth- and eighteenth-century form, the sketch presented people not as individuals but as embodiments of certain professions or personality types.[45] Zhang Xinxin's characters can easily be so interpreted. Individual, even eccentric, as each may be (in comparison to characters in socialist realism)—and much as Zhang wants to transcend the "Marxist-Leninist" idea of typical characters—each chapter does after all communicate only a few interesting corners of Chinese social reality, corners that intrigued the authors. If only in this way, their selection of characters is a means of personal expression. As in oral history, all narration is in the voice of the deponent, and probably hardly any words have been invented. But every word is on the page only because it held Zhang Xinxin's attention.

Is not the authors' representation of *Peking Man*, in an introductory note, as "literature from transcribed oral accounts" (*koushu shilu wenxue*) a little misleading, then? Probably so. But writing down externally derived realities and using tape recordings to back them up is a good strategy for protecting the enterprise from political interference. The often-heard defense that one writes "only fiction" will not work in China, for fiction is expected to be more truthful (representative) than nonfiction itself.

Zhang Xinxin's and Sang Ye's evident fun with language indicates that *Peking Man* is a work of literature. There is arch use of slang, double meanings, and sheer creativity of expression by the folk. Common people who mistakenly assume the intellectual-sounding Zhang and Sang to be representatives of China's official culture even mock the young writers by quoting government slogans "back at them" ("I am *not* exaggerating—I seek truth from facts," says a snack peddler, p. 50).

The authors' construction of a comedy of manners through selectivity is hard to analyze, for we do not know what material they started with. However, we can observe them setting up dramatic confrontations through third-party comments that interrupt a central character's monologue, as when city people on a subway laugh at the malapropisms of a 12-year-old country boy who has fled to Peking from a famine area (p. 548). Sometimes the deponents "coincidentally" bring the silent interviewers into view by repeating—even mocking—their questions. At times they speak to Zhang and Sang as representative young people (meaning, "inexperienced"), as city folk ("educated"), or in the eyes of the farcically assertive but secretly insecure "Mistress Ten-Thousand-aire," as people with low fixed salaries. In the last case, the subject's attempts to poke fun at the differing mores of the educated interviewers are turned back on the subject:

> You need to ask? Bet we got ever'thing you got. Color TV, tape recorder, bi-cycle, refrigerator—and we got a house. Do you have a house? (Authors' note: Husband says: Do you have their education?) Education? Education ain't no use. If you wanna get rich, junior high'll getcha by. You cain't sell education! (p. 87)

There is juxtapositional irony, too. A former child bride who self-lessly joined the Revolution follows a spoiled old man who owes his position to his work abroad but now likes to complain about foreigners (pp. 20–36). A skilled and hopeful truck driver in Shenzhen follows a hopelessly suspicious and self-serving mid-level manager in a Xinhua bookstore (pp. 170–178). The Party theorist who fears the death of communism prepares the way for a smug, time-serving bureaucrat who handles United-Front policy (pp. 259–269). And a badly intimidated cab-aret singer leads into a fellow who is all agog about "The Third Wave" and "Megatrends" (pp. 145–158). Structural ironies are evident even in individual histories. After baring her soul about her singing, what she has to do to stay out of trouble, and the frustrations of her love life, the cabaret girl finishes with this comedown: "How do I make a living? I sell shoes."

An anomaly is the way in which *Peking Man* occasionally pursues data—as if Zhang and Sang were writing history or sociology instead of oral history—much less a personal narrative in the guise of oral history. Their information is interesting, to be sure. The book gives "inside dope" on salaries, social prejudices, and relations in the workplace; in one place we can deduce that Zhang simply asked "What tricks of your trade can you share with us?" (p. 395; cf. p. 172). But so much data can be distracting, as in *Envelope, Postcard, Block-of-Four.* Politics is partly to blame. It is the closed nature of Zhang's society that makes information on how society works so precious, leading to a fixation on how things really get done. Some readers are bound to have read *Peking Man* as a how-to manual. Indeed, many peasants wrote Zhang Xinxin letters asking for advice on how to raise minks for profit, so that they, too, could get rich like "Mistress Ten-Thousandaire."[46]

Although it is impossible to abstract an authorial viewpoint from *Peking Man,* some of Zhang Xinxin's own heartfelt concerns do appear. A young writer relates the pain of not being able to fall out of love with a boy who dated her only for her Peking residence permit. The cabaret singer so in need of self-confidence lists the songs she's not allowed to sing, and tells how her kind were jerked around by the campaign against spiritual pollution. A woman so beautiful that men stop to stare at her ends with the observation (p. 305) "The pity is I don't have anything else to give. No nothing." (Zhang Xinxin has long doubted her own attractiveness.)[47] A young woman whose education was terminated by the Cultural Revolution confides pathetic plans for self-study. And a widow describes how society endlessly subjects her to rumor. Add to this a certain muckraking tone, a calculated assault on myths, an evident desire to show that Chinese people's thinking is different from what the press says, and to preserve historical memory, and we must be part way to understanding Zhang's vision. She told Gayle Feldman, a free-lance writer for *Publishers Weekly,* that she wanted *Peking Man* to "tell people all over the world that the Chinese aren't just a billion blue ants. I also wanted to tell people here that everyone's experience is different—but it also is the same."[48]

The cultural choices in the making of *Peking Man* could hardly be more mixed. The form is Western but the subject matter is Chinese. Zhang Xinxin has not left behind her prior modernist consciousness, even while pursuing history, for the "journalistic novel" as a genre may be called a legacy of modernism. Moreover, if *Peking Man* is to be appreciated as a whole—and I think it is—then pulling it together requires a reading similar to that for *Envelope, Postcard, Block-of-Four. Peking Man* presents a deductive game. To fully understand any given sketch, the reader must figure out what questions led to the printed answers and lines of reflection. Then, how do the individual responses fit into a larger life pattern? Finally, how do the many lives form themselves into one Chinese pattern? The randomness of modern life is allowed to speak for itself, without artificial authorial intervention. If confusion, anomie, and entropy are the only messages we can derive, perhaps they are Zhang Xinxin's, too. One hundred versions of the truth may or may not be intended as a deliberate vision of chaos, but we may be sure that Zhang is still exploring just "how the world works."

LATER EXPERIMENTS

In 1986–1987, Zhang Xinxin and Sang Ye sought to duplicate the success of *Peking Man* with another nonfiction book that speaks in many voices: a fiftieth-anniversary remake of Mao Dun's *One Day in China*. Thousands of Chinese from all walks of life were asked to mail in a manuscript about what they did on 21 April 1986. Chief editors Sang Ye and Zhang Xinxin (the names were displayed in that order)—perhaps with the help of a committee—were to sort through the mess and come up with a book. Because the project was based on written depositions, however, the editors had far less freedom to reconstruct their texts creatively than in *Peking Man*. They could select or reject a deposition, but they were not free to rewrite it. Hence, judging from the excerpts that have been published so far, *One Day in China* lacks the vitality of *Peking Man*.[49]

More interesting is Zhang Xinxin's late 1985 "documentary novel" (*jishi xiaoshuo*) entitled *Zai lu shang* (On the road).[50] This work, too, is a self-conscious appreciation of the present as future history. It could be called a non-generic contribution to the "Searching for Roots" genre made popular in 1985–1986 by the stories of (Zhong) Acheng, Han Shaogong, Zhang Chengzhi, et al., about the enduring, "good-earth" values to be found in China's far rural hinterlands. Yet, once more Zhang Xinxin has found new ways of presenting her social material, and of mocking what she appears to be revering. *On the Road* may even be read as a satire of the "Searching-for-Roots" genre.

The occasion was a solo bicycle trip by Zhang Xinxin along the whole 897-kilometer length of the Grand Canal, from Peking to Hangzhou, in the spring of 1985. She says now that she had perceived a possible crisis coming, at the local levels, in the further implementation of Deng Xiaoping's economic reforms. She wanted to go down to see for herself, and also continue filling in gaps in her own knowledge that she had discovered while writing *Peking Man*. Television reporters and cameramen pursued her, generating a taped television series featuring Zhang, her impressions of the trip, and the things and people she saw.[51]

Stung by intellectuals' criticisms of this venture into television, Zhang went on to write *On the Road*, a literary appreciation of the trip.[52] At first glance, the book seems a collage of very "raw" materials. When the text departs from Zhang Xinxin's own travel experiences and discoveries, it ventures directly into the history and lore of the cities and counties along the way. Zhang retells local legends, searches for historical sites, and describes local customs and festivals. At one point she interrupts her narrative with a substantial block of popular songs and folksongs (pp. 159–172), inexplicably printed one after the other. There are also signs of the gazetteers and tomes about water conservancy she read up on before her trip.

Because Zhang's montage creates a documentary effect (indeed it preserves "documents," including not just the songs but a long quotation in Classical Chinese from a history, pp. 120–121), it toys with reader expectations of *On the Road* as a novel—even more so as linear travelogue—and so brings the book back into Zhang Xinxin's technically modernist creative world. Unrelated scenes are juxtaposed, as in *Envelope, Postcard, Block-of-Four*. Thus the second part of the novel consists of postcards from Zhang to her family, interspersed with subjective narrative not unlike that in *Back Home*. In her narrative voice, Zhang exults at having created postcard literature. Then a second voice is heard, through the medium of postcards written by a television cameraman who is pursuing Zhang Xinxin for the project, and perhaps romantically, too. Confusion of voice and context render the text as difficult in parts as "Theatrical Effects."

Zhang's unprefaced, intertextual album of lyrics must have particularly nonplused her conservative critics. The songs are printed in two parallel rows at the page margins, with a double row of two-character names separating them down the middle. Well over two hundred names appear, in quasi-systematic sequence: "Heavenly Wolf, Heavenly Dog, Heavenly Wine, Heavenly Gatekeeper ... Three Mulberries, Three Pots, Three Pupils of the Eye, Three Piebald Horses ... Wang Qiao,

Wang Ying, Wang Heng, Wang Hai . . ." When readers puzzled at the significance of this wrote to Zhang, she explained that the names were of legendary people and gods.[53] Evidently she transcribed them in order to marvel at the weight of tradition.

In fact, the larger structure of the novel, which may be divided into four major consecutive segments, tells its story in a nonlinear fashion. After observing that everyone is on the move as a tourist these days—a theme that provides a sense of closure when echoed in the brief fourth and final part, which is a montage of diverse conversations overheard on the train back to Peking—the first block of text reflects on Zhang's mental and physical preparations for her trip.

The second part is about the trip itself, with a geographical and historical, sometimes narrowly material, focus. There are, however, frequent ironic reflections on past and present. The northern canal bed is dry and the monuments have been moved into museums, says a postcard to Zhang's little brother, but never mind, the lessons you forget in grade school will be repeated to you verbatim in middle school.

The third and longest part also treats the entire trip; it thus repeats the subject of the second part, but with an emphasis on different, far more subjective themes. The third part directly represents the *feel* of riding a bicycle under different conditions, mixed with the stream of Zhang Xinxin's consciousness as she travels. Songs pop into her head; she experiences the terror of riding along an uneven road in pitch blackness; reflects that she is riding to escape the memory of her ex-husband; and thinks of loving the cameraman. Between her own flights of fancy, Zhang provides telling accounts of brush-ups against unyielding bureaucrats and moving reflections on the place of women in China, viewed in light of own personal experience and the great weight of history.

Though *On the Road* uses both cheery and black humor to taunt Zhang Xinxin's critics with her unconventional claim to have a personal vision, it is also a quest for a lost Chinese past. But it is not a simple nationalistic celebration of Chineseness. Zhang Xinxin said, in interview, that the most illuminating thing about gazetteers is seeing all the things that have been cut out, one by one, in the many revisions of them. Gazetteers "only get you to imagining what our people's culture was like prior to all those constrictions, how our concept of culture kept getting narrower and narrower."[54] Here Zhang Xinxin is not just dealing with the question of destruction during the Cultural Revolution, which embarrasses nationalists in the face of the West. She is confronting the very foundations of Chinese culture, quite aside from the matter of China's place in the world. As in her research for Peking Man, she delights in the cultural richness to be found in China when she can dig it out. But she also worries (as she hinted to Gayle Feldman) that everyone's thoughts may ultimately be about the same. From her research into gazetteers and inquiries along the canal, she has come to fear that Chinese culture may all be about the same, too, from north to south.[55]

Zhang Xinxin the modernist is at first blush very different from Liu Binyan, the guardian of socialism's great "realist tradition." Zhang likes to have fun with the old China, while Liu the Just seems a stern, twentieth-century reincarnation of Judge Bao. But there are similarities between the two writers. Zhang Xinxin's zest to *document* the changes going on in her society is as striking as her desire to record them in new genres and media. Even as he evokes the eternal generalizing power of literature in his reportage, Liu Binyan risks everything by naming real names, so as to have a visible moral impact on the world in his own time. The preface to *Peking Man* has a disclaimer to the effect that names were changed to protect the informants, but in truth, Zhang Xinxin the "pure" literary artist has generally quoted her characters' real names, too.[56] One cannot predict whether she will in future prefer more documentary or more fictive forms. Nor can one say for sure whether she will continue to pursue risky subjects such as problems with the current reforms. In any case, both she and Liu Binyan see Chinese issues transculturally, to use Benjamin Schwartz's term. Neither writer accepts what Schwartz referred to as "one of the more persistent myths of our age": that "History" is "under control."[57] For all her modernism, Zhang Xinxin seems to think that China has more scores to settle with History than with the West.

Part Three
Political Theory

SEVEN

A "Theology" of Liberation?
Socialist Revolution and Spiritual Regeneration in Chinese and Japanese Marxism

GERMAINE A. HOSTON

The founder [of a philosophical system] . . . is not necessarily concerned with the mutual consistency of all his utterances, and on many problems his thought may be fruitfully ambiguous. . . . It is generally the followers who assume the burden of defending the vision against hostile challenge and who must attempt to relate the vision to those aspects of experience which the founder has left out of account.

—Benjamin I. Schwartz

All points of view in politics are but partial points of view because historical totality is always too comprehensive to be grasped by any one of the individual points of view which emerge out of it. Since, however, all these points of view emerge out of the same historical current, and since their partiality exists in the matrix of an emerging whole, it is possible to see them in juxtaposition, and their synthesis becomes a problem which must continually be reformulated and resolved.

—Karl Mannheim

Since the Chinese Revolution swept the Chinese Communist Party (CCP) into power four decades ago, the literature of comparative politics has been enriched by studies offering often profound insights into the reception and adaptation of Marxism in non-European, so-called later-developing societies. Following the example of Benjamin Schwartz's

Chinese Communism and the Rise of Mao,[1] students of revolutionary movements in Asia, Africa, and Latin America have contributed substantially to our understanding of the fate of Marxist theory and practice in non-European societies, but the treatment of this subject matter by Western scholars has remained segregated from the mainstream of the study of Marxist political thought and of comparative political thought as a whole. Asian, African, and Latin American Marxists are discussed almost exclusively by comparativists in the context of developments in Asian, African, and Latin American politics, and their ideas have been depicted as merely "practical" adaptations of a Western revolutionary theory to non-European contexts.[2] Such thinkers tend not to be treated seriously by scholars of Western Marxism, political thought, or intellectual history, and thus their ideas have not been considered as potentially important contributions to Marxism to be contemplated and evaluated alongside the views of European thinkers such as Georges Sorel, Antonio Gramsci, or Karl Marx's own theoretical progenitors.[3]

The reasons for this deficiency in the literature are probably sufficiently self-evident that they need not be belabored here. It is more important to note its consequences: If the ideas of non-European Marxists are routinely discounted as adaptations to the requirements of revolutionary praxis—hence applicable only to the non-Western settings in which they appeared—then their contributions to the larger discourse of political thought cannot be appreciated. If, however, we reexamine the innovative work of non-European thinkers who regarded themselves as advocates of Marx's (admittedly Eurocentric) world view,[4] we discover that important themes of this larger discourse—the nature of modernity, the relationship between objective material forces and human will in shaping human history, and similar concerns—recur across national and cultural boundaries, transcending the particular elements of individual national contexts. Some such themes reverberate not only among Marxist revolutionary theorists of the non-Western world, but also between these thinkers and their West European counterparts. Furthermore, insofar as the innovations produced by thinkers such as Mao Zedong or Sano Manabu departed dramatically from Marx's own views, they often constituted efforts to fill apparent lacunae in his original theory. Thus, Marxism appealed to such thinkers for its diagnosis of the role of material factors in social development and for its critique of industrial capitalism, features which alternative Western political philosophies—such as liberalism or pragmatism—have not offered Yet, their views on what must be added to the "partial" perspectives of a theory that reflected only the West European historical experience[5] may offer to the larger discourse on the nature and legitimacy of modernity insights that bear implications reaching beyond the contexts in which these innovations first emerged.[6]

This study explores one such thematic innovation that emerged repeatedly among Chinese and Japanese Marxists in the first decades of this century and has since been echoed by their contemporaries and successors in Western Europe, Africa, and Latin America. This is the notion that Marx's ideal of genuinely socialist and then communist society cannot be realized unless a regeneration of spirit (*jingshen*) or mind (*kokoro*)—the totality of which on a societal scale comprises culture (*wenhua* or *bunka*)—is undertaken alongside revolutionary change in the socio-economic organization of society. Leading Marxists in China, beginning with Li Dazhao in the May Fourth era and culminating in Mao's advocacy of a cultural revolution, argued that a socialist revolution could save China only if the spirit of the Chinese people—their dispositions toward life and politics—underwent a thorough reconstruction. Such a revolution in the spiritual or cultural realm would supplant the negative attitudes and practices inherited from previous social formations with attitudes and mores appropriate to a new society no longer founded on private exploitation and appropriation. Similarly, leading, if predominantly unorthodox, Marxist theorists in Japan—Takabatake Motoyuki, Kawakami Hajime, Akamatsu Katsumaro, Mizuno Shigeo of the so-called Dissolutionist Faction (Kaitō-ha),[7] and Sano Manabu[8] also stressed this theme in their writings, occasionally linking it to an exceptionalist notion of Japanese spirituality.

This common thread in the writings of Chinese and Japanese Marxists concerning the cultivation of revolutionary consciousness as an essential part of the revolutionary process is consonant with the emphasis on voluntarism of certain Western Marxists: V. I. Lenin's appeal for the creation of revolutionary consciousness as the subjective precondition for revolution in Russia,[9] and Italian Marxist Antonio Gramsci's view that a socialist party must seek to create an alternative ideological "hegemony" before a socialist revolution in an advanced capitalist society can succeed.[10] Unlike Lenin and Gramsci, however, the Marxists treated here linked revolution in the mundane sense with a vision of that sphere of human life that transcends the material world, a vision more conventionally attributed to the purview of theologians than to advocates of a *Weltanschauung* that is widely characterized as atheistic.[11] The intimacy of this connection between spiritual regeneration and socialist revolution is neither casually nor crudely drawn in the works discussed here; indeed, where it is most fully elaborated, this reinterpretation of Marxism comes to function as a sort of "theology of liberation,"[12] in which spiritual or cultural regeneration is targeted along with the transformation of the material world to free man from the alienation from himself and his fellow man that he has experienced heretofore in human history. The implications of this reinterpretation of Marxism are profound. It suggests that these thinkers found Marx's solution to the problem of alienation incomplete, and, further, that they felt that the humanistic concern with the problem of alienation—the central motif of all Marx's work[13]—was best addressed by way of a communal vision of the transcendent. Ironically, this is the very sphere—religion—that Marx had repudiated as a manifestation of the same alienation, the political incarnation of which was the state.[14]

How did Chinese and Japanese advocates of liberation through the coupling of spiritual or cultural regeneration with socio-economic reorganization reconcile their views with Marx's assertions on ideology, religion, and the relationship between material basis and cultural superstructure? How do we account for this pattern of thought among Chinese and Japanese Marxist thinkers? Does it tell us anything about the contexts in which they were operating? More important, what does it contribute to our understanding of Marxism and of Western political thought as a whole? If this pattern of thought were limited to China and Japan, or if it appeared only among "unorthodox" or "atypical" Marxist thinkers in these settings, it would be difficult to extract any meaningful conclusions on its implications for larger issues in Western thought. When we note, however, that this pattern has emerged elsewhere—among Marxist liberation theologians in Latin America, North

African theorists such as Frantz Fanon and Amilcar Cabral, and advocates of radical Black theology in South Africa—its broader significance becomes clear.

This study will trace the emergence of this pattern of Marxist thought in China and Japan, noting commonalities and differences between these thinkers and their West European contemporaries as well as elements shared with similar patterns in Africa and Latin America. It will be noted that Chinese, Japanese, and other non-European Marxists felt the need to inject a transcendentalist perspective into a Marxist theory that too heavily reflected what they often viewed as the excessively materialistic character of the Western (bourgeois) civilization that gave rise to it. Nevertheless, with the benefit of a more catholic perspective, it can be argued more cogently that what Chinese, Japanese, and other non-European Marxists have perceived as a fundamental divergence between East and West in fact comprised tensions or polarities[15] that have been present within Western political thought, as within Marxism itself, from the outset—dualities between the rationalist, materialist, and self-assertive elements identified with modernity in Western thought and their opposites.[16] In questioning the value of what are conventionally assumed to be the attributes of modernity, non-European advocates of a transcendentalist-cum-social revolution response to Western Marxism have posed a provocative challenge to the dominant Western conception of modernity itself, even as this conception is manifested in the conventional presentation of Marxism as an anti-theological—ergo "progressive"—philosophical system.

SPIRITUAL REGENERATION AND MARXIST THOUGHT IN REVOLUTIONARY CHINA

For many years we communists have struggled for a cultural revolution as well as for a political and economic revolution, and our aim is to build a new society and a new state for the Chinese nation. . . . We . . . want to change the China which is being kept ignorant and backward under the sway of the old culture into an enlightened and progressive China under the sway of a new culture. In short, we want to build a new China. Our aim in the cultural sphere is to build a new Chinese national culture.

—Mao Zedong, "On New Democracy"

Marxism first came to China by way of Japan, but it was in China that the issue of spiritual and cultural regeneration found the earlier expression as an urgent appeal among young radical intellectuals. The issue did not immediately surface as a revision of Marxism; this development awaited the Bolshevik Revolution, which demonstrated that a Marxian socialist revolution could occur in societies with "Asiatic" characteristics,[17] in which industrial capitalism had made only limited inroads. Nevertheless, within the first decade of the century, as the Qing struggled to survive Western encroachment and the erosion of faith in traditional values, thinkers who would become founders of the CCP—Chen Duxiu and Li Dazhao—were already suggesting that the key to the physical survival of China lay in the rebirth of its people into a new constellation of values and mores. Early in the cultural renaissance of the May Fourth era, the objective was to replace outmoded and harmful Confucian values and mores with Western "science and democracy"; but, when the Versailles Treaty brought disillusionment with the model offered by the Western powers, the theme of cultural change and spiritual renewal came to be linked with a more critical view of Western capitalist society. Eventually, this theme was manifested in the incorporation of calls for "rectification" and "cultural revolution" into CCP orthodoxy during the 1940s.

It is not surprising that the call for spiritual regeneration should have arisen earlier in China. Japan had effectively responded to the threat posed by Western gunboat diplomacy by means of a (Meiji) "restoration" which revitalized traditional Japanese political values by melding them with German *Staatsrecht* philosophy and neo-Confucian thought to legitimate a highly successful industrialization effort under the tutelage of the state.[18] By contrast, Chinese political leaders in the same era confronted the challenge posed by Western powers armed with values (national wealth and power) which conflicted with those that dominated the Chinese polity;[19] but their responses differed markedly from a Japanese example that drew on a long tradition of philosophical syncretism. The first recourse in China was the *ti-yong* dichotomy, an approach that allowed leaders of the Tongzhi Restoration to undertake industrializing reforms while attempting to preserve philosophical tradition intact. Ironically, the notion that Western technological advances could be emulated without allowing the philosophical perspectives and moral values that undergirded them to disturb the existing pattern of Chinese values also effectively deterred China's reformers from undertaking the kind of creative ideological manipulation that the Meiji oligarchs used so successfully. When nearly half a century of fruitless effort showed the *ti-yong* formula to be untenable, frustration moved a generation of young Chinese intellectuals toward cultural iconoclasm. The legitimacy of the entire Confucian constellation of values came to be challenged.

As Yü-sheng Lin has demonstrated, however, characteristic features of Confucian thought in fact defined the *ti-yong* formula as an aberration. The "totalistic iconoclasm" of the May Fourth New Culture Movement (circa 1915 through 1925) grew directly out of Confucian perspectives on society and polity. In this tradition, the key to changing the world politically and socially lay in a change of "world view" and thereby in a fundamental change of "symbols, values, and beliefs," of culture, in short.[20] Thus, despite the radical rejection of Confucianism in the May Fourth Movement, it should not be surprising that a central tenet of Confucian thought—the view of "spiritual transformation" as a key to effective management of the political realm[21]—should also have resurfaced in the work of Chinese Marxists.

Two factors illuminate how the affirmation of the need for change in the spiritual realm could have been reconciled with the celebration of science (critical rational thought) as the highest priority for China's young intellectuals and with the widespread rebellion against religion that accompanied the rejection of Confucian values. First, a distinction must be drawn between an appreciation of the non-material realm on the one hand and institutionalized "religion," and specifically Confucianism and Christianity, on the other. May Fourth intellectuals attributed primary responsibility for China's malaise to an institutionalized Confucian value system that supported the old political and social order and discouraged democratization by inculcating reverence for hierarchy and passivity into the Chinese people. Similarly, Christianity was reviled for its role in preparing the way for the Western economic imperialism that eventually threatened China's territorial integrity. Such castigation of the political uses of organized religion in China's recent past fueled the anti-religious movement led by the Young China Association (Shaonian Zhongguo Xuehui) in the late 1910s through the early 1920s.[22]

These suspicions did not prevent many, even those who subscribed to Marx's historical materialism, from recognizing the importance of the transformation of spirit in creating a new society in China. This point raises a second issue: the content of the notion of spirit (*jingshen*) in the May Fourth context. Marxists such as Li Dazhao and Chen Duxiu were most certainly not referring to the Judeo-Christian notion of "spirituality" in its denotation of one's relationship to a higher being, but the notion of "spirit" as it occurred in their writings did go beyond mere "consciousness." It referred, as it does today in campaigns against "spiritual pollution" in the People's Republic, to the state of the soul of the Chinese people, to the values and ethics that molded their activity in the material world, and to their sense of hope as opposed to despair. This concern with spirit emerged among Chinese Marxists in the context of a larger controversy over the ontological difference between Eastern and Western civilizations, in which many contrasted a spiritual and passive Eastern "essence" with Western science and militant aggressiveness.[23]

Progressive intellectuals such as Hu Shi and Chen Duxiu, cofounders of *New Youth* (*Xin qingnian*) magazine, advocated Western science and rationalism as the key to saving China. Nonetheless, one must resist the impulse to impose on the Chinese and Japanese contexts the separation between mind and spirit that has dominated Western philosophical discourse since the era of Plato and Aristotle.[24] The terms used by Marxists in China (as in Japan) prescribing the need for change in the non-material sphere embraced the soul as well as the mind (as in *jingshen*), sentiment arising from the heart as well as the rational faculties of the intellect (as in *xin* or *kokoro*).[25] Thus, the ideas of Chinese (as of Japanese) Marxists may be compared fruitfully with those on consciousness posited by Lenin, Gramsci, and other Western Marxists. But they also shared much with the views of those like the French Marxist Georges Sorel, who saw sentiment, aroused through the myth and praxis of the general strike,[26] as a more reliable impetus toward revolution than the sort of deep political consciousness the proletariat would gain either directly through the praxis of production itself (Marx) or through education by a vanguard party (Lenin and Gramsci).[27]

The urgency of the appeal for spiritual change in China was expressed most dramatically by a leading writer of the May Fourth period, a cultural iconoclast who became a Marxist but stubbornly resisted efforts to draw him into the Communist Party. Lu Xun's criticism of traditional Chinese society shared much with CCP co-founder Chen Duxiu's views. Like many other young Chinese, early in the century Lu had gone to Japan to study. He abandoned his initial intention to study medicine, however, when a particularly painful classroom experience convinced him that healing the souls, "changing the spirits" and not merely the bodies, of his countrymen was the sine qua non of China's salvation.[28]

In biting commentary (zawen) and in short stories, Lu Xun expressed his generation's frustration with China's inability to extricate itself from the conundrum created by its forbears' stubborn adherence to traditional values. His "Diary of a Madman" (1918) asserted that Confucian values were not merely an impediment to China's progress along the path to Western science and democracy; they were evil, immoral, cannibalistic in essence. On the surface, Confucianism preached moral rectitude and mutual respect; but "between the lines" of the great classics, Confucianism urged men to feed upon one another, as animals. Yet "[p]erhaps there [were] still children who haven't eaten men? Save the children . . . ," the story concludes.[29] Only those least touched by the poisonous cannibalism of traditional China could be suitably equipped to save it; only by turning away from old self-destructive values and toward the path of "progress" promised by Western industrialized societies could China become a self-assertive, autonomous, and dignified actor in the international community.

This call for spiritual transformation reflected ambivalence concerning the relative merits of Eastern and Western cultures. The Bolshevik Revolution and the nationalist outrage at the Versailles Treaty both heightened the appeal of Marx's critique of Western capitalism and bourgeois democracy and deepened the ambivalence of radical Chinese intellectuals vis-à-vis the West. By the 1920s, Neo-Confucian and even radical Chinese thinkers had noted the pessimism concerning Western civilization that seized European intellectuals after World War I, and began to urge those who would save China to recognize the folly of believing in Western values and technology as the panacea for China's troubles.[30] Such ambivalence concerning the West was reflected from the outset not only in nationalist Li Dazhao's work, but also in a moderation of the views of the more radically iconoclastic Chen Duxiu, particularly with reference to the role of non-material factors in revolutionizing Chinese society.

THE TRANSFORMATION OF SPIRIT AND CONSCIOUSNESS IN CHEN DUXIU. None of the Chinese Marxists discussed here more fully manifested May Fourth iconoclasm than did Chen Duxiu. Commonly depicted as an "internationalist"–like Leon Trotsky, in association with whose views he came to be vilified and blamed for the calamitous Shanghai Coup (1927)–Chen shared Lu Xun's view that, if the Chinese nation-state could not serve its people, perhaps it should perish, along with the Confucian philosophical perspectives that sustained it.[31] Influenced by the social Darwinism of Herbert Spencer and Thomas Huxley, Chen discerned an intimate link between the survival of a people and its ethics. Thus, Chen attributed responsibility for China's national crisis not to imperialism nor to corrupt politicians such as the usurper Yuan Shikai, but to the Chinese people themselves, to their lack of self-consciousness. Even before he launched *New Youth* in 1915, Chen was convinced that the cultivation of new self-consciousness and ethical sensibilities was essential to the future of the Chinese people.[32] As the Marxist elements in Chen's thought took root, this view was incorporated into his Marxism and affected his resolution of the polarities between matter and spirit, historical determinism and voluntarism that were immanent in Marxist thought. In explaining China's failure to match the political and economic growth of Western societies, Chen drew on conventional distinctions between Eastern and Western cultures, but his view more closely approached Marx's negative assessment of "Oriental society" lacking any internal dynamic of change rather than the Neo-Confucian claim of the superiority of China's "national essence" (*guocui*). Chen identified three philosophical axes of difference between East and West. First, competitiveness and struggle rooted in "human nature" were the basis of Western societies, while Eastern peoples such as Chinese, Jews, and Indians sought "rest and repose." Chinese had remained an "inferior Eastern people, loving peace, respecting repose, and . . . [remaining] majestic and refined in appearance"; they preferred to be humiliated rather than to die in battle, and they felt no shame for their abject condition.

Moreover, the stress on individualism manifested in modern Western thought contrasted dramatically with the stress on familial relations and obligations in Chinese thought.[33] While the interests of the state and society might appear to conflict in the West, Chen argued, both state and society rested on the primacy of the interests of the individual. By contrast, Confucian morality rested on values—*xiao* (filial piety) and *zhong* (loyalty)—that reinforced the familial conception of society. To Chen, this signified that China had retained elements of its primitive tribal past and had failed to progress beyond the half-civilized feudal stage.[34] The legacy of China's failure to accede to Western values, even in the face of aggressive intrusion by the European powers, boded ill for the future. Subject to a philosophical perspective that "destroyed . . . human independence and self-respect," "obstructed the liberty of individual desires," "usurped the rights of individuals who were equal in [natural] law," and "cultivated dependency while it destroyed individual productivity," the Chinese people could not hope to liberate themselves from internal and external bondage without a fundamental change of *Weltanshauung*.[35]

At this point, Chen's iconoclasm, and his seduction by Western political values, were nearly total. Much as the "Oriental society" of Marx's conception required the external shock of imperialism to propel it into the mainstream of world history; so too, for Chen, the people of a stagnant China needed the impact of Western values to restore their fortunes.[36] Chen had retained his native tradition's stress on the primacy of moral values cultivated in the conscious mind in determining the fate of the polity; yet he had succumbed completely to Western conceptions of modernity and progress in terms of the content of the self-consciousness to which Chinese were to aspire. Marxism shared the most basic elements of this understanding of "modernity": Belief in the triumph of man over nature through science and technology, industrialization and urbanization at the expense of the peasantry, the primacy of individual self-realization (through socialist organization of economic life), and the view that (religious) faith in the transcendent constituted the objectification and subjugation of man and that it must yield to man's self-assertion as the subject rather than the object of world history.[37]

After the Russian Revolution, Chen's attitudes toward that aspect of the Western conception of modernity that concerned religion became more complex. Initially Chen's disdain for religion matched his rejection of Confucian philosophy. "Increased knowledge of the natural world" through Western science was "the right path to benefit the world and to awaken the people today," Chen wrote in November 1916. Religion did not promote enlightenment. Unaware of Marx's critique of religion, Chen nonetheless closely approximated Marx's equation of religion with "ideology" (as "false consciousness"): Religion was merely self-deceit and only superficially relieved men of their worldly troubles.[38] Yet, Chen appeared to contradict himself on the issue. On the one hand, the critique of religion formed part of an argument against Confucianism as a state religion of sorts. Echoing the American orthodoxy of separation of Church and state, Chen declared, "It is universally true that politics and religion are separate spheres." But he also claimed that Confucianism itself was not really a religion at all.[39] Moreover, he argued, even if one insisted that it was a religion, Confucianism, with its stress on hierarchy and inequality among men, was inferior to Christianity and was fundamentally incompatible with republicanism.[40]

The implication that Christianity was more conducive than Confucianism to republican and democratic ideals, coupled with Chen's long-standing emphasis on the importance of a transformation of values to social change, provided the foundation for the coupling of spiritual change with social revolution in Chen's development as a Marxist. In 1919–1921, as Chen participated in Marxist study groups, he was moved by the "Oriental political apathy" that was spreading among youth influenced by nihilism and anarchism[41] to alter his initial position. By 1920, he had become more convinced that science alone—without some hope-giving faith—could not motivate men to the radical social and political change that China desperately needed. No longer were religion and politics separate spheres: On the contrary, religious faith could move men to meaningful political activity. The only issue was which set of religious beliefs would provide a suitable "theology of hope,"[42] and on this, Chen embraced Christianity as the most promising prospect. In a lengthy article replete with quotations from the four gospels, Chen argued that, despite the evils of the medieval Church and the use of missions to support imperialism in China, Christianity was a major pillar of Western civilization, and he sought to illuminate its contributions to the "successes" of Western civilization and identify those elements that might foster similar greatness in his compatriots.

Chen himself did not accept all the main elements of Christianity on faith: He characterized the creation and the idea of the Holy Trinity as mere myth. But these mythical elements did not invalidate Christianity for Chen. Its "essence" was "faith and love," and such instinct and depth of feeling—lacking in the Chinese Confucian tradition—were critical to moving people to positive action. He rejected as simplistic and inaccurate the conventional wisdom that the East was spiritual and the West a materialistic civilization. Both cultures were rich in "feelings" and "desires," and the difference between the two lay within the content of these sentiments. Eastern peoples tended toward a formal, ritualistic, and superficial "ethical morality" based on intellect and rationality about the nature of the family and society.[43] By contrast, the transcendental element of Christianity revealed a "beautiful, pure religious sentiment" that could not be extinguished by science, Chen asserted, and for that reason he urged that the "lofty character of Jesus"—his spirit of self-sacrifice, forgiveness, and egalitarian brotherly love—should "be nurtured into the blood of" the Chinese people. This was not to say that Christianity should be institutionalized as a state religion: "Christ did not come to save countries, but to save the eternal life of all mankind." Viewed correctly, "Christianity [was] the gospel of the poor," not the tool of those seeking to maintain their privileged positions in the status quo.[44]

Those who have noted Chen's endorsement of Christianity in the past have minimized its significance, perhaps with a view toward stressing the consistency between his early anti-religious convictions and his subsequent stature as a Marxist leader.[45] It is true that Chen's approach to Christianity was more motivated by utilitarian concerns than by a personal conversion experience, and we find scant reference to spirituality in Chen's later writings. Nevertheless, Chen's concern with transcendental factors in social change after the Russian Revolution was consistent with his earlier conviction that attitudes and beliefs were critical to the success of any social revolution in China. This position challenged that component of Western "modernity" that assumes that man cannot be the subject of human history if his view of the world includes a vision of the transcendent. Indeed, Chen asserted the contrary: Only with faith in something that transcended the material world, only with vision that was not bound by the material status quo could Chinese become active subjects rather than passive objects in the drama of human history. This resistance to the "modern" primacy of matter over spirit, rationality over intuition and human sentiment, is even more salient in the thought of Li Dazhao and Mao Zedong.

FROM SPIRITUAL TRANSFORMATION TO CULTURAL REVOLUTION IN REVOLUTIONARY CHINA. As the more nationalistic of the co-founders of the CCP, Li Dazhao moderated the May Fourth attack on China's cultural tradition and tempered Marx's materialism with idealist elements that drew on that tradition. Li's idealism was duly noted in Schwartz's study of the Chinese Communist movement.[46] Here we shall examine this element in Li's thought before his adoption of Marxism and its effect on his own elaboration of Marxism. We will then trace how Chen's and especially Li's views on the role of spiritual transformation in socialist revolution were developed more fully in the notions of rectification and the transformation of souls by Mao Zedong and Liu Shaoqi in the Yan'an era.

The voluntarism that was so pronounced in Li's thought calls into question the notion that Li's idealism shared an Hegelian perspective on the importance of "impersonal historical forces" in social change.[47] There was an essential continuity between what some see as Li's early idealism and his subsequent views as a "mature" Marxist. In his earliest writings, Li showed disdain for religion in general and for Buddhism and Christianity in particular, and is thought to have co-sponsored the Great Federation of Anti-Religionists.[48] Nevertheless, Li also evidenced a belief in liberation through spiritual redemption in terms that are evocative of Biblical language; and, as he became a Marxist, this theme defined the axis along which he himself would revise Marxist thought.

Li was much less uncritically accepting of the most recent trends in Western thought than were Chen Duxiu and other May Fourth intellectual activists. The early unhappy years of the Republic led Li to warn his contemporaries to avoid blind imitation of West European and American political institutions.[49] It was a people's consciousness, rather than changes in political arrangements, that was the fundamental motive force of history, Li argued; shared ideas and values, spiritual "customs," defined a community of people (qun) and motivated them to action. Like Chen, Li blamed China's crisis on the Chinese themselves, for lacking a "spirit that yields to the rule of law and resists cruelty."[50] Under the influence of Leo Tolstoy, he concluded that the true meaning of revolution was for people "to repent of their sins" and to pursue a path of righteousness and morality. There was no path to heaven apart from earth, as in institutionalized Buddhism or Christianity, Li contended; but men, conscious of their sins, should work toward the defeat of sin and evil on earth.[51] Well before Li became a Marxist, then, he placed strong emphasis on the realm of the human heart/mind (xin) and spirit (jingshen): Without spiritual practices, without a strength of spirit and will, the community would cease to exist.[52] This community spirit provided the basis for "rule of the people" (minyi) when Li was drawn to European notions of popular sovereignty and constitutional government in his early years;[53] but it remained important in his analysis of social change even as he was influenced by historical materialism.

Before the Bolshevik Revolution, Li articulated a cosmology based on the primacy of self-consciousness in human history. He shared with Marx and Hegel a dialectical interpretation of history, but at that point his dialectic was not a materialist one. The dialectic between the part and the whole, equality and difference, change and continuity enabled the universe to renew itself continually, but that dialectic was not regulated by changes in the forces and relations of production, nor did it consist in some disembodied spirit, or Geist. Rather, its motive force was human self-consciousness, man's self-consciousness as part of the whole of humanity, as the subject and not the object of history. Consciousness of the possibilities of man's role in the perpetual "springtime" of the renewal of the universe would provide the impetus for the renewal of China.[54] This view, which saw an "unending past and future" in the present, enabled Li to resist radical iconoclasm to affirm the value of China's past: To repudiate the past in its totality deprived one of the possibility of drawing on its best elements to build the future.[55]

Thus, like Chen and Lu, Li's view that the key to resolving China's crisis lay in human consciousness led him to see a special role for China's youth in effecting China's transformation. Despite the atheism that some see in Li's cosmology,[56] Li returned to the religious motif of "sin" and "repentance," and called upon China's youth to repent of their evils to leave the seeds of a better world to the future. China would be renewed through the "self-perfection" of the individual, through the self-cultivation of virtue (*de*) and human kindness (*ren*). Unlike the Confucian conception of these virtues, however, Li saw the standards of morality as changing over time. Hence, where Li was critical of Confucianism, he was so of its absolute and rigid application to an age that its prescriptions could no longer serve.[57] Nor did Li wholly accept Western gnostic conceptions of truth and the value of "objectivity" in discovering that truth. As one scholar has noted, Li held an "existentialist concept in which . . . 'subjectivity' is included within . . . human knowledge . . . [one in which] objective and subjective are [united as] one."[58]

As Li was increasingly drawn to Marxism, these idealist perspectives inspired him to revise the Marxist understanding of the relationship between the material base and superstructure of a society. Conversely, Marxism also prompted him to reformulate his conception of a revolution as consisting in and of spiritual transformation to one in which socialist revolution is powered by the coupling of spiritual and material transformation. For Li, the victory of the October Revolution heralded the "birth of a new spirit . . . of the common self-consciousness of all mankind" in the twentieth century, fulfilling the promise of the self-renewal of the universe. This spirit, he wrote, would finally culminate in the liberation of the individual through socialist revolution throughout the world.[59] Marx's rigorous analysis of economic history helped to account for the victory of Bolshevism, but Li repudiated as dangerous the tendency to use an appreciation of economic factors to produce materialist determinism.[60] One cannot rely solely on material change "to eliminate the evil corruption and the evil nature nurtured in man's prehistory," Li wrote. "We advocate at once reforming the human spirit with humanism, and, at the same time reforming/reconstructing economic organization with socialism. . . . We advocate reconstruction in both the material realm and heart/mind (*xin*), reform of souls (*hun*) and flesh alike.[61] While Li conceded that in Marxism the ideological superstructure could not fundamentally alter the operation of the laws of history,[62] as long as human beings remained unchanged, he argued, a true social revolution was not possible.[63]

Li did not propose to use arbitrary religious-cum-political authority to transform his countrymen into "new men." Indeed, he shared Chen's critical views on the historical abuse of established religious authority.[64] Although Li's perspective shared much in common with traditional Chinese thought on the unity of the way of Heaven (*tiandao*) and humanitarianism (*rendao* or *ren*), he did not share the elitist pretensions of the Confucian legacy. As the worker was changed from a "beast of burden" to a full human being, the intellectual would be transformed spiritually from a "demon" (*gui*) into a genuine human being by participating in workers' and peasants' organizations.[65] Finally, Li took issue with the notion of gaining knowledge as it was represented in the tradition of the European Enlightenment and in Marxism. In seeking revolution through self-consciousness of man's subjectivity in human history, Li concurred with early writings of Marx of which he was yet unaware; but he also saw as critical the role of a subjective—rather than simply objective—truth in liberating mankind.

As Chinese Marxists gained a more "sophisticated" grasp of Marx's original theory, these themes were accentuated rather than abandoned by Mao Zedong and Liu Shaoqi. Neither saw Marxism as a philosophical system that was already complete or necessarily applicable to China in its original form. Mao, distinguishing between "universal" and "particular" elements in all thought systems, asserted that it was essential to produce a new interpretation of Marxism on the basis of the experience of the Chinese Revolution.[66] That reinterpretation would, like Leninism, both make Marxism more complete by testing it against praxis[67] and contribute to Marxism universal as well as particular elements.

Two interrelated aspects of Mao's work have a direct bearing on the theme of spiritual transformation as we have traced its evolution in Lu, Chen, and Li. The first is an epistemology that unifies objective and subjective understanding and balances rational, logical knowledge with the value of instinctive understanding arising out of practice. Mao's dialectical epistemology reflected a mistrust of the hegemony of what Gramsci called "traditional intellectuals" and attributed greater significance to the view from below, such as that which might be articulated by Gramsci's "organic" intellectuals.[68] The second element is the view, also shared by Gramsci, that Marx had understated the ability of superstructural factors—ideology and culture—to impede economic development and socialist revolution. However, unlike Gramsci, who stressed the role of this factor in advanced capitalist societies, Mao and Liu, like Lu, Chen, and Li, saw its significance for less industrialized societies as well. During the Rectification Campaign, first launched in the 1940s, Mao and Liu enhanced Marx's views on the changeability of human nature by drawing on Confucian notions of the perfectibility of man through the cultivation of virtue within the polity and applying them to the problem of achieving a genuinely successful socialist revolution.[69] These two elements ultimately formed the theoretical basis of the notion that cultural revolution is essential to socialist revolution. In addition, these views expressed the rejection of critical elements of Western "modernity"—the assumption that mature industrial capitalism lay in the future of all societies; and the view that the material world and rational knowledge of it have consigned spiritual cultivation to the dustbin of medieval superstition. These views developed outside the Western philosophical tradition strongly resemble challenges to Western modernity once leveled by Sorel and Jean-Jacques Rousseau.[70]

When we examine Mao's approach to knowledge and consciousness, as when we analyze Mao's views on the proper strategy for the Chinese Revolution, we must distinguish between the lip service Mao paid to orthodox Leninist views in order to bolster his claim to CCP leadership and his increasing departures from these views.[71] Thus, Mao deferred to the positivism and empiricism that characterized the Western "science" of which young Chinese intellectuals of the May Fourth era had become enamored. In "On Practice," affirming that "all genuine knowledge originates in direct experience," Mao urged his colleagues to shun a "subjectivist" approach to problem solving: "To be subjective,"

Mao wrote, "means not to look at problems objectively, that is, not to use the materialist viewpoint in looking at problems."[72] Yet, in the context of the whole of Mao's work on the issue, these assertions did not affirm a strictly empiricist approach to knowledge. Mao used freely the term *subjectivity,* with its negative connotations in contradistinction to objective truth. However, the term was used imprecisely in his writings: *Subjectivity* was a charge leveled to attack both exclusive reliance on theories such as Marxism-Leninism without reference to Chinese realities, on the one hand, and reliance on one's own narrow experiences and perspectives to the exclusion of indirect experience, on the other. Here *subjectivity* referred to a "one-sided" approach—either exclusively empiricist or dogmatic theoretically—to knowledge. True knowledge emerged through a dual dialectic. First, there was a relationship between man as the subject of history and his environment. In coming to understand the objective realities that surrounded them by acting in that environment, men and women also changed reality. A second dialectic operated between subjective and objective knowledge, between sensory perception and rational/logical understanding of the world. Praxis played a key role in this dialectic, because it was in applying rational knowledge—based on the application of logic to discrete perceptual observations—to the real world that theories were tested and corrected for reapplication, observation, and reformulation.[73]

This epistemology helped Mao to manifest his instinctive distrust of intellectuals in his *Zhengfeng*-movement writings and eventually in the notion of the mass line.[74] Postulating a symbiotic relationship between intellectuals and the masses of Chinese workers and peasants, Mao came very close to Li's ideas about how intellectuals and peasants could help to transform each others' souls. Mao was far more distrustful than Lenin of the cool, rational logic of intellectuals isolated from physical labor than he was of the spontaneous revolutionary energies of the common people. The latter, reflected in China's long history of peasant rebellions, inspired Mao to seek in China's peasants the motive force for the Chinese Revolution: "In a very short time . . . several hundred million peasants will rise like a mighty storm, like a hurricane, a force so swift and violent that no power, however great, will be able to hold it back."[75] Urging peasants to shed their traditional deference to landlords,[76] Mao saw validity and power in the instinctive, subjective responses of China's peasant masses to their oppression. That was not to say that scientific rational knowledge would have no role: A broader systematic understanding of human experience, a theoretical perspective such as Marxism-Leninism was essential. Yet neither the subjective nor objective, the spontaneous/emotional nor rational/logical alone was sufficient. Intellectuals and peasants each were endowed with only half of what was required to achieve true knowledge and genuine revolutionary consciousness. Praxis by intellectuals and peasants working side by side in the Chinese Revolution would yield the unity of subjectivity and objectivity that Mao described.

Such a large role for subjective consciousness also emerged in Mao's discussion of the relationship between human understanding and "objective" reality itself; this dialectic too was mediated by human consciousness.[77] Like Li, Mao was careful to accede to the materialist requirement that cultural and other superstructural elements be in the final analysis determined by the economic basis of a society. Mao's formulation, however, diminished this relationship to permissive causation.[78] In Mao's view—as in Gramsci's view of the power of hegemony to obstruct social revolution in advanced capitalist societies—it was possible for the superstructure of a society actually to block the further development of the economic basis of society. "When the superstructure (politics, culture, etc.) obstructs the development of the economic base, political and cultural changes become principal and decisive. Are we going against materialism when we say this? No. . . . We also . . . must recognize the reaction of mental on material things, of social consciousness on social being and of the superstructure on the economic base. This [view] avoids mechanical materialism and firmly upholds dialectical materialism."[79] The tension between base and superstructure to which Mao alluded here inhered in Marx's thought from the outset, when he identified the task of the philosopher as changing the world not merely interpreting it.[80] Mao simply illuminated this tension and drew from it implications that Lenin and Gramsci approached but dared not draw.

Lenin had stressed the need for revolutionary theory, but he never claimed that the superstructure could inhibit the development of Russia's economic basis, nor did he envisage the symbiotic relationship between intellectuals and mass that Mao advocated. Gramsci recognized the difference between making socialist revolution in societies with powerful states but weak hegemonies (such as Russia) and in Western bourgeois states based on less coercive power but armed with a stubborn and deeply rooted hegemony; and he argued that revolutions in the latter would have to be prolonged "wars of position" (as opposed to "wars of manoeuvre"). A socialist revolution in such a society could occur only if it was preceded by the creation of an alternative hegemony of values and cultural norms. Only when the majority had been won over to the alternative hegemony of the subaltern classes could the state be smashed and a new socialist order be built.[81]

Gramsci did not envisage this scenario in a non-bourgeois society such as China; nor did he posit a direct link between the cultivation of virtue by individual men and women on the one hand and the establishment of a new hegemony to support a socialist system on the other. These new elements we find in the work of Mao and Liu of the Yan'an period as they drew on Confucian ideas about self-cultivation to enable the transformation of souls to create an "alternative hegemony" in the Shen-Gan-Ning border area. After the CCP's victory in 1949, there emerged an increasing disparity between the views of Mao and Liu on the tension between spirit and matter. This conflict culminated in the Cultural Revolution: Mao's view that spirit could predominate over and actually cause desired material change inspired the Great Leap Forward, and, in response to criticism of that failure, Mao wielded the notions of cultural revolution and spiritual transformation for the sake of stateless socialism against his rivals in the Party bureaucracy. By contrast, Liu had recognized the need for periodic rectifications in the Party, but he was not prepared to accept the notion that spiritual/cultural change alone could overcome China's technological deficiencies and furnish an adequate basis for industrializing China and building socialism at a higher level of development of productive forces.[82]

Nevertheless, during the Yan'an period, Liu, like Mao, drew heavily on Confucian tenets to assert the need for self-cultivation in socialist revolution. His classic work, titled How to Cultivate Oneself to Be a Good Communist in Chinese, is littered with copious references to Confucius and Mencius on the self-cultivation of virtue.

[S]ubjective effort and self-cultivation in the course of revolutionary struggle are absolutely essential, indeed indispensable, for a revolutionary in remoulding himself and raising his own level. . . .

Mencius . . . said that no one had fulfilled "a great mission" and played a role in history without first undergoing a hard process of tempering. . . .* Still more so must Communists give attention to tempering and cultivating themselves in revolutionary struggles, since they have the historically unprecedented "great mission" of changing the world.

---

*From *Mencius,* Book VI, "Kao Tzu," Part II. Mencius lived from 372 B.C. to 289 B.C.[83]

Confucian virtue was cultivated solely through mental labor, contemplation, thus imposing and enforcing an unjust division of labor between mental and physical work and forcing those who worked with their hands to support economically those who worked only with their minds.[84] By contrast, Mao and Liu advocated a kind of self-cultivation that was consistent with Marxian socialist principles in general and with the epistemology we have outlined in Mao's work. Citing Mao "On Practice," Liu argued, "Our Communist self-cultivation must not be divorced from actual revolutionary practice or from the actual revolutionary movements of the laboring masses."[85] This refurbished conception of self-cultivation both helped to legitimate a peasant-cum-intellectual vanguard party and supplied a critical underpinning to the seeds of the idea of cultural revolution already present in the *Zhengfeng* (Rectification) Campaign. Self-cultivation enabled the nurturance of a revolutionary socialist consciousness or viewpoint (*lichang*) among peasants and intellectuals, not merely among those born into the objective material circumstances of wage labor in a capitalist society. Mao recounted that, in his own life, this shift in class viewpoint had occurred through " a long and painful process of tempering" working side by side with workers and peasants. Gradually, revolutionary praxis, including productive labor, led Mao "to feel that compared with the workers and peasants the unremoulded intellectuals were not clean. . . . That is what is meant by a change in feelings, a change from one class to another."[86] Such self-cultivation of proletarian socialist political consciousness in those who did not live in the material conditions Marx described as their origin was no other than a triumph of the cultivation of spirit over matter. As Liu wrote, citing Mencius, "'Everybody can be a Yao or Shun.' . . . [I]t is perfectly possible for our comrades to grasp the theory and method of Marxism-Leninism, take a really conscious and consistent stand as vanguard fighters of the proletariat, really acquire the communist world outlook, never isolate themselves from the current great and deep revolutionary movement of the proletariat and all the labouring masses, and exert themselves in study, self-tempering and self-cultivation."[87] To return to Mao's epistemology, revolutionary consciousness arose from a dialectic between praxis—in revolution itself, not just in a particular kind of productive labor—and the conscious cultivation of a revolutionary viewpoint.

The *Zhengfeng* Campaign was intended to rectify (*zheng*) negative tendencies or styles (*feng*) of work in the Party that conflicted with revolutionary socialist values. It also addressed a larger pair of issues: first, to use Gramsci's terms, the problem of assuring the triumph of the new alternative (socialist) hegemony over the old hegemony; and, second, the related matter of the constant threat of the corruption of virtuous socialist men and women by their exercise of political power as long as the state (and the need for it) continued to exist. Mao failed to distinguish between these two concerns in his work, depicting bureaucratism as arising simply from the "restoration of capitalism."[88] The struggle between the two hegemonies, in this view, would persist and would have to be waged aggressively, because the old ideological superstructure had a life of its own and would not collapse spontaneously as a consequence of radical changes in the socio-economic organization of society. As long as men and women continued to maintain the same conceptions of themselves and continued to treat one another in the manner to which they had become accustomed in all previous social formations, continued to be alienated from one another, in short, there could be no genuine socialist revolution.

The influence of cultural patterns developed under precapitalist societies and capitalism was of particular concern to socialists such as Gramsci and Mao in this respect. Individualism, the primacy of the individual that was at the heart of bourgeois culture, had been a beneficial development historically, helping to break down the oppressive bonds of family, class, and state that had alienated men and women from one another in earlier forms of class society. May Fourth intellectuals had seen in Western bourgeois liberalism's advocacy of the primacy of the individual a useful and attractive tool to wield against the domination of the traditional patriarchal family. Yet this same individualism both reflected and contributed to the ever deepening sense of alienation of individuals in an increasingly atomized society: As Marx claimed, it was in capitalist society that human alienation was greater than it had been in any previous social formation. Mao believed that one could not realistically expect to achieve a victorious socialist revolution one day and on the next suddenly find the alienating attitudes of individualism and feudal loyalties disappear.[89] Where a communitarian society was the ultimate goal, it was necessary to inculcate in men and women a sense of being part of something much larger, the community, for a communitarian society was the ultimate goal. Without the deliberate cultivation of man's self-consciousness as what Marx called a species-being, the artificial schism between public and private man, between the pursuit of individual well-being and the well-being of the society, could not be overcome. The new socialist hegemony would be supported by changes in the economic organization of society, but change in economic structure without the purposeful transformation of souls through the cultivation of socialist virtue in individual men and women would fail to create a genuinely revolutionary kind of society.

As early as the Yan'an era, Liu depicted the relationship between this concern and the problem of bureaucratism differently and perhaps more accurately, since China had never been a mature capitalist society. Liu also perceived the relative autonomy of the cultural and political superstructure in almost Gramscian terms, but he clearly distinguished one set of its implications from the other. To be sure, there was the problem of the lingering influence of the old culture and its threat to revolutionary purity:

> In general, our Party consists of the finest sons and daughters of our country, the vanguard of the Chinese proletariat, but they come from all strata of the old society, and in China today there still exist exploiting classes and the influence of these classes—selfishness, intrigue, bureaucracy and various other kinds of filth. It is the duty of the Communist Party to change existing society, and it is necessary for Communists to remould, cultivate and temper themselves.[90]

Mao too recognized primacy of "feudal" over bourgeois elements in China's culture in this period, and thus he saw the "New Democracy" as a transition period during which the imperialist and feudal elements of Chinese culture could be swept aside.[91] In this sense, for both men, *zhengfeng* was an appeal for revolution in the cultural sphere through the cultivation of proletarian socialist virtue.

In addition, however, Liu saw a second aspect of the need for cultural revolution in the problem of the state. Much as Marx had seen the inherent corruptibility and corrupting influence of state power, Liu saw in the exercise of political power itself a corrupting influence. (Note the irony of this observation in light of Mao's subsequent denunciation of Liu as a bureaucrat, a "capitalist roader" in the highest levels of the Party during the Cultural Revolution.) Marx once remarked, "Society had created its own organs to look after its common interests, originally through simple division of labour. But these organs, at whose head was the state power, had in the course of time, in pursuance of their own special interests, transformed themselves from the servants of society into the masters of society."[92] Liu attributed such a tendency toward the alienation of party cadre from the masses in the 1940s less to the "restoration of [a] capitalism" that had never been dominant in China than to the self-corruptive nature of state power itself. "Some members of our Party," Liu asserted, "cannot withstand the plaudits of success and victory; they let victories turn their heads, become brazen, arrogant and bureaucratic and may even vacillate, degenerate and become corrupted, completely losing their original revolutionary quality."[93] Thus, like Rousseau, both men saw the cultivation of virtue as essential to socialist revolution. But, as in Rousseau, appointing the state or the party as the guardian of virtue was not without its difficulties. Even a temporary proletarian state could degenerate into the same kind of "chains" that had bound men and women under the old state power.[94] Liu and Mao proposed to seek the self-perfection of society through the transformation of souls, through continuous spiritual regeneration.[95]

In making this argument in the context of Marxism, Mao and Liu were able to reconcile a longstanding polarity within the Confucian philosophical tradition. Within Confucian thought, there had been a dialectical tension between the cultivation of virtue in the individual and public service in ordering the world in conformity with Confucian values. The original unity between these two obligations was manifested clearly in the *Analects* and the *Great Learning:* "'He [the superior man, *junzi*] cultivates himself to give rest to the people.' (*Analects,* Book XIV, Chap. xlv)." The two objectives came to be separated, even contradictory, Professor Schwartz notes, under the post-Qin bureaucratic state.[96] Mao's and Liu's stress on the cultivation of virtue and transformation of souls through revolutionary praxis enabled these mandates to be reconciled. Yet their solution generated new tensions between the kind of elitism that often accompanies calls for spiritual change (demanding perhaps a Platonic philosopher-king or Rousseauean Legislator), on the one hand, and the egalitarian ethic fortified with considerably more respect for the instincts of the peasant masses than the Leninist tradition held, on the other.[97] Ultimately, in the quest for "moral transformation," Mao, like Sorel, tried to resolve this new tension by subordinating the preferences of an elite to the spontaneous response of the people to the call to liberation.[98] To be sure, Mao and Liu, Chen and Li subsequently diverged on the precise balance between the roles of spiritual and material elements in social change. But, for all these thinkers, the Chinese people could not even begin the revolutionary process without challenging the accumulated burden of negative attitudes and behaviors rooted in the "customs" and relations of the old society. In this sense, for all these thinkers, the key to launching a successful socialist revolution lay not in the reform of economic and political organization alone, but rather in the transformation of souls.

THE CRITIQUE OF WESTERN INTELLECTUALISM AND THE INJECTION OF YAMATO SPIRIT IN JAPANESE MARXISM

As in China, the theme of spiritual regeneration and socialist revolution emerged repeatedly in the writings of major Japanese Marxists of the interwar period. Like their counterparts in China, Japanese socialists addressed the issue in a manner that implied or voiced explicitly dissatisfaction with the strictly materialist approach of orthodox Marxism-Leninism and with the conception of modernity that it embodied. As we compare the treatment of the issue of spiritual cultivation by Marxist revolutionaries in the two contexts, we are struck immediately by some significant and revealing differences between the two cases, some arising out of profound cultural dissimilarities and others stemming from structural contextual disparities between the two societies. It will be argued, however, that the similarities as well as the differences are helpful for our effort to understand why the issue of spiritual transformation came to be raised so persistently among Marxists in East Asia and the implications of their work for Marxist thought and for the Western philosophical tradition as a whole.

If the theme of spiritual liberation as a component of socialist revolution found its way into the writings of both Chinese and Japanese Marxists, the relationship between its advocates and the organized Communist Party was in Japan quite the opposite of the pattern we have identified in China. In China, the theme of spiritual regeneration was a persistent motif running through the writings of leading figures of the Chinese Communist Party. By contrast, in Japan this theme was pursued only by decidedly unorthodox Marxists; they were thinkers who refused to join the Japanese Communist Party (JCP) at the outset (such as Takabatake Motoyuki) or maintained an ambivalent relationship with the Party (Kawakami Hajime) or, having initially joined or supported the JCP and its activities, ultimately broke all ties with the Party to formulate alternative visions of socialist revolution (such as Akamatsu Katsumaro, the Kaitō-ha, and Sano Manabu). None of these thinkers was able to articulate his views on the role of spiritual cultivation in socialist revolution within the JCP and see them incorporated into the Party's program or methods of operating.

This observation is consonant with the fact that Japanese work coupling socialist revolution with spiritual regeneration tended to show powerful statist and nationalist proclivities, in direct contradiction to the Comintern's stance that there was no legitimate place for nationalism within the Japanese Communist movement. Mindful of the precedents of Japan's humiliating defeat of Russia in 1904–1905 and its protracted occupation of territory in Siberia on the occasion of the Allied intervention against the Bolshevik Revolution, Comintern leaders feared the prospect of Japanese militarism fueled by nationalist fervor, and they actively discouraged nationalism among Japanese Bolshevists. The logic of the Comintern position was straightforward. Lenin and then Nikolai Bukharin had argued that imperialism had divided the world into capitalist and "proletarian" camps. Thus, Comintern officials approved the use of nationalistic appeals to incite wars of national liberation in the less-developed, primarily rural societies that were being exploited by the world's bourgeoisie for raw materials and markets: Such wars would sever the critical link between the advanced capitalist societies of the West and the colonies and semi-colonies that sustained their prosperity. Together, the peasant masses of the East allied with the proletariats of Western bourgeois societies would bring crisis to the world capitalist economy and cause the long-awaited socialist revolution in Western Europe. In this scenario, there was no positive role for nationalism in mature capitalist societies. During World War I, Lenin argued emphatically but fruitlessly that nationalistic appeals were inherently reactionary in advanced capitalistic societies. Nationalism had played a positive historical role in abetting the birth of the nation-state, which in turn had nurtured capitalist industrial economies, and it would play a similar role in helping exploited societies such as China complete their own bourgeois-democratic revolutions through wars of national liberation. But in advanced capitalist societies in the early twentieth century, nationalism had already completed its historical mission and now merely impeded socialist revolution by turning the proletariats of the world against one another.[99]

Japan's position in this schema was ambiguous because of certain incongruities in its pattern of economic development.[100] On the one hand, by the end of World War I Japan enjoyed a flourishing industrial economy with a substantial concentration of capital and a vigorous presence of finance capital. At the same time, capitalism seemed barely to have touched the agrarian sector, which continued to be characterized by high rates of tenancy, extraordinarily small-scale agriculture, and primitive technologies.[101] This dualism in the economic sphere was mirrored in the political realm: The existence of constitutional government and a democratically elected parliament (the Diet) was counterbalanced by the vestment of sovereignty in an emperor considered to be divine, the extraordinary power of the genro, the Privy Council, and the Imperial Household Ministry, a narrowly limited franchise (until universal manhood suffrage was passed in 1925), and the ability of the military high command to override democratic provisions by appealing directly to the emperor.[102]

These authoritarian elements in the political system rested on the coherent and compelling myth of the *kokutai* (national polity) that was disseminated through the nation's universal education system;[103] and this myth would become a prime target for Marxist critics of the "backwardness" and the "semi-feudal" nature of Japanese politics. This was an organic conception of the state that combined elements of traditional Shinto religious thought, Confucian philosophic principles on politics as a moral sphere, and German *Staatsrecht* thought to legitimate the particular form of the Meiji state. Briefly, in this conception, the Japanese nation, the state, was a great family, at the head of which was the emperor. He, and ultimately all Japanese, were said to be descendants of the Sun Goddess, and the closer one was to the emperor, the greater one's claim to the divine.[104] This myth legitimated the state by identifying its roots in the spiritual and physical ties that bound all Japanese: Their very identity as Japanese was bound up with the existence of the state. In this family conception of the state, there could never be—as there could in the Chinese Confucian tradition— any conflict between the ethical values of filial piety (*xiao* or *kō*) and political loyalty to the emperor (*zhong* or *chū*), for *xiao* was subsumed within *zhong*.[105] The continuing deference paid to the *kokutai* conception and the authoritarian elements it supported were cited by Comintern officials and their Japanese Marxist supporters as evidence that Japan's bourgeois-democratic revolution was not yet complete and thus that a proletarian-socialist revolution could not proceed immediately in Japan.[106]

The Comintern, then, took mutually contradictory positions vis-à-vis Japan, and these were especially problematic for those who did not feel that the aspiration to socialism was antithetical to the indigenous values expressed in the *kokutai* conception. On the one hand, the Comintern appeared to discount the signs of advanced industrial capitalism in Japan and to prescribe for Japan's Marxists virtually the same two-stage revolutionary strategy as it offered to barely industrialized China. Nevertheless, fear of Japanese expansionism and recognition of the "advanced" elements of the Japanese economy led Comintern officials to insist not only that there be no nationalistic appeal in the JCP program but also that the Party actively work to eliminate the locus of national identity and focus of Japanese nationalism itself: the imperial monarchy. With some reluctance (notably on the part of Sano Manabu), the JCP accepted this element into its program,[107] and it was left to those outside the JCP mainstream to incorporate nationalistic elements drawn from the *kokutai* conception. Since the emperor was both the spiritual leader of the country and the focus of nationalistic attachment, it is not surprising that those concerned with spiritual cultivation should also have tended to exhibit strong nationalistic and statist inclinations.[108]

This observation highlights a third point of difference between the two cases. As we have seen, Chinese thinkers such as Chen, Li, and Mao tended to be indirect in expressing their misgivings about Western conceptions of modernity. Convinced that, whatever its merits might have been in earlier generations, Confucianism could not serve China's needs in the twentieth century, and rather more inclined than their Japanese counterparts toward a "totalistic" approach to philosophy and cultural values, Chinese thinkers exhibited great caution in disaggregating the separate components of Marxism-Leninism and selecting among them.[109] *Per contra,* Japanese intellectuals saw no need to reject an indigenous value system that had served the country well for generations. Their cultural heritage was one of eclecticism, selective adoption of attractive and useful elements from a variety of non-Japanese cultures—written characters from ancient China, Buddhism from India and China, and industrial technology from the West. These elements were in turn transformed, blended harmoniously with indigenous components, and themselves transmuted into indigenous elements of Japanese society. This tradition of eclecticism had enabled Japan to avoid China's fate under threat from the Western powers. The ability to borrow freely from the congenial ideas of German *Staatsrecht* theorists (such as Georg Jellinek, Johann Kaspar Bluntschli, and Hermann Roesler) and to reinterpret Chinese Neo-Confucian ideas on morality and the body politic in light of Shinto mythology on the divinity of the emperor[110] enabled the Meiji oligarchs to pursue rapid industrialization without risking significant social upheaval. The appeal of socialism in Japan, then, lay less in its radical departure from the old order than in its embrace of values believed to have been affirmed and preserved in Japanese life in the past— community, love of harmony, and the sacrifice of profit for the individual to the well-being of all. Many feared that such virtues were being sacrificed as the drive to compete with the West's industrial capitalism made remarkable gains in the late Meiji era. Endowed with a history of cultural syncretism and concerned lest the Western bourgeois society that gave birth to Marxian socialism have also left its imprint on Marxist-Leninist orthodoxy, Japanese theorists who treated spiritual cultivation were much more frank in expressing their dissatisfactions with that dogma. These Marxists felt no obligation to uphold the orthodoxy on historical materialism and the value and fate of the nation-state when they believed that genuine socialist revolution could not be achieved without devoting considerably more serious attention to the spiritual realm than Marx, Engels, and Lenin had exhibited.

Thus, while we discover in both China and Japan startlingly congeneric endeavors to inject spirituality into the Marxian revolutionary schema, differences between the two cases are also suggestive of how we are to interpret this pattern. In both instances, as in the work of African socialists such as Amilcar Cabral and Julius K. Nyerere and liberation theologians in Latin America and South Africa, this theme contributes to a broader challenge to Western assumptions that posit the essence of modernity in secularization, view history as unilinear and "progressive," and cast economic development in terms of a conflictual relationship between man and nature in the material realm. In China, this challenge emerged in an effort to recreate and reassert men's spirits, to cultivate their souls to rid them of the dehumanizing effects of a coercive interaction with the Western powers resulting in the subjected people's inability to perceive its own subjectivity in human history. The old indigenous value system bore the blame for China's failure to respond decisively to the external threat. Ironically, there the theme of spiritual cultivation was drawn from traditional sources, but it was wielded against those very antecedents; and the struggle against what was old and indigenous diverted attention from what must have appeared—from a traditional Confucian perspective—as the weakness of the entire dualism between matter and spirit in Marx and in the Western philosophical tradition as a whole. In Japan, the issue was never treated in "mainstream writings," nor—as in China or other colonial or semi-colonial societies in Africa[111]—was it pursued as part of a protest against oppression in terms of a need to instill in the soul a new spirit better able to fight oppression. Instead, it arose out of fear of the consequences of too much success in responding to the Western challenge by becoming "modern." As a result, the theme of spiritual cultivation was pursued with a more direct attack on Western assumptions about the nature of modernity and their expression in orthodox Marxism-Leninism. In Japan, as in China, however, the attention devoted to the need to target the spiritual, or "superstructural," realm independently of but alongside the reconstruction of the relations of production in the material world offers a new dimension to Marxist thought. The treatment of this theme by Japan's, as by China's, Marxists parallels but surpasses Gramsci's views on hegemony and revolutionary change by assuming and introducing into Western Marxism a unity between concerns that have been presumed to be separate, even conflicting, elements in Western thought since the time of Aristotle.

Below we shall analyze the issue of the spiritual dimension of socialist revolution as it was treated by Japan's Marxists of the interwar period. The method of discussion must differ slightly from our consideration of the Chinese case because the concern for spiritual regeneration found its way into the work of so many of Japan's Marxists that it would be both tedious and impractical to consider the thought of each in turn. Moreover, since none of those who treated the issue was able to do so within the JCP and integrate it into the party's program, it is not possible to identify the kind of threads that we found in China neatly linking the salience of spiritual regeneration for CCP co-founders Chen and Li with the subsequent institutionalization of the idea by the Party under Mao's leadership. What we can do, however, is identify stages in which several Japanese Marxists incorporated the theme of spiritual cultivation into their work; and we can see the culmination of this effort in the collapse of the JCP in the massive *tenkō* (renunciation of communist ties) movement of the 1930s and the systematic formulation of alternative Japanese socialist programs that incorporated the concern with the moral and spiritual cultivation that many Japanese Marxists found deficient in Marxism-Leninism.

INDIVIDUALISM, MATERIALISM, AND SPIRITUAL REGENERATION IN EARLY JAP-ANESE SOCIALISM. As in China, progressive intellectuals in Japan first imported Marxism as part of an undifferentiated complex of ideas intermingling Christian socialism, Russian anarchism, and other strains of Western socialist thought. By the 1890s, the Meiji oligarchy's industrializing revolution from above began to show impressive results; and the Meiji socialist movement was born, as many feared that this rapid economic change on the Western capitalist model might have ill effects on Japanese social structure and on traditional ethics emphasizing the well-being of the community and social harmony. Japanese intellectuals, then, turned to Western socialism in general and to Marxism in particular to help them launch effective critiques of Japan's increasingly capitalistic and militaristic features. Initially Meiji socialists of different persuasions were unified by opposition to the Russo-Japanese War and by their ethical concern about the negative effects of the Meiji Restoration; but, as more Western socialist works were translated into Japanese and the distinctions among the ideas of Marx, Mikhail Bakunin, and Ferdinand Lassalle, for example, became more clear, intellectuals favoring anarchist, Bolshevist, Christian, and national (or state) socialist approaches, split into factions. Since the family conception of the state served as the nexus of political as well as religious value in Japan,[112] the choice among the ethico-religious versus materialist and statist versus internationalist/anti-statist postures on socialism was closely linked to one's stance vis-à-vis the *kokutai.*

The significance of the ethico-religious component in Japanese Marxism was foreshadowed by the leading role Christian socialists played in the Meiji socialist movement. One of the earliest and most influential groups to introduce Western socialism into Japan, the Shakai-shugi Kenkyūkai (Association for the Study of Socialism) was founded in the 1890s by Christians associated with Tokyo Imperial University and the Unitarian Church in Hongō. This group, which transformed itself into an activist political organization under the new name Shakai-shugi Kyōkai (Association for the Study of Socialism), disseminated the ideas of a wide array of Western socialists, including Claude Henri de Saint-Simon, Charles Fourier, and Lassalle, as well as Marx and Engels.[113] The diverse group included the anarchists Kōtoku Shūsui, Ishikawa Sanshirō, and Ōsugi Sakae; Takabatake Motoyuki, who studied at Kyoto's Christian Dōshisha University; Katayama Sen, who subsequently became Japan's representative in the Comintern; Arahata Kanson, an anarchist follower of Kōtoku who became a leading JCP member; and Abe Isoo, Kawakami Kiyoshi, and Murai Tomoyoshi.[114] Although not all these men were baptized and practicing Christians, many had studied abroad, fallen under the influence of American and Japanese Christians, and were drawn into the socialist movement by the ethical and social reformist concerns of the Unitarian and Congregationalist Churches.[115] They expressed interest in the pacific and moral concerns of socialism by publishing translations of excerpted Western socialist works and articles about the West European and Russian social-democratic movements in the publication *Heimin shinbun* (Commoners' news).[116] In 1905, the pacifist cause having fallen by the wayside, the Commoners' Society was dissolved, the *Heimin shinbun* ceased publication, and there emerged a split between Christian socialists Abe, Kinoshita, Ishikawa, and others who launched the Christian socialist journal *Shin kigen* (New era) and those such as Katayama and Sakai Toshihiko who drew closer to the "materialist" socialism of Marx and Engels and launched a new journal *Chokugen* (Plain talk).[117]

The schism between "materialist" and Christian socialists is readily understandable: What had been introduced into Japan as Marxism thus far was the cruder version of Marxism as systematized by Engels in such writings as *Socialism: Utopian and Scientific*—conveying an unnuanced presentation of Marx's views on religion and consciousness and lacking the expression of profound humanistic concerns addressed in Marx's early writings. At the outset, however, early Meiji socialists saw no conflict either between their Christianity and the socialist aspirations expressed in the "Communist Manifesto" or between their socialism and the traditional religious and social values embodied in the *kokutai*. Indeed, each component reinforced the other. Yet, Christian socialists tended to be anti-statist: hence, Takabatake's abandonment of Christianity before his formulation of a Marxist state/national socialism.[118]

Vehemently opposed to the Russo-Japanese War, Japanese Christian socialists rejected social Darwinist assumptions as they were reflected in international competition among national states as much as their humanitarian concerns led them to repudiate them in capitalist economics. Early in the Meiji period, the Japanese intellectual world had been dominated by the influence of the "British school of economics," but, in the 1890s, Christian socialists played a leading role in developing a critique of British economics and its premise of the primacy of individualism and free unbridled competition. With their oath of higher loyalty, they were prepared to condemn a Meiji regime that invoked the "self-serving demands of the modern state" and "claims of national interest" to pursue rapid industrialization and military adventurism at the expense of large segments of the population left at the mercy of "free" and brutal competition.[119] This was a prominent theme in the two most sophisticated presentations of Marxist thought published circa the Russo-Japanese War—Katayama's *Waga shakai-shugi* (My socialism) and Kōtoku's *Shakai-shugi shinzui* (The essence of socialism). The capitalist principle of "free competition" was identical with the Darwinist notion of the struggle for survival; thus, relying on usurpation, deceit, and cunning, capitalism was in "irreconcilable contradiction" with morality and religion, in their view.[120]

It was this point that finally precipitated the split between Christian socialists and anarchists on the one hand and "materialist" socialists, that is, Marxists, on the other. If, as Kōtoku, Katayama, Ōsugi, and others claimed, capitalism was a systemic "evil," pitting atomized individuals against one another in ceaseless conflict, class struggle was unpalatable to many whose religious convictions sought reconciliation among men and women for many of the same reasons.[121] In accordance with Engels's work, Marxism was for Japan's socialists scientific socialism, and the theory of class struggle was associated with the concept of the survival of the fittest.[122] In this respect, Christian socialists who shied away from class struggle shared the same misgivings that prompted many early to mid-Meiji intellectuals to see in Marxian socialism not values complementary to the communalism of the *kokutai* but rather a threat to it. The challenge posed to the integrity of the *kokutai*, a particularistic conception premised on the uniqueness of Japan's divine imperial line, was exacerbated by the universality of Western socialist thought.[123] This claim was argued by "national-morality" spokesmen such as Tokyo Imperial University professors Inoue Tetsuji-rō and Katō Hiroyuki, and, as we shall see, the issue of particularism remained a stubborn irritant to which Takabatake, Akamatsu, Mizuno, and Sano would respond by modifying the Marxian conception of socialist revolution to accord with the special characteristics of Japan's *kokutai*.

Yet, despite the views of Inoue, Katō, and others, many Meiji (non-Christian) socialists saw no contradiction between their espousal of Western socialism and the values of the *kokutai*. Indeed, the dedication to traditional *kokutai* values of Meiji socialists such as Kōtoku—who was, ironically, executed for *lèse majesté* in 1911—led them to seek in Western socialism a remedy for their ethical concerns about the costs of rapid industrialization. Kōtoku, for example, broke with Christian socialists because he mistrusted what he saw as Christianity's typically Western attribution of higher priority to the individual than to the community. His individualism was that of the *shishi* (noble patriot), and was concerned more with the duties than with the rights of the individual vis-à-vis society.[124] To protect such traditional Japanese values, in Kōtoku's view, moral regeneration had to be a key element of a socialist vision.

Although Kōtoku leaned closer to anarchism than to Marxian social-ism, his treatment of the independent significance of moral regeneration prefigured its prominence in the work of the Marxists discussed here. Influenced heavily by Thomas Kirkup's *An Inquiry into Socialism* (1888), Kōtoku's stress on the need for moral regeneration enabled him to reconcile his socialism with a certain kind of nationalism by separat-ing the statist and national components of the *kokutai* idea. Kirkup had written that "especially in its earliest stages the industrial revolution acted without social or ethical control, and being made the instrument of private gain resulted in the excessive enrichment of the few, and the impoverishment and degradation of the working classes."[125] Like disillu-sioned intellectuals of China under Yuan Shikai, Kōtoku was profoundly disturbed not only by the moral degradation caused by industrial capitalism in the economic sphere but also by the corruption of bureaucratic and party politics in the political arena. For Kōtoku, as for many of his generation, party politics, traditionally suspect in Confucian thought as a means to the pursuit of private rather than public interests,[126] had helped to betray the high moral ideals—"'liberty, equality, and fraternity'"—of the Meiji Restoration. Thus, Kōtoku opposed the statist elements of the *kokutai* conception on the basis of the Confucian tenet that the benefit of the livelihood of the people was the guiding principle of politics.[127] Even when he condemned Japan's military expansionism, then, Kōtoku saw no necessary conflict between the *kokutai* and socialism. The true imperial tradition of the *kokutai* as exemplified in the Emperor Nintoku—whose "great concern" was the well-being of the people"—"was in complete agreement with socialism and absolutely in no way contradicted it": The goals of "peace, progress, and prosperity were common to both."[128] Inasmuch as they pursued these goals while calling for moral regeneration to oppose the perversion of the *kokutai* by bureaucrats and party politicians, Kōtoku and other Meiji socialists saw themselves as legitimate leaders of "a polity that realized the 'true meaning' of this new [Meiji] constitutional state system."[129]

The very same traditional commitment to spiritual cultivation and the dilemmas it posed for Japanese attracted to orthodox Marxism are sharply evident in the career of Kawakami Hajime. A graduate of and lecturer at Tokyo Imperial University (and subsequently at Kyoto Imperial University), Kawakami began his career as a leading figure in the dissemination of Marxian socialist thought in Japan in 1905. In an essay entitled "Shakai-shugi hyōron" (A critical review of socialism) serialized in *Mainichi shinbun* that year, Kawakami criticized prevailing schools of socialism and "social policy" advocates and presented his own interpretation of humanistic socialism. Here, Kawakami sought to achieve an eclectic interfusion of Western socialist thought and traditional Confucian and Buddhist ethical values. As Gail Bernstein's biography attests, by that time the enterprise of spiritual cultivation of the individual as a means of overcoming the evils of existing society had become the central motif of Kawakami's life as a Marxist.[130] Shortly after completing this inaugural series on socialism, Kawakami withdrew from academic life to join Itō Shōshin's Buddhist spiritual cultivation group at the Garden of Selflessness (Muga-en). Although he left the Muga-en after less than a year, his conviction of the importance of the self-cultivation of altruism pervaded Kawakami's influential *Tale of Poverty* (*Binbō monogatari*, 1916) and other writings. Kawakami's appeal to Buddhist and Confucian precepts concerning spiritual cultivation soon led others more acquainted with the complexities of Marxist economic theory (such as former student Kushida Tamizō and JCP leader Fukumoto Kazuo) to castigate him for a mystical and "old fashioned" approach to social problems and a superficial "bourgeois" approach to economics. Kawakami thereupon actively educated himself in Marxist economics, and, through the 1920s, he participated regularly in esoteric controversies over issues such as surplus value and historical materialism and edited two major Marxist serials, *Shakai mondai kenkyū* (Studies on social problems) and *Marukusu-shugi kōza* (Symposium on Marxism).[131] Nevertheless, Kawakami's determination to bridge Marx's historical materialism and traditional Eastern ethical teachings—he viewed Western culture as a whole as materialistic and did not see in Christianity sufficient reason to alter that assessment—delayed his fully committing himself to Marxism. This he felt he could do only after he had resolved the tension he perceived between the primacy of the material world in orthodox Marxism-Leninism and his own belief that spiritual or "mental (*shin-teki*) reconstruction" was the "premise" not the product of revolutionary change in the socio-economic sphere.[132]

Kawakami appeared to have resolved his reservations about historical materialism when finally, at age 50, he fully committed himself to Marxism by joining the JCP in 1932. Having made this commitment after over twenty-five years of study and self-critical reflection, Kawakami was one of the few JCP members who resisted the pressures of imprisonment and adamantly refused to *tenkō* (renounce his ties to the international communist movement). As his commitment to Marxism deepened during the 1920s, Kawakami increasingly endeavored to present himself as a materialist Marxist, one who subscribed to the orthodoxy that culture, religion, and ethics are products and reflections of the sphere of material production.[133] Indeed, Kawakami observed accordingly that Marxism itself was nothing other than "the product of the self-criticism of bourgeois society."[134]

Nevertheless, Kawakami's memoirs reveal that he never fully reconciled the conflict he felt between a vision of socialism premised on a scientific analysis of "objective" material reality and one for which the point of departure was a humanistic view of politics in terms of spiritual cultivation of a higher morality. Why did this dissonance pose such an intense dilemma for Kawakami? Why could he not, having accepted as valid Marx's critique of organized religion,[135] satisfy his other concerns about the role of "superstructural" elements—morality, spirituality, consciousness of self, and "'consciousness of consciousness'"[136]—by extending, in the manner of Mao or Gramsci, Marx's own insights on the ability of superstructure to affect the economic basis of a society? Kawakami was certainly aware of Marx's view on the potentiality of such a mutual effect, and, by the time he committed himself fully to revolutionary Marxism, he was well acquainted with, and cited heavily, Marx's work on consciousness found in early writings such as "The German Ideology" and "The Jewish Question."[137] In the effort to "prove" his Marxist credentials to his critics, however, Kawakami tended to use such writings to buttress his position as a "materialist," and he stressed a fundamental discontinuity with his early efforts to inject "metaphysical idealism" into the scientific realm.[138] Nonetheless, in his autobiography, Kawakami boldly portrayed his ethical idealism and spiritualism as forces drawing him toward Marxism from the very outset. "As Bukharin once said," he recalled, "a true Marxist is materialist in theory but at the same time an idealist in practice."[139] During his imprisonment, in resisting *tenkō* Kawakami cultivated his unyielding belief in Marxism in much the same manner that a traditional *shishi* cultivated moral rectitude and repudiated evils and temptations diverting him from the Way.

This was the imagery Kawakami employed throughout his life to describe his journey as a maturing Marxist. Unlike colleagues like Kinoshita, Kōtoku, and Murai, who were inspired in the same direction by American socialists Richard Ely, Edward Bellamy, and W. D. P. Bliss,[140] the spiritual impulse driving Kawakami toward Marxian socialism was rooted firmly in the Japanese religious tradition. The difficulty for him was that he did not (initially) find within the Marxist theoretical system a call to moral and spiritual self-cultivation that could respond to the social evils Kawakami aspired to resolve through socialist revolution. His instincts told him that social ills reflected the spiritual and moral emptiness in men and women as much as organized religion and immorality reflected the perversity of economic arrangements among men. If one acknowledged causality only in the latter direction, one would be left with a moral relativism that could not possibly serve to produce a genuinely socialist society. Ultimately, while he found insightful much of what historical materialism had to offer to an understanding of how men and women come to make moral judgments, Kawakami could not be satisfied with a position that held no standard of value absolute. Thus, when he was criticized severely by Sakai Toshihiko, a leading JCP member, for lacking a thorough comprehension of historical materialism, Kawakami responded in kind. Acknowledging that, as historical materialism suggested, morality did change with the transition from one mode of production to another, Kawakami also asserted that such a simple formulation was incomplete. It was true that moral or ethical systems metamorphosed in such a way that moral tenets in any given social formation served to legitimate what it was necessary for men and women to do to assure their survival and social reproduction: Ethics that did not find slavery or serfdom objectionable were historical examples of how morality evolved with other social and economic institutions. But, just as Marx wrote of variable and fixed capital, Kawakami asserted, one could draw a similar distinction between variable moralities and "absolute unchanging morals that exist in perpetuity throughout the universe." Without such moral absolutes as represented in a fixed general conception of the Way (*michi*), of God, Buddha, or Heaven, human society was unlikely to be peaceful and felicitous. Moral absolutes enabled one to transcend the morality dictated by the economic needs of the age or of the ruling class in any given stage of human development. Presumably, without them men and women could always contrive to legitimate man's inhumanity to man. Kawakami could not be moved to abandon his belief in the eternal truth of the Way, even if it appeared to others to be contrary to the logic of historical materialism:

In examining social problems, I always stress morality and religious faith. . . . Of course there is no doubt that there are contradictions and some incompleteness (*futettei*) in my thought. But, if believing in an unchanging, eternal, and absolute truth is my "sickness," I cannot possibly separate myself from it, because one should not depart from the Way for a moment. . . . Furthermore, I would like to give thanks to Heaven that I have been able to have such an unchanging, eternal, and absolute sickness in my body.[141]

Mistrustful of any philosophical posture that rendered morality contingent on economic necessities by recognizing only variable ethical principles, Kawakami found in Buddhism and Confucianism reliable guideposts according to which men and women could cultivate themselves the virtues necessary to sustain the self-realization that would be made possible by revolutionary change in the relations of production. As for Mao and Li in revolutionary China, the transformation of individual souls through the cultivation of virtue was an essential concomitant of socio-economic change, one that would not arise spontaneously as a consequence of the socialization of economic production. Although Kawakami was unique among orthodox Japanese Marxists in espousing this perspective, his spiritual commitment was echoed by a group of heterodox national-socialist Japanese thinkers whose Marxism likewise embraced rather than repudiated Japan's political and philosophical traditions.

SPIRITUAL CULTIVATION AND JAPANESE EXCEPTIONALISM IN JAPANESE MARX-IAN NATIONAL SOCIALISM. Kawakami's views were informed by Japanese religious tradition, and he shared with Kōtoku and other Meiji socialists the attraction to Marxian socialism for its trenchant critique of the capitalist economics that was destroying what had been of value in pre-industrial Japan. Kawakami, in adhering to *shishi* ethics, was as much a patriot as Kōtoku, and he maintained that his patriotism often led him to wish (as did orthodox Japanese Bolshevists) for Japan's military defeat for the benefit of socialist Japan.[142] Since his religious ethics were universalistic, however, Kawakami repudiated the particularism and chauvinistic nationalism that would lead other Japanese Marxists to articulate their concern for spiritual cultivation in terms of Japanese exceptionalism and a nationalist/statist interpretation of Marxism.[143]

Those who moved in this direction shared and extended many perspectives that we have already identified in the Meiji socialist movement; but the conflation of spiritual or religious value with the political legitimation of the authority of the emperor produced a repudiation of Western-style modernity on the basis of Japanese exceptionalism. These thinkers saw the *kokutai*—the state under the emperor—as a positive locus of value in Japan, and they opposed the elimination of the emperor system because it was said to represent the distinctive spirit or soul of the Japanese people which must infuse any future Japanese socialist society. Needless to say, this treatment placed these thinkers in conflict with the mainstream of the orthodox Marxist-Leninist movement that was committed to a vision of stateless, internationalist socialism. In defending their heretical views, Takabatake, Akamatsu, Mizuno, Sano, and their followers explicitly challenged not only the universality of the prevailing Western notion of modernity but also its validity in the Western context of its own advocates. To the extent that Marxism itself embodied this conception of modernity, their analyses surpassed the inventive revisionism of Gramsci and Mao on the nature of consciousness to call into question many of the basic assumptions that have constrained Western Marxist theorists.

We can discern these broader implications in the work of Japanese Marxist national socialists because they couched their assertions about socialist revolution in both general and particularistic terms. We see early indications of how the conjunction of doubts about certain general tenets of Marxism with the conviction of Japan's uniqueness engendered the heterodoxy of Marxian national socialism in the work of Takabatake Motoyuki. A relative latecomer to the Meiji socialist movement—he was attracted to Marxism by the *Heimin shinbun* published by Kōtoku, Sakai, and others—by the 1920s Takabatake had distinguished himself as the first to produce a Japanese translation of Marx's *Capital* and as the founder of his own national/state socialist political organization and the first of a series of journals dedicated to that cause. Takabatake came to Marxian socialism through the path shared by many Meiji Christian socialists: Although he abandoned Christianity to join the "materialist" socialist faction by 1906, as a youth Takabatake had converted to Christianity and studied briefly at the Dōshisha University in Kyoto.[144] He then participated actively in the Meiji socialist movement as an advocate of "direct action" under

Kōtoku's leadership and, after the latter's execution, joined future JCP leaders Sakai Toshihiko and Yamakawa Hitoshi in popularizing Marxist thought through the Baibun-sha publishing house and its organs such as *Hechima no hana* (The gourd-flower). Takabatake broke ranks with Sakai, Yamakawa, and other leading Marxists when the immediate aftermath of the Bolshevik Revolution convinced him that Marxism was in fact "statist" in theory and practice. In his view, a true Marxist movement was not dedicated to misguided utopian illusions of an internationalist socialism in which the state would wither away; rather, authentic Marxism properly called for a state socialist movement, and Takabatake dedicated the remaining years of his short life to promoting such a movement.[145]

Within six months of his death in December 1928, Takabatake's Marxian national socialist cause was bolstered by the *tenkō* of the so-called Kaitō-ha (Dissolutionist Faction), a group of young JCP members who had been imprisoned for their communist activities. Led by Mizuno Shigeo and Asano Akira, the Kaitō-ha renounced its ties to the international communist movement, and espoused a Japanese national socialist movement which would seek to establish a socialist Japan under the leadership of the Imperial Household. JCP party leader Sano Manabu, also in prison at the time, sharply criticized the Kaitō-ha initially; but, in June 1933, he and fellow Central Committee member Nabeyama Sadachika also *tenkō*ed, and Sano went on to enunciate his own version of a *kokka shakai-shugi* under the Imperial Household. Finally, the outbreak of war with China with the Manchurian Incident in 1931 appeared to have a similar effect on Akamatsu Katsumaro. Akamatsu had helped found the JCP in 1922, but shortly thereafter broke his ties to that Party. Through the 1920s and 1930s, Akamatsu assumed a variety of ideological postures, but, by 1932, he too had turned to national/state socialism as well. The arguments in favor of *kokka shakai-shugi* wielded by Takabatake Motoyuki in 1919 were echoed and embellished by his successors in this enterprise to address the spiritual dimensions of revolutionary change.

Although Japanese Marxists have not been eager to claim him as one of their number, Takabatake was among Japan's most inventive Marxists. Unlike many of his counterparts acting under Comintern direction within the JCP, Takabatake was widely read in the works of other Western political thinkers such as Thomas Hobbes, John Locke, and Rousseau, as well as in Marxist texts as yet untranslated into Japanese; and, like Akamatsu, he took pride in being "extremely critical" of points on which he believed Marx to have been in error, even as he steadfastly maintained his claim to be a Marxist.[146] Takabatake voiced serious doubts about the validity of Marx's and Engel's historical materialism, for example, which he saw as a reductionist view that attributed excessive causation to economic factors and material relations in explaining political and social phenomena. In Takabatake's view, the ability of so-called superstructural elements to affect the level of the forces of production had been severely understated in Marx's work. No doubt he, like Kawakami, was influenced in this view by the recent example of Japan's rapid industrial growth under the tutelage of the Meiji state. Nonetheless, Takabatake did not feel that one had to subscribe to historical materialism in order to accept Marx's economic theory and his insights into capitalist economics.[147]

Indeed, it was the critique of capitalism and its social and political consequences that made Marxian socialism so appealing to Takabatake and his colleagues in the Meiji socialist movement. The individualism, the primacy of the drive for profit, and the progressively widening gap between rich and poor—these were the foundations of industrial capitalism that threatened the historical integrity of the Japanese people and offended the humanitarian idealism and religious sensibilities of Meiji socialists. Western socialism—understood in opposition to individualism—proposed to eliminate these ills from society, and its Marxian version offered the greatest hope, since the prospect of revolution was said to be based on a scientific analysis of capitalist society rather than on utopian aspirations alone.[148]

Thus, Takabatake objected to capitalism, to bourgeois society in general, but from the outset it was clear that his departures from Marx were closely bound up with a sense of Japanese exceptionalism and a powerful attachment to the mystical dimension of the *kokutai*. Capitalism was most undesirable in Takabatake's view, because its rampant individualism and the economic differentiation and social alienation of one class from another that were both its premise and its consequence perverted and undermined the ties that bound Japanese to one another in the *kokutai*. It was capitalism, not socialism, that was "anti-statist" insofar as its motive force was individual profit, and it placed no value on the state. Unfortunately, however, as capitalism evolved, it could not destroy its enemy in the state, for the state too had become part of the "evil system" of capitalism itself.[149]

Realizing that his sentimental attachment to the Imperial Institution (apart from the state as an abstraction) was inadequate to support his state socialism, Takabatake evolved a sophisticated "functional" interpretation of the state on the basis of which he could repudiate Marx's and Engels's thesis of the withering away of the state under socialism. Drawing on his reading of Western social-contract theory, Takabatake argued that the notion of the withering away of the state manifested a utopian proclivity that conflicted with the rigorous science of Marx's economic theory. Marx and Engels had been wrong to assume that, because the state came to serve the interests of the upper class with the advent of class society, the state had arisen only with and as a result of class conflict. On the contrary, Takabatake argued, the state had originally emerged to serve the interests of all society. It existed not because of class conflict, but because men's natures were fundamentally evil. Men craved society, association with others, but their egoistic impulses constantly set them at odds with one another. As a result, for men and women to live in society, they required some set of organs or institutions to exercise the vital function of "control" or domination over their egoism. "The essence of the state lies in control (domination) . . . and control"—essential to achieve and maintain social cohesion—"precedes exploitation." The state, as the institutional apparatus that exercises this critical function of control or domination, did not evolve as described by Hobbes, Locke, and Rousseau, however. It was not an artificial social contract among individuals. Rather, the state "from the outset develops naturally and unconsciously out of necessity in the preservation of society." It was only subsequently, with the emergence of classes, that the state came to play a role in exploitation and oppression on behalf of the economically dominant classes in each social formation. Since the state originated not out of or because of class conflict but because of flaws in the nature of men, it was unrealistic to expect the state to disappear with the end of classes, for there was no reason to suppose that human nature would change just because of a change in the relations of production. Indeed, the outcome of the Russian Revolution revealed the "huge contradiction between the non-Marxist reality that the state does not disappear even though exploitation disappears and the Marxist theory that the state is the embodiment of exploitation[-based] domination."[150]

Marx had been correct, however, in identifying the effects of capitalist economics on politics. A set of institutions created to serve society had come to dominate it, Takabatake argued, echoing Marx and Engels, and the state had come to serve as the tool of the exploiting classes. The objective of state socialists—those who correctly understood Marxian socialism—was to purge the state of its exploitative elements and restore to it the purity of the legitimate function of domination.[151]

This argument was set in universal terms, but the advocacy of state socialism was intimately connected to Takabatake's sense of Japan's uniqueness. Marx's and Engels's account of the origins of the state was unsatisfactory in general; but still less was their approach positing the state as an oppressive authoritarian institution appropriate, in his view, to describe the Japanese state. On this point, Takabatake assumed a posture of Japanese exceptionalism echoed by Akamatsu, Mizuno Shigeo, and Sano Manabu that bolstered the role of spiritual cultivation in their reinterpretations of Marxism. This assessment of the uniqueness of Japan's state was rooted in the mythology concerning the Imperial Household on which the Meiji conception of *kokutai* had been based. In this view, the individualism of Western bourgeois economics and political thought was alien to Japan, as was the Western concept of the social contract as well as the Marxist critique of the state in its essence as an instrument of class rule. The opposition between the uniqueness of the Japanese "spirit" and this alien complex of Western ideas came to be expressed nicely by those who propagated the *kokutai* conception in official government textbooks in the 1930s:

> [T]he individualistic explanation of human beings abstracts only one aspect of an individuality and overlooks the national and historical qualities. Hence, it loses sight of the totality and concreteness of human beings and deviates from the reality of human existence. . . . Herein lie the basic errors underlying the various concepts of individualism, liberalism and their developments. The nations of the West have now awakened up to these errors, and various

ideologies and movements have sprung up in order to overcome them. Nevertheless, these ideologies and movements will eventually end up regarding the collections of people as bodies or classes, or at the most in conceiving a conceptual state, such things will do no more than provide erroneous ideas to replace existing erroneous ideas and will furnish no true way out or solution. . . .

Harmony such as that of our nation is not a mechanical concert of independent individuals of the same level that has its starting point in [cold] knowledge, but a great harmony that holds itself together by having the parts within the whole through actions that fit the parts. Hence therein are practiced mutual respectful love and obedience, endearment and fostering.[152]

These passages express the organic conception of the state shared by Japan's Marxian national socialists. The conception of the state proffered by Marx and Engels was consistent with the Western tradition of authoritarian political thought and reflected the individualistic bourgeois society in which Marxism was born, Sano argued. "[I]t was only because [Western society and values] became dominant, [that] elements such as egoism, profit-ism, materialism, and class-ism became powerful, . . . and the danger that [state] authority would be above and removed from social life became more serious than in any previous age."[153] Such a narrow class conception of the state was contradicted by Japan's historical experience.[154] Nevertheless, Sano and Mizuno claimed, "mechanistically applying historical materialism" and "adhering blindly" to Comintern analyses offered by Soviet leaders who were ignorant of Japanese realities, members of the JCP tended to "deny completely or at least underestimate" the value of "national (*kokumin-teki*) traditions and [peculiarities of] national character (*kokumin-sei*)." The Comintern's rigid view of the nature of the state in general could not encompass Japan's special characteristics. Yes, Japan was a capitalist society, but its so-called "superstructure" was not necessarily the same as what one would find in Western Europe. Japan was endowed with a "special spiritual civilization" and "special characteristics" to which the CP must respond if a socialist revolution was to succeed in Japan.[155] The Japanese Imperial Household, with its uniquely unbroken line of over 2,500 years, was not merely a tool being wielded by and on behalf of the ruling class of landlords and capitalists; the focus of "national faith," it was bound in a "special relationship" with the Japanese people.[156] As a locus of positive ethnic and spiritual value, and as a tool serving all Japanese to promote community against men's egoistic proclivities, Takabatake claimed, the state was the highest standard, the axis governing "man's moral, political, economic, and all other social life" without which a socialist Japan could not be realized fully and preserved against internal and external threats.[157]

Takabatake, as well as Sano and Akamatsu, couched their affirmations of the state in sufficiently general terms that they could be taken as endorsements of national socialism in any context. Indeed, although he repudiated fascism as a variant of, rather than a departure from, capitalism, Akamatsu praised Hitler for "recognizing that the nation-state was the highest embodiment of a *Volk*, sharing the same culture and historical destiny."[158] Yet, for him, as for the Kaitō-ha, Takabatake, and Sano, the most important attraction of Marxian national socialism was that Marx's thorough critique of capitalism be complemented by an appreciation of the state that suited the Japanese historical experience. In contrast with Western authoritarianism and with the orthodox Marxian thesis that the state existed solely as a product and tool of class conflict, the Japanese imperial state coincided with the *kokutai* and embodied the unity of the Japanese people. In Takabatake's words, "Japan's *kokutai*, along with the core of the state based on an Emperor [descended] from a single (blood) line for ten thousand generations, is always unchanging; the fundamental principle of his rule is *yikun manmin, kunmin ikke shugi* (one monarch, ten thousand people, the monarch and people are a single family); the successive emperors have been so benevolent that they refer to the subjects as their treasure and have displayed a unity of will . . . [between monarch and people.] . . . The brilliant essence of this *kokutai* is itself the source that has nurtured a fierce patriotic consciousness among Japanese that is rare in this world."[159] Thus, national/state socialism represented "an infusion of Marxist wisdom [concerning capitalist economics] into 'Japanese spirit' (*Yamato demashii*);"[160] while orthodox Marxist-Leninists, with their repudiation of the state and the emperor system at the center of the *kokutai*, imposed by the alien leadership of the Comintern, could not possibly appeal to the deepest feelings and spiritual needs of the Japanese people, state socialism would be based on the indigenous spirit (*seishin*) or culture of the Japanese.[161]

If Takabatake, Sano, and other Japanese Marxian national socialists believed that the advocacy of state socialism enabled the fulfillment of the original values of the traditionalist *kokutai* conception, they supported their position in terms that commended this interpretation of Marxism beyond the Japanese context. This argument appealed at one and the same time to "realism" and to spiritual sensibility. It will be recalled that Takabatake repudiated the orthodox Marxist conception of the state as incorrect and unrealistic: The need for the state was dictated not by the emergence of classes but by the most fundamental element of man's nature, his egoism. Marx departed abruptly from the scientific quality of his rigorous analysis of capitalism and fell into utopianism and Hegelian idealism when he claimed that the post-revolutionary state would simply wither away. His vision of proletarian-socialist revolution offered no account of how the egoism and fierce instinct for survival that alienated men from one another, eventually giving rise to class conflict and infusing the state with an exploitative and repressive character, at the outset, would suddenly disappear, eliminating the need for the regulative functions of the state.[162]

Taking up this issue where Takabatake had left it, Akamatsu and Sano drew on "Eastern philosophical perspectives" to propose the need for spiritual revolution to accompany the socialist reorganization of the economic organization of production. After Sano's *tenkō* in June 1933, the vision of an alternative national/statist interpretation of Marxism, one fashioned in accordance with the indigenous *kokutai* conception, not imposed by Russian Comintern leaders who knew little of Japan, began to take shape in Sano's mind. During his remaining ten years in prison, Sano devoted himself to studying Chinese and Japanese philosophical classics with the objective of systematizing his critique of orthodox Marxism-Leninism and explicating more fully the reasons for his disaffection with the Comintern-dominated JCP. As Patricia Steinhoff has noted, many *tenkōsha*, including most notably Sano's partner in *tenkō*, fellow JCP leader Nabeyama Sadachika, experienced their conversion as a "spiritual rebirth," a reawakening to humanistic consciousness from the "inhumanity" of the "cold" class analysis of orthodox Marxism-Leninism.[163] For members of the Kaitō-ha, Nabeyama, and many others, this meant a revival of a sense of self as Japanese, as a member of the unique community that comprised the *kokutai*, and a "spiritual struggle of self-repudiation" for having turned against the *kokutai*.[164] In his earlier years as a follower of Marxism, Sano, like Akamatsu, had not subscribed to the notion that there was any fundamental difference between a materialistic West and a spiritualistic Orient.[165] On rereading Confucian and Buddhist classics, however, Sano became convinced that such basic differences between the West European spirit—prizing rationalism, individualism, and materialism—and the Oriental world view—a pantheistic appreciation of the unity between humanity and the divine, a reliance on intuition rather than rationality, a view of politics as a moral sphere, and an appreciation of man as part of a social community—indeed existed. This meant that, for Marxian socialism to be applicable to the East, and to correct the shortcomings in it resulting from a one-sided emphasis on reason, individualism, and materialism, the positive elements of orthodox Marxism—especially individual self-consciousness—would have to be infused with Eastern philosophical perspectives.[166] In particular, Sano condemned the cold "intellectualism" of the West that allowed orthodox Marxism to treat society and the state in terms of abstract categories such as "class" rather than in human terms.[167] Eastern spiritualism could remedy this defect. The great lesson of the Confucian and Buddhist classics was that the liberation promised by Marxian socialism could be achieved fully only when men and women underwent moral and spiritual self-cultivation in virtue and repented the sins of their egoism. To borrow Takabatake's terms, for the state and society to be purified of their exploitative impure elements, the human beings whom society comprised must undergo spiritual self-cultivation.[168] The Buddhist tradition suggested that socialism was most fundamentally a moral and spiritual struggle between good and evil; and a socialist revolution required a "revolution in human nature."[169] Akamatsu eventually reached the same conclusion: The Confucian and Buddhist traditions dictated that social revolution begin with self-revolution in the human spirit, in a "permanent revolution" of sorts, directed against man's inherent evil tendencies:

> It is not the liberation of the self that is the most important in human life but the deliverance from the self. A real liberation of the self can come [only] after

deliverance. To try to liberate man before his deliverance is to bring human society down to the level of animals. In the face of modern society's confusion and corruption, we must open our eyes to the deep wisdom of the classical Oriental philosophers who taught deliverance rather than liberation.[170]

For Akamatsu, Sano, and Mizuno, then, socialist revolution was above all else a spiritual revolution. It was motivated not by "impure motives, lust for power, or material desires," but by the kind of universal "love" and "enthusiastic" faith one found among Nichiren Buddhists and Christians. Since any revolutionary movement produced, in the course of its struggle, the values and morality that would characterize the post-revolutionary society, Mizuno reasoned, the revolutionary party itself must undergo a constant "self-purging" of corrupt and evil tendencies. Only then could it function effectively as a vanguard leading all Japanese in the spiritual rebirth in which the revolution ultimately consisted. The profound spiritual sensibilities reflected in this view of socialist revolution also contributed to Mizuno's, Sano's, and Akamatsu's turn away from "internationalism," "class struggle," and the destructiveness of violent revolution. "Struggle for the sake of struggle," "destruction for the sake of destruction,"[171] were unattractive abstractions that seemed to have been rooted in the alien experience of Western capitalism and hence were not necessarily applicable to the Japanese context. The resurrection of spiritual values—which bound Japanese of all classes to their Imperial Household—and their placement at the center of the socialist vision promised a more complete restoration of values that were being eroded by Japan's emulation of Western capitalism.

CONCLUSIONS

We have seen that the issue of spiritual cultivation and regeneration as a key component of socialist revolution surfaced repeatedly among Chinese and Japanese Marxists in the first half of this century. In China, this revision was made in Marxist theory as part of an attack on the "reactionary" "feudalistic" values of traditional Confucian thought and culture; but it was also articulated in terms that recalled Confucian tenets concerning spiritual self-cultivation, and the nascent (alien) values of industrial capitalism were targeted by Mao and Liu during the

Yan'an period as bearing dangerous implications for those who would seek to realize Marxian socialism in newly industrializing China. The need for spiritual cultivation as part of an ongoing continuous process of cultural revolution in China not only appeared recurrently in the work of early Marxist thinkers but also became fully incorporated into CCP strategy and tactics. While it was not necessarily stressed uniformly in the later writings of Chen Duxiu and Liu Shaoqi, it is clear that, at the outset of the revolutionary process, these and other Chinese Marxists recognized the paramount need for spiritual preparation and the deliberate cultivation of the values to characterize the new society if a genuinely socialist revolution were to succeed. During the Yan'an era this belief came to be institutionalized in the form of rectification campaigns and criticism-self-criticism as mechanisms designed to propel socialism forward in the sphere of consciousness as well as in the reconstruction of socio-economic organization. Indeed, it might be argued that the kernel of the inspiration for what became the Cultural Revolution lay in this set of beliefs about the need to create a new consciousness, a new spirit to support and reproduce socialist society.

In Japan, by contrast, the possibility of developing this theme— likewise drawing on certain indigenous perspectives on spiritual formation—was ignored by mainstream Marxists of the Comintern-dominated JCP and left to unorthodox thinkers and activists whose critical spirit extended to Marxism itself with respect to such issues as historical materialism and the emperor system. Working this theme into innovative reinterpretations of Marxism, primarily in a nationalist direction, Kawakami, Takabatake, Akamatsu, Mizuno, and Sano explicitly linked their infusion of Japanese spiritualism into Western Marxism to a questioning of the value of modernity as defined in the Western Enlightenment tradition of which Marxism itself was a product.

Despite significant differences between the two categories of Marxists we have examined, certain patterns emerge. In both China and Japan, tensions within Marxist thought rooted in Marx's original conflict between the moral intentionality of the critique of capitalist economics and the claim to scientific probity based on detached observation of men and women in the material world were resolved in the direction of a move away from assumptions defining prevalent Western conceptions of modernity. The value of intuition, sentiment, the non-rational, were affirmed over the presumption of the supremacy of material concerns, rationality, and intellectualism as the motivating forces of human behavior. The assumption that new communities could be fashioned of individuals and classes on an international scale was challenged by faith in the value of and need for spiritual revival based on a sense of national purpose cultivated in an organic polity. Finally, the notion that human "progress" has been driven primarily by impersonal, objective, material forces has given way, in the thought of these Marxists, to the view that human will, consciousness, and the realm of the subjective, were not merely secondary and subordinate to the former but were themselves primary movers of human development. Marx had attacked Hegelian philosophy for being at its core merely "'the speculative expression of the Christian-Germanic dogma of the opposition between spirit and matter, God and the world;'"[172] but a good many Chinese and Japanese Marxists found unsatisfying Marx's effort to transcend this dualism by making one of its elements subordinate to and dependent on the other.

The significance of this pattern in the treatment of spiritual regeneration by Chinese and Japanese Marxists is underscored by the manner in which it has been echoed by spokesmen of other Marxian-influenced liberation movements outside Western Europe. We have already noted this similarity in the work of African socialists Frantz Fanon, Amilcar Cabral, and Julius Nyerere. But still more compelling examples are to be found in the indigenous liberation theologies of Latin America and Black South Africa. Theorists such as José Porfirio Miranda, José Miguez Bonino, and Gustavo Gutiérrez in Latin America and the Reverend Allan Boesak, Itumeleng Mosalo, and Simon Maimela of South Africa have gone beyond the observation that the message of Christianity requires radical action in the material world to incorporate, revising where necessary, Marx's critical perspectives on the evils of class society into a revolutionary new theology of liberation.[173] None of these theologians would take issue with Marx's claim that institutional religion has historically acted as an "opiate of the people." Indeed, they have condemned traditional Christian theology for "a false deliberate reductionism used to limit the understanding of the gospel to the 'spiritual sphere,' to the personal life, implying thereby that Christ's work only touches social structures tangentially and not at their root where social and racial classes struggle to free themselves from political bondage to which they have been subjected by the dominant groups."[174] Since Pope Leo XIII published the encyclical letter *Rerum Novarum* in 1881, Catholic social doctrine has reflected the influence of Marxist thought by criticizing the inequalities of capitalist society, repudiating the commoditization of labor as an affront to human dignity. In the words of Pope Pius XI's encyclical *Quadragesimo Anno* (1931), "Labor . . . is not a mere commodity. On the contrary, the worker's human dignity must be recognized. It, therefore, cannot be bought and sold like a commodity." Nevertheless, while deploring the consequences of trade in human labor in conflict among classes in society and urging the state to adopt social legislation to improve the lot of workers in capitalist societies, in accordance with its historical position as defender of the status quo, the Church has steadfastly rejected socialism, claiming that "[t]he right to private property, even of productive goods, . . . derives from the nature of man."[175] Emerging in contexts exploited by Western capitalism, liberation theologians in Africa and Latin America have challenged these limits of traditional Catholic social teachings, charging that the Church's traditional theology and its social doctrine have served the interests of Western capitalist powers and have made the Church a collaborator in the perpetuation of social injustice. Many of those who pose this challenge to the traditional theology argue that it is based on a fundamental misreading of the original Christian message through the distorting medium of ancient Greek philosophy. Such liberation theologians echo closely the skepticism of the Marxists discussed here concerning predominant Western cultural values and assumptions, perspectives that emerged "in the process of [Christianity's] adaptation to the Graeco-Roman world": the separation of subject from object, the distinction between the material and spiritual realms, and the notion that "there is an essence of God which we can know" through philosophical reflection. Moreover, they go on to argue that the alleged conflict between Marxism and religious faith is false. In their view, this claim is itself premised on the distortion of Christianity into a faith more concerned with other-worldly matters than with the lives of men and women in this world on the one hand, and a vulgar misreading of Marx's humanistic philosophy as it concerns religious faith on the other.[176]

Contemplating these perspectives of liberation theologians in Africa and Latin America alongside the work of the Chinese and Japanese Marxists discussed above, we can discern a fundamental complementarity between the Marxist call for socialist revolution and a religious (whether Buddhist, Confucian, or Christian) commitment to following a Way of the highest morality in this world. As liberation theologians have argued, this compatibility has been obscured by the simplistic understanding of Marx's view of religion that has long been the orthodoxy among Russian and West European Marxists. To be sure, the work of Gramsci and Lukács on consciousness and revolution has alleviated the burden of this vulgar interpretation of Marxism considerably; yet, neither of these thinkers challenged the assumption that Marx's comment on religion as the "opium of the people" represented the whole of Marx's thinking on the subject.[177] It is outside the West European context, where Western assumptions that modernity means the triumph of reason over "superstition" and the end of spiritual hunger with scientific and technological progress are not taken for granted, that we find the fullest appreciation of how spiritual regeneration on the basis of religious faith and socialist revolution in the relations of production can be mutually supportive.

This is not to suggest that there is no approximation of a more sophisticated and nuanced understanding of Marx on religion in the West. Religion plays a dual role in Marx's thought: It is both "an expression of real suffering and a protest against real suffering."[178] Accordingly, as Erazim Kohák has observed, "[I]t is a most problematic step from the claim that religion has been *used*" "as a mystified ideology to justify an unjustifiable social order" "to the claim that such use is its very essence." "Religious faith has to *be there* before it can be *used* to justify oppression," but the simple orthodox formulation neither accounts for the "initial reality of religion" nor recognizes that "religion has served as the ideology of liberation as often as it served as an ideology of oppression."[179] Indeed, the very unorthodox French socialist Sorel appreciated the role of religion and religious myth in achieving revolutionary change. Following Italian philosopher Benedetto Croce, Sorel saw "moral regeneration" as a vital component of socialist revolution and, like Rousseau and many Chinese and Japanese Marxists, questioned "The Illusion of Progress."[180] Neither Sorel nor his Chinese and Japanese counterparts examined here accepted the assumption that, with the empiricism of the Enlightenment and the burgeoning of scientific knowledge, men's and women's souls would no longer thirst for things spiritual as they had in the past. On the contrary, they seemed to share Alexis de Tocqueville's view that "'Religion . . . is simply another form of hope, and it is no less natural to the human heart than hope itself.'"[181] Such hope, a critical aspect of socialist consciousness, could move men and women to revolutionize their world.

This position reveals two fundamental polarities in Marx's own thought. The first has to do with an observation that we have already made with reference to Meiji socialism: Much of the appeal of socialism lay in the desire to preserve what was of value in one's social traditions, relationships, and cultural values that were being eroded by the steady march of technological change and the rise of industrial capitalism. In Marx's own protestations against the ill effects of industrial capitalism and appeal to the real precedent of communist society in man's distant past we can discern precisely such a conservative element. To borrow the language of S. N. Eisenstadt, "The original development of socialism was a reaction to the specific problems, to the forces and contradictions created by the great structural and symbolic upheavals of modernity as it developed in Europe. . . ."[182] This same impulse impelled Meiji socialists to lament the role of capitalism in subverting the humanistic and harmonious bonds of family and nation, and vitiating the spirituality of the organic *kokutai*. Secondly, there was from the outset a tension in Marxism concerning ethical values. Marx's own moral sensibilities were offended by the cruelty of industrial capitalism, even as he saw it as a progressive and "necessary" stage of human social development. Yet Marx also repudiated "abstract morality," insisting that no morality was "timeless and placeless," and that all morality was but partial, class morality.[183] This view was a logical outgrowth of what Straussians have called the modern "project," which was based on the assumption that "all human thought and action are the products of particular changing historical circumstances in which there is no 'natural right,' no fixed ground for reason or eternal and universal judgments."[184]

Yet men and women must somehow be capable of transcending the bounds of their particular historical circumstances if they are to recognize and struggle against the injustices that confront them. Otherwise they are left with the emptiness of complete moral relativism, an uncomfortable position indeed for those who would criticize existing society. Western Marxists who, like the founder, subscribed to Marx's materially constrained notion of consciousness have been no more capable than Marx was of resolving this dilemma; for they, working within this philosophical tradition were no more able than Marx to perceive the constraints imposed upon his perspectives by the context of the bourgeois society in which they lived. Thus, it fell to Chinese and Japanese thinkers operating outside the Western tradition to transcend its bounds to propose an alternative solution to the tensions described here. Their espousal of spiritual regeneration and the transformation of souls represented that solution.

EIGHT

Constitutional Alternatives and Democracy in the Revolution of 1911

DON C. PRICE

THE PROBLEM

Since 1981, the official Chinese campaign to build "socialist democracy" and the students' and intellectuals' unofficial campaign to establish democratic institutions have reminded us of the continued appeal of an elusive goal in modern China—a genuine democratic system. Unlike the question why Chinese civilization failed to produce a scientific revolution, the question why modern Chinese political revolutions have failed to produce a democratic government at least addresses the concerns of those who claimed to have tried. Where efforts were made and obstacles encountered, it makes sense to try to account for failure, even if the question is too large to permit a precise answer.[1]

A variety of answers, not necessarily mutually exclusive, have been proposed. Most of them can be grouped into two broad categories. One category stresses the constraints of the historical moment. Poverty and ignorance, imperialism and national weakness, and profound rifts in the national consensus added up to a crisis which discouraged the tolerance and patience essential to democratic processes.[2] From a larger historical perspective, Marxists have found social and economic development lagging behind the demands of the times, so that the bourgeoisie was too weak to attain bourgeois democracy, and even socialist democracy has been obstructed by the survival of feudal culture. From a non-Marxist viewpoint, others have noted a pattern of nationalistic, authoritarian, statist responses to modern imperialist rivalries in East and West alike.[3]

In this regard, Benjamin Schwartz's analysis of Yan Fu's priorities represents a landmark contribution. An element of liberalism is commonly thought to be essential to the functioning of democracy, but despite the appeal of British liberal thought for Yan Fu, his "concept of liberalism as a means to the end of state power [was] mortally vulnerable to the demonstration that there [were] shorter roads to that end."[4] Liberalism was ultimately of instrumental value in Yan's (and China's) pursuit of wealth and power, and he distorted Western liberal arguments in that direction.

Schwartz's earlier short analysis of Chen Duxiu's shift from liberalism to communism, and other scholars' studies of reform thought in the nineteenth and early twentieth centuries have revealed a tendency to view representative institutions less as an arena and instrument of internal political struggle than as a means for promoting solidarity, economic development, and national strength.[5] Hao Chang's later study of Liang Qichao likewise demonstrated that emerging nationalism amidst the dangers of the modern international world could clearly subordinate individual and political liberty to the interests of the nation. Perhaps this tendency was compounded by a traditionally paternalistic or authoritarian culture.[6]

The other category of explanation invokes China's cultural distinctiveness, suggesting ancient and deeply rooted values and patterns of behavior inhospitable to democracy (in particular, authoritarian attitudes inculcated in the very process of socialization).[7] If the heirs of this culture, including the advocates of democracy themselves, could neither fully understand nor implement the kind of political pluralism, individual freedom, and limits on the powers of leaders and the state which are indispensable to democratic government, this would surely help to explain its failure.

Attempts to gauge the impact of the Chinese psyche on Chinese politics may be overly ambitious, but we are on more solid ground, and perhaps still in the realm of deeply ingrained cultural traits, when we examine patterns of political behavior. It has been argued that an inherited propensity to factionalism constituted an immense obstacle to the establishment of constitutional government (arguably an indispensable component of modern democracy) and persuasive evidence has been offered for the immediate post-Yuan Shikai period in particular.[8] On the other hand, the role of the cultural factor has been challenged most recently by one study that stresses the vigor of representative institutions at the end of the Qing and the dawn of the Republican era, and notes that in the West as well, democratic institutions were the fruit of very protracted struggles.[9] It may be too early to say whether Chinese traditions yield less readily to democratization than those of the West did.

The question remains, in any case: Were Chinese, after all, too bent on unity and collective strength to tolerate a system of institutionalized open political rivalry? Was the pursuit of political liberty illusory from the first?

Perhaps not. Both Yan Fu and Liang Qichao, who bent liberalism to nationalistic ends, were enormously influential, but they were clearly identified with the reformist camp and do not necessarily represent a full spectrum of Chinese political attitudes in the early twentieth century. Revolutionaries, however nationalistic, were more inclined to downplay the risks of revolution in the pursuit not just of liberation from the Manchu yoke and imperialist domination, but from arbitrary and oppressive rule in general. Such liberation does not necessarily imply a commitment to the personal liberties (as opposed to collectivism) generally associated with Western liberalism, nor is it even a sure indication of a genuine commitment to democratic rule. Would-be democrats have not infrequently lapsed into authoritarianism, and Sun Yat-sen, for one, has been criticized for this. Still, the aftermath of the 1911 Revolution has been characterized as a time when "representative government and competitive elections among autonomous political parties came closer to dominating the political process . . . than at any other point in Chinese history." If this is true, the efforts to establish constitutional government at that time deserve close attention.[10] For central to the conflicts over the provisions of the first republican constitution and the implementation of constitutional government was the problem how to reconcile state power with real power in the hands of the governed and how to derive strength from democracy. Amidst these debates and struggles we have an opportunity to examine how concerned the would-be builders of the republic were to combat the threat of post-imperial tyranny,, and how genuinely committed they were to democratization as well as to national strengthening.

CRITICISMS OF QING CONSTITUTIONALISM

By 1911, the issue of constitutional government in China had for several years been the subject of intense debate and eager activity. Limited monarchy had been urged by reformers long before 1905, when the Qing government announced its intention to inaugurate a constitution at an appropriate time. The Qing dynasty, of course, had no intention of relinquishing claim to the traditional source of legitimacy, the Mandate of Heaven, but their position carried little weight among most of the statesmen, pundits, and activists who defended the cause of constitutional monarchy against revolutionaries. For most of the reformers, constitutional monarchy was advocated on the grounds of its practicality, rather than by invoking abstract principles of monarchical legitimacy or loyalty to the Throne. Even Liang Qichao, who preferred for a time to pursue China's modernization by relying on a transitional enlightened absolutism, no longer believed in the Mandate of Heaven. And Liang, too, soon returned to constitutional monarchy. The most important quarrels between such constitutionalists and the revolutionaries were whether the Manchu dynasty, whatever its claim to legitimacy, would surrender any real power under a constitution (as the reformers hoped and the revolutionaries denied), and whether a revolutionary republic would endure and effectively serve the interests of the nation (as the revolutionaries hoped and the reformers denied). Both sides implicitly agreed on the desirability of some form of democratization and on the need for an effective government. Reactions to the dynasty's political moves in its final few years illustrate this point better than the contending theories of the state in which the reformers and revolutionaries couched much of their debate.[11]

As the Qing dynasty formulated and proceeded to implement its plans for constitutional government, partisans of the Throne and representatives of certain vested interests in the bureaucracy worked to prevent the dilution of monarchical power. The Court's concern to preserve supreme authority while instituting a consultative national assembly directed official planning first to the reorganization of the imperial bureaucracy, but this immediately raised the specter of bureaucratic usurpations of royal power. Chinese emperors had for millennia fought to control their bureaucracies.[12] Checks and balances had been devised, albeit on behalf of the monarch, not the people, to prevent the bureaucratic abuse of power. Since the early Ming dynasty the imperial government had tolerated no prime minister, nor were the highest advisory bodies cabinets composed of the heads of boards (ministries). The prospect of confronting a European-style cabinet united under a premier and speaking for the entire administrative bureaucracy was not at all to the Throne's taste.

Some advisers thought the Court might use a national assembly to check the power of a cabinet, but the Court must also have been aware of calculations that a national assembly could serve as the basis for a strong cabinet.[13] Even so, elections were approved. And as it turned out, the provincial assemblies, elected in 1909, in turn elected half the members of the National Consultative Assembly first convened in October 1910, which within two months was calling for a responsible cabinet.[14] After hesitating briefly, the Court responded by announcing the early creation of a responsible cabinet, but then defined responsibility as accountability to the Throne. And then it proceeded, in edicts of 8 May 1911, to affirm its control over the largely Han Chinese bureaucracy by appointing a cabinet packed with Manchus, of whom the majority were members of the imperial clan, under Prince Qing as premier and with another Manchu as one of two vice-premiers.[15]

Since the dynasty's plan for constitutional government had from the outset openly proclaimed that supreme authority was to be reserved for the Throne, revolutionaries were less taken aback than gratified by the anti-Manchu ammunition the new cabinet provided them. But reformers, who had mounted three nationwide campaigns to petition for the immediate establishment of constitutional government, substantially shortening the Court's timetable, had clearly hoped to win real institutional power, and they were bitterly disillusioned.

Was the reformers' quest for power animated by a commitment to democracy? It would appear that in China, no less than Europe, efforts to vindicate the interests of subjects led to more fundamental considerations of the legitimacy of power. In the provinces, assemblies clashed with the Court-appointed provincial governors over taxes, railroad nationalization, foreign loans, and the management of public order. Dissatisfaction over the government's policies led to a search for means to change them, a search that inevitably expressed itself in terms of institutional alternatives. Had there been a national assembly in 1907, some in the lower Yangzi area argued, the officials responsible for the disastrous Shanghai-Nanking railroad loan would have been cashiered. If the rights of the people opposed to the loan were not respected, asked the Shanghai constitutionalist newspaper *Shi bao*, what meaning would a popular assembly or constitutional government have? Ultimately, "[w]hat had begun as quarrels with individual policy-makers ended up as a general questioning of the legitimacy of the imperial system."[16]

As provincial assemblies clashed with Court-appointed officials, the National Consultative Assembly clashed with the Throne's highest advisory body. Anger over the Grand Council's treatment of its recommendations on salt tax and education regulations led to an impeachment of the Councillors and a request that the Grand Council be made responsible to the Assembly, or be replaced by a responsible cabinet.[17] Thus, pressure for a system in which the views of the voters and their representatives could prevail reflected severe dissatisfaction with policies deemed injurious to the popular and national welfare. With regard to the railroad loans, in particular, the more general argument was made that unofficial private and public initiatives would promote local and national welfare better than centralized state domination.[18] Here we may detect an echo of Yan Fu's idea that individual energies needed to be encouraged for collective, national purposes. Indeed, most reformist protests voice no particular concern for the rights of the individual, or of the citizenry, divorced from the collective welfare. Thus the implicit test of a system's legitimacy was its effectiveness in serving the interests of the nation as a whole, rather than its embodiment of natural rights. The constitutionalists' contention was that the "people" could be relied on to make better policy and insure better administration than an emperor or a bureaucracy at liberty to override the people's will. To what extent they were aware that representative institutions rendered governments hostage to chronic tests of strength between contending groups within a divided "people" is not clear. Their willingness to pay this price of democracy remained to be tested.

At the same time that reformers' protests betrayed the weaknesses in their commitment to democracy, some revolutionary attacks on the emerging constitutional order were couched in even more narrowly nationalistic terms. The most significant commentary came from Song Jiaoren and Zhang Shizhao. Song, a founding member of the Chinese Revolutionary League (Tongmeng Hui) recently returned from Japan and working incognito in Shanghai, was the authority on questions of constitutionalism for the revolutionary newspaper, the *People's Stand* (*Minli bao*). Criticizing the new Qing Cabinet in June 1911, Song began by voicing the fear that if the Qing government continued on the same course, China would be lost in ten years. "A nation's strength and prosperity," he said, "depends entirely on the organization of the agencies that wield the power of the state; the cabinet, which brings them all together, is the head of the administration." As the agency upon which "the very life of constitutional government depends," a cabinet should provide united leadership and discharge clearly defined responsibilities.

Unlike other critics, who emphasized their dissatisfaction with the composition of a cabinet dominated by Manchus and imperial clansmen, Song paid a great deal of attention to its organizational defects. He found the all-important conception of responsibility totally confused. To be sure, the *ministers* had a responsibility to serve the *monarch*, but, he insisted, a *cabinet's* responsibility was *to the parliament*, and without a parliament to judge its performance, the concept of responsibility remained empty. This was not all. Arbitrarily modifying their Japanese constitutional model, the Qing government had cluttered up the cabinet with Vice-Premiers and a Managerial Assistant to the Foreign Minister, an obvious device, he charged, to enable individual bureaucrats to shift responsibility to others. With such a system, the purpose of unity of leadership and responsibility was completely subverted.[19]

In London, in the meantime, Zhang Shizhao had been writing articles on the English constitution and commentary on the Qing plans, and sending them back to the *Imperial Daily* (*Diguo ribao*), a legal news-paper published by revolutionaries in Beijing. While the place of publi-cation precluded an openly revolutionary editorial stance, Zhang's criticisms were hardly milder than Song's. Indeed, he anticipated the 8 May edicts with an article entitled "The Freak Cabinet." The essence of a cabinet, according to Zhang, was to bring the ministers of state together to formulate and execute a consistent policy program.[20] Respon-sibility for the execution of policy naturally limited its membership essentially to the heads of ministries. And consistency of policy necessi-tated outward unanimity and secrecy regarding internal debates and dis-agreements in policy formulation. The existing Qing Cabinet,[21] according to Zhang, was simply an organizational novelty, one more high council, an organ of state separate from, and above, the ministries, and bloated with its own staff, secretary, and recorder (compromising confidentiality), and non-ministerial "members" of indeterminate func-tion. Thus, even aside from the questions of its responsibility to a par-liament or its present ethnic composition, Song and Zhang found the very form of the Qing cabinets incompatible with the improvement in governmental effectiveness which the introduction of a cabinet should bring.

Zhang's criticisms were not limited to this initial response, however. In a series of earlier and later articles he described and discussed alter-native forms of constitution, arguing strongly for the superiority of the English model. One article directly addressed the views of the Qing government's Constitutional Commission that, in a country where the government is sovereign (*daquan zhengzhi zhi guo*), as opposed to the parliament, the government must control the parliament, not vice versa. Far from arguing that the government should not control parlia-ment, Zhang declared instead that a model twentieth-century govern-ment *should* wield *decisive* power. This did not, however, mean that the government should be masters of the people, as he proceeded to show by reference to the English system. In England, he explained, the govern-ment, that is, the Cabinet, very much dominates the Parliament, con-trolling the agenda of debate and the flow of legislative action. "I have not seen that any of the countries which the Commissioners character-ize as having 'sovereign governments' can compare with England in its government's ability to control the Parliament," he wrote. If a strong government was their object, he argued, they should advocate the English system. But there, he noted, the strength of the government was due to its being a party government. Why could party government alone attain such power? Because, he answered, only in a party government is the talent and wisdom of the cabinet so markedly superior to that of the other members of parliament that they will accept the cabinet's leadership.[22]

Zhang's argument skipped around the underlying premise of the Constitutional Commission, which was that the power of the *Throne* was to be preserved. But a clear consequence of Zhang's reasoning was that in order for China to enjoy a strong government, power would have to be in the hands of a party, not the Throne. A few days later, he quoted the London *Times*: "The source of all China's perils is her central government's incompetence and fragility. Everyone who knows China knows this, and doubts that there is any quick remedy." Zhang's remedy was party government: "A country cannot survive in the twentieth century without an extremely strong government and such a strong government simply cannot be attained except through party politics."[23] Party government meant representative government, he contended, echoing his earlier articles' argument that the the only way for a country to benefit from a party cabinet would be to have two large parties contesting elections on the basis of distinct alternative programs.[24] Here again, it would appear, representative institutions were recommended for the sake of national strength.

Japan and Germany were the models the Constitutional Commission proposed to emulate. Zhang's analysis of their constitutions followed that of the foremost authority on the English constitution, Albert Venn Dicey, who styled them non-parliamentary executive systems in contrast to Britain's parliamentary executive. According to Dicey, the non-parliamentary executive system had some rationale in federal states, which suffered from unavoidable inherent weaknesses anyway. He also granted that, with outstanding statesmen like Bismarck or Lincoln, a non-parliamentary executive system could occasionally produce impressive accomplishments. But on the whole, they were dangerous or ineffective.[25] In Zhang's opinion, Bismarck's tyranny over the

German Diet was both abnormal and impossible to duplicate and, in imitating Germany, Japan lacked a federation's rationale for separating the legislative and executive branches. Given the fiercely competitive nature of the modern world, even in such apparently successful states as Germany and Japan, he cautioned, such a system might not survive.[26]

Most important, in his view, the success of Japanese or German systems had required a particular historical juncture, with outstanding leadership supplying the impulse for modernization and the charismatic legitimacy to push it through in the absence of any popular, progressive political activism.[27] Lacking these conditions, much less the need for a federative system, China would be choosing a poor alternative if it attempted to follow a German or Japanese model.

Thus, as the Qing Court's plans for constitutional government took ever more concrete shape, both constitutionalist reformers and revolutionaries countered with demands for a representative assembly which would exercise effective control over the government.[28] Moreover, reformers and revolutionaries alike stressed the importance of a responsible cabinet for national strength and solidarity, even survival. While the reformers' rhetoric occasionally invoked the "people's rights," the word *rights* (*quan*) was ambiguous, and could be understood as "powers" in such a way as to suggest something useful rather than inalienable. As for the revolutionaries, Song, and even more explicitly Zhang, professed to find justification for the responsible cabinet system, and by implication, fully representative government, in the fact that no other system could meet China's needs for strong and effective government in a perilous age. In fact, Zhang proclaimed himself willing to "regress" to the Japanese model, or even an unconstitutional enlightened despotism, if those who disagreed with him could show how that would lead to a stronger government.[29]

THE DEMOCRATIC ALTERNATIVE

Such arguments for democratization do suggest a nationalist motivation which was not necessarily democratic at heart. On the other hand the nationalistic rhetoric itself may belie a predisposition to seek democratic rather than authoritarian remedies. It was possible to make an excellent *prima facie* case for Germany and Japan as models of rapid national self-strengthening. Can it not be, then, that in stressing the virtues of a responsible cabinet from the standpoint of national survival, an ulterior motive of many revolutionaries and reformers was precisely to counter monarchist arguments for German and Japanese models which they found unacceptably undemocratic? The writings of Zhang Shizhao and Song Jiaoren give some reason to think so, for both of them were concerned to link or reconcile the independent or even potentially conflicting values of democracy and national strength.

The surviving 1910–1911 articles of Zhang Shizhao suggest, indeed, that he was no less concerned with political justice than with national survival. In fact, his first article on constitutional government, entitled "What is 'No Taxation without Representation'?" invoked Edmund Burke's doctrine of the natural right to dispose of one's property in order to show the direct relation between the freedom-loving British and American spirit of constitutionalism and the idea that the people must exercise the right to tax themselves. Zhang concluded with a poignant reminiscence. "If I admire the British and American ideals and hope to apply their principles," he wrote, "how can I relate them to our existing fiscal arrangements? Unfortunately, I can find no relation between such disparate things. I remember the expression of rage on my old father's face when we took 3,000 cash as the equivalent of one silver tael to the county office to pay the tax on our few *mou* of poor land. . . Suddenly descending from Burke's sublime doctrines, I fear to think how ridiculous this reality would appear to him."[30]

Shortly thereafter, Zhang responded to reports of the illiberal new Qing press code with a ringing affirmation of the freedom of the press, British style. Here he invoked Dicey's authority on the principle that the function of the law was to define crimes to be punished upon conviction, not to prevent transgressions by controlling behavior. *"If the government is forever monitoring the people out of a constant concern lest they break the law, it treats the citizens no better than animals or criminals* . . . [All sorts of preventive detention would be justified on this principle, and] how unimaginably imperiled would human rights (*renquan*) be!" Publishers' guarantee deposits, he stated, were nothing but payments against fines to be levied on crimes which might be committed.[31]

Moreover, freedom of the press was, like freedom of speech and correspondence, not a public but a private right. Once the government
invaded private rights with compulsory licenses, Zhang wrote, it could
promulgate a code of sexual morality, require everyone to pay for a sex
license, and demand daily reports from husbands and wives on the previous night's activities.[32]

From Burke and Dicey, Zhang had enthusiastically appropriated two
important principles of the English tradition: that freedoms are to be
abridged only to bring a suspect to trial or as punishment for a proven
crime, and that the state may use the people's property only to the
extent, and in ways, that they authorize. "Our people's sovereignty (*zhu-
quan*) was stolen by the government thousands of years ago," he wrote,
"and it goes without saying that it will be hard to retrieve . . . [but in the
absence of unremitting effort on our part,] what fears or scruples will
deter this wretched government from continuing its usurpations!"[33]

Zhang's espousal of personal and political liberties had not always
coexisted so easily with his nationalism. He had for several years, in
fact, set them aside in favor of pursuits he judged more helpful to the
nation. In 1905, disillusioned with his own inchoate revolutionary radicalism and convinced that China required something like Japan's level
of education more than political revolution, Zhang Shizhao had resisted
his friends' urgings to join the Revolutionary League and had gone to
Scotland to study. His 1911 articles clearly reflect a happy discovery
that the revolutionary goal of representative government not only
embodied important autonomous values but was, in the form of majority party government, an ideal instrument for the pursuit of national
strength.

Song Jiaoren's evolving political thought likewise reflects an independent element of protest against power wielded in defiance of the wishes
of the ruled. His growing disenchantment with the Japanese model of
national strengthening and his growing sensitivity to institutional guarantees of genuinely representative government reflect a serious effort to
achieve national strength without sacrificing the ultimate values of a
kind of universal political progress he saw as essentially democratic.

His first public pronouncement on constitutional government in
1905 expressed his understandable suspicion that the Manchus would

never yield real power, whatever trappings of constitutionalism they adopted to divert their critics' attacks. Song's anti-Manchuism probably also drew his attention to provisions in the political systems of Prussia and Russia, which, he noted, reserved real power to the monarchies, despite the existence of representative national assemblies.[34]

Such comments need not be read as evidence that Song was committed to liberal government as early as 1905. Indeed, Japan's triumph over Russia in 1905 made an extremely favorable impression on Song, in exile there at the time. His initial admiration of Japan was based not on the virtues of her constitutional system but on the patriotism and civic and martial virtues of her people, assiduously fostered by her leaders. For this approach to government, with its stress on paternalistic leadership and popular morale, he could find support in Western as well as Eastern wisdom, and he was for a time inclined to the view that institutions were of strictly secondary importance compared to the personal qualities of a people.[35]

The more Song learned about Japanese politics, however, the less he was inclined to dismiss institutions. By 1911, thoroughly disillusioned with the Japanese government's abuse of its power, he pronounced Japan a constitutional country in name only, ruled in reality by cliques of militarists. This judgment appeared in his September 1911 articles in *The People's Stand* on the change of the Japanese Cabinet. His attack on the Japanese political system was clearly directed against the Qing plan to preserve monarchical power through an imperially granted Japanese-style constitution.[36]

By this time Song had long been alert to the ways in which different constitutional systems could either give or deny real power to the electorate. The existing transitional organs of the National Assembly and the prime ministership only encouraged his suspicions that China's people would win no power under a Qing constitution, for the National Assembly was nothing but an administrative organ, and the Throne could appoint or dismiss the prime minister at will.[37]

But as Song considered the ways in which the people might wield power, he was forced also to consider the idea that giving power to the people meant taking power from the government, with a consequent weakening of the nation. Among other sources, Song's recently completed translation of Kobayashi Ushisaburô's massive treatise, *Comparative Public Finance*, drew his attention to this problem.[38]

Kobayashi clearly showed the historical necessity for elected legislatures to gain some control of the national purse—to approve taxes and expenditures—if the people were to be protected from arbitrary and oppressive government.[39] The power of the purse had long been recognized by Chinese revolutionaries and reformers alike as a powerful weapon in people's struggles for control over their governments.[40] But it was a clumsy and dangerous weapon, because it threatened paralysis of a government whose budget the legislature could refuse to approve. Kobayashi cited examples of deadlocks in such systems as the American and Australian, where the legislature had theoretically unrestricted control over the budget, and he pointed out that the same problem in France exposed that country to grave international danger. "Yet this is generally the effect of the budgetary process under the European and American constitutions," he wrote, "which they can remedy only where they interpret the legislature's power as limited."[41] Thus, in some countries, including England, fixed or long-term expenditures (although theoretically open to legislative revision at any time) were effectively removed from annual budgetary review while the Meiji constitution, which did not treat the budget as legislation at all, protected the Japanese government from budgetary pressure on the part of the Diet.[42] The effect of Kobayashi's analysis was to suggest that Western countries (including England) avoided the difficulties of treating the budget as legislation to the extent that their practice approximated Japanese theory. Japan may have pointed the way to fiscal and political stability for Kobayashi, but for Song Japan was no model of constitutional government. He had concluded, in fact, that the system of executive budgeting which bypassed legislative control enabled the Japanese government to manage finances and the national economy in ways contrary to the people's interests and wishes, and over which they had no control.[43]

Kobayashi's satisfaction with the Japanese system reflected a judicious statist attitude. He recognized the value of struggles over the purse in establishing constitutional government. He deplored the oppressive and arbitrary mobilization of national resources in the pursuit of rulers' personal ambitions. He admired Adam Smith's contributions to the modern understanding of the relations between free enterprise, the national economy, popular welfare, and state finance. But he also saw an expanded role for the state in the national economy as the wave of the future. He cited with evident approval the ideas of German theorists influenced by English budgetary practice, according to which the "life or death" of the state should not be held hostage to annual legislative budgeting. Thus, although he was critical of the Japanese government's recent financial policies, he did not suggest that greater legislative power was the remedy.[44]

While his treatment of the history of finance could, up to a point, support Song's democratic and nationalistic inclinations, Kobayashi saw a conflict between the powers of the people's representatives and the effective conduct of the nation's business by the government, and favored the government. Song, to the contrary, felt that the government's freedom from control by the legislature was itself a threat to the national interest. How, then, could the requirements of national strength be reconciled with democracy? Certainly Kobayashi's association of German theory with English practice could hardly commend the English model to Song. If Kobayashi's work could only pose a dilemma for Song, Zhang Shizhao, to whom Song acknowledged a great debt of gratitude for his articles on English government, provided an answer.[45]

Directly addressing the connection between the legislature's power of the purse and the coordination between the legislature and the executive, Zhang cited the British constitutional authority Walter Bagehot. In Bagehot's analysis, civilized government depended on the support of the legislature, especially in the matter of taxation. The government required taxes to do its work, and it was up to the legislature to impose them by its laws. "If the persons who have to do the work are not the same as those who have to make the laws," he wrote, "there will be a controversy between the two sets of persons. The tax-imposers are sure to quarrel with the tax-requirers." Recognizing a built-in tendency to conflict between an executive which could be "crippled" by legislative resistance and a legislature "spoiled" by its lack of responsibility for the performance of the executive, Bagehot located the nub of the problem in the question whether the two "sets of persons" are the same. The American separation of powers, he argued, led to quarrels and difficulties. The English union of legislative and executive eliminated them.[46]

Thus, for Bagehot and for Zhang, the answer to the problem of maintaining representative control without impairing executive effectiveness certainly did not lie in close *parliamentary* control of the budget. To be sure, Zhang contended that the principle of no taxation without representation lay at the heart of the English constitution. It was not as if taxes and representation were two things, he argued, one given by the people to the government and the other given by the government to the people. Rather, taxes *remained* the people's money and the government consisted of representatives chosen by them to manage that money.[47] But despite the importance of this sacred principle, Zhang did not contend that the British budgetary process in itself enabled the parliament to control the government, and Song knew already, from Kobayashi if not from other sources, that this was not the case.[48]

The answer to the contradiction between executive and legislature and, by extension, between strength and democracy, lay rather in the unity of the parliament and the cabinet. It was not by wielding the club of budgetary control that parliament controlled the government; rather, the cabinet's dependence on parliament for its very incumbency gave parliament firm, albeit indirect, control over the budget. In Zhang's analysis, England's was the most representative government possible, because there was no power higher than that of the elected representatives. The parliament was, as he put it, "omnipotent."[49] Consequently, the English system precluded destructive deadlocks between the branch of the government charged with conducting the business of the state and the branch charged with ensuring that this was done in accordance with the interests of the people. And while the cabinet had sufficient power to conduct its business expeditiously, the state further derived the strength that flowed from unity with its people. It was precisely the prospect of this kind of solidarity uniting all Chinese, from commoners to the highest officials, that, he contended, China's foreign oppressors feared.

Essential to the functioning of such a system was the party cabinet and competition between two major parties for an electoral majority.

The majority view in parliament guided the cabinet because the cabinet was drawn from the leaders of the majority party. The alternative—a cabinet of bureaucrats—Zhang argued, could hardly coexist with a real parliament.[50] This led him into a further discussion of real political parties and the functioning of a two-party system. Real parliamentary parties, he explained, existed to offer the voters real alternatives on important policy matters so that the policies of the party in power would be generally acknowledged as representing the views of the majority in the nation, while the party out of power could continue to argue for its policies in an effort to replace the party in power.[51]

Reiterating these points in other articles, Zhang explicitly criticized the American system as one which, by its separation of the three branches, weakened the government. In fact, he contended, with the anomalous exception of Japan, non-party cabinets were successful only in federations (a weak system to begin with) like Germany and America, and even there, a party cabinet could probably function more effectively.[52]

The English union of parliament and cabinet thus provided Zhang with a way to achieve the maximum policy coherence, operational efficiency, and financial stability without sacrificing government responsiveness to popular opinion.

Song's full debt to Zhang was not immediately evident. Most of Song Jiaoren's commentary on constitutional issues in 1911 was written too early to have been influenced by the articles in which Zhang explained Bagehot's and Dicey's ideas. Moreover, Song's attacks on the government to mid-1911 took a somewhat different tack from Zhang's. Zhang wrote as if China's provincial and national assemblymen could establish the English system in China in the teeth of Court opposition. For Song, it was important to show that efforts to establish any representative government would be frustrated as long as the Manchu dynasty remained. For his purposes it was enough, then, to show how disastrously the Qing constitutional guidelines deviated from sound constitutional provisions, for which he took the responsible cabinet system as a standard. Not only had the Court compounded the evils of their "semiautocratic" Japanese model by adding features that favored the evasion of administrative responsibility. It had violated its own edicts in adopting budgetary measures without the consent of the National

Assembly. "The budget system, the levying of taxes and contracting of debts are the basic elements of national financial administration," he wrote. "Not a single constitutional country denies its legislative organs the power to approve them, and thus to check the executive offices and prevent them from taking decisions at will. It is in this principle that the spirit of constitutional government resides."[53]

Perhaps the issue could not have been put much differently given Song's concern to show that the Court would not yield any power to representative organs. Before reading Zhang's later articles Song was still inclined to identify the purse strings with the reins by which the people could control their rulers, and was unprepared to show how the disadvantages of an adversarial relationship between legislature and government might be overcome.[54] If Song was still unable to see how ingeniously the English system married democracy and strength, it was perhaps because he was only slowly coming to see England's democratic potential.

In the meantime, Song had taken a keen interest in another series of articles by Zhang Shizhao, which he reprinted in his own newspaper.[55] These articles reported the recent struggles in the Parliament between Commons and the House of Lords, which with its veto had blocked policies strongly favored by the people's elected representatives. In 1910, this struggle approached its climax, culminating with a decisive victory for Commons in Asquith's parliamentary reform of 1911. Zhang's series broke off before the new Parliament was convened, but Song reported on the final victory in one of his most important articles, "England's Parliamentary Revolution."

England, for Song, had been a strongly conservative country, in which the power of the aristocracy severely limited the power of the people. The victory of Commons, however, provided clear evidence of the irresistible march of progressive trends throughout the world in the twentieth century. Not only had the principle of democracy triumphed; the reform had also permitted the passage of socially progressive tax measures, reminiscent of the Revolutionary League's goal of land equalization. Song's omnivorous readings in psychology, anthropology, and history had equipped him with a view of progress as the product of large, impersonal trends and forces, operating through a series of stages. What the English example showed and what Song so ecstatically hailed in this article was the universal modern trend from partial representative government to fully democratic government committed to social and economic justice.[56] Indeed, the developments in English politics may have reminded Song of the hopes voiced by his colleague Zhu Zhixin in 1906, that the workers' political movement might capture a parliamentary majority and carry through a peaceful social revolution in England within twenty years.[57] If England's conservative traditions had distracted Song's attention from the virtues of her system as a model for China, the parliamentary reform of 1911 quickly overcame that difficulty, and developments in China before the end of the year were to confirm Song in his conviction that China must adopt the responsible cabinet system.

THE RESPONSIBLE CABINET SYSTEM AFTER THE REVOLUTION

As the constitutionalists' patience with the Qing government wore thin and China edged closer to revolution, prospects for cooperation between revolutionaries and constitutionalists began to brighten. In advocating a responsible cabinet in a legal Beijing newspaper, Zhang Shizhao and its revolutionary publishers must have been intent on driving a wedge between reformers and government by encouraging constitutionalist demands which the government would be certain to refuse. Song's *The People's Stand* pursued a similar course, applauding the insistence on self-government but calling on the constitutionalists to give up on the Qing. Thus, disregarding Sun Yat-sen's blueprint for a transitional revolutionary dictatorship, major organs of revolutionary propaganda were, by 1911, endorsing a system that the constitutionalists found attractive. Such propaganda was tribute to the vigor and strength of the reformers' constitutionalist movement, and it provided a natural basis for collaboration between revolutionaries and constitutionalists when the Revolution broke out.

Collaboration took concrete form in the wake of the Wuchang mutiny on 11 October, as assemblies in province after province declared independence of the dynasty, and revolutionaries worked with them to establish interim governments. On the question of the national government, however, it took some time to establish a consensus on the nature of the new polity. Sun Yat-sen was committed to the separation of powers in a five-power system, some provincial leaders favored provincial autonomy in a federal system, and many in the revolutionary camp felt the need for strong and relatively unfettered executive leadership.

Such leadership was written into the provisional constitution of the revolutionary government of Hubei which Song Jiaoren helped draft in early November. It provided for a military governor elected independently of the legislature, and vested in him the command of the armed forces and the authority to appoint his executive officers without consulting the legislature. Although the budget was to be approved by the legislature, it was to be drawn up by the executive, which was also empowered to take extraordinary finance measures subject to post facto ratification by the legislature.[58]

These provisions testify eloquently to the revolutionaries' enthusiasm for executive strength at the expense of legislative control, but they probably are a less accurate indicator of Song's constitutional ideals at the time than of the immediate requirements of the revolutionary situation.[59] The campaign to establish a responsible cabinet system of government that Song began in late November would occupy him until his death. In the process, he had first to overcome widespread sentiment among his own fellow revolutionaries in favor of the presidential system as well as suspicions that he himself was angling for the post of premier. To the extent that he succeeded, it was due more to their fears of Yuan Shikai as president than to his own persuasiveness.[60]

Song's views clashed with those of Sun Yat-sen. By late December of 1911 when Sun Yat-sen returned to China to claim the presidency, his comrades had long since offered it to Yuan Shikai, a man generally favored by constitutionalists, pending successful negotiation of the transfer. Sun himself, puzzlingly enough, insisted on the eve of his election that the Tongmeng Hui work for the establishment of a presidential system, arguing that an elected chief of state, particularly at such a time of crisis, should not be reduced to a figurehead in a parliamentary system. The leader, he felt, should be free to act decisively.[61] Despite vigorous opposition on Song's part, Sun Yat-sen's demand carried the day. But by early March, when a provisional constitution was hastily passed just before Yuan was to succeed Sun, it represented a cross between Song's conception of a responsible cabinet system and Sun Yat-sen's presidential system, a compromise designed both to link the executive to the legislature and to prevent a still rather strong president from abusing his authority.[62]

Despite the hybrid nature of the provisional constitution, the revolutionary camp characterized it as a responsible cabinet system. Zhang Shizhao, writing in Shanghai for *The People's Stand*, continued to advocate this system. And when constitutional issues arose over Yuan's exercise of his authority in mid-1912, the Revolutionary League headquarters in Beijing would proclaim that the provisional constitution was modeled on the French. The legislature, they argued, was the highest organ of government, and the real power was vested in the cabinet, as the locus of executive responsibility subject to supervision by the legislature. With that responsibility, embodied in the requirement that presidential orders be countersigned by the cabinet, went the exposure to attack and impeachment by the legislature. While the cabinet's responsibility shielded the presidency from such indignity, it rested on the power of countersignature, without which "the cabinet would be no more than a tool of the president, and the whole meaning of a responsible cabinet would be lost."[63] The reality of politics in 1912 defied this theory, however, and in a draft platform written for the victorious Nationalist Party in 1913, Song Jiaoren was to make the establishment of a truly unitary responsible cabinet polity the first major plank. China currently operated under the "name, but not the reality, of a responsible cabinet system," he wrote, and he proposed to rectify that by giving the cabinet sole authority for drafting executive orders and putting it under a prime minister elected by the lower house.[64]

In the meantime, constitutionalist support for a responsible cabinet constitution continued to solidify. Even before the Wuchang uprising, perhaps anticipating that the dynasty would persist in a suicidal course, Meng Sen and his Friends of the People Translation Society had begun the study of James Bryce's famous *The American Commonwealth*, a distinguished British ambassador's comprehensive analysis of American politics which became a standard textbook in the English-speaking world and had long been available in Japanese translation. In October

1911, a Chinese translation was undertaken by Meng and eight colleagues. Some of them were founding members of the Tongyidang, which proceeded to publish the first volume when it was completed in April 1912, as part of the party's efforts to provide political education to the citizens of the new Republic. At the same time, the Tongyidang published another translation by the same Translation Society on the French constitutional system. It is hard to escape the inference that, once the goal of a parliamentary system under a constitutional monarchy was no longer an option, the question whether the Republic should follow the presidential or cabinet model became a matter of intense interest to former constitutionalists. It is unknown whether the translation on France survives, nor what the original was. The translation of Bryce does survive, and it did not present the reader with a positive evaluation of the American constitutional system, which the translators took to be the foremost example of a presidential government.

Like Dicey, to whom his book was dedicated, and Bagehot, whose basic comparison of Britain and America he follows, Bryce was a firm believer in the overall superiority of a parliament and a responsible cabinet. This is not to say that he did not admire the government and politics of the United States. Indeed, he greatly appreciated the success of the Americans in avoiding tyranny, but he thought they had done so partly in spite of, and partly thanks to, a seriously defective and ineffective system.[65] Having listed the results of the American separation of legislative and executive powers, he concluded:

> We may include these defects in one general expression. There is in the American government, considered as a whole, a want of unity. Its branches are unconnected; their efforts are not directed to one aim, do not produce one harmonious result. The sailors, the helmsman, the engineer, do not seem to have one purpose or obey one will, so that instead of making steady way the vessel may pursue a devious or zig-zag course, and sometimes merely turn round and round in the water.

This system, he declared, "work[ed] better than [it] ought to work," thanks largely to the people's peculiar political talents and ability to "mak[e] the best of bad conditions." "Such a people," he concluded, "can work any constitution." Notwithstanding his admiration for the Americans' political genius, he was constrained to warn, "The danger for them is that this reliance on their skill and their star may make them heedless of the faults of their political machinery, slow to devise improvements which are best applied in quiet times."[66]

About the same time that the translation of Bryce appeared, a more direct indication of the lessons that constitutionalists drew from Bryce's work appeared. This was the *Discussion of Guidelines for the Establishment of the Chinese State*, ghost-written by Liang Qichao and published in mid-April of 1912 by Tang Hualong's Society for Deliberation of the Establishment of the Republic (Gonghe Jianshe Taolun Hui). This pamphlet stressed the grave perils that faced China in a fiercely competitive international arena, and called for a unified country and a protectionist and interventionist economic policy promoting economic development through private enterprise. "Henceforth," Liang wrote, "China has no alternative but to use her government to forge her people into a single unit to compete with the outside world. We will turn our entire population into the soldiers of a single army as it were, or students in a single school."[67] And to those who feared that a strong government would abuse its power, it argued that a weak government would not necessarily be any better, and insisted that republics trusted their chief executive officers.[68]

Despite this quasi-fascist rhetoric, the pamphlet went on to recommend the kind of parliamentary/responsible cabinet system described in Zhang Shizhao's articles and in Bryce's work, repeating the same arguments for them. (Indeed, the differences between this pamphlet and Liang's pre-revolutionary writings on constitutional systems lead one to suspect that Liang had in the meantime been very much influenced by Zhang Shizhao.) The strongest government, he now asserted, was one in which the highest officers in the executive branch were drawn from the legislative, so that both branches were fused into a whole. The key to the system the pamphlet recommended was the competition of two major political parties, which would serve as the basis for a responsible cabinet. In such a system, it argued, there was a natural harmony between the leadership of the executive branch (the cabinet), and the majority party in the legislature. The strength of the executive power in this system lay in the prime minister's unchecked authority to appoint his own cabinet. But his incumbency depended on the popularity of his party and, if the majority of the parliament turned against him, his government could be forced to resign, as periodically happened in England. Such a system, the pamphlet argued, guaranteed that the power of the government would not be used in a way contrary to the wishes of the people.[69] The competition of two strong parties was essential to the working of such a system. Upon losing its majority, a cabinet must promptly yield to the other party, otherwise the parliament would be reduced to mere window-dressing and the people have no recourse but revolution, as happened with the defunct Qing dynasty.

Other means of preventing the abuse of state power were not to be recommended. Provincial autonomy, an alternative that had been advocated by Hu Hanmin, was unacceptable as a counterweight against possible tyranny at the center, for national unity required that local authorities be appointed by the central government. And in the central government itself, Liang and his colleagues rejected the separation of the legislative and executive branches as a way of checking the power of the executive. (These were two decisive reasons for rejecting the American model.)[70]

This *Discussion of Guidelines* has been interpreted as a part of Liang's strategy of establishing an enlightened despotism under Yuan Shikai behind a facade of party government.[71] While Liang certainly proposed this to Yuan in his letter of 13 February 1912, his rhetoric in that letter more likely masks an intention to win an indispensable place for himself as Yuan's adviser, helping him to cope with a genuinely representative system. Had the recommendations in this pamphlet been adopted, Yuan's constitutional power would have been effectively reduced to appointing his prime minister, and his unofficial power would have depended heavily on his ability to win popular approval for his plans. Whatever Liang's motives, the system endorsed in this pamphlet provided a far stronger check on the president, and far greater unity of executive and legislature, than the provisional constitution then in effect. Moreover, he voiced grave warnings against possible threats to the Republic.

In advocating a government made strong by the strength of its representative institutions, Liang endorsed a keen vigilance regarding the conditions of genuine representative government. The parliament, he said, must be free of military coercion, and public debate and elections must be absolutely free, in order for the majority to win the acquiescence of the minority. Thus, he carried on the constitutionalists' tradition of demanding real power from the Qing, and pinpointed a major threat in the early Republican period to the kind of government they advocated: military power. And in a postface to the pamphlet, he endorsed the competition as well as the cooperation of the two-party system. "Life stagnates in the absence of contending camps," he wrote. "And though one camp exist, if it has no rival, then there will be an unbalanced, overbearing government of the proud and powerful, leading in the extreme case to absolutism (*zhuanzhi*). Absolutism does not require a dictator. Since ancient times democracies have also suffered this evil and perished from it." Those too timid to struggle for the policies they thought best would have only themselves, not their adversaries, to blame and would not deserve the sacrifices of "the valiant men who for decades had shed their blood for freedom and the welfare of the country."[72] It is still unclear whether this pamphlet, published after Yuan had assumed the presidency, was intended to temper his ambitions, or reflected an unrealistic fear that high-riding revolutionary extremists would attempt to establish a party dictatorship, or was a general attempt to consolidate support for an elite representative government against threats from whatever quarter.

By mid-1912 China had adopted a provisional constitution that many were prepared to characterize as providing for a responsible cabinet system of government, while support among former revolutionaries and reformers was growing for a full-fledged responsible cabinet system for the new Republic. The emerging consensus reflected a school of thought then, and still, widespread in the West, according to which the English model provided the most effective form of representative government, avoiding defects that plagued the American system.[73] The English (or, in its Republican variant, the French) system enjoyed growing approval despite Sun Yat-sen's argument that in her hour of crisis China needed a popular president who could act relatively free of legislative restraints.

The contemporaneous political scene illuminates the practical implications of the English model's continuing popularity. A number of incidents after Yuan assumed the presidency were quickly, and accurately, interpreted by the more militant revolutionaries as moves by Yuan first to eliminate any potential military opposition, and then to eliminate the restraints on his power that had been written into the provisional constitution. In the face of this challenge to republicanism, other revolutionaries looked forward to the upcoming general elections and the adoption of a permanent constitution as the means to check Yuan's ambitions.

Sun Yat-sen's public pronouncements reflected a somewhat different position. Yuan's attempt to contract a foreign loan through his Minister of Finance, bypassing his Prime Minister, aroused a storm of protest and did not succeed. But when, reneging on a solemn promise, Yuan appointed Wang Zhixiang Southern Pacification Commissioner instead of military governor of Zhili, and did so despite his Prime Minister's refusal to cosign the appointment, provoking the resignation of Tang Shaoyi and all the Tongmeng Hui members in his cabinet, Sun was prepared to dismiss the "political disputes" in Beijing as the results of "economic difficulties." And after Yuan's summary execution of the revolutionary officers Zhang Zhenwu and Fang Wei, Sun did not interrupt his plans to meet and consult with Yuan on national policy, proclaiming his faith in Yuan's reliability. After meeting Yuan, Sun publicly reassured Huang Xing that Yuan was not to blame for this incident, and went on to recommend that Yuan be retained for a second term as president.

Sun never went as far as Zhang Taiyan did, to recommend publicly that Yuan should be free of constitutional constraints, and that the rights of the people must be sacrificed for the sake of national survival. But he did contend that Yuan was capable of doing good, and should not be provoked—presumably by irresponsible criticisms or attempts to tie his hands—to do evil. This assessment reveals much about Sun's hopes and fears for China under Yuan.[74] The issue was not how much power a president should have, but how Yuan would use it. If forced to fight for power, Yuan would fight, exposing China to more division, suffering, and danger. But given enough latitude in the exercise of power, Yuan might use it to China's benefit.

Generally speaking, prominent constitutionalists tended through 1912 to distrust former revolutionaries more than they did Yuan Shikai, whom, like Sun, they viewed as a stabilizing element in critical times.

In the course of the Revolution, they abandoned, at least for the time being, the principle of a party cabinet, and did not even insist that Yuan Shikai respect the powers of the non-party cabinet. Whether from fear of the revolutionaries or of imperialism, many of them came to Yuan's defense when he was attacked for behaving like a dictator. Like Sun Yat-sen, most constitutionalists, whatever their theoretical preference for representative government, were unwilling to insist on it in a crisis.

It is clear that, despite broad agreement on the suitability of the British model and the two-party competition, there remained some, even among revolutionaries, who were inclined to prefer strong-man rule, and many whose priority on unity was so strong as to discourage conflicts between parties, or challenges to the power of the incumbent leader.

Thus, political thought and action at the beginning of the Republican era presents a mixed picture. The consensus between the moderate revolutionaries and the constitutionalists should not be obscured by the continued hostility and distrust between them.[75] That hostility and distrust prevented a broad united front between them against Yuan, without destroying their agreement on the value of a government which effectively represented the voters. Even when, in their feud with the Tongmeng Hui, the constitutionalists viewed Yuan as an ally, their ideologues were still arguing for a system that would give them power through a responsible cabinet. Indeed, the often deplored adulteration of the revolutionary ranks by previous non-revolutionaries during the conversion of the Tongmeng hui into the Guomindang suggests how many former constitutionalists were prepared to line up against Yuan. And the Guomindang's resounding victory in the general election further indicates that a strong plurality of China's elite electorate were prepared not only to support the principle of a responsible cabinet, but also to vote against Yuan.[76]

Although the base of support for parliamentary government among the elite is sometimes criticized as insufficiently firm, it was broad, and surprisingly persistent. Even after Song Jiaoren's assassination, the failure of the second revolution, departures of Guomindang parliamentarians from Beijing, and defections under the pressure of Yuan's threats and blandishments, the new parliament's constitutional commission proceeded to produce a Temple of Heaven constitution designed to subject the president and the cabinet to the control of the parliament. Only after Yuan had dissolved the parliament was he able to achieve the kind of constitution he wanted, and that only by presidential fiat.

TRADITIONS AND THE PRECONDITIONS FOR DEMOCRATIZATION

What does this review of the constitutional alternatives tell us about the failure of democracy in China? Did it flow inexorably from a deeply rooted cultural intolerance for liberal politics, or from the preeminent claims of state power in an age of emergent nationalism, from a configuration of social forces insufficiently modernized to support a pluralistic government, or from other even more accidental or exogenous factors in the historical moment?

Exogenous and accidental factors must certainly be given their due. Indeed, they loom so large that one might think it unnecessary to look elsewhere for explanations of the failure of democracy in the early Republic. Whatever his motives, Yuan Shikai was certainly crafty and ruthless, and commanded formidable military forces which he was fully prepared to use. Dislodging Yuan would have required civil war, and few were prepared to ignore the threat of increased foreign encroachment in that event. Moreover, the powers supported Yuan at a time when any central government would have to seek foreign loans. In fact, one of the weapons that had served to check the power of the English kings' governments from the outset—the crown's ancient dependence on the voluntary financial support of the propertied classes—was lacking in China. The propertied classes had little to offer Yuan, and for the most part expected him to seek foreign loans.

Foreign threats and Yuan's wiles were not the only obstacles, for memories of the Taipings and Boxers and recent incidents of popular unrest could raise the specter of social upheaval in a context of domestic political instability. In a country with so many peasants and such a small bourgeoisie, considerations of security could favor an authoritarian regime. Had the level of modern commercialism, ideas, and elite political activism been as high all over China as in the hinterland of Shanghai, advocates of constitutional order might have been strong enough to find other alternatives besides Yuan and the radicals. Had China's enormous peasantry and lower classes not harbored such a terrifying potential for disorder, elites may have felt less inclined to buy order at the price of dictatorship.[77] What is interesting is that all these considerations did not produce unanimous elite support for Yuan. But for the entire array of historical circumstances, it is not inconceivable that Yuan would have been checked or ousted well before 1916. Conversely, these circumstances surely gave pause to men who otherwise might have felt more inclined to fight for the establishment of representative government.

Even if such obstacles might have defeated a movement genuinely committed to democracy, however, this does not preclude the possibility that the apparent support for democratic forms belied a far stronger preoccupation with national goals and deep-rooted cultural attitudes unfavorable to democracy. The prominence of the concern for China's survival is not to be denied, and its anti-democratic potential is sometimes reflected in the pro-democratic writings of revolutionaries and constitutionalists. Liang Qichao's argument that the perilous international struggle demanded the adoption of a government as strong as the British, so as to transform the nation into "soldiers of a single army" and "students of a single school," are reminiscent of Sun Yat-sen's later denunciations of the excessive individual liberty that had turned China into a "sheet of loose sand." Zhang Shizhao's avowed readiness to revert to the Japanese or German model if they could be shown to make China stronger may mask an ulterior commitment to democratization, but such rhetoric demonstrates the ambient nationalist priorities to which constitutionalism might be sacrificed.

How, then, would nationalism demand the sacrifice of a sound constitutional order? To be sure, nationalism and *individualism* were an unstable compound, and the transience of Spencerian liberalism's appeal as the solution to China's weakness was evident in the efforts to build the new Republic. But proponents of democratic government at this juncture were hardly talking about the usefulness of individual liberty for national strength. They were preoccupied with the problem of avoiding the divisive dangers of democracy as they sought to escape the trammels of autocracy. This led them to reject not only the Japanese and German models for their authoritarianism and potential instability but also the American, with its separation of powers, for its institutional weakness. That did not exhaust the democratic alternatives, however, for the English model showed how to eliminate tyranny while preserving a strong executive and achieving the stability, strength, and unity that popular support could provide, all at the same time. But while the English system served England's national purposes well, exogenous and accidental circumstances could prevent its effective functioning in China, and if the English system could not be made to work there, for whatever reason, then nationalism would naturally demand something else.

It remains to consider whether values and habits of thought and action deeply rooted in a distinctively Chinese cultural tradition precluded a genuine commitment to democracy and its prerequisites. We are not yet in a position to gauge the impact in the Republic's infancy of the factionalism which proved such an obstacle under the warlords. Suspicions and animosities between constitutionalists and revolutionaries certainly weakened the cause of democratic government.[78] While these two camps could agree in theory on the value of a responsible cabinet system, their failure to unite in insisting on the implementation of such key elements of that system as the party cabinet and cabinet approval of high-level appointments resulted in a president more powerful than the cabinet. The fragmentation and reassembling of political groups in 1912 was a striking enough phenomenon, but perhaps less important in the failure of the initial republican experiment than a conservative-radical rift that was more ideological in character than factional. In fact, it is a tribute to the vitality of the republican ideal that Song Jiaoren was able to put together such a large and successful coalition as the Guomindang, which might have produced a party cabinet had it not been for Song's assassination and the political repression that followed. Subsequent Chinese experience may make it difficult to imagine that two large parties could ever have contested political supremacy in a responsible cabinet system, but the experience of India and Japan suggests that factions and dominant parties *in themselves* are not necessarily incompatible with considerable political pluralism.

What of ancient Confucian paternalism, the idea that rulers and ruled must be bound by bonds of trust, that government must proceed on the basis of harmony rather than conflict, and that the interests of the collective must not be challenged by lesser groups, much less individuals? Are not these ancient values reflected in Chinese constitutions which have treated rights as something granted by the state, not inhering in the person?[79] How can democracy take root where such a tradition prevails?

In the modern American mind, the separation of powers, guarantees of individual liberty, political equality, and inalienable individual rights solidly enshrined in a stable constitution and protected by the watchful eye of an independent judiciary are inextricably linked with the idea of democracy. But reflection on China's English model and her English mentors reminds us that these things are not essential to representative government.[80] In fact, the lack of them may lead us to wonder whether Bagehot's England should be considered a democracy. The assumption that the cabinet is implementing the wishes of the majority undermines the rationale for parliamentary oversight of the executive, and the permanent bureaucracy is shielded from committee investigations. To the present day, Her Majesty's civil service is far less accountable to the public than the American bureaucracy, and freedom of the press in England far more circumscribed.[81] Nevertheless, even Bagehot's England meets Schumpeter's minimal criteria for a "pluralist democracy," and the democratization of England was to proceed apace after his day. By 1914, Dicey, facing the inevitable with less optimism than Song, wondered how the historian writing in 1950 or 2000 would "sum up the final outcome of democratic government in England."[82]

In any event, whatever degree of democracy the "mother of parliaments" has generated in the present grew out of a political tradition the mainstream of which did not, even in modern times, evaluate its government on the basis of democratic theories. The nineteenth-century parliamentary-reform acts which "established the broad principle of political democracy" in England were, in fact, passed by men who "had no belief in the kind of political democracy implicit in universal suffrage and the equality of electoral districts and who feared that the introduction of such a system would lead to the tyranny of the illiterate many over the cultured few."[83]

Bagehot, Bryce, and Dicey represented a kind of pragmatic, flexible conservatism far more concerned with the workability of institutions and the national well-being than with the theoretical basis of their legitimacy. Their pragmatism confronts us with striking ironies as we compare their thought with that of their Chinese disciples, for their mid-Victorian liberalism[84] contains elements of the culturalism, commitment to the welfare of the national collective, and elitism that we are likely to view as impediments to democracy in China. We find, moreover, that where the Chinese saw strength in the more democratic and progressive features of the late Victorian system, the British whose authority they invoked found it in the more elitist traditions.[85]

Too concerned about the ramifications of institutional transplants in different cultures even to recommend correcting the evils of American government by English-style reforms, it is unlikely that Bryce would have rushed to recommend the English system for China. Bagehot, likewise sensitive to the influence of national culture on the functioning of political institutions, proclaimed the choice between presidential and parliamentary government the only practical one for "first-rate nations," and did not conceal his opinion as to which was better for new countries formed by English colonials. But it is unlikely that he would have expected the English system to take root in such exotic soil as China's.[86]

No less ironic is the fact that new features of the English system which impressed Zhang and Song as components of strong and effective popular government disturbed Bagehot and Dicey. Their pragmatism led both to value qualities of collective elite leadership that conflicted with the party discipline which Zhang Shizhao hailed as the root of "strong" government. Bagehot, in particular, thought little of partisanship which would place the implementation of a well-defined platform above moderate bipartisan support, and he valued the leadership of a trusted statesman above party "tenets." Dicey lived to see party government in full swing, and to inveigh against its evils, fearing that a majority party would abuse its power to contravene the wishes of "the nation."[87] Unlike Zhang, neither was prepared to assume that the proper function of leaders was primarily to implement the party platform democratically chosen by an electorate.

Their distrust of strong *party* government does not, however, reflect a distrust of strong *government*. Bagehot was happy that, in contrast to the handiwork of the American constitution-makers who "shrank from placing sovereign power anywhere," the English constitution was "framed on the principle of choosing a single sovereign authority, and making it good."[88] "The material necessities of this age," Bagehot declared, "require a strong executive; a nation destitute of it cannot be clean, or healthy, or vigorous like a nation possessing it."[89] Moreover, trust was essential to the functioning of this government, trust between the people and their representatives (see below) and between the representative body and the executive, which Bagehot called "a board of control chosen by the legislature, out of persons whom it trusts and knows, to rule the nation."[90]

And while "free government" was surely one of the most treasured values of these Victorians, they were themselves fully committed to the goals of national power and prestige. Dicey, the legal authority, fretted over the dangers majority rule posed for Britain's greatness, and defended the suspension of jury trial and *habeas corpus* to keep Ireland in the United Kingdom.[91] Bagehot, complaining of the troubles occasioned by the exclusion of Parliament from treaty making, claimed that this defect was mitigated by patriotism. "English statesmen and English parties have really a great patriotism," he wrote. "[T]hey can rarely be persuaded by their passions or their interest to do anything contrary to the real interest of England, or anything which would lower England in the eyes of foreign nations." Moreover, it was a merit of the English system that the "people" could, in times of emergency, "choose a ruler for the occasion," a man with the "great qualities, the imperious will, the rapid energy, the eager nature fit for a great crisis," who "when he feels the steady power of England behind him, will advance without resistance, and will strike without restraint."[92]

Most ironic of all, perhaps, if we suspect that the Chinese desire for strong government distorted their understanding of Western democracy and liberalism, is their British mentors' rejection of natural rights as an impediment to the effective functioning of their system. Neither Bagehot nor Dicey saw any conflict between genuine representative government and the reservation of a politically dominant role for a privileged, public-spirited elite of electors and their representatives, in whom the power of the state was concentrated. Their elitism was coupled with a pragmatic approach to politics according to which the criterion of the best "free" government, or "self-government" was simply that the "people" think it the best, and in the best of these, "certain persons" judged "by common consent . . . to be wiser than others," are granted a disproportionate voice in the representation."[93] For them, the franchise was not a right but a "gift."[94] Like Marx, Bagehot viewed the abstract "notions of political equality" put forward by spokesmen of the disenfranchised capitalists primarily as a justification for their own demands for power. But unlike Marx, he sympathized with their real demands, not with their speculative principles. Not only were equal political rights not sacred; they were a disadvantage. "The masses of Englishmen," he wrote, "are not fit for an elective government."[95] He thought it natural and preferable that the electoral system represent the politically competent and articulate elements in a country and declared, "I do not consider the exclusion of the working classes from effectual representation a defect in *this* aspect of our parliamentary representation." Indeed, he feared the prospect in England of the masses' deciding policy questions as parties representing the "higher orders" competed for their support. "I can conceive of nothing more corrupting or worse for a set of poor ignorant people," wrote Bagehot, "than that two combinations of well-taught and rich men should constantly offer to defer to their decision, and compete for the office of executing it." Bagehot feared changes for the worse after the Reform Act of 1867, claiming that "the deference of the electors to their betters was the only way in which our old system could be maintained."[96]

Thus, in the eyes of its most sympathetic Victorian analysts, the virtue of the British government lay not in "supposed checks and balances" to prevent the concentration of power, nor in its guarantee of sacred and inalienable universal rights, but in the fact that it served the country well, and generally commanded the trust of the public. The views of Bagehot and Dicey were on the conservative side of the liberal spectrum, and more democratic trends were to carry the day by the early twentieth century; but the significant point here is that British social and political democratism grew out of the social, political, and intellectual background they described.

Their commitment to representative government was no less genuine for the fact that they found the rights of individuals best protected in England by a system in which the majority were governed by their betters,[97] and deplored partisan struggle, subordinating the potential claims of majority and minority alike to the security of the nation as a whole. Most important, they favored the unification of authority in the interest of the nation as a whole, so long as it remained accountable to the electorate. The coexistence of such priorities with a political system that was becoming increasingly democratic in England should warn us against the over-hasty identification of traditional "Confucian" values as a legacy that has foreclosed the option of democracy in China. If Mencius expected those who labored with their muscles to support and be governed by those who labored with their minds, so did Bagehot. And if Bagehot, who found the "dignified" aspect of government, particularly the loyalty to the symbol of monarchy, of more vital importance to the lower than the upper orders, this finds some echo in the patently fictitious claims of monarchical sagehood endorsed by the later imperial order in China. One need not overdraw the parallels between paternalistic Chinese and English elitism and the value both put on the maintenance of social order and preservation of the national interest. The fact remains that, if these cultural factors were compatible with democratization in England, they cannot in themselves explain why it stalled in China. Indeed, we might be led to wonder whether open political competition and accountability are not compatible with even more collective and less individualistic orientations and laws than England's. Assuming a consensus of respect for the views and political rights of substantial minorities, if not of individual eccentrics and rebels, it is not clear why individual liberties should be an indispensable precondition of democracy.

Examining another admirer of England, Benjamin Schwartz showed how Yan Fu's nationalist perspective not only distorted the thought of Herbert Spencer and John Stuart Mill, but at the same time, and perhaps more importantly, illuminated the affinity of their individualism and liberalism with the modern Faustian spirit which exalted energy, collective progress, and national wealth and power. And then, by examining Yan Fu's identification of individualism with energy and virtue, he invited our attention to the individualist values that Yan and Spencer missed. Less subtlety is required to draw analogous lessons from a juxta-position of Chinese arguments for the responsible cabinet system with the older patriotic and paternalistic elements in the thought of Bagehot and Dicey. If Mill and Spencer strove to limit the power of the state and preserve the broadest scope for individual freedom, Bagehot and Dicey (no statists, themselves) did not hesitate to talk of the national prestige or the interests of the Empire, nor to justify the English system on the grounds of its service to the whole community, while consigning the majority of the population to political passivity. If Chinese distorted such men's thought, it was in making them out to be better democrats than they were. This distortion may have arisen in part from an igno-rance of the changes in the Victorian constitution, but despite the gen-eral trend toward democracy, the continuing rationale of the system was not grounded in any abstract theory about rights. The distinctive En-glish constitution was generally valued by Englishmen not on abstract theoretical grounds but for its success in achieving many goals, both lib-eral and nationalist. Progress along the road to democracy did not depend on a preexisting commitment to natural rights or a distrust of government power.[98]

But while inalienable rights and a division of powers to uphold their constitutional guarantees are not essential to "pluralist democracy," it does not follow that there were not cultural differences between the two traditions operating to the disadvantage of democracy in China. If repre-sentative government flourished in nineteenth-century England without a doctrine of inalienable rights, it rested historically on the basis of jeal-ously guarded elite privileges which the Crown was bound to respect and which had been defended and extended in struggles that had converted the "appendages of a monarchy . . . into the essence of a republic."[99] China had no counterpart to the Magna Carta or the Cromwellian Republic. British subjects had no inalienable rights, but neither did their kings,[100] and Bagehot drew attention to an inveterate distrust of executive power—the successor to royal power. "[O]ur freedom," he wrote, "is the result of centuries of resistance . . . We have, accordingly, inherited the tra-ditions of conflict, and preserved them in the fullness of victory . . The natural impulse of the English people is to resist authority."[101]

Despite an apparent contradiction with his characterization of the English as a deferential people, Bagehot's account here confirms a sort of communitarian (not familistic) conception of nation and government. English government succeeds because the lower classes trust the upper classes to govern, and the upper classes, in the persons of their elected representatives, are sufficiently practical, moderate, responsible, and patriotic to serve the nation well. Kings, however, proved far more useful as symbols of the sacred dignity of government than as rulers, in which capacity they were as likely to be bad as good—so bad, in the case of James II, as to provoke his people to change the dynasty.[102] In China, when the virtue of a dynasty ran out, the royal power did not become a matter of negotiation between a new emperor and the elite who chose him, but was restored intact to a new dynasty whose victory demonstrated its virtue and its claim to unchecked authority legitimized by the Mandate of Heaven. If Englishmen, on the other hand, were used to being governed by their "betters," their "betters" were not organized into an ideally monolithic pyramid of virtue with sovereignty concentrated at the very apex. Not only did the institution of Parliament legitimize effective opposition to the king's wishes, effectively dividing sovereignty; the political process tended further to divide Parliament into the supporters of the king or his ministers and the "loyal opposition," rendering contests between them a matter of course rather than evidence of insubordination or sedition. It was upon that basis that the Victorian union of Parliament and executive in the party cabinet was built.

In the nature of elite privilege, perhaps, lies the greatest distinctively Chinese cultural impediment to representative government, although it was clearly but one factor. The privileges of the Chinese elite were not rights which they they had won in contests with the Throne, and had certainly never included the right to vote on their taxes or on the uses to which taxes were put. They renounced monarchy in 1911 after just a few years' open struggle for legislative power at the national level. Their desire to wield power in a constitutional system is attested by the fact that many of those who chose to support Yuan continued to call for a responsible cabinet. But the power they had lately come to demand was not securely theirs in the early Republic, nor was the demand for it always firmly fixed in their own minds. The brevity of China's "tradi-

tion of conflict" surely handicapped elite resistance to Yuan's usurpations, while the tradition of imperial rule lent some credibility to Yuan's
appeal to reestablish rule by virtue and claim to bypass elected assemblymen as a spokesman for the "people's will."[103] Yuan failed, but not
before destroying the new republic's constitutional order. Not even
under the Guomindang, which in many ways served their interests, did
China's upper classes as a whole control the national government, and
after 1949 their power on the mainland was utterly broken.

The movement for democracy in the infant Republic had drawn support from its promise to promote the interests of the elite, the interests
of the nation, and progress to a more democratic future. It was vulnerable to the fear that elite and national interests would suffer more from
domestic strife than from dictatorial rule. Its most loyal supporters—
men like Zhang Shizhao and Song Jiaoren—were those who were most
inspired by the visions of an even more democratic future and alert to
the democratic potential of representative institutions as elite privilege
evolved into general rights. Even they were not uniformly committed to
the values of individualism and personal liberty, but they were determined to make government accountable to an electorate. Unfortunately
for their cause, the elite on which their strategy depended was not up
to the task they assigned it. Song paid for his miscalculation with his
life, and Zhang, frustrated by bitter experience, abandoned the strategy
altogether.

Part Four
Culture and Methodology

Continuities between Modern and Premodern China: Some Neglected Methodological and Substantive Issues

THOMAS A. METZGER

THE DURKHEIMIAN CONCERN IN CONTEXT

In the study of intellectual history and society today, no concern is more central than that with the relation between the self and the group. Worry about the rootless or anomic individual pervades the study of "advanced" societies, while objections to authoritarianism, collectivism, dependency, and particularism fill the pages of monographs about "developing" societies. The overarching ideal animating both kinds of worries was summed up most succinctly in Emile Durkheim's classic study of suicide, which sought a kind of balance between group and self, a social structure freeing the individual from the "too strict tutelage" of society while yet providing her or him with the advantages of belonging to "a cohesive and animated society."[1]

In the case of China, the mainstream Western view has been that Confucian norms emphasized the importance of the group at the expense of the individual's freedom, spontaneity, creativity, and moral autonomy. Directly or indirectly, this view has been held by many of the greatest Western thinkers, ranging from Kant, Hegel, Marx, and John Stuart Mill to Max Weber.[2] In "On Liberty," expressing a view of history almost as teleological as Marx's, the father of modern liberalism saw his Western world as representing "the more civilized portions of the species"[3] but not yet sufficiently grasping the truth expressed by Wilhelm von Humbolt: "'The end of man, or that which is prescribed by the eternal or immutable dictates of reason, and not suggested by vague and transient desires, is the highest and most harmonious development of his powers to be a complete and consistent whole,'" a goal requiring "the free development of individuality." Thus Mill denounced the "despotism of custom" and said: "We have a warning example in China." China, he said, was "provided at an early period with a particularly good set of customs" but had "become stationary." The reason for the lack of progress in China was that the Chinese had "succeeded . . . in making a people all alike, all governing their thoughts and conduct by the same maxims and rules. . . . if they are ever to be farther improved, it must be by foreigners."[4]

Western scholarship today often avoids Mill's teleology and ethnocentrism and is based on far greater understanding of Chinese culture, but the Western mainstream view remains that, in Confucian culture, the autonomy of the self is either not present or attenuated. The most recent authoritative version of this mainstream view is that of Professor Benjamin I. Schwartz, one of the most erudite, meticulous, perspicacious, and influential China scholars ever produced by the West. His position can be summed up as follows. In conceptualizing the desirable way to live, Confucian thought emphasizes "roles" instead of more indeterminate, spontaneous ways of thinking and acting. The term *role*, originally borrowed by sociology from the theater, refers to a conventionally fixed set of social expectations to which individual behavior should conform. All roles are hierarchically ordered in Confucian thought, Schwartz maintains. This is so partly because Confucianism "accepts unblinkingly what it regards as the need for hierarchy, status, and authority within a universal world order." It is so also because, in Confucianism, hierarchy has a certain sacred, cosmic aspect. Moreover, in this hierarchical order, most people end up accepting a status unequal and inferior to that of the more gifted minority morally qualified to lead them. Still more, even when this minority is revealed as morally incompetent, respect is owed to the positions of authority they occupy, as illustrated by the deferential behavior of Confucius at the courts of hereditary aristocrats, whom he actually regarded as morally deficient

(*Lunyu*, Chap. 10, 13.20). True, Confucius did combine hierarchy with non-hierachical, indeed non-differential qualities such as some ultimate sense of equality, reciprocity, mutual respect or love, and moral autonomy. These are the qualities of the "man of integrity" (*junzi*) applying equally to all roles. Yet these qualities were less important than the need to respect the actual structure of hierarchy, status, and authority. This is the judgment at the heart of Professor Schwartz's position. Writes Professor Schwartz about Mozi: "As in the case of Confucius, the initiative for enabling all men to 'love each other and benefit each other' lies with those above. The authority that resides in the political order is still overwhelming."[5] Thus, as Schwartz sees it, according to Confucian thought, the horizontal or universalistic moral relations between people are based less on the sense of morality within the individual than on the initiatives of those above him in the vertical structure of society.

This Western view represented by Professor Schwartz is certainly close to that of many Chinese scholars, especially those influenced by the iconoclasm of the May Fourth Movement. Probably the most systematic Chinese work of this sort in recent years is that of Yang Guoshu, a Professor of Psychology at National Taiwan University and a leading liberal thinker.[6] Lacking Schwartz's nuanced analysis of Confucian ideas, he is interested in widespread social orientations and without qualifications sees the "traditional" culture as "collectivistic" and "authoritarian" (see below).

Going back to the 1920s, however, a broad trend in China developed which we can call modern Confucian humanism, which is represented by scholars as different as Tang Junyi (1909–1978) and Princeton's Yingshih Yü, and which in effect argues that Confucian thought was well on the way to finding that balance between self and group called for by Durkheim. According to these humanists, Confucian thought if not society not only attended to the needs of group life but also emphasized the dignity of the individual; the autonomy of the individual, as he put morality above the cues of immoral authority figures; the grounding of this autonomy in the individual's independent access to "transcendent," cosmic values; and so the construction of society as the accumulation of such autonomous individual efforts concretely to realize these transcendent moral goals. From the standpoint of this ideal, status, hierarchy, and authority had no significant existence except as a result of autonomous moral efforts on the part of individuals to "serve" others in order both "to realize fully what the self should be" and to "help all other persons or things realize what they should be" (*chenji, chengwu*). Far from seeing ideal Confucian society as emphasizing hierarchy, Tang Junyi said that in it "all the different kinds of relationships between human beings . . . equally cluster around the character of the individual as spokes do around the hub of a wheel."

Crucial to this humanistic position as a whole is the idea of "transcendence" as a capacity freeing the individual from the normative dictates of other people. This idea was already basic to the six books Feng Youlan wrote in the late 1930s and early 1940s to establish his own Confucian philosophic system. Inspired by Xiong Shili, however, the New Confucians emphasized the relations between this transcendence and the moral subject. The idea of "inner transcendence" was already used by Tang Junyi in 1951. In his 1984 book on the relation between modernization and the nature of Chinese culture, Professor Ying-shih Yü based his analysis of the latter on this idea.[7]

When we look at this controversy about Confucian attitudes toward authority and moral autonomy, much can be clarified by first noting that our subject matter is not social reality but "the world of thought," to use Professor Schwartz's term. Even if social reality in the imperial period was not so empty of love and mutual respect as some scholars seem to think, disparity between ideals and actual behavior is common in any culture. The question at stake here is not whether Chinese social practice was more or less authoritarian than Western but whether the Confucian vision of life put primacy on individual moral autonomy. It also seems clear that, if we identify the core of this vision with the conceptual ground shared by the three classical masters of Confucianism—Confucius (551–479 B.C.), Mencius (ca. 371–289 B.C.), and Xunzi (ca. 298–238 B.C.)—the modern Chinese humanists' emphasis on moral autonomy is more in accord with the documentary data than Professor Schwartz's interpretation, as I have tried to argue elsewhere.[8] Even Xunzi, regarded as the most "authoritarian" of the three, heavily emphasized individual moral autonomy.

If, however, the data are so clear, why do so many scholars still see

Confucian thought as failing to provide an adequate basis for individuality? One reason is that many see such a basis as requiring not only moral autonomy but also what Max Weber called a "unified personality." His idea connotes the modern, Western, individualistic idea of personality, which Steven Lukes analyzed.[9]

Recognizing that the latter was alien to Confucian thought, we Westerners have to avoid presuming that ideals we cherish are the only ones revealing the authentic self. Most of us greatly value the way this modern Western tradition has constructed the self: the emphasis on privacy; the skeptical approach to the problem of knowledge, facilitating criticism of authority figures ("epistemological pessimism," as one may term it);[10] the Dionysian, "romantic" approach to the emotions, including the profound ways in which the relations between emotional, sexual, moral, and religious tendencies were explored by Rousseau, Dostoyevsky, and Freud; the emphasis on economic and political rights; and even the philosophies defining the individual as the ontologically ultimate human unit. Yet, much as we may cherish these ideas, it is hard to discern any trans-cultural standards by which they necessarily amount to the "best" or the most "authentic" construction of the self.

If, then, the Durkheimian issue can be thus resolved in favor of Confucian thought, it would seem to follow that there is no major controversy remaining about the extent to which Confucian values meet the requisites of modern life. After all, as discussed below, there already is much agreement on both sides of the Taiwan Strait about which of these values meet these requisites, which do not. If scholars agreed about whether the Confucian conceptualization of self meets the needs of modern Chinese emphasizing the moral autonomy of the individual, the process of revising Confucian culture to make it accord with modern values could seemingly go on free of basic controversy.

In fact, though, even if the Durkheimian issue can be thus resolved, unresolved questions remain. This paper argues that there are basic aspects of the Confucian tradition that have been little noticed, that have continued to be influential in modern times, and that may be not entirely compatible with the modern Chinese goal of democracy. These aspects, therefore, should be described and then evaluated in the light of this goal. The one discussed here can be called "optimistic this-worldliness." It seems, therefore, that while scholars continue to fear that the alleged authoritarianism or dependency of the Confucian tradition may impede democratization, they should instead be debating whether "optimistic this-worldliness" does.

Making this point is difficult, however, because Confucianism's optimistic this-worldliness has taken the form not only of ideas basic to explicitly Confucian texts but also of the very conceptual framework used today by most Chinese intellectuals when they discuss and evaluate the Confucian tradition. They see themselves as standing on an analytical platform—often referred to by them as "reason" and "morality"—which is above or outside the Confucian tradition, and which allows them to evaluate the latter by referring to trans-cultural, universal standards. Yet, to some extent at least, this platform is more culture-bound than they realize, since it has been much affected by their inherited "optimistic this-worldliness." Thus, if we want to describe and critique the Confucian tradition and its influence on modern Chinese thought, we need to expand our topic to include the mode of thought used by Chinese today when they discuss culture, history, and modernization.

If this argument is on track, we should be able to identify such a culturally distinctive, contemporary Chinese world of intellectual discourse, to make clear how it differs from other major modes of contemporary discourse, to explain how it is rooted in the Confucian tradition, and to show how it may or may not impede the pursuit of democracy in China.

This paper tries to begin this task. I begin by describing a largely unnoticed disparity between the basic Chinese and Western ways of discussing culture, history, and modernization. Many regard these two worlds of discourse as homologous, but they are heterologous to a large extent. This heterology or disparity, I then argue, stems from the great continuity between modern and premodern Chinese thought. Second, looking at more overtly or explicitly traditional cultural elements, I turn briefly to more familiar problems of continuity and discontinuity in modern Chinese history, note the lack of controversy about many of them, and touch on the Durkheimian issue. Finally, I try to deal with the issue of optimistic this-worldliness, trace this attitude back to the tradition, note its impact on Chinese ideas about history, culture, and modernization, and touch on its normative implications.

One can easily illustrate the widespread Western and Chinese belief that, in discussing culture, history, and modernization, Chinese intellectuals have largely broken with their traditional orientations and now discuss these issues using basically Western perspectives, thus forming a kind of global internally homologous seminar on these issues with the West as Professor. John Dunn, a brilliant British political theorist, recently dipped into the literature on China and concluded that, as Chinese sought to "secure the practical advantages of Western technique," they gradually experienced "cultural subjection." Thus they "deserted the solidary culture of China which had millennially dominated its own private world and affiliated themselves instead with the invasive culture of the barbarians."[11] Conversely, when Yang Guoshu and Wen Chongyi in 1982 edited *The Sinification of Research in the Social and Behavioral Sciences*, they saw these disciplines in Taiwan precisely as experiencing this "cultural subjection" and so as badly in need of conscious efforts to given them an authentically Chinese character doing justice to the data about Chinese behavior and social patterns.[12]

Where, then, is the illusion? Most generally, we should keep in mind that, if, besides scientific or technical writing, the three leading contemporary Western intellectual trends are socialism, existentialism, and that mix of positivism and ethical skepticism identified with modernity by Alasdair MacIntyre and others,[13] only socialism had a serious influence on modern Chinese culture. Neither has there been much impact made by some other cultural patterns crucial in the West, such as Christianity or the conservative political tradition stretching from Aristotle through Burke. Thus the contemporary Chinese and Western intellectual worlds are certainly disparate to an important extent.

But the disparity important here is that pertaining to the conceptualization of history, culture, and the criteria of successful modernization. With regard to these three issues, the subjection of Chinese to

Western thinking has been greatly limited, and the disparity between Chinese and Western discussions remains basic. Therefore, putting their specific research results into the context of their own, distinctively Chinese views about the nature of history, culture, and modernization, Chinese social scientists like Yang Guoshu have already Sinified their scholarly investigations without being entirely aware of this fact.

Let us first look at the problem of conceptualizing history. The leading contemporary Chinese schools of thought—generally speaking, these are modern Confucian humanism, Chinese liberalism, the doctrine of the Three Principles of the People, and Chinese Marxism[14]—all examine the problem of traditional values by trying to set up a full-scale philosophical system somewhat like Hegel's. Thus they seek a system that solves all epistemological, ontological, and cosmological problems and establishes teleological principles of historical development defining both necessary historical stages and the moral mission of the heroic or enlightened individual in the present. That is, they all assert that a certain kind of knowledge—Marxist theory, say, or empirical, psychological, statistical research, or concrete historical data put into a Western, anthropological framework, or a Kantian exegesis of experience, or some eclectic combination of Habermas and Wittfogel—supersedes all other knowledge claims. This knowledge is viewed as based on "reason" (*lixing*), a term comfortably used by most Chinese today in a broad way denoting not only logic but also certain moral norms seen as universal or necessarily authoritative for the writer's audience. These norms revolve around the ideal of *dagong wusi* (unreserved commitment to the public good without any clinging to selfish interests).

Given this epistemological-ontological-ethical framework, "society" is then defined in terms of certain basic components, such as ecotypes or classes, which interact in a "necessary" way forming a series of "stages" of development, such as the agricultural and the industrial, or the feudal, the capitalistic, and the socialistic. The coming stage being identified with "reason" and "morality," the historical process as factually described inherently furnishes the moral norms people today should follow. "Ought" is thus deduced not from "is" but from "was" or from "about to be." Moreover, as criteria of successful modernization or historical evolution, these norms are invariably formulated in a perfectionist, utopian way (see below).

At the same time, however, moral and intellectual confusion in the present is seen as an unavoidable aspect of historical evolution. Despite the pervasive belief in "democracy," Chinese intellectuals usually endorse the actually articulated views of the majority only selectively and commonly view them as "unscientific" or "feudalistic." It is commonly asserted that most people have not understood what the proper form of knowledge is, have failed to grasp the principles of history, cling to the norms of an obsolete historical stage, and so cannot use their reason to appreciate the norms and policies appropriate to the coming era. Evaluated according to perfectionist criteria, China's current condition is perceived as a predicament, and progress is regarded as depending on the ability of "intellectuals" to propagate the correct understanding of the world. Propagating it, they carry out what Wm. Theodore de Bary recently called "prophecy," denouncing the radical, systematic failure of Chinese civilization in the present. To the extent that Marxism is blamed for this failure, many Chinese intellectuals define the rise of Chinese Marxism as just another stage in the pathological development of Chinese culture.

It is obvious that such a teleological vision of history is common to Chinese Marxism, the doctrine of the Three Principles of the People, much modern Confucian humanism, or, say, the thought of the nationalistic Hu Qiuyuan. Strikingly enough, however, it is basic also to the thought of a scholar, Yang Guoshu, who, as a Professor of Psychology at National Taiwan University, has long been immersed in American behavioral science and has devoted himself to the use of statistical survey methods to analyze personality changes in Taiwan during the last decades.

To be sure, Professor Yang does employ a distinctly descriptive concept of personality and culture in much of his work. Yet he puts his statistical findings about psychological changes in Taiwan into the context of a historical, teleological process. That is, he uses seven concepts (some having many sub-categories) to analyze societies in general: physical environment, ecotype, social structure, form of socialization, personality and types of behavior, way of thinking (for example, "mysticism" or respect for science), and form of government (for example, democracy). Seeing the ecotype as the main causative factor, he depicts the contrast between "traditional, agricultural" and "modern, industrial" society in China in terms of these seven concepts.[15] Thus, he describes Taiwan's current development as one transforming an "agricultural," "collectivistic," "hierarchical," "monistic," "authoritarian," "particularistic," "closed," unscientific, and undemocratic society into an "industrialized," "individualistic," "egalitarian," "pluralistic," "universalistic," "open," scientific, and "democratic" society. As Fingarette might say, there is no choice here. Virtually any Chinese accepting his analysis would hope to hasten China's entrance into the later historical stage, which is thus depicted as both an imminent fact and a moral norm.

Because Yang's analysis is presented as fully scientific, he can with great persuasiveness depict any Chinese still believing in Confucian values as mistakenly clinging to the "collectivism" of an increasingly obsolete historical stage. Moreover, according to him, most Chinese today are still mired in this misunderstanding: "First of all, we see that in Taiwan and Hong Kong, a new, modern Chinese society has already emerged, and in these new Chinese societies, a new, modern kind of Chinese has gradually appeared, but the Chinese who live in these Chinese societies lack experience with this new kind of Chinese society and lack the slightest understanding of this new type of Chinese person."[16] In other words, the articulated views of the majority are out of accord with the objective moral norms Chinese should follow.

A passionate believer in democracy and a prolific, widely respected liberal writer, Yang thus sees Chinese progress as depending on not only the full enactment of democratic political procedures but also the evolution of the ecotype as well as intellectual efforts such as his to bring a true understanding of historical change to the Chinese population. At the same time, he argues energetically and with unqualified optimism that, based on this true understanding, the intellectual and moral consensus of society will be strengthened as freedom increases. In his eyes, that is, consensus in a democracy will not be limited to agreement about the procedures with which to arrive at decisions; it will also include "consensus about what is objectively right and wrong from the standpoint of the public good" (*gongshi gongfeide gongshi*). He even predicted in 1986 that, once laws limiting political freedom in Taiwan were abolished, tensions would end between those seeking Taiwan independence and those adhering to Chinese nationalism.[17]

Chinese intellectuals often combine such an optimistic, teleological vision of history with the assumption that a brief normative formula can be found which will epitomize the historical direction Chinese should take. The classic case, of course, is Zhang Zhidong's "Chinese learning as the foundation, Western learning for instrumental adaptation." The continuing Chinese search for the right formula is illustrated by some remarks made by the prominent Taibei intellectual and editor Wei Zhengtong at a conference organized in Beijing in 1988 by the Academy for the Study of Chinese Culture (Zhongguo Wenhua Shuyuan):

> In this regard, I especially want to refer to Professor Lin Yü-sheng, here with us today. More than twenty years ago, writing a letter in English to Mr. Yin Haiguang, he brought up the idea of "creative transformation" (*chuangzao-xingde zhuanhua*). Mr. Yin was tremendously excited and repeatedly stated that this concept is of the greatest value. In Taiwan, during the early 1960s some emphasized "wholesale Westernization" and so provoked a debate about Chinese and Western culture. . . . In the 1970s, the slogan of "modernization" replaced "wholesale Westernization," becoming a new trend. Comparatively speaking, "modernization" is a relatively neutral term, but the difficulties that later were seen in the theory of "modernization" became increasingly numerous. In the last ten years, people have begun to reexamine this concept, and it has been criticized a lot. Gradually there has arisen a tendency for Professor Lin's concept of "creative transformation" to replace "modernization" in the discussion of these issues. If now one would wish to write an essay, one could trace the changes from "wholesale Westernization" to "modernization" and then to "creative transformation" and so could grasp how in Taiwan, under the influence of Western culture, there was a gradual transformation in the attitudes with which people reflected back on their own existence and sought to deal with the question of Chinese culture. "Creative transformation" is a concept not just widely used in Taiwan. Even in Hong Kong, even indeed on the Mainland, some people have turned to it. I think that when Professor Lin Yü-sheng brought up the term "creative transformation" as a lodestar for cultural work in China, he certainly made a great contribution.

Professor Lin then interjected: "I only hope it's more than a word."[18]

Again, what is significant here is not the particular conceptualization of change advanced by Professor Lin and so enthusiastically endorsed by even so astute an intellectual as Wei Zhengtong, who wrote an excellent book on *Xunzi* and edits a sophisticated periodical in Taibei, *Zhongguo luntan*. Nor need one ask whether there is any substantive difference between "creative transformation" and other well-known slogans, such as the old *jiwang kailai* (Continue all that is of value in the past while opening China up to all new possibilities). The important point is that the Chinese pursuit of the right formula of cultural change continues as an intellectual project few if any Chinese have any doubts about.

Paradoxically, this pursuit itself exemplifies the "intellectualism" Professor Lin once analyzed as an aspect of Chinese culture. More specifically, it exemplifies the widespread belief that cultural change is not a matter of cumulative, disparate, and ad hoc intellectual, artistic, social, organizational, economic, and political efforts scattered throughout society but rather a controllable unifiable process that can and should be guided by intellectuals who have discovered the single, correct philosophy of history. To use William Graham Sumner's distinction, cultural change is "enacted," not "crescive," when it is normative, that is, proceeds as it should. It is, then, a matter of transformative, not accommodative, action. Subject to the guidance of intellectuals pursuing the right theory of cultural change, it is "Napoleonic," to use Tolstoy's distinction between Napoleon's belief that leaders can control the course of history and General Kutuzov's belief that leaders can only adjust themselves to historical forces largely out of their control. The desire to control history by conceptualizing the boundary between two entities (tradition and modernity) also meshes with Neo-Confucian habits of mind.[19]

This emphasis on normative theory as the key to enacted cultural change has largely shaped Chinese use of the word *wenhua* (culture). True, Chinese make abundant use of an Anglo-American anthropological literature that deals with culture in a largely descriptive way, trying to minimize "value judgments." It looks at "what people think and value" (F. G. Bailey) rather than at what they *should* value and the cultural factors either helping or preventing them from valuing what they should value. In Chinese discussions about Chinese culture, however, the emphasis is overwhelmingly on distinguishing between the undesirable and the desirable aspects of the cultural heritage, the "poisons inherited from the feudal period" (*fengjian yidu*) and the culture's "finest essence" (*jinghua*), to use the Mainland terms. The criteria with which this allegedly objective distinction is made are either explicitly identified with "reason" (*lixing*) as an absolute, trans-historical, trans-cultural standard or are undiscussed, being treated as self-evident.

Thus looking at Chinese culture in a normative way, distinguishing between the bad parts that should be expunged and the good ones that should be further developed, Chinese intellectuals often discuss Chinese culture completely ignoring those aspects that are amoral or alogical—for instance, the Confucian assumption that the center of the polity has enormous power morally to transform society, or that history includes a period of morally perfect government. What Chinese discussions of Chinese culture seldom display is the desire of a Robert Redfield just to stare at a way of life, try with a minimum of prejudgment comprehensively to describe everything one can observe, think about how all these facets form or do not form a whole, and only then cautiously raise the question of how morally to evaluate them.

In fact, when discussing "culture," Chinese intellectuals typically depict a particular society as not only creating a culture but also acting in relation to reason and morality as universal principles. To be sure, this ambiguity can be found in Western writing too. Yet because historicism, ethical skepticism, and cultural relativism have been so influential in the West, Western intellectuals often worry about this ambiguity, sensitive to the contradiction between the idea of universal morality and that of morality as a cultural product. No such sensitivity can be found in the thought of Hu Qiuyuan, whose way of theorizing about these matters is much less controversial in Taiwan than his nationalistic conservatism:

> What is culture? Facing their natural and international environments and trying to ensure their survival and progress, people base themselves on man's nature and capabilities and create cultures. Because the nature of man is the same, there are no basic differences between the world's cultures. The essential creative power of all cultures lies in the human desire for true values, reason, morality, and knowledge. Cultures vary or rise and decline because their structures and circumstances, both internal and external, differ, and because such internal and external factors interact in different ways.[20]

This outlook is typical of the Chinese intellectual world. In 1989, a scholar in Sichuan sent me a photograph with an inscription defining "culture" precisely as a process based on universal norms: "*Wenhua shi meiyou guojiede*" (Culture is without national boundaries). One famous book after another analyzes Chinese culture in an emphatically normative way by depicting it as a determinate entity that either does or does not accord with norms regarded by the author as universally or intrinsically valid. Standard examples of this genre are Tang Junyi's *Zhongguo wenhuazhi jingshen jiazhi* (Chinese culture and its value for the realization of the human spirit), a classic first published in 1953; Yin Haiguang's *Zhongguo wenhuade zhanwang* (An appraisal of Chinese culture and its prospects), a major iconoclastic document banned in Taiwan when first published there, in 1966, but republished there in 1988; and Ying-shih Yü's much admired *Cong jiazhi xitong kan Zhongguo wenhuade xiandai yiyi* (The modern relevance of Chinese culture: A discussion from the standpoint of the traditional value system), published in 1984 in Taiwan. An entirely normative concept of culture is basic also to Wei-ming Tu's defense of Confucian values in his *Ruxue di san qi fazhande qianjing wenti* (Reflections on the dawning of the third era in the evolution of the Confucian tradition), published in 1989.

In thus adopting such a normative concept of culture, Professor Tu of course was in accord with Mainland as well as other Chinese intellectual trends. For instance, at the above-mentioned conference in Beijing on Chinese culture, Zhang Dainian made a typical comment: "In China's traditional culture are lots of good things, which are hard to preserve, while the bad things are hard to eradicate."[21] Equally illustrating this normative perspective on the Mainland is Lin Jinquan's preface to Li Zonggui's 1988 book on Chinese culture: "How to construct a cultural and intellectual system appropriate to the structures of modernization, that is, how to construct a socialistic civilization based on the human spirit and fitting China's distinctive national character, thus became a most important and real problem for everyone, whether those on the higher or the lower rungs of society."[22] In terms of its ideological basis, Mao's "cultural revolution" also presupposed a normative concept of culture as something formed by people pursuing intrinsically valid ideals.

Indeed, in Chinese intellectual life today, there is no prominent tendency to doubt that human reason, with a limited amount of empirical data, can construct a grand philosophical system making clear the principles according to which cultures as integrated wholes and history as a series of stages develop; that these principles are normative or moral ones which reason can use to distinguish between the good and the bad in cultures and in history and to describe history as a teleological process moving toward a good end, namely the ultimate merging of all cultures on the basis of universally valid ideals; and that, by grasping these principles and propagating them, the intellectual members of a culture can demonstrate the correct way to control its development. Even Lao Siguang, an astute, cosmopolitan philosopher based in Hong Kong and well aware of historicism, ethical skepticism, and the problem of cultural relativism, entertains no such doubts, or at least feels no need to deal with them when addressing his Chinese public. This can be seen from both his 1981 book on Chinese modernization and the articles setting forth his most recent thoughts about this question in three 1988 issues of *Zhongguo shibao*.[23]

These assumptions, moreover, often are linked to sublime if not utopian criteria of successful modernization. True, many Chinese today, like many foreign social scientists or journalists, use more modest criteria of success, including statistical indices comparing developments in China to those in other developing countries. Lao himself emphasizes practicality. There is, however, a strong Chinese tendency to ignore such empirical comparisons and instead to use as the criterion of successful modernization a problem-free historical stage theoretically depicted as imminent if only something can be done about the "vested interests" (*jide liyizhe*) and intellectual confusion currently dominating the political center and so preventing the normal development of society.

Selfishness and intellectual confusion, even in the political world, are thus perceived as abnormal, eminently avoidable forms of human behavior. In other words, just as with the Confucian vision of a golden age (the Three Dynasties), normal political behavior is defined not in an a posteriori way, by observing behavior and inductively determining what is usual, but in an a priori way, by assuming that normal people would act in an ideal way were they not hampered by removable obstacles. This a priori approach to the problem of political practicality, entirely contrary to the Western mainstream, especially the Aristotelian, the Machiavellian, and the modern liberal or Millsian traditions, was at the heart of Confucian this-worldliness and remains prevalent in China today.[24]

To be sure, many Chinese take with a grain of salt those visions of imminent societal perfection and moral harmony (*datong*) put forward by modern Chinese ideologues since Kang Youwei. Yet these visions have indeed had great meaning for millions of them. Moreover, these visions are not more striking than the many ways that sublime criteria of success are taken for granted here and there in various conversations or writings. Hu Qiuyuan's writings are replete with them. When the psychologist Yang Guoshu speaks of social mobility and social justice in that "open society" into which, he hopes, Taiwan will turn, he does not use empirical studies about the extent to which concrete modern democracies like the United States have realized these ideals. He just states as a fact: "In an open society, the individual's social status and position depend on your own ability, efforts, and accomplishments."[25] When, in April 1987, the two biggest Taiwan newspapers (*Zhongguo shibao* and *Lianhebao*) created great excitement by publishing a debate about political-social issues between Ding Bangxing and He Huaishuo, both intellectuals assumed that their nation was headed for disaster unless the citizenry would become not only law-abiding and hard-working but also truly virtuous. (Ding decried the prevalence of selfishness, while he built his case on the pervasive lack of sincerity.)

When one makes a single list of criteria out of all such cliché expectations or commonly used standards of public behavior and political performance, one can see how much Chinese criticize their present life by referring to a priori, high ideals rather than empirical comparisons: Citizens should be selfless and totally sincere, not just moderately civic-minded; stratification should exhibit not only a comparatively high rate of social mobility but also the morally perfect distribution of power, prestige, and wealth; intellectual life must be based on an objectively valid moral consensus (*ren tong ci xin, xin tong ci li*) and cannot just amount to a confusing marketplace of contradictory ideas mixing the good with the bad; democratization must be total and immediate and lead to a polity uninfluenced by selfish interests; the economy must achieve not only a comparatively good record but also technological independence and lack of dependence on foreign markets; China must be quickly unified and develop into the equal of any superpower rather than just seeking national security in regional terms.[26]

I would argue, therefore, that, when we consider ideas about culture, history, and the criteria of successful modernization, there is a great disparity between the Chinese and the Western intellectual mainstream. According to a variety of widespread Chinese attitudes that are seldom questioned in Chinese circles, the Chinese today find themselves in a disastrous situation but could successfully control their fate by using reason, which, without depending greatly on empirical data, can establish moral and factual truths and create an all-encompassing theory depicting the teleological unfolding of history, deriving sublime criteria of successful modernization from this historical process, and using these criteria morally to evaluate political developments and the various cultural traditions of the world. Thus ego's moral imperatives are objectively, publicly, and clearly given to him or her by the objective structure of life, whether history, culture, or reason.

The Western intellectual mainstream is different. Tolstoyan doubts about the human ability to "control" historical change are prevalent. Though John Stuart Mill still spoke of "reason" as finding moral "truths," Alasdair MacIntyre and others have shown how Humean skepticism has risen in the West to erode the hope of finding objective, impersonal standards of morality. Teleological assumptions can be uncovered in Western writing, but the attempts to construct theories of history and culture have faltered as many scholars have sought maximally to base the study of human life on empirical data and have attacked Hegel. Thus, when John A. Hall tried to construct even a modest theory of history, he noted that he was swimming against a mainstream formed by Raymond Aron, Isaiah Berlin, and Karl Popper. Utopian ideals are not fashionable, and cultural anthropology emphasizes descriptions, not moral evaluation.[27] Finally, discussions of morality often emphasize indeterminate private hopes or impulses, not historically promulgated moral principles.

My point here is not to claim that either outlook is more valid than the other but merely to describe the disparity between them. My hope is that the examples cited here will convince the reader that this disparity exists. If it exists, it has important historical implications.

If it exists, the thesis of Western cultural hegemony over China has to be revised. Similarly, such heterology is hard to reconcile with the thesis that modern Chinese thought is largely discontinuous with the Confucian intellectual tradition. Professor Schwartz is at the forefront of the scholars who have seen the modern Chinese intellectual discourse as largely shaped by Western ideas, but I presume below to argue that this modern Chinese vision of modernity is rooted in the optimistic this-worldliness of Confucianism and arose as this Confucian outlook was combined at the turn of our century with a new surge of optimism about the current development of the world.

Looking at the problem of the continuity of Confucian culture in modern times, therefore, I have argued that there is a widespread Chinese way of discussing this problem, that this Chinese way is very different from that of the Western intellectual mainstream, and that this Chinese way of discussing Chinese cultural continuity itself illustrates this continuity.

This argument can be read as a criticism of modern Chinese intellectuals, a claim that they tried but failed to analyze completely the culture they grew up in. They have seen themselves as gazing down on their inherited culture while standing above it on a platform of universal reason, but actually their intellectual platform has been itself largely made out of a culturally specific set of categories they inherited.

It may well be, however, that we could thus criticize anyone trying to make sense out of cultural change. Any such intellectual effort may necessarily be a muddy mixture of reflexivity and culturally inherited presuppositions. Instead of criticizing Chinese intellectuals for underestimating the continuity of their culture, therefore, we can wonder at its expansiveness and flexibility. Adopting a drastically new picture of the physical world, of technology, of world geography, of world history, and of the desirable forms of economic-political organization, Chinese in modern times easily combined that picture with ways of thinking they had long been accustomed to, especially certain epistemological, historical, and ethical perspectives. These inherited perspectives remained basic to the universe of discourse into which they fitted this new picture. Moreover, noting the disparity between this universe and our own Western one, we Westerners have slowly learned or should learn that the "epistemic power" (John Dunn) of either form of discourse is not necessarily superior to that of the other. How do we determine *the* right way to think about human life? What are the trans-cultural criteria with which to evaluate different worlds of discourse? Does any world have a monopoly on the ability to make life better? With our current cultural presuppositions, we may think it nonsense to see ego's moral responsibilities as publicly and objectively given to him or her by the structure of history, but this vision may be justified as needed to make life better in a particular cultural situation.

The purpose of this essay is to obtain an overview of the factual continuities linking premodern and modern China as well as of the agenda of normative issues implied by these continuities. Our discussion so far has concentrated on intellectual categories that, to a large extent, were inherited unconsciously. This kind of cultural continuity has often been noted, as illustrated by Paul Tillich's remark that Marx was deeply influenced by Christian ethics, or Tang Junyi's remark that Chinese Marxism was deeply influenced by indigenous ideals, such as the ideal of "the whole world as one family."[28]

This kind of factual continuity raises a normative question: To what extent should this unconscious heritage be uncovered and revised? Discussing this heritage further below when we look at "optimistic thisworldliness," we shall touch on this normative question. At this point, however, we should turn from this unconscious heritage to look at the question of more overtly traditional continuities, functional and dysfunctional.

Overt Continuities and the Normative Agenda They Entail

Repeatedly identified by a large variety of Chinese and non-Chinese scholars, certain explicit or overt aspects of the traditional culture have been almost universally seen as persisting and as incompatible with modernity. This evaluation goes back to the Chinese reformers at the turn of the century such as Yan Fu, Liang Qichao, Tan Sitong, and Sun

Yat-sen.[29] Currently, Mainland writers on Chinese culture very much emphasize these aspects, seeing them as persisting to a large extent under communism and as greatly responsible for the Mainland's failure to modernize. Their preoccupation with this problem, for instance, is shared by Professor Wei-ming Tu and pervades his 1989 book recording his intellectual interactions with them on the Mainland in 1978–1987, *Reflections on the Dawning of the Third Era in the Evolution of the Confucian Tradition.* In Taiwan, this sense of wallowing in the "poisons inherited from feudalism" is far less prominent in writings about politics and culture, but few doubt that certain inherited ways of living were correctly discarded or should be still further revised.

To a large extent, these rejected traditional patterns are those which Chinese have come to regard as incompatible with the requirements of a society strongly focused on instrumental rationality, the instrumental means logically needed to pursue the distinctively modern goal of maximizing national well-being in a material sense. This is what Max Weber called *Zweckrationalität,* a concept intellectuals like Lao Siguang have explicitly picked up to conceptualize the central modern values. This perspective on Chinese modernization makes sense when we note that both of the Chinese governments today are far more directly preoccupied with economic development than was any imperial government through the nineteenth century. A great discontinuity with the tradition has indeed occurred, as Professor Schwartz long ago made so clear in his classic work on Yan Fu.

We perhaps could theoretically define this pursuit of instrumental rationality by discussing efforts to maximize economic incentives and minimize transaction costs. Further to define what "instrumental rationality" means for modern Chinese, however, one has to describe the traits they have focused on as incompatible and as compatible with this goal.

If we look at the philosophical analysis of Chinese culture published in Canton in 1988 by Li Zonggui and the largely psychological analysis of this subject published in Taibei that same year by Yang Guoshu, one finds much the same list of dysfunctional factors, except for Li's focus on modes of knowing, and except for a terminological difference: Li sees these phenomena as aspects of the inherited "feudal society," while Yang uses "traditional, agricultural" instead of "feudal."

First, an excessive emphasis on authority, group-centered life, and the family in particular is seen as preventing the development of a population focused on the good of the nation, equality under law, and the free and full development of the individual. Sexism has been part of this syndrome. Second, the tradition was excessively focused on agriculture, neglecting commerce and industry. Third, the traditional modes of knowing neglected the critical and rigorous development of logic and epistemology, insufficiently pursuing "dispassionate analysis," the differentiation of topics, factual accuracy, practical efficacy, and natural science. Instead, although emphasizing the systematization and unification of knowledge, these "traditional" or "feudal" cognitive modes followed an intuitive, pan-moralistic way of merging philosophy with natural science, ontology, cosmology, and religion. Fourth, these cognitive modes were connected to an insufficient emphasis on the innovative acquisition and application of new information. Fifth, formal and informal modes of political organization developed complementing the above social, economic, and epistemological patterns, especially the Confucian monarchy and exploitative kinds of bureaucratic and patron-client relations.[30]

While scholars with virtual unanimity have agreed on the need to discard these dysfunctions, there is also much scholarly agreement that a variety of traditionally inherited norms facilitate modernization, according with the goal of instrumental rationality, especially those emphasizing family cohesion, frugality and savings, hard work, respect for authority, respect for education, academic competition, competition in the economic marketplace, and certain bureaucratic skills.[31] Moreover, despite the epistemological syndrome noted above, appreciation for modern science and technology quickly developed in the twentieth century, frequently in harmony with explicitly Confucian values. Indeed, humanistic and religious objections to science have been weaker in China than in the West, as Ying-shih Yü has observed.

Based on wide scholarly agreement, these two lists not only refer to historically persisting aspects of the traditional culture but also roughly make clear a normative program concretely defining instrumental rationality, and consisting of two complementary efforts, discarding the dysfunctions and cultivating the desirable traits. To be sure, this program involves many subtleties and ambiguities. For instance, familism is to be discarded while family cohesion and harmony are to be promoted, and respect for authority is to be cultivated while authoritarianism is to be eliminated. Such subtleties, however, are integral to social life, and, presumably, dealing with them is mainly a matter of creative social practice.

As scholars have compared the requirements of modernity to the more explicit or overt aspects of the tradition, therefore, the point of controversy that has proved to be the hardest to resolve has centered on the Durkheimian problem of authority and autonomy. Durkheim and contemporary thinkers like Robert N. Bellah have raised the normative standard of society that both avoids authoritarian manipulation and knits the individual together with the local and the broader community, cultivating "those habits of the heart that are the matrix of a moral ecology, the connecting tissue of a body politic."[32] This standard has been seen as implying "individualism." Because of the great differences in the ways that cultures construct the self,[33] however, we can with less ambiguity speak of "the self-propelled adult." This refers to the location of decision making in the case of the many options faced in adult life, whether residential, occupational, intellectual, political, or moral. These choices can be made for the adult by a local customary group, such as a family, or by the state as it changes its "line" to mobilize society,[34] but the "self-propelled adult" makes them himself or herself on the basis of reflection and of norms acquired through childhood socialization, education, and other personal experience.

It is clear that in Taiwan's economic, social, moral, and intellectual life, the institutionalization of the self-propelled adult has gone very far, while in the political realm, this legitimization of adult autonomy has become stronger since the reforms of 1986 and can be traced back at least to the lively elections of 1977.[35] It is also clear that this legitimation, based on all three of the leading ideological trends in Taiwan—Chinese liberalism, modern Confucian humanism, and the official doctrine of the Three Principles of the People—has been a process of ideological communication filled with references to Confucian writings allegedly exalting the dignity and moral autonomy of the individual.

But does this contemporary image of Confucian values accord with their actual historical character? As already mentioned, scholars today disagree on how to answer this question. According to Chinese humanists, the scholarly study of Confucian texts reveals a moral vision that either wholly or to an important extent coincides with the modern goal of individual moral autonomy. This view today is at least partly followed even by Mainland scholars like Li Zonggui, who emphasizes not only the dysfunctional aspects of Confucian culture listed above but also the pervasive emphasis of traditional Chinese thought on "morality": "In the society of traditional China, there universally was a kind of deep sense of moral responsibility for history. This point applies equally to thinkers, ordinary scholars, and the common people."[36] On the other hand, Li's kind of emphasis on Confucian morality is also not far from the ways in which Benjamin Schwartz and Yang Guoshu see Confucian morality as de-emphasizing individual autonomy (see section on the Durkheimian Concern above).

Obviously unable to settle this controversy here, I can only offer three reasons why I support the humanists' view. First, Professor Yang not only describes Confucian orientations in a reductionist way, deducing them from organizational needs and not analyzing what Confucian writings said. He also fails to consider all the basic organizational needs of the traditional society. Focusing entirely on the need for authority and harmony within the small group carrying out agricultural work, he ignores the need of such small groups for a peaceful if not helpful political environment. This need logically implies the need to cultivate leaders who can distinguish between the greater good of the whole community and narrower interests, and who can autonomously pursue this greater good in the face of particularistic pressures. Thus even if one agrees with Professor Yang that one can infer the nature of social orientations from organizational needs, the agricultural ecotype in imperial China implied a need for moral autonomy as much as for group solidarity. Second, the view of traditional China as agricultural is true on the whole but not the whole truth. Third, if one wants to argue that Confucian thought put respect for authority figures above moral autonomy, one has to weigh the evidence to the contrary, such as Xunzi's central emphasis on the dignity and moral autonomy of the individual in his chapter on proper filial behavior ("Zi dao pian"), where he states: "Follow morality, not the ruler; do what is right, do not obey your father [if he is making a moral mistake]."[37]

THE PROBLEM OF OPTIMISTIC THIS-WORLDLINESS

Looking at the relation between Confucian culture and modernization by focusing on the explicit or overt aspects of the tradition, therefore, scholars have tended to agree about many traditional traits, evaluating them as desirable or dysfunctional, while also disagreeing about whether the modern Chinese goal of moral autonomy and pluralism is essentially consistent with Confucian ideals. What this discussion has neglected is the possibility that there is a contradiction between modern Chinese goals and the less consciously transmitted aspects of the Confucian heritage. While scholars worrying about the compatibility of the inherited culture with modern life have focused on the Durkheimian issue of autonomy, the more urgent problem may be optimistic this-worldliness.

This has been alluded to above as basic to the rise of a certain teleological vision of history and to the great optimism with which many Chinese today define the criteria of successful modernization. Especially because this teleological vision has often been used iconoclastically to identify the traditional culture with its dysfunctional aspects and to reject it, scholars today still often see this teleological vision as largely constructed out of ideas imported from the West. Indeed, no one has argued this case more effectively than Professor Schwartz and Professor Hao Chang, whose recent study of Tan Sitong gives Western influences major credit for Tan's transformative vision, even while richly documenting Tan's central preoccupation with the Confucian ideal of a society uniformly based on mutual empathy and respect (*ren*).[38] Nevertheless, more work is needed, I believe, on the relation between this modern Chinese teleological vision, going back to Tan's generation at the turn of the century, and indigenous concepts.

Professor Wang Ermin has pointed to the convergence at the turn of the century between Western evolutionism and the indigenous New Text vision of history as moving upward toward an epoch of moral perfection (*taiping*).[39] Apart from such consciously discussed doctrines, however, we should take into account the most basic, culturally inherited assumptions shared by Chinese as they faced the new situation imposed on them by the West.

These included what can be called "optimistic this-worldliness." Confucian thought since Zhou times largely posited sublime political goals and the existence of extremely efficacious means available in the human struggle to reach these goals. Thus, in general, Confucians not only put forward the goal of a government fully based on absolute morality (*renzheng, dezhi*) but also believed that this goal was completely practicable. Its practicability was obvious, in their eyes, because sages had obtained absolute moral-political wisdom which had been transmitted down to the present, even though in a partly unclear way; because the sages' perfect rule in the distant past demonstrated its practicability; because the cosmos existed as an inspiring moral presence, whether in the form of outer order or inner feeling; because the individual lacked original sin and so could fully grasp and act on that cosmic presence; and because the very nature of the polity was such that any moral person heading it would almost immediately have an enormous transformative effect on the whole society, dissolving immorality throughout China if not the whole world. Among all such assumptions, none was more important than "epistemological optimism," the belief in the ready availability of enough absolute moral knowledge to evaluate everyone perfectly and totally reform the political order.

With the goal of totally moral government thus realized, total justice in this world would be effected, that is, every individual would be perfectly evaluated by the government and receive exactly the rewards or punishments he or she deserved. In other words, all status, power, and wealth would be distributed in a morally perfect way. There would be no hierarchy out of accord with the moral needs of any individual. This perfect distribution of rewards and punishments thus would not depend on any divine bar of judgment in the afterlife. Indeed, the idea of punishment and rewards in the afterlife did not even exist in China until a century or two after the birth of Christ, as Buddhist influence in China became significant.

Confucian thought, of course, fully recognized the pervasive presence of evil and suffering. In particular, it persistently perceived the current polity as failing to evaluate individuals properly and so failing to distribute rewards and punishments (especially status) in a moral, just way, and it persistently perceived all individuals, except for the barely remembered sages, as failing fully to identify themselves with the inherently elusive though divine presence of the cosmos. Yet Confucians viewed this persisting failure to reach their sublime goals as occurring despite the full practicability of these goals, which in turn was based on the wonderfully sufficient epistemological, psychological, institutional, and cosmological *setting* of all human efforts in the present. (I believe that the many discussions of Confucianism as "humanism" often look at the Confucian "concept of man" while neglecting the Confucian perception of the setting of human life.)[40]

This highly optimistic, this-worldly view of the polity is at odds with the much more pessimistic view of the Western mainstream, from Plato, Aristotle, and St. Augustine through Machiavelli, Hobbes, Locke, the American Founding Fathers, John Stuart Mill, and twentieth-century liberal thought. Where Confucius believed he could quickly reform any government that hired him, Socrates said that, if an honest man tried to serve as an official, he would shortly be killed by his enemies. As Professor Hao Chang has argued, this Western emphasis on the "dark" side of human nature has been basic to the Millsian or liberal tradition of democratic thought in the West, though the optimism of the Rousseau-Hegel-Marx tradition is comparable to that of the Confucian.[41]

In modern China, however, the traditional heritage of optimistic this-worldliness fully merged with liberalism and humanism, not only Marxism. That is, despite much discussion about how the Western impact shattered the traditional world view of the Chinese and threw them into a state of "disorientation," Chinese intellectual circles at the turn of the century came to be filled with a new optimistic feeling that great moral progress in the organization of mankind was at hand.[42] I would argue that this new optimism, logically consistent with the Confucian belief that the highest moral-political goals are attainable in the present, was the indispensable basis of Mao's utopianism and personal appeal. At the very least, this new optimism defined current societal changes as part of a worldwide trend (*shijiede chaoliu*) carrying mankind almost inevitably from its present miserable historical stage to a pleasing if not perfect future. Undoubtedly, the rise of this optimistic vision has much to do with those widely shared teleological assumptions described above regarding the nature of history, culture, and the criteria of successful modernization, though just how much is still debated.

Yet, whether these assumptions stem more from the indigenous world view or from Western ideas, they imply a normative agenda: Are these assumptions valid? Should Chinese continue to use them? This agenda certainly raises questions far beyond the scope of this paper, especially since one would have to figure out how to define the criteria by which such assumptions should be evaluated.[43] How can one decide whether the bluntly teleological theory of history so prevalent in contemporary China is or is not preferable to the anti-Hegelian thinking common in Western circles today? If one accepts the plausible view of Lao Siguang and others that the key challenge presented by modern life is how to combine an emphasis on instrumental rationality with a commitment to the moral-spiritual foundations of society, are these widespread Chinese views about the inherently moral structure of human life less helpful than some others?

Unable here to deal with such questions, we can, however, at least note that whether optimistic this-worldliness can be successfully combined with political pluralism is an open question. Use of these sublime criteria of successful modernization to criticize government turns political disagreement into a series of Manichaean, black-and-white confrontations, as illustrated by the ROC's political history in recent years.[44] From this standpoint, the normative agenda of Chinese modernization should include the question of how to establish reasonable criteria of political success. This discussion has not yet been forcefully developed in China, despite Hu Shi's famous call for "tolerance" in criticizing the government and Hao Chang's well-known article on how democratization requires awareness of the human weaknesses that necessarily infect political life (*you'an yishi*). My own hope is that Chinese intellectuals will increasingly consider the distinction made in the section on Disparate Worlds above between the a priori and the a posteriori way of determining what is politically practicable. This point indeed coincides with Lao Siguang's emphasis in his 1988 *Zhongguo shibao* interview on reducing political expectations to what can actually be accomplished. Clearly, some such reduction is needed if Joseph Schumpeter was right when he correlated democracy with a public style of moderate political criticism.

Yet, despite their quest for "self-awareness" (*zijue*), Chinese intellectuals have done little to identify Confucianism's culturally distinctive optimism and to consider to what extent this heritage might impede their efforts to establish political pluralism in China. Themselves typically filled with great optimism, Chinese iconoclasts identified Confucian culture with the dysfunctions listed above but took for granted that Confucianism's optimism was just a normal if not universal way of thinking, not a culturally distinctive trait. Similarly, the Confucian humanists have seen nothing distinctive or controversial about this optimism. In discussing Kant, for instance, Tang Junyi assumed that Kant's "experience" was the same universal given about which Confucians philosophized. But Kant did not posit a past historical period of morally perfect experience. His "experience" was just the morally imperfect or neutral experience available to anyone any time. In Neo-Confucian terms, Kant identified "experience" with only the realm of "already issued feelings" (*yifa*).

Similarly, Professor Ying-shih Yü holds that Confucius's principles were essentially just inferred from observable experience and so were quite practicable.[45] Yet Confucius himself granted that he had never personally been in the presence of a sage, and his vision of a distant, morally perfect past was also not based on personal observation. In other words, his idea that people could become morally perfect and establish morally perfect government was not based in the slightest on observed experience.

It was based on an optimistic faith he conflated with the historical record. Chinese today still tend to conflate it with the universally observable, factual character of human life, instead of separating out this faith as a culturally distinctive pattern and critically evaluating it in relation to their current goal of modernization and democratization. To a large extent, therefore, their conceptualization of history has remained rooted in their historical tradition.

CONCLUSION: THE AXIAL ROOTS OF CHINESE MODERNITY

Yet, however one may criticize the ways in which Chinese intellectuals discuss Chinese modernization, it seems clear that modern Chinese life, whether in Taiwan or on the Mainland, is still deeply influenced by the traditional cultural heritage. In other words, an exceptionalist view of Chinese modernization is hard to defend, since cultural change in modern China is, after all, a mix of continuities and discontinuities, just as cultural change normally is.

True, many Chinese scholars, such as Lao Siguang, believe that China's premodern cultural heritage has suffered from a peculiar incompatibility with modern values, while in the West the transition from tradition to modernity went far more smoothly. Yet, from the breakup of the medieval world through World War II, the West also had to endure one horrible upheaval after another. How can one measure the amount of suffering and disorientation on one side to prove it was "more" than on the other? On the contrary, the Chinese vision of a peculiarly Chinese incongruity with modern values is very likely just a concept meeting certain modern Chinese ideological needs, not a balanced way of looking at history, just as is the common Chinese claim that there is no ideological or cultural crisis in the West comparable to the Chinese one. East and West, the discontinuities with tradition have often been experienced as a painful state of disorientation and intellectual crisis but have nevertheless been intertwined with major continuities. Should we envy those many societies today that entered the modern era barely aware of it, continuing in their traditional ways without undergoing any "cultural crisis"?

Thus distinguishing between the more overt and the less conscious continuities, we can make a good case that both have been important in twentieth-century China. The Chinese case, therefore, testifies to the great persistence of the cultural orientations formed during what Karl Jaspers and S. N. Eisenstadt have called the "axial age." According to their view, during the first millennium B.C. some societies, such as the Chinese, the Hindu and Buddhist, the Greek, and the Jewish, came to define life in terms of a systemic gap between the ideal world and the given, mundane world, and each of these "axial civilizations" developed its own distinctive ways of defining the nature of this gap, the ways in which to close it, and the institutional nature of the elites responsible for closing it. True, there is dispute about the extent to which axial orientations have persisted in the context of modernization. S. N. Eisenstadt sometimes views them as largely superseded by this context in the case of modern China. Yet Robert N. Bellah and his colleagues have analyzed contemporary U.S. culture as still rooted in the Judeo-Christian and Greco-Roman traditions of the West's axial age.[46] Ying-shih Yü similarly views China's anciently formed orientations as persisting today, and the evidence presented in this paper supports his position.

Scholars, after all, already agree that many currently persisting cultural traits in China are tradition-rooted. The main remaining point of controversy with regard to these much-discussed issues is the Durkheimian one of authority and autonomy. Moreover, as this essay has argued, there is another, less noticed line of continuity with the tradition, the link between China's traditional optimistic this-worldliness and prevalent contemporary Chinese ways of discussing history, culture, the criteria of successful modernization, and the issues of political conflict. In all these complex ways, then, major continuities persist between China's axial roots and a variety of intellectual, institutional, and behavioral patterns in China today, despite the discontinuities that occurred when China adopted the widespread modern emphasis on instrumental rationality.

How to understand this mix of continuities and discontinuities is a matter of factual, historical inquiry. Yet how this mix is understood shapes the agenda of normative issues with which Chinese and others are concerned today. Precisely to distinguish between the good and the bad in the tradition may be not entirely possible, not to mention agreeing on all the criteria needed for this task. Amidst these ambiguities, however, some questions are central: Will all of China be able to focus on instrumental rationality by revising inherited patterns? Will all of it be able to fashion a society based on the self-propelled adult? Can pluralism and individual autonomy best be furthered by invoking Confucian values? Will the criteria of successful modernization be realistically re-examined and discussed in the light of an a posteriori understanding of practical economic-political development?

TEN

The Place of Values in Cross-Cultural Studies: The Example of Democracy and China

ANDREW J. NATHAN

The proper role of the investigator's values in social scientific and historical studies is no longer as intensely debated as it once was. So far as I know, no one now seriously disputes the view, prominently identified with Hume and Weber, that fact and value statements are different in kind and need to be based on different kinds of arguments. But the strict behavioralism or "naturalism" that argued that social-science inquiry, to be valid, must be entirely value-free, has yielded among most practitioners to the acknowledgment that the investigator's values unavoidably influence at least the choice of topic and approach and the language of description and analysis. Beyond this, many historians and social scientists believe that value judgments may legitimately be made in the course of an inquiry, as long as they are clearly expressed as such and are separated from statements of fact. Some argue further that social inquiry is incomplete without an ethical dimension and that reasoned argument about value issues should be a standard part of social science research. Some even hold that ethical judgment constitutes social science's main reason for being and the ultimate source of its meaning. In one way or another, all these views recognize that values play a legitimate role in social science inquiry alongside empirical analysis.[1]

Scholarship in cross-cultural studies is capable of being as value-free and empirical as scholarship in which the investigator studies people or events within his or her own culture—which is to say, value-free and empirical within the limits of the human sciences. This is true even in the limiting case of works whose main subject is the values of another culture, provided that they treat the values they are describing in an objective way, in the sense that they describe them comprehensively, fairly, and with insight.[2] To be sure, the fact that an author is describing another culture's values in the language of his own culture introduces special problems of translating and interpreting value-laden concepts, whose meanings are in some sense changed just by being rendered in another language. Yet the challenge this presents is one of translation in its broadest sense rather than of evaluation.

But, as students of foreign cultures, we often reach the point at which, for one reason or another, we wish to make an explicit value judgment. Sometimes it is precisely because cultures differ about the values concerned that cross-cultural study of a particular issue is intellectually compelling in the first place, or has practical significance. We may study another culture to seek new ethical and moral perspectives for ourselves, or because we hope to influence others to accept our values. At the same time, citizens from the country the area specialist is studying often invite dialogue by showing a lively interest in our judgments of their country's political, legal, social, or economic performance.

The problem the area specialist confronts at this point is whether the values that form the ultimate ground of judgment in a given study ought to be those of the culture being studied or those of the investigator. Actually, value judgments made in the course of scholarship on one's own culture also face this problem whenever the values of the judger and the judged are different, as can easily happen in societies of any complexity. What I have to say will apply to this situation of what we might call domestic cross-cultural judgment as much as to the problem of international cross-cultural judgment, but it is in the latter that the issue is especially felt.

To be more precise, two possibilities confront an investigator who wishes to make an explicit, reasoned value judgment as a component of scholarly research about a foreign society. The choice I will argue for is to base the judgment on values in which the investigator believes. Even if the values chosen have some supporters in the subject society, the investigator chooses them because he or she believes in them. These are most likely to be values based in his own society, although that is not strictly necessary to my analysis of the problem. This choice is founded on the claim that values the investigator believes to be valid can validly be applied to societies other than his own—what might be called evaluative universalism.

The second choice, which I think is the one in principle preferred by most area specialists, is to base the judgment on values the investigator finds among those indigenous to the subject society. Even if he shares these values, he chooses them because they are native to the society he is judging. These may be among the dominant values there, or they may be the values of a minority. In either case, their choice as the standard of evaluation is founded on the claim that a society can validly be judged only by values that are among its own. I label this position cultural relativism, narrowing that term for the purposes of this essay to one of its meanings.[3]

The problem of evaluative universalism versus cultural relativism as methodologies of evaluation in cross-cultural studies should not be confused with a separate difficulty that has more often been discussed: whether and how members of one culture can understand, or interpret, the ways of thinking of other cultures.[4] This is a question of how to know or understand, rather than how to evaluate or judge. Evaluation and understanding are intimately related in several ways, one of which I shall discuss later, but the two procedures are different and so are the problems of carrying them out cross-culturally. Similarly, the question whether it is appropriate to apply foreign value standards to another culture is not the same as whether it is appropriate to apply foreign analytical frameworks—for example, whether it makes any sense to refer to the Chinese National People's Congress as a legislature, or to speak of it as performing the rule-making function; or to refer to the casting of ballots in China as voting or as the performance of the interest-articulating function.[5] The use of such concepts might sometimes be a prelude to evaluation, and may even tend to create a bias toward either positive or negative evaluation, depending on how they are used. But the problems of categorizing and evaluating remain separate ones.

Nor, third, do I wish to discuss in detail whether value judgments may be made at all in social science inquiry (although many of the arguments adduced below pertain to this broader problem as well as to the narrower one on which I wish to focus) or whether value statements can be epistemologically meaningful. I address myself to the area specialist who has made an empirical study of some aspect of a foreign culture, in the process overcoming to the extent possible the problems of translation, understanding, interpretation, and analysis, who now wants to make a value judgment, and who assumes, at least for the time being, that such a judgment conveys some kind of meaning. In short, I wish primarily to discuss not why we want to make value judgments or whether we are allowed to do so, but how to do so: to give not so much a philosopher's account of the problem as a practitioner's.

Cultural relativism has its roots in the aspiration of the modern social sciences to treat a diverse humankind with an equalizing objectivity.[6] In its effort to rise above racism, modern anthropology adopted the theory that each society's culture serves its own functional needs. Functionalism in turn became the basis of modern sociology and political science, and through them of area studies. As a professional tool of post-World War II American area studies, relativism especially recommended itself as a corrective to our society's nineteenth- and early-twentieth-century missionary impulses. The pioneers of area studies believed that Americans must reconcile themselves to the fact that their way of life was not going to sweep the world. Other cultures must be understood on their own terms in order to avoid confrontations that no one would profit from. In China studies in particular, relativism represented an attempt to temper the nativism which from the 1950s on threatened to produce disastrous misunderstandings of Asian communism.

John K. Fairbank, for example, worried that "th[e] difference in values between Chinese and Americans makes it easy for each to regard the other as essentially immoral. Our great power rivalry can be superheated by the moral righteousness that is second nature to both peoples."[7] He warned the American public in 1946: "It is because we apply our political faith to China directly, with no allowance for Chinese conditions, that our thinking has become confused. . . . We cannot expect democracy in China soon or on our own terms, but only on terms consistent with Chinese tradition, which must be gradually remade."[8] Reaffirming this argument with characteristic wryness nearly forty years later he commented: "Liberals do get themselves between fires! I was committed to viewing 'communism' as bad in America but good in China, which I was convinced was true. This led me to claim China and America were different 'cultures' or 'social orders'—also true. It followed that area specialists like me had esoteric knowledge of these cultural-social differences between China and America. The question was whether we could impart it to our fellow citizens. . . . It was a tall order but the only way to keep American policy on the right track."[9]

Throughout the post-war era, practitioners of China studies have continued to see themselves as needing constantly to correct the culturally biased misunderstandings and impatient judgmentalism of non-specialists. For example, a 1971 collection of essays by younger China scholars opened with the declaration: "One frequent reason for the inadequacy of our policies is that they are based on assumptions that grow out of the application of norms external to China. Negative judgments are rendered because the questions asked and the norms applied are derived from other civilizations. Thus the politics of the People's Republic is decried because it fails to conform to cherished Western notions, like the rule of law, separation of powers, and institutional pluralism. . . . For a new generation this will not do. . . . We must try to come to an understanding of modern Chinese history which appreciates the Chinese understanding."[10] Similarly, a 1979 symposium of essays sponsored by the Asia Society was based on the premise that "a judgment about China's human-rights record must be made, but only after choosing our yardstick with care. It is no good looking at our own cherished values, labeling them universal values, then asking if the Chinese are human enough to adhere to such 'universal values'. . . . A billion people live in China—and we don't. . . . Ultimately the values of the Chinese people—their priorities, views about the world, and ultimate beliefs—must be a key testing ground of any theory about China."[11]

Perhaps, as Paul Hollander has argued, the call for cultural relativism in many cases masked what was really the projection of personal values, critical of American society, onto the Chinese revolution under the claim that they were Chinese values.[12] In this sense it was not authentic relativism, but instead a convenient mask for what was, in the terms of this essay, actually a universalistic but negative evaluation of one's own society. But the fact that a relativist disguise was deemed useful for such a critique is tribute to the fact that relativism had become the conventional wisdom of area studies. As such, relativism existed before and lasted after the era of American self-disillusionment during the Vietnam War, and its influence has extended to virtually all points of the political spectrum.

Thus, relativism has largely survived the turn toward negativism which American feelings about China took shortly after the purge of the "Gang of Four."[13] The new negativism was fueled in part by gradually increasing (although hardly complete) Chinese honesty about the past, by revelations that became available because of improved Western access to China,[14] and by the increased sophistication of China specialists, as scholarship advanced, about the actual functioning of Chinese society.[15]

The earlier paradox of the West praising China most warmly just when it least deserved it was replaced by a new paradox: Skepticism and disillusionment grew widespread just as Chinese-Western relations were improving and China was ending the worst abuses of the Maoist era. Some commentators deplored China's backwardness or authoritarianism, while others expressed pessimism about the prospects for modernization. Some criticized China from the left for abandoning Maoism. By the late 1980s, the mood of American China specialists was sufficiently critical to permit some 160 scholars to sign an open letter protesting the removal of Hu Yaobang from the post of Party General Secretary and the purge of three leading intellectuals from the Chinese Communist Party, an act of adverse public judgment on the actions of the Chinese Communist Party so far as I know unprecedented among such a broad spectrum of China scholars since at least the 1950s.[16]

But these developments constituted only a modest, and mostly inarticulate, shift in the direction of what I have labeled evaluative universalism.[17] This is perhaps partly because the Chinese have been making negative judgments of their own errors and shortcomings at the same time as Westerners have been doing so, with the result that many of the values involved (for example, development) and many of the evaluations (for example, that Mao behaved tyrannously) appear to be shared, at least at a certain level of generality, by both sides. To the extent that American critics confirm what Chinese critics have said, a clear clash of value premises is avoided and with it the need to clarify the problem of which set of values is being used as a basis for judgment. In addition, evaluative works by political scientists and economists in particular often sidestep the issue of value selection by applying criteria of "growth" or "performance," derived from their disciplines, which are putatively accepted by and thus applicable to all cultures.[18]

But much of the apparent new agreement on values is merely verbal, and disappears when broad concepts like development, democracy, or human rights are analyzed more closely for their specific meanings within different cultures. Similarly, many apparently universalistic values describing such economic or political "system outputs" as welfare, security, equity, freedom, or justice are not understood or ranked the same way in different societies. In many areas, such as the proper limits of state power or the role of law, the differences between the two cultures' preferences are too obvious to be papered over by any formula. Thus the problem remains, because in many respects the values of the two societies remain different, even if they no longer seem to be as different as they once were.[19]

Before the choice that is faced in making value judgments about another society can be explored further, it is necessary to be precise about what it consists of. It is often conceived as a choice between applying Western values to a foreign country and applying its own values. But this way of stating the problem ignores the likelihood that there is a diversity of values on the question at issue within the culture of the judger, within that of the judged, or within both. Taking this fact into consideration, the choice between universalism and relativism can only be defined as I did at the outset—as a choice between values in which the investigator believes and values that are found in the subject society.

The problem takes the simplified our-culture-versus-theirs form only if two conditions exist. The first is that the cultural mainstreams of the two societies are distinctly identifiable and fundamentally opposed on a given issue. To be sure, this is not an uncommon situation. It is certainly the case with the example of democracy and China. The mainstream democratic values of both China and America are relatively easy to identify, and they are different. What is called democratic pluralism (defined further below) is recognized by its critics and supporters alike as the dominant conception of democracy in the West.[20] And in China, even most critics of the official notion of socialist democracy share some of the core values embodied in that concept, for example, that democracy should be conducive to social harmony.[21]

The second condition is that the outside analyst chooses to apply the mainstream values of his own society. This is also a common situation, but not inevitable. I can illustrate with two examples. Maurice Meisner in *Mao's China* operates as an evaluative universalist, but he does not apply the dominant values of his own society to China. He evaluates the performance of the Chinese political system against standards of humanistic socialism which he applies not because of their Chinese provenance (although he argues these values are grounded in Chinese communism) but because he believes in their validity himself.[22] Otherwise, he would not be able to continue to evaluate Chinese socialism by these values even as he marks an almost complete erosion of commitment to them on the part of most Chinese. On the other hand, in a recent article, Thomas A. Metzger employs essentially Western values to evaluate Chinese politics, but feels able to do so only because he is able to locate their proponents within the Chinese context. He argues that "one cannot expect a society to realize options not clearly conceptualized by a good number of its more influential members."[23] In other words, one's standard of evaluation should be chosen from among those available within the society being evaluated, although the outsider has the latitude to choose for this purpose whichever of the indigenous outlooks most closely resembles his own.

The point of these examples is that standards applied under the rubric of evaluative universalism need not be those that are dominant or even widely influential in the analyst's own culture, nor need the standards applied by the cultural relativist necessarily be unpopular ones in his own society. And, although cultural relativism is often linked with a positive evaluation of a foreign culture and evaluative universalism with a negative one, these linkages are not inevitable either.

Three arguments are usually given against the rendering by a foreigner of judgments on aspects of another society based on his own values. First, to judge by other than native values is arbitrarily to impose an outside standard without moral justification. We have no right to do this; it is a form of interference or cultural imperialism. Second, it makes no sense to the people being judged. The values applied have no intellectual foundation in the society they are being applied to, because such societies lack a tradition of these values and the values are not widely supported there (although there may be a few supporters, out of tune with their own society). The outside values are abstract words, with no cultural referents. Third, applying outside values exerts no useful effect. Since the values we seek to impose have no roots and few supporters in the target society, insisting upon them is an empty exercise that is not going to persuade anyone or change behavior. Indeed, our values would not work if transplanted to most other societies, because most non-Western societies lack the prerequisite cultural, economic, and social conditions. For example, people in poor countries lack the economic security, educational backgrounds, and sense of individuality necessary for Western standards of human rights or democracy to function successfully.

The first argument is apparently based on a misunderstanding of what making a value judgment entails. The metaphors of imperialism and sovereignty are inappropriate. Evaluation is an intellectual act, not an act of coercion; an act of communication, not of excommunication. It is the opposite of the kind of denigration labeled by Edward Said as "Orientalism."[24] A value judgment is a way of respectfully sharpening and focusing discussion, not ending it. It involves defining, defending, and applying a value so that others may become informed of it and may respond if they wish. Applying values in which one does not believe, were it even intellectually feasible to do so, would defeat the process of communication.[25] As Gerald James Larson has pointed out, "The glossing over of important differences in the name of civility may, in fact, be the worst kind of uncivilized behavior."[26]

In fact, evaluative universalism amounts to little more than the almost tautological position that a value is a standard in the validity of which the person holding it believes. As both Bernard Williams and Geoffrey Harrison have pointed out, the opposite position is both incoherent and contradictory: First, from the fact that different cultures' values are different, it derives an injunction for moral relativism which does not logically follow; then it contradicts itself by applying this injunction universally.[27] By contrast, evaluative universalism is logically consistent. It does not make the untrue claim that one's values are or must be universally accepted, but only states the intention to apply them oneself in a consistent manner, both inside and outside one's own society. A certainty of having absolute answers is thus no more a prerequisite of rendering a judgment for advocates of evaluative universalism than it is for advocates of cultural relativism. If anything, the opposite is more nearly the case: The more controverted one recognizes the issues to be, the more appropriate evaluative universalism becomes, because it is all the more important to communicate clearly and to explain to those who apparently disagree with us what we really think.

Nor is the application of one's own values an exercise in arbitrariness. As noted earlier, it is generally accepted that evaluative or moral reasoning is different in kind from empirical or scientific reasoning. But this does not mean that values are simply a matter of taste about which no argument is possible. There are standards of logic and reasoning that are applicable to ethical or evaluative argument.[28] Frank Fischer, for example, following Paul Taylor,[29] identifies four stages in evaluation — verification, validation, vindication, and rational choice. Some of these stages involve the empirical assessment of a situation against value-derived criteria, others the derivation of the criteria themselves or the defense of the values on which they depend. Thus valid evaluation entails both careful argumentation about the values involved and empirical research about the situation to which they are being applied. One need not accept Fischer's highly articulated version of what evaluative reasoning entails to agree that people can discuss value issues more or less reasonably.

If this were not the case, then to be sure the argument for evaluative universalism would fail. For then there could be no logical warrant for applying one's own values to a foreign culture, or even for applying them within one's own culture to groups or individuals who do not happen to share them. No reasoned discourse about values would be possible among those who disagreed. This indeed seems to be the ultimate, if normally unacknowledged, argument of the relativist. It is a counsel of intellectual despair that suggests that values are so irrational or immutable that only people who already agree on them have any business discussing them.[30]

Indeed, in the hands of some of its practitioners cultural relativism goes even further than this. It requires the application of value standards from the subject society, not only when the evaluator finds some he is able to agree with but even when he does not. The prerequisite for discussion, then, is to give up whatever there is to discuss. For example, the reporter Hans Koningsberger in his widely read *Love and Hate in China* wrote, "What right do we Westerners have, freshly back home from plundering the world for four centuries, fat and rich and worried about calories, what nerve do we have really, to poke around here and see if there's dust on the political piano, and worry so nobly whether these people, whose former drowning or starving by the millions didn't make our front pages, have enough democratic rights?"[31] And a Quaker delegation of the early 1970s argued, "The American social experience of pluralism and diversity and the relatively ungoverned U.S. economy do not constitute a lens through which Americans can successfully examine the basis of Chinese society."[32] What such viewpoints forget is that, in the words of Bernard Williams, "*De gustibus non disputandum* is not a principle which applies to morality, [and] 'When in Rome do as the Romans do' . . . is at best a principle of etiquette."[33]

Besides the difficulties with cultural relativism already mentioned, such judgment by abdication of judgment carries insoluble methodological problems. The more authoritarian a society is, the less we know about any differences that exist within it about value issues, the more united it appears. By no coincidence, objections to foreign value judgments are voiced most often and most loudly by authoritarian governments, not by private citizens under authoritarian regimes nor by the citizens or the governments of open societies. Since modern societies are seldom unanimous on value questions, which values from the subject society should we select to apply to it? How does one apply standards one does not find convincing? What does one achieve by doing this? The relativist position provides no independent footing from which to call into question whether the standards promoted by the dominant forces in a society are, in fact, generally accepted there.

For example, in the Mao period, most cultural relativists acknowledged that the Chinese system appeared totalitarian to Western eyes, but in their view it was inappropriate to take account of this in our analyses because the perception itself was based on Western individualism. This was a value the Chinese were thought not to share because no Chinese at the time dared to express it. On the one hand, a truthful book by Ivan and Miriam London about violence and subsequent disillusionment among the Red Guards was widely disbelieved by China specialists because of the apparent anti-Communist stance of its authors.[34] On the other, Western scholars attempting to evaluate China by what they thought were Chinese standards reached a series of erroneous conclusions: One scholar found that "May 7 cadre schools are reasonably successful in revolutionizing many cadres";[35] another that "[Chinese industries] have equaled the most progressive and democratic experiments taking place in various corporations of western Europe";[36] and the Quaker delegation concluded that "[China's] political system . . . is willingly supported, in our opinion, by the great majority of the Chinese people."[37]

Objective information thoroughly understood is obviously a prerequisite to a meaningful value judgment. But, less obviously, the relationship can also run the other way. Evaluation can serve as an aid to understanding by spurring skepticism.[38] By contrast, suspending one's standards of judgment in order to try to evaluate another society by what we take to be its standards can lead us to lose our critical footing in dealing not only with values but also with facts.

Cultural relativism, in short, led into not only a moral but also a cognitive dead end. The relativist position adopted in order to prevent missionary zeal from clouding our understanding of the non-Western world led in some cases to an equal but opposite kind of self-deception. Precisely when, as we know now, the Chinese people's alienation from the Maoist system reached its height, so did the vogue of Maoism among China specialists in the West. The lesson we should draw from this experience is that, so far from there being no moral justification for applying one's own values to another society, there really is no justification, moral or intellectual, for applying any values but one's own to any society.

Strictly speaking, this line of thinking disposes of all three arguments against evaluative universalism. For if there is no choice but to apply the values one believes in, then it does not matter how difficult it is to make oneself understood to persons in the subject culture (the second argument)—although we should do our best to overcome obstacles to understanding—or how remote are the values being applied from those that have any realistic possibility of being realized (the third argument). A value judgment, after all, is not a prediction. For example, to argue that Chinese democracy is inadequate by some chosen standard does not require proof that an adequate form of democracy is actively possible there. If it is indeed the case that a better form of democracy is not an available option, this fact confirms the evaluation instead of altering it, and perhaps helps to explain why an inadequate form of democracy persists. There are other logical weaknesses in these two arguments as well. The second seems to exclude the possibility that, through communication across cultural lines, people might come to understand something for the first time; the third appears to deny that societies change or respond to international opinion.

But it may be interesting to address directly the factual assumptions at the base of these two remaining arguments. How often is it the case that an outside evaluation actually holds a society to a value standard that we know for certain its members can neither understand nor achieve? It is of course impossible to answer this question for every possible case of a society evaluated along some dimension by a foreigner. The example of a Westerner's evaluation of Chinese democracy may continue to serve as an example. Because it is a "hard case," it suggests how rarely it can be true that a set of outside values on an important human issue are completely irrelevant to a given society's thinking and possibilities. Another good example would be the application to China of the idea of human rights as embodied in the Universal Declaration of Human Rights.[39] The arguments for that example would be closely parallel to the ones presented below.

The evaluative standard I applied in *Chinese Democracy* is "pluralist democracy," a concept that traces its lineage to Joseph A. Schumpeter's *Capitalism, Socialism, and Democracy*.[40] It is an avowedly minimalist standard that defines democracy as government that is rendered at least potentially responsive (or accountable) to the public by means of three institutions: open, competitive elections; freedoms of speech and publication; and the right to organize politically. In Schumpeter's sense of the term, political systems as structurally diverse as the American, British, Indian, and West German are democratic because each has an open competition for political office; on the other hand, a society might be quite open and free, and might be ethnically, economically, or culturally pluralistic, like Yugoslavia, without being deemed a pluralist democracy in Schumpeter's sense.

Some have argued that pluralistic democracy is not really very democratic.[41] Several quite different but still Western conceptions of democracy have been offered in its place, including notions of corporatist democracy, participatory democracy, and socialist democracy, all of them gaining substantial scholarly and political support.[42] Even though this debate is unlikely ever to be settled, for the purposes of the present essay the discussion can proceed on the basis of the fact that the writer believes that pluralism is the form of government most efficacious in protecting individual rights and achieving responsive government.[43] Since pluralism is reasonably easy to apply as an evaluative standard (it is not hard to determine whether its three defining conditions are present or absent), and it is a realistic rather than utopian standard (quite a few countries in the world fulfill it), nothing seems to stand in the way of applying this standard to China if one believes in it, unless we find that it is blocked by the force of the remaining two arguments against evaluative universalism.

The second argument would hold that China lacks the cultural and intellectual foundations for pluralist democracy. In fact, however, we know now that interest in pluralist democracy is strong there. The Democracy Movement of 1978–1981 first revealed the existence of a small number of serious thinkers who advocated in China what amounts to the pluralist theory of democracy. There is no evidence that they read Schumpeter or other contemporary Western democratic theorists, nor was their vision of democracy a fully Americanized one.[44] Nonetheless, through a combination of some familiarity with Western texts and concepts on the one hand and, on the other, by dint of their own thinking about the political situation they faced, they came to the view that free elections, freedom of political organization, and the right of free speech are the necessary minimal institutions needed to render leaders accountable. Public expression of these notions was initially limited to a small circle of students and workers. But support for them steadily widened, so much so that, by the mid-1980s, the notion that Western-style democracy suits China had become almost faddish, especially among intellectuals and younger, urban party members.[45]

Some of the more conservative party elders tried to stem this development. For example, the attack on pluralism was a major theme in the Anti-Bourgeois Liberalization Campaign of 1987. Senior party leader Peng Zhen stated that the bourgeois liberalizers "advocated something called 'pluralism,' which in reality is a negation of [Communist] Party leadership. They wanted to organize a political party that opposed socialism, that stood against the Communist Party."[46] *Guangming ribao* carried an article entitled "The Two-Party System is Not Suited to China's National Conditions."[47] Yet, even the official notion of political reform contained some elements of Schumpeterian pluralism—among them, the idea that government should be accountable to the people, and the insight that the mechanisms necessary for this included meaningful elections at least at the local level and an active press functioning independently of those it was licensed to criticize. By early 1989, however, the official vision of political reform remained limited to such measures as political consultation, decentralization of administrative powers, and the establishment of a civil service system—all "under the leadership of the Communist Party." As then-Party Secretary Zhao Ziyang stated at the Thirteenth Party Congress in November 1987, "We will never abandon [the advantages of our own system] and introduce a Western system of separation of the three powers and of different parties ruling the country in turn."[48]

The fact that few, if any, foreign specialists on China anticipated before 1978 that Western-style democratic ideas would gain the degree of importance in China that they did warns against a closed, deterministic view of what outside ideas members of a culture are capable of understanding. In any case, our knowledge of premodern Chinese culture and modern intellectual history should have deterred us from arguing that pluralist democracy had no potential cultural roots and no possible intellectual future in China. After all, what is required in the realm of culture or ideology for democracy to flourish are not replicas of specific Western values, but values that perform similar functions in supporting democratic institutions. J. Roland Pennock, for example, suggests in *Democratic Political Theory* that democracy requires widespread acceptance of such values as dignity, autonomy, and respect for persons; belief in individual rights; trust, tolerance, and willingness to compromise; commitment to democratic procedures and values; public spirit; and nationalism, among others.[49] In this perspective, the question is not whether key Western values find exact equivalents in China, but whether the Chinese tradition contains values that can potentially serve as their functional equivalents in supporting political institutions that—although they too may not be cognate to Western ones—fulfill the criteria of pluralist democracy.

Recent scholarship has revealed or re-emphasized the existence of a number of proto-modern, proto-liberal, and even proto-democratic values in the Chinese tradition which could conceivably serve as some of the building blocks of a Chinese democratic political culture.[50] They include such ideals as the morally autonomous individual, the absolutely just ruler, the responsibility to protest injustices at any personal cost, the responsibility of the government for people's welfare, and the ordinary person's responsibility for the fate of the nation. In imperial times, these values were not used to shake China's autocracy. But, in modern times, they have been used quite directly—with little, if any, Westernization—to justify resistance to both the Guomindang and the CCP. We learned recently that such values motivated at least a few Chinese to resist the Maoist dictatorship at its height. For example, Liu Binyan's controversial reportage, "The Second Kind of Loyalty," told the story of two men who insisted on protesting injustice under Mao at great personal cost.[51] Liu's own career as an investigative reporter, for which he was purged from the party in 1987, provides another example. The vitality of these ideas in the 1980s was further demonstrated by student demonstrations, insubordinate writings and actions by ideological theorists and literary and art workers, and pressure by journalists for more freedom to write critically. In these events, Western rationales for intellectual freedom—for example, as an innate human right, or as contributing through a marketplace of ideas to the discovery of truth—were relatively unimportant.[52] Instead, traditionally based values served as the main justification for the growth of a pressure movement demanding democratization in a Schumpeterian direction. Thus, while the Chinese tradition does not necessarily contain functional equivalents of all the values needed for democracy, it contains strong versions of some of them.

Nor, of course, is the Chinese tradition a stagnant reservoir. In "responding" to the West, Chinese thinkers neither discarded nor blindly reaffirmed tradition, but created a synthesis by absorbing selected but numerous elements from Western thought into conceptual patterns already in existence or in the process of coming into being. Thus, when a concept like human rights was adapted into the Chinese framework, although it lost its Western associations of uninfringeable, legally based individual claims against the state, it gained strength from Chinese notions of personal sacrifice in the cause of justice and truth. Similarly, democracy, originally a Western concept, is today a cherished Chinese value. Although its meaning is sharply contested and few Chinese understand it in the Schumpeterian sense, almost all Chinese throughout the century have understood it to include such ideas as government responsiveness, just government, and the right of ordinary citizens to be informed and express opinions about politics.

Even Chinese Marxism—a separate tradition which China adopted from outside—is not devoid of notions that can be interpreted to support pluralistic political institutions. Marx himself and many of the early Marxists envisioned the politics of the socialist period as democratic in the Western bourgeois sense.[53] Although Marxism in China today is officially used only to support the non-pluralist concept of socialist democracy, a number of Chinese thinkers have explored its democratic implications. For example, the theorist Wang Ruoshui was criticized and fired from his job in 1983 because, his critics claimed, his exposition of the concepts of alienation and socialist humanism had politically pluralist implications.[54] Fang Lizhi, an astrophysicist and university administrator, was purged from the party in early 1987 after giving a series of lectures which allegedly offered encouragement to the student demonstrations of late 1986. The transcripts of the lectures show Professor Fang, then still a Party member, arguing from a Marxist standpoint for, among other things, complete freedom of thought and speech; exclusion of the Party from most policy decisions; resistance to the Party by intellectuals when it makes errors; and the idea that democratic rights are inherent and not given by the state.[55]

That both Chinese traditions, the domestic and the imported, are capable of reinterpretation and development in pluralist-democratic directions is also suggested by the late 1980s political reforms in Taiwan. Although the Guomindang, the ruling party there, does not espouse Marxism, it is structurally modeled on the Communist Party of the Soviet Union and until recently made claims, similar to those of the Soviet and Chinese Communist Parties, to the right to exercise undivided and uncontested rule. To this degree, the Guomindang is, like the CCP, a Leninist party. But in 1986–1987, the Guomindang allowed the formation of several opposition parties, most importantly the Democratic Progressive Party, and took a series of other significant steps to ease restrictions on freedoms of the press and political organization. For the time being at least, the Guomindang retains unchallenged electoral dominance, which leaves the reformed system well short of full pluralist democracy by Schumpeter's definition, but the changes it has made are in the pluralist direction.[56] The Taiwan experience demonstrates that a society within the Chinese culture area, with political institutions not unlike those on the mainland, is capable of evolving in a pluralist direction.

The Taiwan example may seem irrelevant, however, because Taiwan's level of economic and educational development is much higher than that of the mainland. This brings us to consideration of the third argument against evaluative universalism, that it is futile to apply standards that the subject society lacks the preconditions to fulfill. In his classic article "Economic Development and Democracy," Seymour Martin Lipset has shown that democracy is closely correlated with several indicators of economic development—industrialization, urbanization, wealth, and education.[57] According to G. Bingham Powell, Jr., democracies with lower levels of economic and social development are less stable.[58] Since China is one of the poorest countries in the world, it may seem clear that it lacks the preconditions for stable democracy. Many Chinese intellectuals appear to believe this. While struggling for more freedom for themselves, they oppose any reform that would put substantial power into the hands of the peasants, who they feel are so superstitious, anti-intellectual, and anti-foreign that their rule would be disastrous for intellectual freedom and modernization.[59]

But China's economy is growing. GNP per capita was $300 in 1980, already above the level found in the three poorest stable democracies in the 1970s, and, if the goal of quadrupling national income by the year 2000 is achieved, GNP per capita will match or exceed the level enjoyed by the eight poorest democracies in the early 1970s (India, Sri Lanka, the Philippines, Turkey, Costa Rica, Jamaica, Chile, and Uruguay in ascending order of wealth).[60] China's level of literacy in the 1982 census was already as high as that of several democracies (India, Sri Lanka, the Philippines, and Turkey), and the 1985 decision to extend compulsory education to nine years, despite difficulties in implementing it, suggests that the educational level of the populace will continue to rise.

How tight, in any case, is the relationship between democracy and a specific level of economic development? In Lipset's argument, development was thought to support democracy not so much because of the direct effect of wealth on politics but because a more developed society had a higher degree of stability and consensus, less polarization, and more involved, participant citizens. China appears to have achieved many of these preconditions at a lower level of GNP per capita than has been required in some other countries. China, for example, has a relatively equitable distribution of wealth, excellent means of political communication which reach even its illiterate citizens, and strong police and military institutions that are more than equal to the task of controlling civil disorder. Although poll data are lacking to prove it, China also appears to have many of the elements of a "civic culture" (that is, a set of public attitudes conducive to the stable functioning of a democratic regime). These include a relatively high degree of consensus on some basic political values (including nationalism, modernization, and the desire for order); widespread acceptance of the communist regime as legitimate, although it may not be especially well liked; and a certain degree of alienation from politics, which reduces expectations directed at the political system.[61] Even if one argues that all this was achieved because China has had an authoritarian regime, the fact that such conditions now exist suggests that a democratic transition is not out of the question.[62]

In short, a Western-based evaluative statement about Chinese democracy is not only valid on its own, as I argued in the first half of this essay, but is relevant to the Chinese situation. Perhaps the foregoing discussion has illustrated one dimension of this relevance—in stimulating a critical analysis of the factors in the empirical situation that seem to favor or to block development in the valued direction. More directly, Western values are relevant to China because they are of interest to the intellectuals there and have played a role in the party's internal discussions about political reform.

In the end, it is the view that holds that one culture's values are not relevant to another that turns out to be insular, because it blinds itself to the reality of a cross-cultural dialogue that it thinks ought not to occur but does. It is those who hold Western-style rights or democracy irrelevant to China who are behaving prescriptively rather than those who acknowledge that democracy has been declared relevant by the Chinese themselves, whatever they make of it in the end. If there is any cultural arrogance at play, it is not on the part of those who enter into international dialogue in good faith.

That evaluative universalism seems to make more sense today than it did forty or twenty years ago is no doubt as much a creature of historic context as the dominance of cultural relativism has been. This essay is written in an era of resurgent American self-confidence and of transitions to democracy in Asia and Latin America. My arguments may be used to justify the promotion by America of democracy abroad or to support the international lobbying of human-rights organizations. But whatever philosophical validity universalism has extends beyond its historical context. And its policy implications are not fixed. The New Left among social scientists in the 1960s called for the freedom to evaluate in order to attack, not defend, the institutions of American democracy. The policy implications of evaluative universalism depend on the values that are applied.

Evaluative universalism by no means requires a return to the missionary mode of promoting Western values. It is not a call for proselytism but an expression of the belief, first, that value differences when they exist can, and can only, be honestly expressed, and second, that beliefs originating in different societies can fruitfully be confronted with one another, compared, and judged, even though disagreement is expected to persist. Just as Western values are a valid basis for a judgment of Chinese society, Chinese values are valid for those who believe in them to apply in judging Western society. "Those who do not like [intellectual] prisons," says Karl Popper, ". . . will welcome a discussion with a partner who comes from another world, from another framework, for it gives them an opportunity to discover their so far unfelt chains, to break them, and thus to transcend themselves."[63]

This call for dialogue, however, should not be read as a last-minute concession to the relativist position that all values are equally valid. One can favor dialogue about democracy while still holding that one form of democracy is superior to other forms. One can recognize that this is not a question that will ever be settled conclusively for everyone while holding, without inconsistency, to the view that there are a preponderance of arguments in favor of one position. Again to quote Popper, "From the fact that we can err, and that a criterion of truth which might save us from error does not exist, it does not follow that the choice between theories is arbitrary, or non-rational."[64]

The implications of this conclusion trespass beyond the boundaries of my original topic to suggest an anti-relativistic point of view that applies as much within as between cultures, as much to scientific as to moral reasoning, and as much to the problems that I said I was not going to discuss in detail (understanding, interpretation, the validity of making value judgments at all) as to the practitioner's issue of how to make cross-cultural value judgments that I have attempted to focus on. This was unavoidable, because the problems we face as practitioners of area studies are, after all, at bottom the same as those faced by searchers after knowledge generally, even within cultures. Our problems are only a special, and perhaps in some respects an especially clear, case of everyone's problems. Perhaps it is precisely in area studies, where both the obstacles to and the achievements of understanding are so conspicuous, that we have earned the right to affirm most strongly the potentialities of understanding.

The major issues of the Western tradition—democracy, rights, individual and society—are no longer the West's alone, if they ever were. Benjamin I. Schwartz has always argued that on the great questions the answers may have varied, but the questions are transcultural. After two centuries of intense contact, the language of political discourse around the world has become Westernized; or to put it in a better way, once-Western issues have become part of international discourse. How non-Western thinkers deal with originally Western ideas has become an important part of the history of these ideas. The "foreign areas" are part of the world—they are the greater part. For this reason, area studies cannot treat itself as detached from the great issues. A major task of area studies is to learn enough of the language and cultures of other societies to carry out cross-cultural discussion of common concerns with minimal misunderstanding. What is at stake here ultimately is the value Benjamin Schwartz holds most dear—"the possibility of a universal human discourse."[65]

Notes
Index

Notes

INTRODUCTION

1. *The Closing of the American Mind: How Higher Education Has Failed Democracy and Impoverished the Souls of Today's Students* (New York: Simon and Schuster, 1987). Schwartz addressed Bloom's theses critically in lectures at Harvard University, the University of Illinois, and elsewhere in 1987.
2. "The Religion of Politics: Reflections on the Thought of Hannah Arendt," *Dissent* 17.2:144–161 (March-April 1970).
3. Benjamin I. Schwartz, *The World of Thought in Ancient China* (Cambridge: Harvard University Press, 1985).
4. Benjamin I. Schwartz, *In Search of Wealth and Power: Yen Fu and the West* (Cambridge: Harvard University Press, 1964), pp. 1–2.
5. Ibid., p. 2.
6. Ibid.
7. *Chinese Communisim and the Rise of Mao* (Cambridge: Harvard University Press, 1951), p. 1.
8. Ibid., pp. 1–2.
9. *The World of Thought in Ancient China*, p. 1.
10. Ibid., p. 2.
11. *In Search of Wealth and Power*, p. 2; see also *The World of Thought in Ancient China*, pp. 13, 413.
12. Ibid.
13. *In Search of Wealth and Power*, p. 239 and passim.
14. Ibid., pp. 242–243.
15. Ibid., p. 247.
16. The phrase appears in *The World of Thought in Ancient China*, p. 14.

1. SOME REFLECTIONS ON THE PROBLEMS OF THE AXIAL-AGE BREAKTHROUGH IN RELATION TO CLASSICAL CONFUCIANISM, BY HAO CHANG

1. Benjamin I. Schwartz, *The World of Thought in Ancient China* (Cambridge: Harvard University Press, 1985) pp. 2–3.
2. Ibid., p. 53.
3. Eric Voegelin, *Israel and Revelation* (Baton Rouge: Louisiana State University Press, 1956), pp. 16–45, 52–115.
4. Ibid., pp. 1–11.
5. For the Shang king as chief Shaman, see K. C. Chang, *Art, Myth, and Ritual: The Path to Political Authority in Ancient China* (Cambridge: Harvard University Press, 1983) pp. 44–55.
6. I am referring here to the doctrine of the Mandate of Heaven as spelled out in the *Book of Documents* (*Shu Jing*) and the *Book of Poetry* (*Shi Jing*). See also Ch'en Meng-Chia, "Myths and Magic of the Shang Dynasty" (in Chinese) *Yenching Journal of Chinese Studies* 20:485–576. (December 1936)
7. Hsu Fu-kuan, *Renxinglun shi* (A history of views of human nature; Taizhong: Donghai University Press, 1963), pp. 36–46.
8. Schwartz, *The World of Thought in Ancient China*, pp. 51–52.
9. *Xinyi sishu duben* (A newly translated primer of Four Books; San-min shu-ju, Taibei, 1957). *Lunyu* (Analects), pp. 68–70, 77, 88, 230.
10. Ibid., pp. 82, 83, 101.
11. Ibid., pp. 54, 96, 83, 159.
12. Ibid., p. 103.
13. Ibid., pp. 137, 188.
14. Ibid., p. 203.
15. Ibid., p. 117.
16. Ibid., p. 118.
17. Ibid., pp. 79–80.
18. Ibid., p. 99.
19. Ibid., p. 122.
20. Ibid., p. 114.
21. Ibid., p. 191.
22. Ibid., p. 129.
23. Ibid., p. 77.
24. Ibid., p. 240; see also *Mengzi* (Mencius), pp. 288–289.
25. Ibid., p. 294.
26. Ibid., p. 273.
27. Ibid., pp. 454–455.
28. Ibid., pp. 453–455.
29. Ibid.

30. Ibid.
31. Ibid., pp. 476, 517.
32. Ibid., pp. 297, 313, 484.
33. Ibid., p. 455.
34. Ibid., p. 429.
35. Ibid., pp. 436, 479.
36. *Xunzi* in *Sibu congkan zibu*, XI, 119.
37. Ibid., "Wang-zhi pian" (On the kingly institution), V, 56.
38. Ibid., p. 56; also see, "Jundao pian" (On rulership), VII, 88.
39. Ibid., VII, 83.
40. Ibid., "Hsiu-shen p'ien" (on cultivation), I, 8–13; II, 16.
41. Ibid., II, 16–17.
42. Ibid., II, 16.
43. Ibid., IV, 44; V, 56.
44. Vol. XX, 206.
45. Feng Youlan, *Zhongguo sixcangshi* (A history of Chinese philosophy; Hong Kong, 1959), pp. 437–455.
46. Xinyi sishu duben, *Zhongyong* (The mean), p. 17.
47. Ibid., pp. 46–47.
48. *Li Ji jingzhu jingyi* (The Book of Rites annotated), ed. Wang Mengou, Vol. I, Chs. 5 and 6, pp. 163–241.
49. William Edward Soothill, *The Hall of Light, A Study of Early Chinese Kingship* (London: Lutterworth Press, 1951), pp. 22–65.
50. Chen Mengjia, *Yinxu pucizongshu* (A synthesis of the oracle bone inscriptions of the Yin tombs; Peking, Kexue chubanshe, 1956), pp. 590–594.
51. *Liji jingzhu jingyi*, Ch. 6, "Yueling" (Monthly ordinance), pp. 201–241.
52. Ibid.
53. Dong Zhong-shu, *Chungiu fanlu* (Luxuriant dew of the Annals of Spring and Autumn) in *Sibu congkan*, 1st ser. (Shanghai: Commercial Press, 1929–1936), II, 61–62.
54. Xu Fuguan, *Renxinglun shi*, pp. 47–51.
55. *Xinyi sishu duben*, Lunyu, p. 72.
56. Ibid., Mengzi, p. 269.

2. *A Language of Continuity in Confucian Thought*
by Don J. Wyatt

Author's note: Research support for this essay was provided by a summer grant from the Middlebury College Faculty Professional Development Fund. A preliminary version was presented to the fifth biennial conference of the International Society for Chinese Philosophy at the University of California, San Diego, 12–17 July 1987. I thank all of those conference participants who offered helpful suggestions for revision, particularly Professors Kwong-loi Shun, Kwang-Sae Lee, and David D. Kuo. I extend special thanks to Professor Ronald C. Egan for his thoughtful comments on the essay in its inception and to Professors Chad Hansen and Craig Ihara for their careful readings and earnest reactions near the time of its completion.

1. Fung Yu-lan, for example, in his *The Spirit of Chinese Philosophy*, E. R. Hughes, tr. (London: Routledge & Kegan Paul Ltd., 1947), p. 2, has taken an apologist position in which he contends that Chinese philosophical this-worldliness "cannot be said to be either wholly right or wholly wrong," and he argues instead for what he terms the "world-transcending" quality of Chinese philosophy. Fung articulates this same view again but without specific reference to the "world-transcending" quality of Chinese philosophy in *A Short History of Chinese Philosophy*, Derk Bodde, ed. (New York: The Macmillan Company, 1948), pp. 7–8. In his *The Story of Chinese Philosophy* (New York: Washington Square Press, 1961), p. xix, Ch'u Chai is more approving of the this-worldliness thesis, stating that Chinese philosophy "has seldom separated itself from ethical and practical needs." Angus Graham states in his essay "The Place of Reason in the Chinese Philosophical Tradition," in Raymond Dawson, ed., *The Legacy of China* (Oxford: Oxford University Press, 1964), p. 54, that, "if we can make any safe generalization about the whole of Chinese philosophy, it is that interest has always centered in human needs, in the improvement of government, in morals, and in the values of private life. Philosophers have seldom shown much concern for truths which serve no obviously useful purpose." For some brief but useful observations on the characteristics of the idea of Chinese philosophical "this-worldliness" in specific contrast to the apparent "other-worldly" orientation of Indian thought, see Frederick C. Copleston, *Philosophies and Cultures* (Oxford: Oxford University Press, 1980), pp. 39–41.

2. Fung, *Spirit of Chinese Philosophy*, p. 2.

3. Hu Wei, *Zhongyong zhuzhu jiuzheng* (Taibei: Zhongguo zixue mingzhu jicheng bianyin jijinhui, 1978), *zhang* 23, pp. 511–516. James Legge, *The Doctrine of the Mean*, Vol. I, *The Chinese Classics*, reprinted from the last editions of Oxford University Press, 3rd ed. (Hong Kong: University of Hong Kong Press, 1960), p. 417. My translation differs markedly from Legge's in this instance. For more information on the emphasis on the common and the ordinary in the *Zhongyong*, see Fung Yu-lan's *Short History of Chinese Philosophy*, pp. 166, 174–176.

4. Frederick W. Mote, *Intellectual Foundations of China* (New York: Alfred A. Knopf, 1971), pp. 26–27.

5. Chad D. Hansen, "Ancient Chinese Theories of Language," *Journal of Chinese Philosophy* 2.3:261 (June 1975).

6. *Lunyu* 15.17. D.C. Lau, *Confucius, The Analects* (London: Penguin Books, 1979), p. 134. For the most part, my own translations of the *Lunyu* will closely adhere

to Lau's. There will, however, be occasional divergence, as in the passage given here.

7. *Lunyu* 7.21. Lau, *Confucius, The Analects*, p. 88.

8. Donald J. Munro, *The Concept of Man in Early China* (Stanford: Stanford University Press, 1969), p. 117.

9. Ibid., p. 118.

10. *Lunyu* 15.41. Lau, *Confucius, The Analects*, p. 137.

11. *Xunzi* (SBBY ed.) (Shanghai: Zhonghua shuju, 1927), 1.3a. Burton Watson, tr., *Hsun Tzu: Basic Writings* (New York: Columbia University Press, 1963), p. 17.

12. Qian Mu, *Zhuangzi zuanjian* (Hong Kong: Dongnan yinwu chubanshe, 1951), p. 1. Burton Watson, tr., *The Complete Works of Chuang Tzu* (New York: Columbia University Press, 1968), pp. 29–31.

13. Ibid., p. 16. My own translation of this very difficult passage follows those put forth by Lin Yutang in *The Wisdom of China and India* (New York: Random House, 1942), p. 638, and by Wing-tsit Chan in *A Source Book in Chinese Philosophy* (Princeton: Princeton University Press, 1963), p. 185.

14. Pierre Do-Dinh, *Confucius and Chinese Humanism*, Charles Lam Markmann, tr. (New York: Funk & Wagnalls, 1969), p. 133.

15. E. R. Hughes, "Epistemological Methods in Chinese Philosophy," in Charles A. Moore, ed., *The Chinese Mind: Essentials of Chinese Philosophy and Culture* (Honolulu: University of Hawaii Press, 1967), pp. 79–80. Some authors have chosen to regard this controlling aspect of the Chinese language (especially the written language) as overweening and oppressive. John Fairbank, for example, has written of what he terms the "tyranny of language" in traditional China and has emphasized its social drawbacks. He, for instance, links the retardation in the development of Chinese science with the prior failure to develop a more comprehensive speculative logic. Fairbank also sees the almost autonomous status the Chinese language eventually achieved through the sanction of Confucianism as having constricted the parameters of traditional thought and thus having posed the threat of serious moral consequences to anyone who might have doubted the content of the language. He writes: "To question the Confucian virtues would have been to deny the existence of the written characters which expressed them." See his *The United States and China*, 4th ed. enlarged (Cambridge: Harvard University Press, 1948), pp. 76–79.

16. Munro, *Concept of Man in Early China*, pp. 117–118.

17. *Lunyu* 13.3. Lau, *Confucius, The Analects*, p. 118.

18. See the commentary of Arthur Waley in *The Analects of Confucius* (London: Allen & Unwin, 1938), p. 172.

19. *Lunyu* 2.23. Lau, *Confucius, The Analects*, p. 66.

20. Support for the perceived primeval nature of analogical reasoning is widely available and broadly based. William James (1842–1910) wrote: "Men, taken historically, reason by analogy long before they have learned to reason by abstract

characters." See William James, *The Principles of Psychology*, Vol. II (New York: Henry Holt, 1890), p. 363. The contemporary political scientist and philosopher Bertrand de Jouvenel is probably even more emphatic in simply stating: "No procedure comes more naturally to the mind than looking for analogies." See Bertrand de Jouvenel, *The Art of Conjecture*, Nikita Lary, tr. (New York: Basic Books, 1967), p. 63.

21. A. C. Graham, *Reason and Spontaneity* (London and Totowa, NJ: Curzon Press; Barnes & Noble, 1985), p. 52.

22. Ibid.

23. J. David Bolter, *Turing's Man: Western Culture in the Computer Age* (Chapel Hill: University of North Carolina Press, 1984), p. 22. For more on the importance of analogy among the ancient Greeks and its role in argumentation, see also R. G. Collingwood, *The Idea of Nature* (Oxford: Oxford University Press, 1945), pp. 8–9, 19–20, 35; F. E. Peters, *Greek Philosophical Terms: A Historical Lexicon* (New York/London: New York University Press/University of London Press, 1967), p. xi; and G. E. R. Lloyd, *Polarity and Analogy: Two Types of Argumentation in Early Greek Thought* (Cambridge: Cambridge University Press, 1966), pp. 176–180.

24. Benjamin I. Schwartz, *The World of Thought in Ancient China* (Cambridge: Harvard University Press, 1985), pp. 175–179.

25. Ibid., p. 176.

26. *Lunyu* 5.13. Lau, *Confucius, The Analects*, p. 78.

27. *Lunyu* 17.2. Lau, *Confucius, The Analects*, p. 143.

28. Shu-hsien Liu, "The Use of Analogy and Symbolism in Traditional Chinese Philosophy," *Journal of Chinese Philosophy* 1.3/4:328 (June/September 1974) and A. S. Cua, "Uses of Dialogues and Moral Understanding," *Journal of Chinese Philosophy* 2.2:132 (March 1975). See also Cua's earlier article "The Logic of Confucian Dialogues," in John K. Ryan, ed., *Studies in Philosophy and the History of Philosophy*, Vol. IV (Washington, D.C.: The Catholic University of America Press, 1969), pp. 25–26.

29. *Lunyu* 5.10. Lau, *Confucius, The Analects*, p. 77.

30. See Lau, *Confucius, The Analects*, p. 204.

31. Wang Chong, *Lunheng* (Shanghai: Saoye shanfang, 1923), 9.2b. See also the translation appearing in Alfred Forke, *Lun-heng: Philosophical Essays of Wang Ch'ung*, Part I, reprinted from the last 1907 edition (New York: Paragon Book Gallery, 1962), p. 399.

32. See D. C. Lau, *Mencius* (London: Penguin Books, 1970), pp. 235–263.

33. I. A. Richards, *Mencius on the Mind: Experiments in Multiple Definition* (New York: Harcourt, Brace, 1932), p. 44.

34. Chad Hansen, *Language and Logic in Ancient China* (Ann Arbor: University of Michigan Press, 1983), p. 124.

35. A. C. Graham, *Studies in Chinese Philosophy and Philosophical Literature*

(Singapore: Institute of East Asian Philosophies, 1986), pp. 42, 45.

36. Schwartz, *World of Thought*, p. 263.

37. Ibid., p. 175.

38. Munro, *Concept of Man in Early China*, p. 136.

39. Schwartz, *World of Thought*, p. 176.

40. Munro, *Concept of Man in Early China*, p. 136.

41. See Schwartz's opinion in *World of Thought*, pp. 263, 275.

42. *Mengzi*, SBBY ed. (Shanghai: Zhonghua shuju, 1930), 11.2b–3. This chapter designation corresponds to the first part of the sixth book, which is more conventionally denoted as 6A. Lau, *Mencius*, pp. 160–161.

43. See Lau's opinion in *Mencius*, pp. 160–161, 241–243.

44. Schwartz, *World of Thought*, p. 265.

45. The *locus classicus* for this description of human nature is the opening line of the *Zhongyong*. For an informative discussion of the role of this Heaven-bestowed *xing* in the Mencian idea of religion, see Schwartz, *World of Thought*, pp. 288–290.

46. Schwartz, *World of Thought*, p. 265.

47. See, among others, the opinion expressed by Lin Yutang in *The Wisdom of Confucius* (New York: Random House, 1938), pp. 273–274.

48. Carsun Chang, *The Development of Neo-Confucian Thought*, Vol. I (New York: Bookman Associates, 1957), pp. 133–134.

49. Ibid., pp. 105–108. See also Wing-tsit Chan's *Neo-Confucian Terms Explained* (New York: Columbia University Press, 1986), chiefly p. 124. This work is an annotated translation of the *Beixi ziyi* by Chen Chun (1159–1223).

50. Cheng Yi, "Henan Chengshi yishu," in *Er Cheng quanshu*, Ji Yun, ed. (Danyatang chongyin, 1908), 18.27a–b. See also 19.6b. Here Cheng Yi makes the intriguing statement: "As for saying 'men are similar by nature,' this is a reference to the nature with which everyone is endowed. But this is not referring to the foundation or root of nature. Now, as for the foundation of nature of which Mencius spoke, this is the correct way of speaking of nature."

51. Ibid., 18.24b–25.

52. This is not to deny, however, that Mencius elsewhere offered positive conceptual discussions of *xing*. For a thoughtful discussion of the conceptual bases of Mencius's knowledge of human nature, see Willard J. Peterson's "The Grounds of Mencius' Argument," *Philosophy East and West* 29.3: 307–321 (July 1979). See also Donald J. Munro, *Images of Human Nature: A Sung Portrait* (Princeton: Princeton University Press, 1988), pp. 88–89.

53. Cheng Yi, *Er Cheng quanshu*, 19.6.

54. Ibid., 18.24b. For a brief but elucidating discussion of Cheng Yi's equation of nature with *li* and its implication for the problem of evil, see Graham, *Reason and Spontaneity*, pp. 59–60. Cheng Yi's this-worldly analogical arguments are numerous and wide-ranging. In 19.10, for example, he makes the following

remark concerning instincts (*liangneng*): "Everything in the world has instincts. Just like the common everyday birds in building their nests: actions like these, to be sure, are clever traits. These are their instincts and they do not require study. People, as well, when first born, only have the task of suckling the breast, which is not learned behavior. But everything else in life is study and humans only acquire wisdom at great detriment to their instincts."

55. The dialectical tension between *xing* and *cai* continued to be particularly influential in the thought of later Neo-Confucianists such as Dai Zhen (1723–1777). For more on this issue in Dai Zhen's thinking, see Fung Yu-lan's *A History of Chinese Philosophy*, Vol. II, Derk Bodde, tr. (Princeton: Princeton University Press, 1953), pp. 657–663 and Wing-tsit Chan's *Source Book in Chinese Philosophy*, p. 719.

56. Zhu Xi, *Zhuzi quanshu*, Li Guangdi, ed. (Yuanjianzhai yuzuan, 1713), 42.27a–b.

57. Schwartz, *World of Thought*, p. 175.

58. Ibid., p. 179.

59. Zhu Xi, *Zhuzi quanshu*, 42.6b–7.

60. Ibid., 42.7b–8b. Man's attempt to learn about himself through comparison of himself with animals of course has a long history. Interestingly, there are marked parallels between these attempts in the West and in China. For an insightful account of the history of this development in the Western tradition, see Kenneth Bock's *Human Nature and History: A Response to Sociobiology* (New York: Columbia University Press, 1980), pp. 7–35.

61. Donald J. Munro, "The Family Network, the Stream of Water, and the Plant: Picturing Persons in Sung Confucianism," in Donald J. Munro, ed., *Individualism and Holism: Studies in Confucian and Taoist Values* (Ann Arbor: University of Michigan Press, 1985), p. 261. The retention and affirmation of analogical argumentation in the dialogues of Song and later Chinese thinkers is itself a significant indicator of the extreme contrast in the distinct developments of the Chinese and the Western philosophical traditions. In the West, especially after Aristotle (384–322 B.C.) and the emergence of the classic syllogism argument form, there began a gradual tendency to try to abandon analogical constructions altogether in favor of arguments expressed purely in terms of variables (A, B, x, y, etc.) and eventually mathematical symbols. The result has been that analogical reasoning has become largely relegated to the dubious realm of "informal" logic or the "quasi-logical." Moreover, particularly within the last century, many Western philosophers have even attempted to exclude such argumentational forms as analogy from the discipline of logic entirely. See the discussion of analogy as a "quasi-logical argument" from Henry W. Johnstone, Jr., *Validity and Rhetoric in Philosophical Argument: An Outlook in Transition* (University Park, PA: The Dialogue Press of Man & World, Inc., 1978), pp. 98–99.

62. In contrast to its overwhelming acceptance and prevalence in Confucian argu-

ment, it is interesting to note that the employing of ordinary language has always had a dubious position in the history of Western philosophy. One scholar, Michael Scriven, has in fact observed: "The argument from ordinary language has a remarkable status in philosophy in that it is regarded by many philosophers as fallacious or even vicious, and by many others as foundational, indeed unavoidable." See his "The Argument from Ordinary Language," in James H. Fetzer, ed., *Principles of Philosophical Reasoning* (Totowa, NJ: Rowman & Allanheld, 1984), p. 261.

63. Benjamin Schwartz, "Some Polarities in Confucian Thought," in Arthur F. Wright, ed., *Confucianism and Chinese Civilization* (Stanford: Stanford University Press, 1959), p. 12.

64. S. C. Humphreys, *Anthropology and the Greeks* (London: Routledge & Kegan Paul, 1978), pp. 213, 227, 272. Aristotle is considered to have been the leading fourth-century professionalizer of Attic philosophy. For a discussion of his view that the philosopher, by virtue of his service of the intellect and contemplation of truth, is less dependent on society and rightly stands apart from it, see H. C. Baldry's *The Unity of Mankind in Greek Thought* (Cambridge: Cambridge University Press, 1965), pp. 90–92.

65. This is, of course, the central and overall theme of Munro's *The Concept of Man in Early China*. See his "Preface" and first chapter, "Human Nature and Natural Equality" (pp. 1–22) for the straightforward explication of this theme. For a stimulating analysis of this thesis, Chinese ideas of social mobility, and their joint application to the development of Chinese historiographic sensibilities and writings, see Donald E. Brown, *Hierarchy, History, and Human Nature: The Social Origins of Historical Consciousness* (Tucson: University of Arizona Press, 1988), pp. 61–69.

3. *YAN FU'S UTILITARIANISM IN CHINESE PERSPECTIVE*, *BY HOYT CLEVELAND TILLMAN*

I would like to thank Ying-shih Yü, On-cho Ng, Don Wyatt, Phil Williams, and the editors of this volume for their comments on an earlier version of this essay. I also appreciate research support extended by the College of Liberal Arts and Sciences at Arizona State University.

1. Benjamin I. Schwartz, *In Search of Wealth and Power: Yen Fu and the West* (Cambridge: Harvard University Press, 1964).

2. Joseph R. Levenson, *Liang Ch'i-ch'ao and the Mind of Modern China* (Cambridge: Harvard University Press, 1953), and his *Confucian China and its Modern Fate: The Problem of Intellectual Continuity* (Berkeley: University of California Press, 1958). For a survey of U.S. historiography of the period, see Paul A. Cohen, *Discovering History in China: American Historical Writing on the Recent Chinese Past* (New York: Columbia University Press, 1984).

3. Mizoguchi Yūzō, "Chūgoku ni okeru ko shi gainen no tenkai," *Shisō* 669:19–38 (1980).

4. See Deng Guangming's discussion of editions of Chen Liang's works in his introduction to the revised edition of *Chen Liang ji* (Beijing: Zhonghua, 1987).

5. See especially material in Jiang Guanghui, "On the Yan-Li School of Utilitarian Confucianism and its Place in History," *Social Sciences in China* 6.3:186–205 (1985); Wu Chunshan, *Chen Tongfu de sixiang* (Taibei: Guoli Taiwan Daxue Wenxueyuan, 1971), passim. See Thomas Bartlett's Princeton PhD dissertation on Gu Yanwu. On-cho Ng, "Text in Context: *Chin-wen* Learning in Ch'ing Thought" (PhD dissertation, University of Hawaii, 1986), especially Chapters 2–4, uses Chen as the baseline for background on Qing trends in historicism and vitalism. I have discussed the issue of influence in "Ch'en Liang on the Public Interest and its Relation to Laws," in Conrad Schirokauer and Robert Hymes, eds., "Ordering the World" (submitted to the ACLS-SSRC series on China at the University of California Press).

6. Benjamin I. Schwartz, *The World of Thought in Ancient China* (Cambridge: Harvard University Press, 1985).

7. "Proto-Nationalism in Twelfth-Century China? The Case of Ch'en Liang," *Harvard Journal of Asiatic Studies* 39.2:403–428 (1979).

8. Schwartz, *World of Thought*, p. 149.

9. John Rawls, *A Theory of Justice* (Cambridge: Harvard University Press, 1971), p. 558, quoted in Schwartz, *World of Thought*, p. 159.

10. *Mozi xian gu*, commentary by Sun Yirang, *Xinbian zhuzi jicheng* ed. (Beijing: Zhonghua, 1986), 12.47:405; tr. with slight modification from Schwartz, *World of Thought*, p. 159.

11. Schwartz, *World of Thought*, p. 160.

12. *Mozi xian gu* 1.4:19, tr. Schwartz, *World of Thought*, p. 166.

13. Rawls, p. 178, quoted in Schwartz, *World of Thought*, p. 329.

14. Schwartz, *World of Thought*, pp. 260–261.

15. Ibid., pp. 261–280 passim.

16. Chen Liang, *Chen Liang ji* (Beijing: Zhonghua edition, 1974) 21:334; revised and enlarged edition (1987) 29:396.

17. *Utilitarian Confucianism: Ch'en Liang's Challenge to Chu Hsi* (Cambridge: Council on East Asian Studies, Harvard University, 1982).

18. *Mencius* 7B/24; Cf. tr. D. C. Lau, *Mencius* (Baltimore: Penguin Books, 1970), p. 198.

19. *Chen Liang ji* 4:40–41; rev. ed. 4:40–41.

20. Ibid. 20:293; rev. ed. 28:352–353.

21. Ibid. 9:97–99; rev. ed. 9:100–102.

22. Ibid. 9:98–99; rev. ed. 9:101–102. *Mencius*, 1B/5 (Lau, pp. 65–66) offers a similar argument.

23. For instance, *Chen Liang ji* 19:262; rev. ed. 27:321.

24. See discussion in *Utilitarian Confucianism*, Chap. 2.
25. Zhang Zai, *Zhang Zai ji* (Beijing: Zhonghua edition, 1978), *Zhengmeng* 17:62, tr. Wing-tsit Chan, *A Source Book in Chinese Philosophy* (Princeton: Princeton University Press, 1963), p. 497.
26. *Chen Liang ji* 14:167–168; rev. ed. 23:260–261.
27. Ibid. 19:253; rev. ed. 27:312.
28. Ibid. 25:383; rev. ed. 33:445.
29. Ibid. 4:40–41; rev. ed. 4:40–41.
30. Ibid. 10:103–104; rev. ed. 10:105–106.
31. Ibid. 10:103; rev. ed. 10:106–107.
32. Ibid. 25:379; rev. ed. 33:441.
33. Ibid. 20:273–274; rev. ed. 28:333.
34. *Chen Liang ji* rev. ed. only 11:124–125.
35. *Chen Liang ji* 14:164; rev. ed. 23:254.
36. *Chen Liang ji* rev. ed. only 11:122–123, 13:153, 15:170. Regarding the negative side of laws, Chen's premises are similar to the ones Schwartz identified in Confucius, *World of Thought*, p. 327; see especially *Analects*, 2/3. For more discussion of these issues, see my "Ch'en Liang on the Public Interest," and also "Ch'en Liang on Statecraft: Reflections from Examination Essays Preserved in a Sung Rare Book," *Harvard Journal of Asiatic Studies* 48.2:403–431 (1988).
37. *Chen Liang Ji* 16:199–201; rev. ed. 23:255–256. See also discussion in *Utilitarian Confucianism*, pp. 96–97.
38. *Chen Liang ji* 20:275–276; rev. ed. 28:334–335.
39. Schwartz, *Wealth and Power*, especially pp. xii, 238–244.
40. Quoted in ibid., p. 39; see also pp. 38–41, 70–72, 166.
41. Ibid. especially pp. 152–153, 165–166.
42. Ibid. p. 60.
43. Quoted and tr. by Schwartz, *Wealth and Power*, p. 126; see also pp. 113–114, 116, 122–125.
44. Ibid. especially pp. 73, 121, 141, 237–247.
45. Ibid. especially pp. 67–68, 171–172, 222, 229–232, 237–247.

4. THE MORAL WORLD OF HEBEI VILLAGE OPERA, BY DAVID ARKUSH

1. Li Jinghan and Zhang Shiwen, eds., *Dingxian yangge xuan* (A selection of operas from Dingxian; N.p.: Zhonghua pingmin jiaoyu cujinhui, 1933; Reprint, 4 vols [Minsu congshu #38–41], Taibei: Orient Cultural Service, 1971). All references to plays in this paper are to this collection; page numbers are the same in the original edition and the Taiwan reprint. An English version is available, but the quality of the translations is uneven: Sidney D. Gamble, ed., *Chinese Village Plays from the Ting Hsien Region* (Amsterdam: Philo Press, 1970). These operas have not been much studied; there is little besides Chao Weipang,

"Yang-ko: The Rural Theatre in Ting-hsien, Hopei," *Folklore Studies* 3.1:17–38 (1944), and Judith Johns Johnston, "A Critical Study of the 'Ting-hsien Yang-ko Hsuan'" (PhD dissertation, Florida State University, 1978).

2. One illiterate old actor named Liu Luobian sang and recited for them seven hours a day for half a month. On the performance of Dingxian operas, largely overlapping information can be found in: *Dingxian yangge xuan*, preface and introduction; Li Jinghan, *Dingxian shehui gaikuang diaocha* (Survey of social conditions in Dingxian; Beiping: Zhonghua pingmin jiaoyu cujinhui, 1933), pp. 336–340; Gamble, *Village Plays*, "Introduction"; and Sidney D. Gamble, *Ting Hsien: A North China Rural Community* (Stanford: Stanford University Press, 1954), pp. 329–335. On how actors shaped drama to meet audience desires, there is also much evidence in published oral histories by North Chinese folk performers.

3. For a thoughtful discussion of how folktales of an East African people contain "hidden and disturbing speculation" about the moral order, see T. O. Beidelman, *Moral Imagination in Kaguru Modes of Thought* (Bloomington: Indiana University Press, 1986).

4. The virtue of a wife's fidelity to her husband is a more prominent concern. In three operas, the main character is an upright woman whose willingness to sacrifice her honor for the sake of a higher loyalty to her husband is held up for admiration. In *Miaojin gui* (The gold-lacquered chest), she has been carried off by river pirates who killed her husband, an official. She chooses not to preserve her honor by committing suicide, but instead to live on as the pirate chief's wife for three years until she can have him brought to justice and her husband avenged—only then does she commit suicide. Similarly, in *Daoting men* (At the door to the rear hall), the abducted widow of a murdered man decides not to commit suicide, this time on the grounds that she is pregnant and the child might be a son, whom she should raise to carry on the family line (if it is a daughter she will commit suicide). In *Longbao si jiangxiang*, the man wrongly accused of murder is finally released when his loyal wife puts her chastity and reputation at risk in order to entrap the real murderer. These murder stories *are* somewhat moralizing; but fidelity and even love between spouses is a very different value than filial piety.

5. The precise meaning of this title eludes me. It seems to mean something like "Two Lovers Visit a Grave."

6. James C. Scott, *Weapons of the Weak: Everyday Forms of Peasant Resistance* (New Haven: Yale University Press, 1985), particularly pp. 314–350.

7. Similarly, *Sha xu* (To kill a son-in-law) presents a good man who, returning home rich with imperial rewards for his military valor (a sort of reciprocity), gratefully rewards the father-in-law who had taken care of him when he was poor. This exemplary recognition of obligations, even in changed circum-

stances, is contrasted with the behavior of the evil father-in-law, who murders him out of greed for even more of his riches.

8. Three rather interesting plays show an ordinary young peasant woman meeting a man who is destined to found a dynasty. The emperor-to-be is in lowly circumstances but the woman recognizes his imperial destiny from supernatural signs, such as dragons emanating from his head while he sleeps. She then contrives to have sex with him and get him to promise to make her empress after he ascends the throne, thus rising with him to the pinnacle of society (*Liu Xiu zou guo* [Liu Xiu flees the country], *Zhu Hongwu fangniu* [Zhu Hongwu tends cows], *Bai tao po* [The white grass slope]).

9. Max Weber, *The Religion of China*, tr. Hans Gerth (New York: Macmillan, 1964), pp. 230, 227, 237. The literature on this subject and on Weber is large. I have found particularly helpful: C. K. Yang's introduction to Weber, *The Religion of China*; the essays by S. N. Eisenstadt and Gary G. Hamilton in *Max Weber in Asian Studies*, ed. A. E. Buss (Leiden: E. J. Brill, 1985); Wolfgang Schluchter, "The Paradox of Rationalization: On the Relation of Ethics and World," in Guenther Roth and W. Schluchter, *Max Weber's Vision of History* (Berkeley: University of California Press, 1979); Gary G. Hamilton, "Patriarchalism in Imperial China and Western Europe," *Theory and Society* 13:393–425 (1984); Thomas A. Metzger, *Escape from Predicament* (New York: Columbia University Press, 1977); and Stephen Molloy, "Max Weber and the Religions of China: Any Way Out of the Maze?" *British Journal of Sociology* 31:377–400 (1980). Weber's denial of transcendence to high Confucianism has been widely criticized; here we are concerned with popular culture. Weber talks often of the sib, or lineage, but the principle of patriarchal domination with which he is concerned is found equally in the family. There are no references to lineages in the Dingxian operas.

10. Pp. 188, 223: "vegetarians" means Buddhist practitioners.

11. *Jiang Shichuang xiuqi*, p. 596; *Xiaogu xian*, p. 727.

12. This business of vows has implications for the matter of business trust which so interested Weber. While it might be argued that it is a lack of trust and honesty among the Chinese that makes them have to resort to religious oaths, it seems to me more significant that, at least on the evidence of these operas, belief in supernatural sanctions was effective in making people keep their word when sworn, and that in this respect folk religious beliefs were conducive to trust among strangers. It is possible, of course, that this is just a dramatic convention, and does not reflect how people really felt and acted.

13. *The Religion of China*, p. 200.

14. Ibid., pp. 227, 225.

15. Benjamin I. Schwartz, *The World of Thought in Ancient China* (Cambridge: Harvard University Press, 1985). For a well worked-out example based on fieldwork in Taiwan, see Emily Martin Ahern, *Chinese Ritual and Politics* (Cambridge: Cambridge University Press, 1981).

16. *Zhuang Zhou shan fen, Yang Fulu tou qin.*
17. *Fan tang.*
18. *Shuang suo gui,* pp. 63–64. The idea of a union of political and divine authority is reinforced by a scene in another opera in which a grand fairy (*da xian*) warns fox fairies that the Jade Emperor will be angered if they harm the future emperor (*Bai cao po,* p. 222).
19. This view of gods and officials working together to right wrongs underlines the importance of what Schwartz (*World of Thought,* p. 37) called the basic Chinese "concept of a total all-embracing social and cosmic order." To be sure, these plays about the bad being punished and the good rewarded doubtless contained an element of wishful thinking about the perennial problem of evil. But people must have accepted the premise of a political-moral universe at least partially or plays based on it would not have been popular. It is impressive to see the strong presence of this idea in twentieth-century folk culture so many centuries after the formative age Schwartz was discussing.
20. *Jiang Shichuang xiuqi.*
21. *Longbao si jiangxiang.*
22. *Daoting men.*
23. *Gao Wenju zuo huating.*
24. *Jiang Shichuang xiuqi,* p. 600; *Wang Mingyue xiuqi,* p. 570; *Xiaogu xian,* 720; and *Gao Wenju zuo huating,* 585.
25. *Miaojin gui.*
26. *Yang Fulu tou qin.*
27. Schwartz, *World of Thought,* p. 411.

5. IN SEARCH OF MODERNITY: SOME REFLECTIONS ON A NEW MODE OF CONSCIOUSNESS IN TWENTIETH-CENTURY CHINESE HISTORY AND LITERATURE, BY LEO OU-FAN LEE

1. The discussion of post-modernism was the result of the impact of the American theorist Fredric Jameson's recent lecture tours of Beijing (Fall 1985) and Taipei (Summer 1986). See a collection of his lectures in Chinese, translated by Tang Xiaobing, *Hou xiandai zhuyi yu wenhua lilun* (Post-modernism and cultural theory; Xian: Shanxi shifandaxue chubanshe, 1986).
2. Lung-kee Sun, "Chinese Intellectuals' Notion of 'Epoch' (*Shidai*) in the Post-May Fourth Era," *Chinese Studies in History* 20.2:44 (Winter 1986/87).
3. James Reeve Pusey, *China and Charles Darwin* (Cambridge: Council on East Asian Studies, Harvard University, 1983), p. 15.
4. Ibid., p. 37.
5. Hao Chang, *Chinese Intellectuals in Crisis: Search for Order and Meaning, 1890–1911* (Berkeley: University of California Press, 1987), pp. 51, 52.
6. Ibid., p. 52; Pusey, p. 5.

7. Quoted in Pusey, p. 51.
8. Stephen Toulmin, *Human Understanding*, Vol. I: *The Collective Use and Evolution of Concepts* (Princeton: Princeton University Press, 1972), p. 331.
9. Ibid., p. 334.
10. Ibid., pp. 321–322.
11. Yan Fu, "Yuanqiang" (Origins of power), in *Yan Jidao xiansheng yizhu* (Posthumous writings of Yan Fu; Singapore: Nanyang xuehui reprint, 1959), pp. 98–99.
12. H. Stuart Hughes, *Consciousness and Society* (New York: Vintage Books, 1958), pp. 38–39.
13. Benjamin Schwartz, *In Search of Wealth and Power* (Cambridge: Harvard University Press, 1964), p. 46.
14. Ibid., p. 243.
15. Chen Duxiu, *Duxiu wencun* (Collected works of chen Duxiu; Hong Kong: Yuandong reprint, 1965), 1:41.
16. The three Beijing University scholars are Chen Pingyuan, Qian Liqun, Huang Ziping; see their symposium, "Ershi shiji Zhongguo wenxue" (Twentieth-century Chinese literature), serialized in *Dushu* 1–3 (January–March 1986). It was later published as a book, *Ershi shiji Zhongguo wenxue sanren tan* (The symposium of three on twentieth-century Chinese literature; Beijing: Renmin wenxue chubanshe, 1988).
17. See Bonnie McDougall, *The Introduction of Western Literary Theories into Modern China, 1919–1925* (Tokyo: The Center for East Asian Cultural Studies, 1971), Chap. 1.
18. Chen Zhengmo, *Xiandai zhexue sichao* (Currents of contemporary philosophy; Shanghai: Shanwu, 1933).
19. Chen Changheng and Zhou Jianren, *Jinhua lun yu shanzhong xue* (Evolution and eugenics; Shanghai: Shangwu, 1923).
20. Ibid., p. 5.
21. Ibid., pp. 7–8.
22. Ibid., pp. 26–27.
23. Chow Tse-tsung, *The May Fourth Movement: Intellectual Revolution in Modern China* (Cambridge: Harvard University Press, 1960), p. 333.
24. Hughes, p. 114.
25. Zhang Dongsun, *Xin zhexue luncong* (Discussions on new philosophy; Taibei: Tianhua reprint, 1979), pp. 350–365.
26. Ibid., p. 321.
27. Li Shicen, *Li Shicen lunwen ji* (Collected papers of Li Shicen; Shanghai: Shangwu, 1924), I, 9.
28. Ibid., pp. 8–9.
29. Ibid., p. 13.
30. Ibid., pp. 17–18.
31. Ibid., p. 18.

32. Ibid., pp. 31–35.

33. Hughes, p. 118.

34. Ibid., p. 34.

35. Sun, p. 52.

36. Ibid., p. 52.

37. Ibid., pp. 65–66.

38. Thomas A. Metzger, "Comments on Leo Ou-fan Lee's Paper at the Breckinridge Conference on Individualism and Holism" (23 July 1981; unpublished), pp. 5–6.

39. Leo Ou-fan Lee, *The Romantic Generation of Modern Chinese Writers* (Cambridge: Harvard University Press, 1973), Chaps. 2, 14.

40. Lung-kee Sun, personal letter to the author dated 13 January 1988. In writing this paper, I am much indebted to his research and insights.

41. Monique Chefdor, Ricardo Quinones, and Albert Wachtel, eds., *Modernism: Challenges and Perspectives* (Urbana: University of Illinois Press, 1986), p. 1.

42. Malcom Bradbury and James McFarlane eds., *Modernism 1890–1930* (New York: Penguin, 1976), p. 23.

43. Ibid., p. 14.

44. Matei Calinescu, *Faces of Modernity: Avant-Garde, Decadence, Kitsch* (Bloomington: Indiana University Press, 1977), pp. 20, 22.

45. Ibid., p. 41.

46. Ibid., p. 41.

47. Ibid., p. 44.

48. Bradbury and McFarlane, p. 50.

49. McDougall, Chap. 1.

50. See a recent collection of Mao Dun's critical essays, *Mao Dun wenyi zalun li* (Miscellaneous essays on literature by Mao Dun; Shanghai: Shanghai wenyi chubanshe, 1981), Vol. I.

51. Ibid., pp. 6–8.

52. The first Chinese introduction of Freud, published in *Dongfang zazhi* in December 1916, was a translation of a popular piece by a certain Dr. H. Addington, "The Marvels of Dream Analysis" from an American journal, *McClure's* (November 1912). Since the piece was in the spirit of popular science, not strictly speaking a scholarly treatise (as Freud himself intended his theory to be), the Chinese version seems well in line with the emergent temper of introducing Western knowledge as a way to modernity. The subsequent Chinese discussions of Freudian theory generally followed this mode of popular inquiry without delving seriously into the aesthetic implications of the Freudian notion of the subconscious on modern literature. For this I am indebted to the research of my student Mr. Jicheng Lin.

53. See Donald Munro ed., *Individualism and Holism in Chinese Thought* (Ann Arbor: University of Michigan Press, 1985).

54. Sanford Schwartz, *The Matrix of Modernism: Pound, Eliot, and Early Twentieth-Century Thought* (Princeton: Princeton University Press, 1988), p. 30.

55. For a discussion of Kuriyagawa Hakuson's influence on Lu Xun, see my book, *Voices from the Iron House: A Study of Lu Xun* (Bloomington: Indiana University Press, 1987), pp. 33, 92.

56. The information is based on my extensive interviews with Shi Zhicun and Xu Chi, poet and essayist, in 1986.

57. *Xiandai* 4.1:6 (1934).

58. Ibid.

59. Raymond Williams, *The Country and the City* (New York: Oxford University Press, 1973), Chaps. 16, 19.

6. THE CULTURAL CHOICES OF ZHANG XINXIN, A YOUNG WRITER OF THE 1980S, BY JEFFREY C. KINKLEY

Portions of this essay were originally presented at "The Fifth Quadrennial International Comparative Literature Conference in the R. O. C." convened at Tamkang University, 10–14 August 1987. I thank my colleagues there for their criticisms and advice.

1. Benjamin I. Schwartz, "Introduction," in Schwartz, ed., *Reflections on the May Fourth Movement: A Symposium* (Cambridge: East Asian Research Center, Harvard University, 1972), pp. 2, 4. Schwartz has implicitly reconfirmed this viewpoint in his Chapter 8, "Themes in Intellectual History: May Fourth and After," in *The Cambridge History of China* (Cambridge: Cambridge University Press, 1983), XII, 406–450.

2. Representative of the new emphasis on the late Qing in Western studies of modern literature (independent of Schwartz's influence) is Milena Doleželová-Velingerová, ed., *The Chinese Novel at the Turn of the Century* (Toronto: University of Toronto Press, 1980). Schwartz's student Leo Ou-fan Lee emphasizes the late Qing in his Chapter 9, "Literary Trends I: The Quest for Modernity, 1895–1927," in *The Cambridge History of China*, XII, 451–504.

   Studies of modern Chinese journalism by students of Schwartz and John K. Fairbank include Paul A. Cohen, *Between Tradition and Modernity: Wang T'ao and Reform in Late Ch'ing China* (Cambridge: Harvard University Press, 1974), and Leo Ou-fan Lee and Andrew J. Nathan, "The Beginnings of Mass Culture: Journalism and Fiction in the Late Ch'ing and Beyond," in David Johnson, Andrew J. Nathan, and Evelyn S. Rawski, eds., *Popular Culture in Late Imperial China* (Berkeley: University of California Press, 1985), pp. 360–395.

3. Benjamin I. Schwartz, *In Search of Wealth and Power: Yen Fu and the West* (Cambridge: Harvard University Press, 1964). On Liang Qichao, besides Leo Ou-fan Lee and Andrew J. Nathan, see Hao Chang, *Liang Ch'i-ch'ao and Intellectual*

Transition in China (Cambridge: Harvard University Press, 1971). On "cosmopolitanism," Joseph R. Levenson, *Revolution and Cosmopolitanism: The Western Stage and the Chinese Stages* (Berkeley: University of California Press, 1971). Schwartz uses the term *breakthrough generation* in his "Introduction" to *Reflections on the May Fourth Movement*, p. 2.

4. Studies of other turn-of-the-century thinkers by Schwartz's students include Charlotte Furth, ed., *The Limits of Change* (Cambridge: Harvard University Press, 1976); see also her *Ting Wen-chiang* (Harvard University Press, 1970); Hao Chang, *Chinese Intellectuals in Crisis* (Berkeley: University of California Press, 1987); Lin Yü-sheng, *The Crisis of Chinese Consciousness* (Madison: University of Wisconsin Press, 1979); Don C. Price, *Russia and the Roots of the Chinese Revolution, 1896–1911* (Cambridge: Harvard University Press, 1974); and James Reeve Pusey, *China and Charles Darwin* (Cambridge: Council on East Asian Studies, Harvard University, 1983). Then there are studies of individual thinkers: Maurice Meisner, *Li Ta-chao and the Origins of Chinese Marxism* (Cambridge: Harvard Univerity Press, 1967); Guy S. Alitto, *The Last Confucian* (Berkeley: University of California Press, 1979); Noriko Kamachi, *Reform in China: Huang Tsun-hsien and the Japanese Model* (Cambridge: Council on East Asian Studies, Harvard University, 1981); Joey Bonner, *Wang Kuo-wei: An Intellectual Biography* (Cambridge: Harvard University Press, 1986); and Leo Ou-fan Lee, *Voices from the Iron House: A Study of Lu Xun* (Bloomington: Indiana University Press, 1987). Schwartz and Fairbank also were of some inspiration to Jerome B. Grieder, author of *Hu Shih and the Chinese Renaissance* (Cambridge: Harvard University Press, 1970), and David Tod Roy, author of *Kuo Mo-jo: The Early Years* (Cambridge: Harvard University Press, 1971). Studies of later Chinese thinkers by students of Schwartz include those by David Arkush, Merle Goldman, Chang-tai Hung, Barry Keenan, Kwok-sun Luk, and me.

Schwartz's critique of Levenson, "History and Culture in the Thought of Joseph Levenson," is in Maurice Meisner and Rhoads Murphey, eds., *The Mozartian Historian: Essays on the Works of Joseph R. Levenson* (Berkeley: University of California Press, 1976), pp. 100–112 (quotation, p. 111). Levenson was a kindred spirit and beloved sparring partner of Schwartz's.

5. For works in translation, see Liu Binyan, *People or Monsters?*, tr. Perry Link (Bloomington: Indiana University Press, 1983). On Liu's reportage, see Rudolf G. Wagner, "Liu Binyan and the *Texie*," *Modern Chinese Literature* 2.1:63–98 (Spring 1986). On Liang Qichao and reportage, see Yin-Hwa Chou, "Formal Features of Chinese Reportage and an Analysis of Liang Qichao's 'Memoirs of My Travels in the New World,'" *Modern Chinese Literature* 1.2:201–217 (Spring 1985).

6. For example, Liu Binyan at the end of 1986 still felt that writing should be about social concerns and the new reforms—that it was worrisome if more than one out of five Chinese authors went in for aesthetic exploration beyond the

bounds of realism. See Leo Ou-fan Lee, "Cong liang ge wenxue huiyi kan Zhong-guo wenhua de fansi" (Ruminations on Chinese culture, proceeding from two literary conferences), *Jiushi niandai* 203:78–79 (December 1986). Liu, who has always shown a capacity for growth, has gone through a great deal in recent years, including a second expulsion from the Communist Party in 1987. And his recent articles, such as one in the January 1987 issue of *Fazhi wenxue xuankan* (Selections from literature about the legal system), brought to my attention by Michael Duke, show considerable willingness to throw over the traces even more and work outside the political (and so possibly literary) culture of the Communist Party as he has known it. I would not freeze the bold and unconventional Liu Binyan into place forever as a cultural conservative, but Zhang Xinxin was in any event already well along on her own independent path.

7. Benjamin I. Schwartz, *Chinese Communism and the Rise of Mao* (Cambridge: Harvard University Press, 1951), p. 4.

8. Helmut Martin, "Social Criticism in Contemporary Chinese Literature: New Forms of pao-kao-Reportage by Chang Hsin-hsin," an essay to be published in Taibei by Academia Sinica, revised from Zhang Xinxin and Sang Ye, *Peking Menschen*, German translation ed. by Helmut Martin (Köln: Diederichs, 1986), postscript. Carolyn Wakeman, "Fiction's End: Zhang Xinxin's 'New Approaches to Creativity,'" 1987 essay. For an overview of the kinds of Chinese criticisms of Zhang Xinxin, see "Zhang Xinxin zuopin taolunhui ceji" (Forum on the works of Zhang Xinxin: Notes from the sidelines), *Wenxue yanjiu dong-tai* 117:17–18 (15 April 1984).

9. I discussed the new criticisms of Zhang Xinxin with her in Shanghai, 5 November 1986. For a friendly and concerned reaction to Zhang's shift to journalism, see the published correspondence between Li Hui (cultural editor of the *Beijing wanbao*) and Zhang Xinxin, "Dianxing, huangdan ji qita" (Models, the Absurd, and other things), *Waiguo wenxue* 1985.11:47–49 (November 1985). Zhang in interview said that she knew Liu Binyan and wanted to put him into *Beijingren* (a work discussed below). He consented to be interviewed. However, she did not follow up, because Liu Binyan had been interviewed so many times he was repeating himself.

Henry S. Resnik, "When America Was Singing 'Buddy, Can You Spare a Dime?'" *Saturday Review* 53:27–30 (18 April 1970), already characterized Lewis and Terkel (one of Zhang Xinxin's models) as practitioners of "journalistic tape-recorded novels." Note that one of Zhang Xinxin's recent promoters is Xiao Qian, an ex-modernist writer-journalist.

10. Pan Yuan and Pan Jie, "The Non-Official Magazine *Today* and the Younger Generation's Ideals for a New Literature," in Jeffrey C. Kinkley, ed., *After Mao: Chinese Literature and Society, 1978–1981* (Cambridge: Council on East Asian Studies, Harvard University, 1985), pp. 193–219.

11. I have been influenced by recent works on literary modernism by intellectual

historians such as Frederick R. Karl, *Modern and Modernism* (New York: Atheneum, 1985), and Daniel Joseph Singal, *The War Within: From Victorian to Modernist Thought in the South, 1919–1945* (Chapel Hill: University of North Carolina Press, 1982).

12. Interview with Zhang Xinxin, Shanghai, 5 November 1986.

13. Wakeman, "Fiction's End."

14. Interview with Zhang Xinxin, 5 November 1986. She says she learned about psychology in fiction through translated novels by authors such as Henry James and Proust.

15. Wakeman, "Fiction's End." See also *Zhang Xinxin xiaoshuo ji* (A collection of short stories by Zhang Xinxin; Haerbin: Beifang wenyi chubanshe, 1985), pp. 429–431.

16. *Zhang Xinxin xiaoshuo ji*, pp. 119–245. Wakeman's essay traces modernist tendencies in Zhang's early fiction, including this story. In a letter to me of 8 June 1987, Zhang insisted that this story is autobiographical only in certain surface aspects.

17. *Zhang Xinxin xiaoshuo ji*, pp. 260–279.

18. Zhang Xinxin, "Theatrical Effects," tr. Jeffrey C. Kinkley, *Fiction* 8.2/3:155 (1987).

19. Ibid., p. 147. See Liang Heng and Judith Shapiro, *Intellectual Freedom in China After Mao* (New York: Fund for Free Expression, 1984).

20. *Zhang Xinxin xiaoshuo ji*, pp. 304–326. My translation.

21. Interview with Zhang Xinxin, 5 November 1986. Transformation from a human to an animal is a Kafka theme, as Wakeman and Martin point out, but the plot of "Orchid Madness" is nearly a carbon of Ionesco's *Rhinoceros*. Zhang told me in interview that the derivative quality of the story's plot diminishes it in her estimation. Still, she may be too hard on herself. The "madness" she explores differs in substance, cause, and manifestations from the madness (fascism) that is the subject of *Rhinoceros*.

22. On the origin of "Orchid Madness," see "Dianxing," p. 51. In interview, Zhang indicated that she was writing of orchid mania in Changchun; the citizens of Changchun even came to hate her because of the bad publicity the story brought them. Since Changchun is not mentioned by name, though, the city's mania must already have been known through the press, though *People's Daily* reported on orchid mania (in Anshan) only a year later, on 16 June 1984. See "'Fengkuang' de junzilan jiaoyi" (The "mad" trafficking in *junzi* orchids), cited in Bi Hua, "Rongxu zuojia zou zai zhengzhijia de qianmian" (Let authors travel ahead of politicians), *Jiushi niandai* 175:103 (1 August 1985). Perhaps *People's Daily* got this title from Zhang's story; perhaps reporters tagged the word *madness* to the story in 1983 and Zhang assimilated it. See note 36.

23. Gayle Feldman, cited below, has followed Zhang's hardships. Wang Yu said, in a seminar on Zhang Xinxin convened by Marsha Wagner at Columbia University, 2 May 1987, that Zhang finally got her diploma a year late. Since then, we have learned that critics intended to assail Zhang Xinxin again in early 1987.

However, the January 1987 hullabaloo over Liu Xinwu's alleged insult to the Tibetan people while editor of *Renmin wenxue*, which led to his temporary firing from that post, distracted critics from Zhang.

24. Zhang Xinxin, "Xing yun er–dui 26 ge wenti de huida" (Lucky me–my answers to 26 questions), *Wenhui yuekan* 57:13 (10 February 1985). *Beijingren* was first published, serially, in the form of individual character sketches, in *Meizhou Huaqiao ribao* (New York), 1984–1985. Fifty-eight sketches, slightly revised, were published for the first time in China in the January 1985 issues of *Zhong-shan* (Mt. Zhong), *Shanghai wenxue* (Shanghai literature), *Shouhuo* (Harvest), *Wenxuejia* (Writers), and *Zuojia* (Authors). Some of those were reprinted in *Xiaoshuo yuebao* (Short story monthly) 65 (May 1985). Still more characters were printed in *Zuojia* 1985.3 (March 1985) and *Shanghai wenxue* 94 (1 July 1985). Finally, the whole book of 100 characters (like the 100 in Terkel's *American Dreams*) appeared from the Shanghai wenyi chubanshe in August 1986. All page number citations hereafter refer to this paperback edition. On pp. 613 and 616, Zhang further discusses her shift to journalism.

   Much of *Beijingren* (64 sketches) is now translated under the title *Chinese Lives*, ed. W. J. F. Jenner and Delia Davin (New York: Pantheon, 1987). Not all the literary aspects of the book that I speak of in this essay can be appreciated in the translation. There have been excisions within individual sketches, particularly of interactions between the interviewers and interviewees. The sketches selected for translation were put into a new thematic order and generally flattened out for an Anglo-American public that presumably mainly wanted concrete knowledge about China. Another, less polished, edition of 39 sketches, is out under the title of *Chinese Profiles* (Beijing: Panda Books, 1986). That book ends with a statement about *Beijingren* by the authors, but the paragraphs have all been reordered.

25. *Zhang Xinxin xiaoshuo ji*, pp. 365–428. Kris Torgeson has translated this into English for her BA thesis at Wesleyan University. Information on Wang Meng from an 8 June 1987 letter from Zhang.

26. Zhang Xinxin, *Feng pian lian*, *Shouhuo* 52:4–92 (25 February 1985).

27. Contrary to Zhang's statement in "Xing yun er," p. 13, the symbols are not internationally known. The International Postal Union does not use them, and old-timers in the U.S. Postal Service have never heard of them. But, as Zhang admits in the same article, she is not a collector herself. If she were, she might not have thought the hobby so strange and obsessive.

28. I came to this conclusion after a fruitless search of Chinese postal albums, then read Zhang's own admission that she invented the story of the stamp after hearing local Shandong tales about the robbery. The latter is in *Hui lao jia, Zhang Xinxin xiaoshuo ji*, p. 368.

29. I analyze Chinese post-Mao detective formulas in *After Mao*, pp. 89–129. On older Chinese popular fiction, see Perry Link, *Mandarin Ducks and Butterflies* (Berkeley: University of California Press, 1981).

30. Zhang Xinxin, "Xing yun er," p. 13.
31. Interview with Zhang Xinxin, 5 November 1986.
32. Zhang speaks about reaching the masses through *Peking Man* and her television series *People Along the Canal* in "Dianxing, huangdan ji qita," pp. 50–51. See also the essay by Martin and *Beijingren*, p. 613. Since *Peking Man*, Zhang has continued writing popular reportage and working for television. She is filming *Envelope*. I do not agree with Martin that the novel mainly spoofs (instead of exploiting) the detective genre, except insofar as Zhang satirizes everything all the time. In that vein, there is a facetious reference to Agatha Christie (p. 71) and so forth.
33. Li Hui and Zhang Xinxin, "Dianxing, huangdan ji qita," p. 51.
34. C. T. Hsia, "The Scholar-Novelist and Chinese Culture," in Andrew H. Plaks, ed., *Chinese Narrative* (Princeton: Princeton University Press, 1977), pp. 266–305.
35. Lu Min, "Xin chao zhong de zhongshengxiang" (A new-wave view of creation), *Zhengming* 97:56 (1 November 1985). The piece "Wanyuanhu huzhu," in *Beijingren*, pp. 83–89, originally bore the word "taitai," which in mainland China has a satirical edge because the word is considered old-fashioned. Courtesy Wang Yu, Columbia seminar, 2 May 1987.
36. The old collector in *Envelope*, Xu Banghan, struck me as a possible composite of the coin-collecting "Old Man" (*Beijingren*, pp. 61–67) and the "First Customer," pp. 20–29. The retired folk reminded me of the ones at Baotou, pp. 505–515. There is a reverse link between *Peking Man* and "Orchid Madness." A *junzi* orchid specialist who is featured in *Peking Man* (pp. 470–475) gives information about the introduction of the orchid into China similar to that in "Orchid Madness." Zhang said in interview that she went up to interview a real flower maniac only after she wrote her story.
37. Wang Yu, Columbia seminar, 2 May 1987.
38. Interview with Zhang Xinxin, 5 November 1986. Wang Yu, at the Columbia seminar, said that she suggested the interviewing project, while Sang Ye introduced the idea of using Terkel for a model. That sounds plausible. In *Beijingren*, pp. 610–611, Sang Ye evidences familiarity with Terkel's *Working*. Zhang Xinxin in interview said she had not read *Working*; she added that only *American Dreams* and *The Good War* were translated into Chinese. Terkel interviews famous people as well as people on the street, and the occupational emphasis of *Working* also seems evident in *Peking Man*.
39. The idea for Terkel's first oral-history book, *Division Street*, came from Terkel's publisher friend André Schiffrin, who had read Jan Myrdal's *Report from a Chinese Village*. Ronald J. Grele, ed., *Envelopes of Sound* (Chicago: Precedent, 1975), pp. 21–22.
40. Terkel, cited in Grele, p. 12.

41. James Hoopes, *Oral History* (Chapel Hill: University of North Carolina Press, 1979), pp. 13–14.

42. Cullom Davis, Kathryn Back, and Kay MacLean, *Oral History: From Tape to Type* (Chicago: American Library Association, 1977), pp. 51–52. See also Willa K. Baum, *Transcribing and Editing Oral History* (Nashville: American Association for State and Local History, 1977).

43. Helen Epstein, "Tape It Again Studs," *The Washington Post Book World*, 5 October 1980. Lawrence Goodwyn, "In the Right Kind of Trouble," *The New Republic* 183:30–32 (15 November 1980).

44. *Beijingren*, p. 612, alludes to this, and I nailed it down in my 5 November 1986 interview. Zhang said she reordered topics of conversation.

45. C. Hugh Holman, *A Handbook to Literature*, 3rd ed. (Indianapolis: Bobbs-Merrill, 1972), p. 90.

46. Interview with Zhang Xinxin, 5 November 1986.

47. See Zhang Wei, "Women Writers Through Three Generations," *Beijing Review* 29.9:24 (3 March 1986).

48. Gayle Feldman, "Extracts from an Interview with Zhang Xinxin (September 1986)," unpublished.

49. Sang Ye and Zhang Xinxin, *Zhongguo yi ri* (One day in China), began publication in *Meizhou Huaqiao ribao*, 18 October 1986. Over 1,700 letters were received. Thirty or so, most of them shorter than the typical character sketches in *Beijingren*, were printed serially, through January-February 1987. Then publication petered out to a couple pieces a month; by the summer, the series seemed to have been discontinued. I note, from the original 18 October announcement, that *One Day in China* was a project with a 9-person editorial committee. The members are, in order, Liu Binyan, Xiao Qian, Deng Youmei, Yuan Ying, Bi Shuowang, Dong Yueshan, Li Xiaolin, Wang Yu, and Guo Zhaoqing. Liu Binyan, for one, ran into political difficulties in early 1987. On Mao Dun's project, see Sherman Cochran and Andrew C. K. Hsieh, with Janis Cochran, eds., *One Day in China* (New Haven: Yale University Press, 1983).

50. Zhang Xinxin, *Zai lu shang* (Hong Kong: South China Press, distributed by Joint Publishing Co., May 1987), retrospective preface dated 22 April 1986 (the next day after the "One Day" in China; see note 49).

51. Zhang Wei, p. 23. Interview with Zhang Xinxin at another Columbia University seminar convened by Marsha Wagner, 7 November 1987.

52. Interview with Zhang Xinxin, Shanghai, 5 November, 1986.

53. *Zai lu shang*, p. 4.

54. Interview with Zhang Xinxin, Shanghai, 5 November 1986.

55. Ibid.

56. Ibid.

57. Benjamin I. Schwartz, "Introduction," *Reflections on the May Fourth Movement*, p. 12.

7. A *"Theology" of Liberation? Socialist Revolution and Spiritual Regeneration in Chinese and Japanese Marxism,* by Germaine A. Hoston

The author wishes to thank Benjamin I. Schwartz, Baba Hiroji, Ishida Takeshi, William E. Connolly, Carl N. Edwards, Van H. Gardner, Thomas Schindler, Patricia G. Steinhoff, and Mbulelo V. Mzamane for their contributions to the preparation of this paper. The author is also grateful for the helpful suggestions and patient encouragement of Paul A. Cohen and Merle Goldman. Special appreciation is due to Ian J. MacAuslan for patient and stimulating discussions of the issues addressed here. Valuable research assistance was provided by Wang Li-Shing, Ma Junling, and Elizabeth Peterson. The financial support of the Rockefeller Foundation, the Social Science Research Council, the National Endowment for the Humanities, and The Johns Hopkins University is gratefully acknowledged.

1. Benjamin I. Schwartz, *Chinese Communism and the Rise of Mao* (Cambridge: Harvard University Press, 1951).

2. The reliance on Comintern and official Party documents in many early studies has reinforced this perception of Asian Marxists as offering little of value in the realm of political thought. See, for example, George M. Beckmann and Genji Okubo, *The Japanese Communist Party, 1922–1945* (Stanford: Stanford University Press, 1969); Gail Lee Bernstein, "The Russian Revolution, the Early Japanese Socialists, and the Problem of Dogmatism," *Studies in Comparative Communism* 9.4:327–348 (Winter 1976); Conrad Brandt, *Stalin's Failure in China 1924–1927* (Cambridge: Harvard University Press, 1958; New York: W. W. Norton, 1966); Robert C. North, *Moscow and Chinese Communists,* 2d ed. (Stanford: Stanford University Press, 1963); and Richard C. Thornton, *The Comintern and the Chinese Communists, 1928–1931* (Seattle: University of Washington Press, 1969). Neither the Comintern's role in creating the disastrous experience of the CCP in the late 1920s nor the ignorance of its leadership on matters concerning Japan can be denied. An examination of Comintern and official Party documents alone, however, cannot produce an adequate picture of independent innovations in Marxist thought of the sort that one would find in non-programmatic writings of Marxists inside and outside the official Communist Parties.

3. There are, of course, exceptions to this generalization, which make the pattern that much more pronounced. The exceptions with reference to China and Japan, the focus of the present study, include the following: On China, Benjamin I. Schwartz, "China and the West in the 'Thought of Mao Tse-tung,'" in *China in Crisis,* eds. Ping-ti Ho and Tang Tsou (Chicago: University of Chicago Press, 1968), I, 365–379; Benjamin I. Schwartz, "The Reign of Virtue: Some Broad Perspectives on Leader and Party in the Cultural Revolution," in *Party Leadership and Revolutionary Power in China,* ed. John Wilson Lewis (Cam-

bridge: Cambridge University Press, 1970); Frederic Wakeman, *History and Will* (Berkeley: University of California Press, 1973, Campus Books, 1975); and, to a limited extent, Arif Dirlik, "The Predicament of Marxist Revolutionary Consciousness: Mao Zedong, Antonio Gramsci, and the Reformulation of Marxist Revolutionary Theory," *Modern China* 9.2:182–211 (April 1983); and on Japan, see Germaine A. Hoston, "Between Theory and Practice: Marxist Thought and the Politics of the Japanese Socialist Party," *Studies in Comparative Communism* 20.2:175–207 (Summer 1987); Germaine A. Hoston, *Marxism and the Crisis of Development in Prewar Japan* (Princeton: Princeton University Press, 1986), especially Chap. 7; and Germaine A. Hoston, "Marxism and National Socialism in Taishō Japan: The Thought of Takabatake Motoyuki," *Journal of Asian Studies* 44.1:43–64 (November 1984). It is also interesting to note that, to the extent that innovations by thinkers such as Mao Zedong or Takahashi Kamekichi are noted, their pedigree as "genuine" Marxists is more readily questioned—even by their own countrymen—than is that of their European counterparts. See the debate between Richard Pfeffer and Benjamin I. Schwartz in *Modern China* in the mid-1970s on Mao and Marxism; the discussion in Tang Tsou, "The American Political Tradition and the American Image of Chinese Communism," *Political Science Quarterly* 77.4:570–600 (December 1962); and Germaine A. Hoston, "Marxism and Japanese Expansionism: Takahashi Kamekichi and the Theory of 'Petty Imperialism,'" *Journal of Japanese Studies* 10.1:1–30 (1984). Note that, in this study, as in the articles cited above, Chinese and Japanese names appear in accordance with customary usage, surnames first.

4. We shall refrain here from establishing arbitrary criteria according to which we may judge whether these thinkers are "genuinely" Marxists or not. The thinkers discussed below regarded themselves as Marxists—having adopted such concepts as "mode of production"—and were explicit about those aspects of Marx's original theory and method to which they subscribed and those to which they did not.

5. To the extent that Marx spoke of an "Asiatic" mode of production and "Oriental" society, Marx knew little of Asia, and these terms were used imprecisely to refer to a pattern that was opposite to that experienced in the West. "Oriental societies" were said to have no internal dynamic of social change that could lead them to evolve autonomously into feudal and then capitalist modes of production. Oriental societies were said to be incapable of developing private property as it has become known in the West, because of the repressive power of a despot who was the sole owner of the land and people of the society. See Germaine A. Hoston, "State and Revolution in China and Japan: Marxist Perspectives on the Nation-State and Social Revolution in Asia" (PhD dissertation, Harvard University, 1981), Chap. 5; and Hoston, *Marxism and the Crisis of Development*, Chap. 6. On Marx and "Orientalism," see Edward W. Said, *Orientalism* (New York:

Pantheon, 1978; Random House, 1979), pp. 2–3, 153–156, 206. For Marx's views on the Asiatic mode of production and Oriental society, see Karl Marx, *Pre-Capitalist Economic Formations*, tr. Jack Cohen, ed. Eric J. Hobsbawm (New York: International Publishers, New World Books, 1965); and Karl Marx, "Preface to a Contribution to the Critique of Political Economy," pp. 3–6, and "The British Rule In India," pp. 653–658, both in *The Marx-Engels Reader*, ed. Robert C. Tucker, 2d ed., rev. and enlgd. (New York: W. W. Norton, 1978).

6. I am indebted to my colleague William E. Connolly for guidance on the current debate among Western philosophers such as Karl Löwith, Martin Heidegger, and Hans Blumenberg on the legitimacy of the concept of modernity. For an introduction to this discourse, see the Translator's Introduction by Robert M. Wallace to Hans Blumenberg, *The Legitimacy of the Modern Age* (Cambridge: MIT Press, 1983), and the "Review Essay" on the same by Martin Jay in *History and Theory* 24:183–195 (1985).

7. The Kaitō-ha was a group of imprisoned members of the Japanese Communist Party (JCP) who, in 1929, declared that they would seek to build socialism on the basis of the Japanese Imperial Household. See Germaine A. Hoston, "Emperor, Nation, and the Transformation of Marxism to National Socialism in Prewar Japan: The Case of Sano Manabu," *Studies in Comparative Communism* 18.1:32–33 (Spring 1985).

8. The orthodox Kōza-ha might be added to this group, inasmuch as they claimed that vestiges of "feudalism" and "Asiatic" features continued to characterize the superstructure of Japanese society, thereby making an immediate proletarian-socialist revolution in Japan impossible. Nevertheless, this group did not write extensively on the need for spiritual/cultural revolution alongside material change, nor did its members stress spirituality and cultural revolution as a distinct element that needed to be incorporated actively into Marxism-Leninism. See Hoston, *Marxism and the Crisis of Development*, Chaps. 6–7.

9. This, of course, was the essential point of "What Is To Be Done?" written in 1903. See Robert C. Tucker, ed., *The Lenin Anthology* (New York: W. W. Norton, 1975), especially pp. 23–33, 50.

10. In Gramsci's work, "hegemony"—acceptance of or consent to the legitimating principles of a political system—is contrasted to "domination," which is rule resting on coercion, on the state's monopoly on the use of force. Gramsci argued that, in a less developed capitalist society, such as 1917 Russia, the revolution resembled a "war of manoeuvre," for it was sufficient to attack the state power directly: Unsupported by a highly developed civil society resting on a firm ideological consensus, the tsarist state and then the fragile provisional government crumbled in 1917. By contrast, in advanced capitalist societies, the hegemony exercised by the bourgeoisie was powerful, reinforced by schools, media, and other elements of civil society. See Antonio Gramsci, *Selections*

from the Prison Notebooks, ed. and tr. Quinton Hoare and Geoffrey Nowell Smith (New York: International Publishers, New World Paperbacks; and London: Lawrence & Wishart, 1971), pp. 238–239, 243.

11. Here the term *theology* is defined broadly to refer to that which "articulates a particular vision of the transcendent." (Louis Dupré, "Spiritual Life in a Secular Age," *Daedalus* 111.1:30 [Winter 1982: "Religion"].)

12. For this phraseology I am indebted to Gustavo Gutiérrez's articulation of this conception of theology within the Judeo-Christian tradition. According to Gutiérrez, a "theology of liberation" is "critical reflection on historical praxis . . . a theology which does not stop with reflecting on the world, but rather tries to be part of the process through which the world is transformed." (Gustavo Gutiérrez, *A Theology of Liberation*, tr. and ed. Sister Caridad Inda and John Eagleson [Maryknoll, N.Y.: Orbis Books, 1973], p. 15.)

13. This author does not subscribe to the Althusserian view that there was a major epistemological break between the "young" and the "mature" Marx. The conception of alienation developed in Marx's early works furnished the philosophical basis for the critique of capitalist society presented in later writings. The fundamental problematique thus remained consistent throughout all Marx's writings. On this controversy, see Alan Wolfe, "New Directions in the Marxist Theory of Politics," *Politics and Society* 4.2:132 (Winter 1974); Jean Hyppolite, "Marxisme et philosophie," in Jean Hyppolite, *Etudes sur Marx et Hegel*, 2d ed., Bibliothèque philosophique (Paris: Editions Marcel Rivière et Cie., 1965), pp. 109–110; and John Plamenatz, *Karl Marx's Philosophy of Man* (Oxford: Oxford University Press, 1978), pp. 209–210.

14. See Karl Marx, "Contribution to the Critique of Hegel's *Philosophy of Right*: Introduction," pp. 53–65; Karl Marx and Friedrich Engels, "The German Ideology: Part I," especially pp. 148–163; and Karl Marx, "On the Jewish Question," pp. 26–52, all in Tucker, ed., *Marx-Engels Reader.*

15. For the conceptualization of this problem in terms of "polarities," I am indebted to Benjamin I. Schwartz's usage in "China and the West;" and "Some Polarities in Confucian Thought," in *Confucianism in Action*, ed. D. Nivison (Palo Alto: Stanford University Press, 1959), pp. 50–62.

16. Compare Benjamin Schwartz's caveat against the potentially simplistic presumption that Mao's view that "the key to the good society lies in the transformation of souls into selfless parts of the whole" came from peculiarly Chinese philosophical antecedents, such as the Confucian emphasis on *wusi* (unselfishness). Schwartz argues that the roots of this theme in Mao may also be found in the tension within the Western philosophical tradition between the view of history as a "moral drama," on the one hand, and the notion that history is made by objective forces in the "technico-economic sphere," on the other. See Schwartz, "China and the West," pp. 365–366.

17. In the writings of George Plekhanov, Leon Trotsky, and Lenin, Russia's "Asi-

atic" features differentiating it from Western Europe figured heavily in their accounts of Russia's laggard economic development. See Samuel H. Baron, "Plekhanov's Russia: The Impact of the West upon an 'Oriental' Society," *Journal of the History of Ideas* 19.3:390, 392–393, 396–400 (June 1958); V. I. Lenin, *The Development of Capitalism in Russia: The Process of the Formation of a Home Market for Large-Scale Industry*, rev. 2d ed. (Moscow: Progress Publishers, 1964), especially pp. 176–177; and Leon Trotsky, *1905*, Eng. ed. (New York: N.p., 1971), pp. 3–8, 12–15, 38–39. Geography was stressed as the most significant factor causing divergent paths of development in East and West in Plekhanov's *Fundamental Problems of Marxism*. This work, one of the first of Russian Marxism to be introduced into China and Japan after the October Revolution, was translated into Japanese and widely read by 1925.

18. See Ishida Takeshi, *Meiji seiji shisō shi kenkyū* (Studies in the history of Meiji political thought; Tokyo: Mirai-sha, 1954), pp. 3–149; and Hoston, "State and Revolution," I, 218–238. In a recent study, Carol Gluck takes issue with the implication of Japanese historiography on *tennō-sei* thought (the orthodoxy legitimating the Meiji state on the basis of the sanctity of the imperial institution); but her account of the formation of that *tennō-sei* ideology in willy-nilly fashion does not gainsay the fact that official efforts were made to systematize this orthodoxy, to disseminate it through the educational system, and to wield it both to legitimate the Meiji state's industrializing activities and to counter its potentially destabilizing social effects. (See Carol Gluck, *Japan's Modern Myths: Ideology in the Late Meiji Period* [Princeton: Princeton University Press, 1985].) For accounts of official and scholarly efforts to articulate and disseminate this *kokutai* thought, see Nakase Juichi, "Meiji kenpō moto ni okeru tennō-kikan-setsu no keisei" (The formation of the emperor-organ theory under the Meiji constitution), *Hōritsu jihō* 34:59–71 (April 1962); Ukai Nobushige, "Kenpō ni okeru no chi'i: kikan to shite no tennō to shōchō no tennō" (The position of the emperor in the constitution: The emperor as organ and the emperor as symbol), *Shisō* (Thought) 336:504–511 (June 1952); and Ukai Nobushige, "Minobe hakushi no shisō to gakusetsu: sono rekishi no igi" (The thought and theory of Dr. Minobe: Their historical significance), *Hōritsu jihō* 20:45–49 (August 1948).

19. See Benjamin I. Schwartz, *In Search of Wealth and Power: Yen Fu and the West* (Cambridge: Harvard University Press, 1964), pp. 12–13.

20. Yü-sheng Lin, with a foreword by Benjamin I. Schwartz, *The Crisis of Chinese Consciousness: Radical Iconoclasm in the May Fourth Era* (Madison: University of Wisconsin Press, 1979), pp. 27, 6n.

21. Schwartz, *In Search of Wealth and Power*, p. 12. I am not suggesting here that Confucianism was in fact a "religion" in imperial China. But Chinese critics like Chen Duxiu rejected it in association with religion in general because of its character as a dogma of moral values that functioned to legitimate imperial rule

and the existing social order in the same manner that state churches in the West legitimated the political and social status quo. Certainly there is a meaningful similarity between the notion of the Mandate of Heaven and the Divine-Right-of-Kings doctrine of medieval Europe.

22. See Chow Tse-tsung, "The Anti-Confucian Movement in Early Republican China," in *The Confucian Persuasion* (Stanford: Stanford University Press, 1960), pp. 296–303; Neander C. S. Chang, "The Anti-Religious Movement," *The Chinese Recorder* (Shanghai) 54.8:459–467 (August 1923); and Chow Tse-tsung, *The May Fourth Movement: Intellectual Revolution in Modern China* (Cambridge: Harvard University Press, 1960), pp. 320–327. The interpretation here differs from the treatment presented in Chow's book, which does not draw this distinction between institutionalized religion and concern with the spiritual sphere.

23. Cf. Guy S. Alitto, *The Last Confucian: Liang Shu-ming and the Chinese Dilemma of Modernity* (Berkeley and Los Angeles: University of California Press, 1979), pp. 10–12.

24. This is a key point in the argument made by Mexican liberation theologian José Porfirio Miranda. See Miranda, *Marx and the Bible: A Critique of the Philosophy of Oppression*, tr. John Eagleson (Maryknoll: Orbis Books, 1974), especially pp. xix–xx; and A. Francke, "Plato's Doctrine of Truth," tr. John Barlow, in William Barrett and Henry D. Aiken, eds., *Philosophy in the Twentieth Century: An Anthology*, Vol. II (New York: Random House, 1962), especially p. 270.

25. In some instances, most notably in the work of Japanese Marxists Sano Manabu and the Kaitō-ha members, the cry for spiritual regeneration was accompanied by an explicit questioning of the value of Enlightenment empiricism and the assertion of the validity of non-rational (sentimental and spiritual) claims to understanding. (This point is explored below.) To the extent that it questions the notion that truth is accessible only through the "objective" reflection of an enlightened elite (such as Plato's philosopher-king), the epistemology presented in Mao's "On Practice" also fits into this category: In both cases, the intuitive and subjective faculties of persons engaged in real life are elevated to the level of objective reason. These thinkers drew much closer to that element in Marx that stresses consciousness arising out of the praxis of production and revolution than to the sophisticated comprehension of the exploitative nature of production as a whole that Marx undertook and that Lenin saw as inaccessible to those engaged in production itself. See n. 26 below.

26. See Georges Sorel, *Reflections on Violence* (1906), tr. T. E. Hulme (New York: Peter Smith, 1941), especially Chap. 4; and Georges Sorel to Benedetto Croce, 26 February 1898, in "Lettere a Benedetto Croce," *La Critica* 25:1–7 (20 March 1927).

27. Marx and Engels declared the necessity for the "alteration of men on a mass scale," "an alteration which can only take place in a practical movement, a *revolution*," as a condition "for the production on a mass scale of . . . communist

consciousness;" but men would be moved to revolution through consciousness of their dehumanization in production through the experience of industrial production itself. Despite the absence of advanced capitalism in China, the emphasis on the subjective element in Chinese and Japanese Marxism (as in Lenin's critique of Eduard Bernstein's economics) had less to do with the desire to legitimate a socialist revolution in a less-developed country than with the conviction that, even in an advanced industrial setting, the experience of factory production was inadequate to impel the transformation of spirit sufficient to initiate a socialist revolution and to create a new society free of exploitation. See Karl Marx and Friedrich Engels, "The German Ideology," in Tucker, ed., *Marx-Engels Reader*, p. 193 (emphasis in original); "Alienation and Social Classes" (an excerpt from Karl Marx and Friedrich Engels, *The Holy Family: A Critique of Critical Criticism* [1845]), in Tucker, ed., *Marx-Engels Reader*, p. 134; Karl Marx, "Economic and Philosophic Manuscripts of 1844," in Tucker, ed., *Marx-Engels Reader*, pp. 80–82; V. I. Lenin, "What Is To Be Done?" in *The Lenin Anthology*, ed. Robert C. Tucker (New York: W. W. Norton, 1975), pp. 49–59; and Antonio Gramsci, "The Modern Prince," in Antonio Gramsci, *Selections from the Prison Notebooks*, ed. and tr. Quintin Hoare and Geoffrey Nowell Smith (New York: International Publishers; London: Lawrence & Wishart, 1971), pp. 129–133.

28. Lu Xun, "Preface to *A Call to Arms*," in *The Complete Stories of Lu Xun*, tr. Yang Xianyi and Gladys Yang (Bloomington: Indiana University Press and Foreign Languages Press, 1981), pp. vi–vii.

29. Lu Xun, "A Madman's Diary," in *Complete Stories of Lu Xun*, pp. 4, 12.

30. See the influential series of lectures collected in Liang Shuming, *Dong-Xi wenhua ji qi zhexue* (Eastern and Western civilizations and their philosophies; Shanghai: Commercial Press, 1922); Chen Jiayi, "Dongfang wenhua yu wuren zhi daren" (Eastern culture and our major responsibility), *Dongfang zazhi* (Eastern miscellany) 18.1:19–38 (10 January 1921) and 18.2:9–25 (25 January 1921); and the discussions in Alitto, *Last Confucian*, Chaps. 4–5, and Chow, *May Fourth Movement*, pp. 327–332.

31. Chen Duxiu, "Ouxiang pohuai lun" (On the destruction of idols; 15 August 1918), in *Duxiu wencun* (Collected writings of [Chen] Duxiu), 3 vols. (Hong Kong: Yuandong tushu gongsi, 1965), I, 229.

32. This was the point made in Chen Duxiu, "Aiguoxin yu zijuexin" (Patriotism and self-consciousness), *Jiayin zazhi* (Tiger magazine) 1.4:1–6 (1915); see the discussion in Peng Ming, "Wusi shiqi de Li Dazhao he Chen Duxiu" (Li Dazhao and Chen Duxiu in the May Fourth period), *Lishi yanjiu* (Historical studies) 6:48 (1962).

33. Compare the stress on this feature of Western liberal thought as a basis for a "concept of justice" in the work of the contemporary American political philosopher John Rawls. See his *A Theory of Justice* (Cambridge: Harvard University

Press, 1971), pp. 3–4. For the convenience of his argument, here Chen collapsed the disparate elements of the Daoist, Legalist, Buddhist, and Confucian traditions into one category. In a subsequent article, Chen did differentiate among the various currents of Chinese philosophy in order to refute the view that Confucianism alone constituted China's "national essence." See Chen Duxiu, "Xianfa yu kongjiao" (Constitutionalism and Confucianism), in *Duxiu wencun*, I, 106–110.

34. It is a curious reflection of Chen's acceptance of social Darwinism at this point that he should have characterized the aggressive warlike peoples who subjugated China as civilized and those of the East who preferred repose as only "semi-civilized."

35. Chen Duxiu, "Dong-Xi minzu genben sixiang zhi cha'i" (Differences in the basic thought of Eastern and Western peoples), 15 December 1915, in *Duxiu wencun*, I, 35–38; Chen Duxiu, "Rensheng zhenyi" (The true meaning of human life) 15 February 1916, in *Duxiu wencun*, I, 183–184; Chen Duxiu, "Wuren zuihou zhi juewu" (Our final self-awakening), 15 February 1916, in *Duxiu wencun*, I, 49, 55; and Chen Duxiu, "Xianfa yu kongjiao," I, 103–104, 116.

36. Chen, "Wuren zuihou zhi juewu," I, 55–56.

37. Compare the discussions in Yves Chevrier, "De l'Occidentalisme à la solitude: Chen Duxiu et l'invention de la modernité chinoise," *Etudes chinoises* 3:7–34 (1984); and Yves Chevrier, "Utopian Marxism: 'Populist Strains' and Conceptual Growth Pains in Early Chinese Marxism, 1920–1922," in *Reform and Revolution in Twentieth Century China*, ed. Yü-ming Shaw (Taipei: National Chengchi University, Institute of International Relations, 1987), pp. 34–35. Compare the formulation offered by Martin Jay, discussing the Western conception of modernity as it is treated in Hans Blumenberg's work: " . . . what defines the modern is precisely its attempt to ground itself on the basis of self-assertion rather than theological dispensation" (Jay, "Review Essay," p. 187). "Self-assertion," for Blumenberg, refers not to "the naked biological and economic preservation of the human organism by the means naturally available to it. It means an existential program, according to which man posits his existence in a historical situation and indicates to himself how he is going to deal with the reality surrounding him and what use he will make of the possibilities that are open to him" (Blumenberg, *Legitimacy of the Modern Age*, p. 138).

38. Chen, "Xianfa yu kongjiao," pp. 104–106, 110–111; and Chen Duxiu, "Zai lun kongjiao wenti" (More on the question of Confucianism), 1 January 1917, in *Duxiu wencun*, I, 129–130.

39. Chen, "Zai lun kongjiao wenti," I, 130–134.

40. Chen Duxiu, "Jinri Zhongguo zhi zhengzhi wenti" (The problem of politics in China today), 15 July 1918, in *Duxiu wencun*, I, 224–225; Chen, "Xianfa yu kongjiao," I, 103–111; Chen, "Zai lun kongjiao wenti," I, 129–130; Chen,

"Wuren zuihou zhi juewu," I, 55–56; and Chen Duxiu, "Jiu sixang yu guoti wenti: zai Beijing Shenzhou Xuehui jiangyan" (Old thought and the question of the national polity: A lecture at the Beijing Shenzhou Learned Society), 1 May 1917, in *Duxiu wencun*, I, 149–151.

41. See Nomura Kōichi, "Chūgoku ni okeru Marukusu-shugi (I): Sono keisei katei ni tsuite no nōto" (Marxism in China: Notes on the process of its formation), *Shisō* 486:1653 (December 1964).

42. I have borrowed the phraseology of the theologian Jürgen Moltmann's work *Theology of Hope* (New York: Harper and Row, 1967); Jürgen Moltmann, "The Revolution of Freedom: Christians and Marxists Struggle for Freedom," in his *Religion, Revolution and the Future*, tr. M. Douglas Meeks (New York: Scribner's, 1969), pp. 65–66. Cf. Peng, "Wu-si shiqi de Li Dazhao he Chen Duxiu," p. 62; and Lee Feigon, *Chen Duxiu: Founder of the Chinese Communist Party* (Princeton: Princeton University Press, 1983), pp. 143–144.

43. Chen Duxiu, "Jidujiao yu Zhongguoren" (Christianity and the Chinese), 1 February 1920, in *Duxiu wencun*, I, 417–422. In this respect, Chen agreed with the views presented in Liang Shuming's essays on Eastern and Western civilizations. See Chen Ruoshui, "Liang Shuming yu 'Dong-Xi wenhua ji qi zhexue'" (Liang Shuming and *Eastern and Western cultures and their philosophies*; Taibei: Wenxue chubanshe, 1977), pp. 217–223. Also see Chen Duxiu, "Jidujiao yü Jidujiao-hui" (Christianity and the Christian Church), in *Duxiu wencun*, I, 659ff.

44. Chen, "Jidujiao yu Zhongguoren," I, 422–430.

45. See, for example, Chow, *May Fourth Movement*, pp. 321–322, 326; and Feigon, *Chen Duxiu*, pp. 144–145.

46. See Schwartz, *Chinese Communism and the Rise of Mao*, pp. 11–12.

47. Ibid., p. 11; cf. Maruyama Matsuyuki, "Ri Taishō no shisō to sono haikei: shisō to taikeika to jissen to no kankei ni tsuite" (Li Dazhao's thought and its background—on the relationship between the systematization of thought and practice), *Rekishi hyōron* (Historical review) 87:50 (August 1957).

48. Tatsuro and Sumiko Yamamoto, "Religion and Modernization in the Far East: A Symposium, II: The Anti-Christian Movement in China, 1922–1927," *Far Eastern Quarterly* 12.2:144–145 (February 1953).

49. Li Dazhao, "Yiyuan-zhi yu eryuan-zhi" (Unicameralism and bicamerialism), cited in Satoi Hikoshichirō, "Ri Taishō no shuppatsu: 'Genchi' ki no seiron o chūshin ni" (Recommencement of Li Dazhao, mainly on [the basis of] his political arguments in the "Statesmanship" [*Yanzhi*] Period), *Shirin* (The Shirin or the Journal of History) 40.3:197 (May 1957).

50. Li Dazhao, "Guoqing" (The state of the nation), 10 November 1914, in *Li Dazhao xuanji* (Selected writings of Li Dazhao; Beijing: Renmin chubanshe, 1962), pp. 6–7; and Satoi, "Ri Taishō no shuppatsu," p. 194.

51. Li Dazhao, "Torusutoi-shugi no kōryō" (April 1913) and "Yüansha" (September

1913), both cited in Kondō Kuniyasu, "'Minkoku' to Ri Taishō no ichi: Shingai kakumei kara goshi undō e" (The "Republic" and the position of Li Dazhao: From the 1911 Revolution to the May Fourth Movement), *Shisō* 477:290–291 (March 1964); and Satoi, "Ri Taishō no shuppatsu," pp. 196–197, 203.

52. Li Dazhao, "Fengsu," cited in Maruyama, "Ri Taishō no shisō to sono haikei," pp. 47–48.

53. Li Dazhao, "Minyi yu zhengzhi" (Rule of the people and politics), 15 May 1916, in *Li Dazhao xuanji*, p. 40; Li, "Kongzi yu xianfa" (Confucius and the constitution), 30 January 1917, in *Li Dazhao xuanji*, p. 77. See also the discussions in Maurice Meisner, *Li Ta-chao and the Origins of Chinese Marxism* (New York: Atheneum, 1977), pp. 31–32; Nomura Kōichi, "'Goshi' jidai no nashonaru na shikō: Ri Taishō ni tsuite" (Nationalistic thought during the May Fourth period: On Li Dazhao), *Shisō* 453:290–291 (March 1963); and Shimamoto Nobuko, "Go-shi ki ni okeru jūgatsu kakumei no eikyō: Ri Taishō no shisō o tōshite" (The influence of the October Revolution on the May Fourth Movement: Ideas of Li Dazhao), *Shiron* (Historica) 14–15:27 (March 1966).

54. Li, "Jin," pp. 95–96; and Li, "Qingchun," p. 76. See also Nomura, "Kindai Chūgoku no shisoka: Ri Taishō to Marukusu-shugi" (A thinker in modern China: Li Dazhao and Marxism), *Shisō* 464:179–180 (February 1963); Nomura, "'Go-shi' jidai," pp. 286–288, 291–292; Kondō, "'Minkoku' to Ri Taishō," p. 293; Maruyama, "Ri Taishō no shisō," p. 51; and Shimamoto, "Go-shi ki ni okeru jūgatsu kakumei no eikyō," pp. 27–28. Compare Marx on man's consciousness of himself as a species-being and as the subject of human history in: "On the Jewish Question," in Tucker, ed., *Marx-Engels Reader*, p. 46; and "Economic and Philosophic Manuscripts of 1844," in Tucker, ed., *Marx-Engels Reader*, pp. 106–125.

55. Li Dazhao, "Jin" (The present moment), in *Li Dazhao xuanji*, pp. 93–94; and Li Dazhao, "Qingchun," (Spring), in *Li Dazhao xuanji*, pp. 67–68, 72, 74; cf. Nomura, "'Go-shi' jidai no nashonaru na shikō," p. 288.

56. Kondō, "'Minkoku' to Ri Taishō," pp. 293–294.

57. Li, "Jin," p. 96; Li Dazhao, "Ziran de lunliguan yu Kongzi" (The naturalistic view of ethics and Confucius), in Li, *Li Dazhao xuanji*, p. 78; cf. Maruyama, "Ri Taishō no shisō," pp. 51–52.

58. Kondō, "'Minkoku' to Ri Taishō," p. 294; Nomura, "'Go-shi' jidai no nashonaru na shikō," pp. 292–293.

59. Li Dazhao, "Bolshevism de shengli" (The victory of Bolshevism), 15 November 1918, in *Li Dazhao xuanji*, pp. 117–118; Li Dazhao, "Pan . . . ism zhi shibai yu Democracy zhi shengli" (The defeat of Pan . . . ism and the victory of democracy), 15 July 1918, in *Li Dazhao xuanji*, pp. 107–108; Li Dazhao, "Shumin de shengli" (The victory of the masses), 15 November 1918, in *Li Dazhao xuanji*, pp. 110–111.

60. See Li Dazhao, "Weiwu shiguan zai xiandai shixueshang de jiazhi" (The value

of historical materialism in contemporary historiography), 1 December 1920, in *Li Dazhao xuanji,* pp. 334–340.

61. Li Dazhao, "Wo de Makesizhuyi guan" (My Marxist views), 11 May 1919, in *Li Dazhao xuanji,* p. 194.

62. See Kondō, "'Minkoku' to Ri Taishō," p. 294; and Zhang Jingru, *Li Dazhao tongzhi geming sixiang de fazhan* (The development of Comrade Li Dazhao's revolutionary thought; Wuhan: Hubei renmin chubanshe, 1957), p. 38.

63. Li Dazhao, "Jingsheng jiefang" (Spiritual liberation), 8 February 1920, in *Li Dazhao xuanji,* p. 309; Kondō, "'Minkoku' to Ri Taishō," p. 296; and Nomura, "Kindai Chūgoku no shisōka," p. 188.

64. See, for example, Li Dazhao, "Fa-E geming zhi bijiao guan" (A comparative perspective on the French and Russian revolutions), 1 July 1918, in *Li Dazhao xuanji,* pp. 101, 103; and Li Dazhao, "Wuzhi biandong yu daode biandong" (Material change and ethical change), in *Li Dazhao xuanji,* pp. 261–265, 272–273.

65. See Maruyama, "Ri Taishō no shisō to sono haikei," pp. 50–51; Li Dazhao, "Qingnian yü nongcun" (Youth and the village), 20–23 February 1919, in *Li Dazhao xuanji,* pp. 146–150; and Kondō, "'Minkoku' to Ri Taishō," p. 296.

66. Mao Tsetung, "On Contradiction," in Mao Tsetung, *Selected Readings from the Works of Mao Tsetung* (Peking: Foreign Languages Press, 1971), pp. 107–108; and Mao Tse-tung, "Reform Our Study," in Mao Tsetung, *Selected Works of Mao Tsetung,* 5 vols. (Peking: Foreign Languages Press, 1967), III, 24. See also the perceptive analysis on this point in Raymond F. Wylie, "Mao Tse-tung, Ch'en Po-ta and the 'Sinification' of Marxism, 1936–1938," *China Quarterly* 79:447–480 (September 1979).

67. "The history of human knowledge tells us that the truth of many theories is incomplete and that this incompleteness is remedied through the test of practice. Many theories are erroneous and it is through the test of practice that their errors are corrected." Mao Tsetung, "On Practice," in Mao, *Selected Readings,* p. 77.

68. For Gramsci, both kinds of intellectuals could come from any social class, but "traditional" intellectuals acted as "the dominant group's 'deputies' exercising the subaltern functions of social hegemony and political government." By contrast, "organic intellectuals" maintained their connections with their own class of origin (e.g., peasantry or proletariat), and articulated its ideas. (Antonio Gramsci, "The Intellectuals," in Gramsci, *Selections from the Prison Notebooks,* pp. 4, 12. Also see Joseph V. Femia, "Hegemony and Consciousness in the Thought of Antonio Gramsci," *Political Studies* 23.1:40–41 [March 1975].) Cf. Nigel Todd, "Ideological Superstructure in Gramsci and Mao Tse-tung," *Journal of the History of Ideas* 35.1:153 (1974); and Dirlik, "Predicament of Marxist Revolutionary Consciousness," passim. Mao, of course, had no knowledge of Gramsci's writings on this subject, which were published in Italian only a dec-

ade after Gramsci's death in 1937. Cf. Qu Qiubai, "Zhengzhi yundong yu zhishijieji" (The political movement and the intelligentsia), *Xiangdao zhoubao* (The guide weekly) 18:147–148 (January 1923).

69. "The human essence," Marx asserted, "is no abstraction inherent in each single individual. In its reality it is the ensemble of the social relations." (Karl Marx, "Theses on Feuerbach," in Tucker, ed., *Marx-Engels Reader*, p. 145.) See also Benjamin I. Schwartz, "The Philosopher," in *Mao Tse-tung in the Scales of History*, ed. Dick Wilson (London: Contemporary China Institute Publications, 1977), p. 15; Benjamin I. Schwartz, "The Reign of Virtue: Some Broad Perspectives on Leader and Party in the Cultural Revolution," in *Party Leadership and Revolutionary Power in China*, ed. John Wilson Lewis, Contemporary China Institute Publications (Cambridge: Cambridge University Press, 1970), pp. 166–169; and Donald J. Munro, "The Malleability of Man in Chinese Marxism," *China Quarterly* 48:609–640 (September–November 1971).

70. On Sorel's view on the decadence of modern society, see Jack J. Roth, "Revolution and Morale in Modern French Thought: Sorel and the Sorelians," *French Historical Studies* 3:206ff (Fall 1963). For Rousseau's critique of the decadence and corruption of modern civilization, see Jean-Jacques Rousseau, "Discourse on the Sciences and Arts (First Discourse)," in Jean-Jacques Rousseau, *The First and Second Discourses*, ed. with an Introduction and Notes by Roger D. Masters, tr. Roger D. and Judith R. Masters (New York: St. Martin's Press, 1964), pp. 31–64. Professor Schwartz has offered a superb analysis of how Rousseau's perspective on history as "moral drama" is incorporated along with the conflicting optimistic view of history as "techno-economic progress" in Marx's thought. See "China and the West," pp. 368–370.

71. See the illumination of this tension in Schwartz, *Chinese Communism and the Rise of Mao*, especially Chaps. 12–13. The issue of the orthodoxy versus heresy of Mao's thought, of course, formed the core of the controversies between Professor Schwartz and Karl Wittfogel in the 1950s and between Schwartz and Richard Pfeffer in the 1970s. See K. A. Wittfogel, "The Legend of 'Maoism,'" *China Quarterly* 1:72–86 (January–March 1960) and 2:35–42 (April–June 1960); Richard M. Pfeffer, "Mao and Marx in the Marxist-Leninist Tradition," *Modern China* 2.4:421–460 (October 1976); and Schwartz, "Essence of Marxism Revisited," pp. 461–472.

72. See Mao, "On Practice," p. 73; Mao, "On Contradiction," p. 100; and Mao Tse-tung, "Reform Our Study" (May 1941), in Mao, *Selected Works*, III, 20–21; and Mao Tse-tung, "Rectify the Party's Style of Work" (1 February 1942), pp. 35–38.

73. Mao, "On Practice," pp. 80–81.

74. For a succinct expression of the "mass line," see Mao Tsetung, "Get Organized!" (29 November 1943), in Mao, *Selected Readings*, p. 301.

75. Mao Tsetung, "Report on an Investigation of the Peasant Movement in Hunan" (March 1927), in Mao, *Selected Readings*, p. 24.

76. See, among many examples, Mao Tsetung, "The Situation and our Policy after the Victory in the War of Resistance against Japan" (13 August 1945), in Mao, *Selected Readings*, pp. 334–335. See also the vivid portrayal of the interplay between the peasantry and the CCP in William Hinton, *Fanshen: A Documentary History of Revolution in a Chinese Village* (New York: Alfred A. Knopf, and Random House, 1966).

77. Mao, "On Practice," p. 80.

78. Ibid., p. 79; and Li, "Wuzhi biandong yu daode biandong," passim. Cf. the discussion of Gramsci on this point in Femia, "Hegemony and Consciousness," p. 38.

79. Mao, "On Contradiction," p. 116.

80. Marx, "Theses on Feuerbach," p. 145.

81. On Lenin, see "What Is To Be Done?" For Gramsci's views, see Antonio Gramsci, "State and Civil Society," in Gramsci, *Prison Notebooks*, pp. 235–239; and Walter Adamson, *Hegemony and Revolution* (Berkeley and Los Angeles: University of California Press, 1980), especially Chaps. 6 and 7.

82. For a superb discussion of these differences between Mao and Liu on China's development strategy, see Jack Gray, "The Two Roads: Alternative Strategies of Social Change and Economic Growth in China," in *Authority, Participation and Cultural Change in China* (Cambridge: Cambridge University Press, 1973), pp. 109–157.

83. Liu Shao-chi, *How to Be a Good Communist (Lectures Delivered at the Institute of Marxism-Leninism in Yenan, July 1939)* (Boulder: Panther Publications, 1958), pp. 5–6.

84. Ibid., pp. 19–20, 73–74, 86.

85. Ibid., p. 6.

86. Mao Tse-tung, "Talks at the Yenan Forum on Literature and Art" (May 1942), in Mao, *Selected Works*, III, 73.

87. Liu, *How to Be a Good Communist*, pp. 9, 12–13.

88. See, e.g., Mao Tsetung, "On the Correct Handling of Contradictions among the People" (27 February 1957), in Mao, *Selected Readings*, p. 445. The most obvious weakness of Mao's formulation (and of Marx's similar identification of bureaucracy with the emergence of the modern capitalist state) lies in its failure to account for the long history of Chinese bureaucracy, which had arisen long before the sprouts of capitalism appeared in China. One solution to this difficulty might lie in the claim that we find in the work of Max Weber, for example, that there was a qualitative difference between such Chinese bureaucracy and "modern" legalistic, technocratic bureaucracy. See Max Weber, *Economy and Society*, ed. Guenther Roth and Claus Wittich, 2 vols. (Berkeley and Los Angeles: University of California Press, 1978), Chap. 11. A major reason for the periodic recurrence of the debate on the Asiatic mode of production among Chinese Marxists from the 1920s to the present may well lie in the need to

account for this characteristic of precapitalist China by recourse to the notion of "Oriental despotism." See Hoston, "State and Revolution," Chap. 5.

89. Some might claim that the terms *alienation* (*yihua*) and *atomization* were themselves alien to Mao, but it is clear that the content of these concepts was not. In Marx's work, the emergence of classes and eventually the extreme primacy of the individual were both reflections of man's alienation from his fellow man and from himself as a "species being." The particular formulation of this phenomenon that we find in Marx was itself a product of the maturation of bourgeois society, in which the individual actually comes to see himself as "alienated" from society and from himself; hence it is not suprising that we should not find this precise terminology in Mao's works. We do find in his and other pre-1949 writings, however, an appreciation of how patrimonialism, allegiance to precapitalist class identities, and even "bourgeois" liberalism pose profound impediments to the emergence of the communitarian spirit essential to a socialist society. Interestingly, while Mao accepted Marx's view that divisions among men could be overcome only by means of class struggle, Japanese Marxists Sano Manabu and Akamatsu Katsumaro (see below) saw even this "classism" of Marx as a manifestation of man's alienation in bourgeois society.

90. Liu, *How to Be a Good Communist*, pp. 73–74.

91. Mao Tse-tung, "On New Democracy," in Mao, *Selected Works*, II, 369–370.

92. Karl Marx, "The Civil War in France," in Tucker, ed., *Marx-Engels Reader*, p. 627. Cf. the following observation by Engels: "In possession of the public power and the right of taxation, the officials now present themselves as organs of society standing *above* society." (Frederick Engels, *Origin of the Family, Private Property and the State*, ed. with an Introduction by Eleanor Burke Leacock [New York: International Publishers, New World Paperbacks, 1972], p. 230.)

93. Liu, *How to Be a Good Communist*, pp. 7–8.

94. See Jean-Jacques Rousseau, "Discourse on the Origins of Inequality" (Second Discourse), in Rousseau, *First and Second Discourses*; and Jean-Jacques Rousseau, *The Social Contract*, tr. with an Introduction by Maurice Cranston (Harmondsworth and Baltimore: Penguin Books, 1968), p. 49.

95. Liu, *How to Be a Good Communist*, p. 86.

96. Schwartz, "Some Polarities," p. 52.

97. Mao Tse-tung, "The Great Union of the Popular Masses," tr. Stuart R. Schram, *China Quarterly* 49:87 (1972).

98. Roth, "Revolution and Morale," pp. 205–206.

99. See Nikolai I. Bukharin, *Imperialism and World Economy* (New York: International Publishers, 1929), Chaps. 10, 11, and 13; Hoston, *Marxism and the Crisis of Development*, pp. 56–60; Kazama Jōkichi, *Mosukō to tsunagaru Nihon Kyōsantō no rekishi* (History of the Japanese Communist Party in relationship to Moscow), ed. Sano Manabu and Nabeyama Sadachika (Tokyo: Tenman-sha, 1951), pp. 176–187; Stephen F. Cohen, *Bukharin and the Bolshevik Revolution* (New

York: Random House, 1971, Vintage Books, 1975), pp. 25–43. For Lenin's views, see V. I. Lenin, "Imperialism, the Highest Stage of Capitalism," in Tucker, *Lenin Anthology*, pp. 234–259 passim; and György Lukács, *Lenin: A Study in the Unity of his Thought*, tr. Nicholas Jacobs (Cambridge: MIT Press, 1971), pp. 50, 59.

100. For a fuller exposition of the difficulty of fitting Japan into this schema, see Hoston, "Marxism and Japanese Expansionism," pp. 22–27.

101. On the Japanese dual economy, see Kazushi Ohkawa and Henry Rosovsky, *Japanese Economic Growth: Trend Acceleration in the Twentieth Century* (Stanford: Stanford University Press, 1973), pp. 37–38; Tsunehiko Watanabe, "Industrialization, Technological Progress, and Dual Structure," in *Economic Growth, the Japanese Experience Since the Meiji Era*, ed. Lawrence Klein and Kazushi Ohkawa (New Haven: Economic Growth Center, Yale University Press, 1968), pp. 114–134; Takahashi Kamekichi, *Nihon shihon-shugi hattatsu shi* (History of the development of Japanese capitalism), rev. and enlgd. ed. (Tokyo: Nihon Hyōron-sha, 1929), p. 255.

102. See Shūichi Kato, "Taishō Democracy as the Pre-Stage for Japanese Militarism," in *Japan in Crisis: Essays on Taishō Democracy*, ed. Bernard S. Silberman and H. D. Harootunian (Princeton: Princeton University Press, 1974), pp. 224–225.

103. See Harold Joseph Wray, "Changes and Continuity in Japanese Images of the *Kokutai* and Attitudes and Roles Toward the Outside World: A Content Analysis of Japanese Textbooks, 1903–1945," PhD dissertation, University of Hawaii, 1971; and Ishida Takeshi, "Ideorogii to shite no tennō-sei" (The emperor system as ideology), *Shisō* 336:39 (June 1952).

104. During the Sino-Japanese War, this argument was used to legitimate the Japanese incursion into China. See the excellent analyses in Masao Maruyama, "Theory and Psychology of Ultra-Nationalism," and "Thought and Behaviour Patterns of Japan's Wartime Leaders," pp. 93–94, both in Masao Maruyama, *Thought and Behaviour in Modern Japanese Politics*, ed. Ivan Morris, expanded ed. (London: Oxford University Press, 1968). On the incorporation of the myth of divinity into *kokutai* thought, see Robert Cornell Armstrong, *Light from the East: Studies in Japanese Confucianism* (Toronto: University of Toronto, 1914), p. 3; David Magarey Earl, *Emperor and Nation in Japan: Political Thinkers of the Tokugawa Period* (Seattle: University of Washington Press, 1964), pp. 67, 221; and Robert N. Bellah, *Tokugawa Religion: The Values of Pre-Industrial Japan* (Glencoe: The Free Press, 1957; Boston: Beacon Press, 1970), pp. 99–100.

105. To quote the late Tokugawa thinker Yoshida Shōin, "'It is only in our country that sovereign and subject are united, and that loyalty and filial piety converge.'" (Yoshida Shōin, *Shiki Shichisoku*, quoted by Robert King Hall, ed., *Kokutai no Hongi: Cardinal Principles of the National Entity of Japan*, tr. John Owen Gauntlett [Cambridge: Harvard University Press, 1949], p. 90.) See also

Takeda Kiyoko, "Tennō-sei shisō no keisei" (The formation of the emperor-system ideology), in *Iwanami kōza: Nihon rekishi* (Iwanami symposium: Japanese history), 21 vols., Vol XVI: *Kindai* (Modern times), (Tokyo: Iwanami, 1962), III, 269–270, 297–303; Joseph Pittau, *Political Thought in Early Meiji Japan, 1868–1889* (Cambridge: Harvard University Press, 1967), pp. 132, 145; and Feng Yu-lan, "The Philosophy at the Basis of Traditional Chinese Society," in *Ideological Differences and World Order: Studies in the Philosophy and Science of the World's Cultures*, ed. Filmer Stuart Cockow Northrup (New Haven: Yale University Press, 1949), pp. 22–30.

106. [Communist International], "Nihon Kyōsantō kōryō sōan" (Draft program of the Japanese Communist Party; 1922), pp. 5–8; G. Voitinsky, "Nihon ni okeru kaikyūsen (Sankō ronbun)" (Class struggles in Japan [Reference paper], pp. 10, 15–17; [Communist International], "Nihon mondai ni kansuru ketsugi (ni-nana tēze)" (Resolution on the Japan problem, 1927 Theses), pp. 30–32, 44; and [Communist International], "Nihon ni okeru jōsei to Nihon Kyōsantō no ninmu ni kansuru tēze (san-ni tēze)" (Theses on the situation in Japan and the responsibilities of the Japanese Communist Party), pp. 81–85, all in *Kominterun Nihon ni kansuru tēze shū* (Collected Comintern theses on Japan), comp. Ishidō Kiyotomo and Yamabe Kentarō (Tokyo: Aoki Shoten, Aoki Bunko, 1961). All the Comintern theses except the 1931 Draft Political Theses emphasized the primacy of the semi-feudal elements and the need for a two-stage revolution. See Hoston, *Marxism and the Crisis of Development in Prewar Japan*, Chap. 3, and pp. 207–220; and the translations of the theses and discussion in George M. Beckmann and Genji Okubo, *The Japanese Communist Party, 1922–1945* (Stanford: Stanford University Press, 1969). For a Japanese Marxist critique of the ideology supporting the emperor system, see Hirano Yoshitarō, "Burujoa minshu-shugi undō shi" (History of the bourgeois-democratic movement), in *Nihon shihon-shugi hattatsu shi kōza* (Symposium on the history of the development of Japanese capitalism), 7 vols. and supplement (Tokyo: Iwanami Shoten, 1932–1933, reissued, 1982), III, 5–7, 18–20; and Hirano Yoshitarō, "Jiyū minken: Sono seishitsu, undō no gendo, naibu-teki kihon tairitsu no kiso kōsatsu" (Civil rights: An examination of their character, the limits of the movement, and the basis of its fundamental internal contradictions), *Kaizō* (Reconstruction) December 1933: 2–22.

107. Kazama, *Mosukō to tsunagaru Nihon Kyōsantō no rekishi*, pp. 89–90.

108. Kawakami Hajime was the exception to this nationalistic/statist tendency.

109. See Yü-sheng Lin's characterization of the May Fourth tendency toward cultural iconoclasm. (See his *Crisis of Chinese Consciousness*.) Li Dazhao, the least "totalistic" in his iconoclasm, most explicitly questioned the "materialism" of Marx's approach. As Meisner has noted, Li "found wholly unpalatable the Marxist de-emphasis on the role of ethical and spiritual factors in history." (Meisner, *Li Ta-chao*, pp. 92–93.)

110. See Atsuko Hirai, "Ancestor Worship in Yatsuka Hozumi's State and Constitutional Theory," in *Japan's Modern Century: A Special Issue of Monumenta Nipponica Prepared in Celebration of the Centennial of the Meiji Restoration*, ed. Edmund Skrzypczak (Tokyo: Sophia University and Charles E. Tuttle, 1968), pp. 41–50; S. An, "Meiji shoki ni okeru Doitsu kokka shisō no jūyō ni kansuru ichi kōsatsu: Burunchuri to Katō Hiroyuki o chūshin to shite" (The reception of J. C. [*sic*] Bluntschli's Theory of the State by Hiroyuki Katō in early Meiji Japan), in *Nihon Seiji Gakkai nenpō, 1975: "Nihon ni okeru Sei-Ou seiji shisō* (Annual bulletin of the Japanese Political Science Association, 1975: "Western Political Thoughts in Japan"; Tokyo: Iwanami Shoten, 1976), pp. 121, 140–142; and Walter Dening, "Confucian Philosophy in Japan. Reviews of Dr. Tetsujirō Inoue's Three Volumes on this Philosophy," *Transactions of the Asiatic Society of Japan* (Tokyo), Vol. XXXVI, pt. 2 (1908), pp. 116ff.

111. The most compelling account of the psychological damage inflicted on black persons victimized by colonial rule can be found in Frantz Fanon's *Black Skin, White Masks* (originally titled *Peau Noire, Masques Blanches* and published in 1952) tr. Charles Lam Markmann (London: Pluto, 1967; New York: Grove Press, 1967); and *Wretched of the Earth* (originally titled *Damnés de la terre* and published in 1961), tr. Constance Farrington, with a Preface by Jean-Paul Sartre (New York: Grove Press, 1963). Similarly, Amilcar Cabral, the late Marxist revolutionary leader of Guinea-Bissau, stressed the need to counter the efforts to repress and destroy indigenous culture that were, he argued, essential to the colonial effort. See his "National Liberation and Culture" (1970), pp. 39–56, in *Return to the Source: Selected Speeches of Amilcar Cabral*, ed. Africa Information Service (New York: Monthly Review Press, 1973); and "Identity and Dignity," in *Return to the Source*, pp. 59–63. Julius K. Nyerere's position bears an even closer resemblance to that of the Japanese theorists discussed here; for he claimed that pre-colonial society in Tanganyika and Zanzibar was essentially communitarian, egalitarian, even socialistic, and that class differences, individualistic materialism, and exploitation were introduced only with the imposition of colonialism. His view, then, both appealed to the traditional values that existed before contact with the West and led him to espouse a cultural revolution against "bourgeois" values. Neither Nyerere nor Cabral nor Fanon, however, laid significant stress on spiritual cultivation as such, and in this they differ from the Chinese and Japanese writers discussed here and from the African and Latin American thinkers considered below.

112. Takeda, "Tennō-sei shisō no keisei," p. 269.

113. Matsuzawa Hiroaki, *Nihon shakai-shugi no shisō* (Japanese socialist thought; Tokyo: Chikuma Shobō, 1973), p. 26; and Onabe Teruhiko, *Nijū seiki* (The Twentieth Century), Vol IV: *Meiji no hikari to kage* (Light and shadows of the Meiji period; Tokyo: Chūō Kōron-sha, 1978), p. 465.

114. *Nihon shakai undō jinmei jiten* (Biographical dictionary of Japan's social move-

ment; Tokyo: Aoki Shoten, 1979), s.v. Takabatake Motoyuki, Ishikawa Sanshi-rō, Katayama Sen, Arahata Kanson, Abe Isoo, Kawakami Kiyoshi, Murai Tomoyoshi, and Ōsugi Sakae.

115. Abe Isoo, Katayama Sen, and Murai Tomoyoshi all studied in the United States at universities associated with Congregationalism or Unitarianism. Both Abe and Murai were baptized into Christianity circa 1880 under the influence of Nii-jima Jō, a Japanese educator who had studied at Amherst College, became a practicing Christian, and founded Dōshisha University as a Christian college in Kyoto. Abe went to the United States in 1891 to study "social problems," and the value of the Bible as an historical source; he studied at Hartford Theological Seminary (Congregationalist) for three years, where he read Edward Bellamy's *Looking Backward* and came to believe that socialism provided the solution to poverty. After studying at Berlin University for several months and observing socialist activity in Glasgow, Abe returned to Japan in 1895 as a Christian social-ist. He became the head of the newly rechristened Shakai-shugi Kyōkai in 1900; co-founded, with Katayama and Kōtoku, Japan's first socialist party (ordered to dissolve the same day) in 1901; joined other Christian socialists to publish the journal *Shin Kigen* (New era) after the Russo-Japanese War; and, in 1920, was a founder of the Japanese Fabian Society. Katayama studied at Grinnell College, a Congregationalist school, and at Andover (Congregationalist) and Yale semi-naries and returned to Japan in 1895. Converting to Christianity during his stay in the United States, Katayama was influenced by Richard Ely's *Social Aspects of Christianity*. Murai also studied at Andover Theological Seminary and, on returning to Japan, became a preacher at the Hongō Unitarian Church, stressing social issues. (See Takeuchi Yoshitomo, "Nihon no Marukusu-shugi" [Japanese Marxism], in *Marukusu-shugi* II [Marxism], ed. Takeuchi Yoshitomo, Gendai Nihon shisō taikei [Outline of contemporary Japanese thought], 21:8–9 [Tokyo: Chikuma Shobō, 1965]; and Hyman Kublin, "The Japanese Socialists and The Russo-Japanese War," *Journal of Modern History* 22.4:325 [December 1950].) On the reformist orientation of Unitarianism, see Robert Kelley, *The Cultural Pattern in American Politics: The First Century* (New York: Alfred A. Knopf, Borzoi Books, 1979), p. 204; and David Walker Howe, *The Unitarian Conscience: Harvard Moral Philosophy, 1805–1861* (Cambridge: Harvard University Press, 1970). The first Unitarian Church in Japan was founded by A. M. Knapp in 1887. (*Kirisuto-kyō dai jiten* [Encyclopedia of Christianity], rev. and enlgd. ed. [N.p.: Kyōbun-kan, n.d.], s.v. Unitarian; and Murakami Shigeyoshi, *Nihon shūkyō jiten* [Encyclopedia of Japanese Religion; Tokyo: Kōdan-sha, 1978], p. 355.)

116. Arahata Kanson, *Kanson jiden* (Autobiography of [Arahata] Kanson), 2 vols. (Tokyo: Itagaki Shoten, 1948; Iwanami Shoten, Iwanami Bunko, 1975), I, 99, 100, 111–113, 132–135; *Nihon shakai undō jiten*, s.v. Kōtoku Shusui; and Ara-

hata Kanson, _Nihon shakai-shugi undō shi_ (History of the Japanese socialist movement; Tokyo: Mainichi Shinbun-sha, 1949), pp. 107, 108.

117. _Nihon shakai undō jinmei jiten_, s.v. Sakai Toshihiko; and Arahata, _Nihon shakai-shugi undō shi_, p. 106.

118. _Nihon shakai undō jinmei jiten_, s.v. Takabatake Motoyuki. In the _kokutai_ conception, one could not easily prescind the state from the nation; thus, the term _kokka shakai-shugi_ is translated here as both state socialism and national socialism. On the introduction of Marxism into Japan, see Hoston, "State and Revolution in China and Japan," I, 44–55; and Koyama Hirotake, _Nihon Marukusu-shugi shi_ (Tokyo: Aoki Shoten, 1956), pp. 13–14.

119. See Nobuya Bamba and John F. Howes, ed., _Pacifism in Japan: The Christian and Socialist Tradition_, with a Foreword by Robert N. Bellah (Vancouver: University of British Columbia Press, 1978). Quotations here are taken from H. D. Harootunian's review of this book in _The American Historical Review_ 85.3:697 (June 1980).

120. Matsuzawa, _Nihon shakai-shugi no shisō_, pp. 36–40.

121. Ibid.; and Kida Jun'ichirō, _Meiji no risō_ (Ideals of the Meiji period; Tokyo: San'ichi Shobō, 1965), p. 213. Cf. the orthodox Roman Catholic opposition to "class struggle" in Marxism and liberation theology on the same grounds. See Catholic Church, Pope 1926–1937 (Pius XI), "Atheistic Communism" (Encyclical letter _Divini Redemptoris_, 19 March 1937), in _Sixteen Encyclicals of His Holiness Pope Pius XI_ (Washington, D.C.: National Catholic Welfare Conference, 1926–1937), pp. 7–9. Significantly, like Sano, Pope John Paul II has criticized Marxism as reflecting the same materialism and economism that are characteristic of bourgeois society as a whole. These perspectives, in his view, are thus "incapable of providing sufficient and definitive bases for thinking about human work, in order that the primacy of man over the capital instrument, the primacy of the person over things, may find in it adequate and irrefutable confirmation and support." See Catholic Church, Pope John Paul II, _On Human Work_ (Encyclical _Laborem Exercens_, 14 September 1981; Washington D.C.: United States Catholic Conference, 1981), pp. 24, 29–30. This was also true of Li Dazhao, who preferred to project the imagery of the survival of the fittest and class struggle to the international arena rather than to relations among Chinese. See Li Dazhao, "Jieji jingzheng yu huzhu" (Class struggle and mutual aid), 6 July 1919, in Li, _Li Dazhao xuanji_, pp. 222–225; and Li Dazhao, "You jingjishang jieshi Zhongguo jindai sixiang biandong de yuanyin" (An economic interpretation of the causes of changes in modern Chinese thought), 1 January 1920, in Li, _Li Dazhao xuanji_, pp. 295–302.

122. Takeuchi, "Nihon no Marukusu-shugi," p. 12; Matsuzawa, _Nihon shakai-shugi no shisō_, pp. 35–36; and Kuno Osamu and Tsurumi Shunsuke, _Gendai Nihon no shisō—sono itsutsu no uzumaki_ (Contemporary Japanese thought: Five whirl-

pools; Tokyo: Iwanami Shoten, 1956, Iwanami Shinsho, 1978), p. 33 and Chap. 2 passim.

123. See Ishida, "Ideorogii to shite no tennō-sei," p. 39; George Wilson, *Radical Nationalist in Japan: Kita Ikki, 1883–1937* (Cambridge: Harvard University Press, 1969), p. 22; and Bellah, *Tokugawa Religion*, pp. 13, 14.

124. Fred G. Notehelfer, *Kōtoku Shūsui: Portrait of a Japanese Radical* (Cambridge: Cambridge University Press, 1971), pp. 49, 56–59, 66–75; and Nakamura Katsunori, "Kōtoku Shūsui no shōgai to shisō" (The life and thought of Kōtoku Shūsui), *Hōgaku kenkyū* (Legal studies) 30.11:22–23 (November 1957).

125. Thomas Kirkup, *An Inquiry into Socialism* (New York: N.p., 1888), p. 41, quoted in Notehelfer, *Kōtoku Shūsui*, p. 77.

126. See Frederic Wakeman, Jr., "The Price of Autonomy: Intellectuals in Ming and Ch'ing Politics," *Daedalus* 101:35–70 (Spring 1972).

127. Fred G. Notehelfer, "Kōtoku Shūsui and Nationalism," *Journal of Asian Studies* 31.1:34–35 (November 1971); cf. Matsumoto Sannosuke, "Atarashii seiji ishiki no hōga: sono shikaku to mondai" (The germination of a new political consciousness: Perspectives and problems), in *Kindai Nihon seiji shisō shi* (History of modern Japanese political thought), 2 vols., ed. Hashikawa Bunzō and Matsumoto Sannosuke, Kindai Nihon shisō shi taikei (Outline of the history of modern Japanese thought), no. 3, ed. Miyazawa Toshiyoshi and Ōkouchi Kazuo (Tokyo: Yūhikaku, 1971), pp. 7, 9–12.

128. Kōtoku Shūsui, "Shakai-shugi to kokutai" (Socialism and national polity), 1902, in Kōtoku Shūsui, *Shakai-shugi shinzui* (The essence of socialism; Tokyo: Iwanami Shoten, Iwanami Bunko, 1953), pp. 73–74.

129. Matsuzawa, *Nihon shakai-shugi no shisō*, pp. 27, 29–32.

130. Gail Lee Bernstein, *Japanese Marxist: A Portrait of Kawakami Hajime, 1879–1946*, (Cambridge: Harvard University Press, 1976); and *Nihon shakai undō jinmei jiten*, s.v. Kawakami Hajime.

131. Koyama, *Nihon Marukusu-shugi shi*, p. 19; Moriya Fumio, "Nihon ni okeru Marukusu-shugi no seiritsu" (The establishment of Marxism in Japan), *Gendai to shisō* (Modern times and thought) 39:125 (March 1980); and Amano Keitarō, *Kawakami Hajime hakushi bunkenshi* (A bibliography of the writings of Dr. Hajime Kawakami; Tokyo: Nihon Hyōron Shinsha, 1956).

132. Kawakami Hajime, "Shin-teki kaizō to butteki kaizō," 1921 (Psychic reconstruction and material reconstruction), in Kawakami Hajime, *Kawakami Hajime chosakushū* (Collected writings of Kawakami Hajime; Tokyo: Chikuma Shobō, 1964), X, 199–201; Kawakami Hajime, "Roshiya kakumei to shakai-shugi kakumei," 1922 (The Russian Revolution and socialist revolution), Kawakami, *Kawakami Hajime chosakushū*, X, 228–230.

133. Kawakami Hajime, "Yuibutsu shikan ni kansuru jiko seisan," 1928 (A settlement of accounts with myself on historical materialism), pt. 9, *Shakai mondai kenkyū* (Studies on social problems), 87:30 (October 1928).

134. Kawakami Hajime, "Yuibutsu shikan ni kansuru jiko seisan" (pt. 1), *Shakai mondai kenkyū* (Studies on social problems), 77:5 (February 1927); cf. Bernstein, *Japanese Marxist*, p. 169.

135. Kawakami Hajime, "'Shihon' ni arawareru yuibutsu shikan no danpen" (Fragments of historical materialism manifested in *Capital*), in Kawakami Hajime, *Yuibutsu shikan kenkyū* (Studies in historical materialism; Tokyo: Kōbundō, 1921), pp. 151–156.

136. Bernstein, *Japanese Marxist*, pp. 168–169.

137. Kawakami Hajime, *Marukusu-shugi no tetsugaku-teki kiso*, 1929 (The philosophical foundations of Marxism; Tokyo: Kōdo-sha, 1949), pp. 269–270.

138. Kawakami Hajime, *Jijōden* (Autobiography), 5 vols. (Tokyo: Iwanami Shoten, 1952), I, 205–206, 211; III, 196; and Kawakami Hajime, "Yuibutsu shikan to risō-shugi" (The materialistic interpretation of history and idealism], *Shakai mondai kenkyū* (Studies on social problems) 11:365–376 (December 1919), passim.

139. Kawakami, *Jijōden*, III, 198.

140. Martin Bernal, *Chinese Socialism to 1907* (Ithaca: Cornell University Press, 1976), pp. 76–79, 94–96; and *Nihon shakai undō jinmei jiten*, s.v. Abe Isoo, Murai Tomoyoshi, and Nishikawa Kōjirō.

141. Kawakami Hajime, "Kahen no tōtoku to fuhen no tōtoku," 1919 (Variable morality and invariable morality), in Kawakami, *Kawakami Hajime chosaku-shū*, X, 175–176, 179–183.

142. "'Those *shishi* who aspire to the revolutionary reform of the political system of the nation sometimes ardently wish for their country's defeat. Their attitude is derived from sincere feelings of patriotism in its true sense.'" (*Jijōden*, quoted in Bernstein, *Japanese Marxist*, pp. 168, 80–81.) Cf. Kawakami, *Jijōden*, III, 196–197.

143. See his critique of Japanese national socialists in Kawakami Hajime, "Kokka shakai-shugi no riron-teki kentō" (A theoretical examination of national/state socialism), *Chūō kōron* (Central review) 47.6:2–36 (June 1932).

144. *Nihon shakai undō jinmei jiten*, s.v. Takabatake Motoyuki. A fuller exposition of his thought is presented in Hoston, "Marxism and National Socialism in Taishō Japan."

145. Takabatake died at 42 of stomach cancer. Tanaka Masato, *Takabatake Motoyuki: Nihon no kokka shakai-shugi* (Takabatake Motoyuki: Japan's national socialism; Tokyo: Gendai Hyōron-sha, 1978), Chaps. 3–5; and Tanaka Masato, "Takabatake Motoyuki ron: Taishō shakai-shugi no bunka" (On Takabatake Motoyuki: The differentiation of Taishō socialism), *Shirin* 53.2:41–44 (March 1970).

146. See Takabatake Motoyuki, *Marukusu-gaku kenkyū* (Studies on Marxism; Tokyo: Daitō-kaku, 1919), pp. 37–39, 51; Tanaka, *Takabatake Motoyuki*, p. 299; and Akamatsu Katsumaro, "Kyōsantō kōzai ron" (On the merits and demerits of the Communist Party), *Chūō kōron* (Central review) June 1929:31.

147. Takabatake, *Marukusu-gaku kenkyū*, pp. 41–47.

148. Takeuchi, "Nihon no Marukusu-shugi," pp. 10–11; Matsuzawa, *Nihon shakai-shugi no shisō*, pp. 42–43. Similarly, Akamatsu condemned capitalism as anarchistic and unethical (given the primacy of the pursuit of profit); by contrast, socialist production was "controlled, planned, and oriented to the welfare of the populace." George O. Totten, "The National Socialism of Akamatsu Katsumaro," paper prepared for presentation at the American Political Science Association Annual Meeting, 30 August–2 September 1984, Washington, D.C., p. 20; and Akamatsu Katsumaro, *Shin kokumin undō no kichō* (The keynote of the new national movement; Tokyo: Manrikaku, 1932), p. 148.

149. Takabatake Motoyuki, "Kokka shakai-shugi no hitsuzen-sei" (The necessity of state socialism), in Takabatake Motoyuki, *Hihan Marukusu-shugi* (Criticizing Marxism; Tokyo: Nihon Hyōron-sha, 1934), pp. 184–185; and Takabatake Motoyuki, "Kokka shakai-shugi no seisaku" (The policies of state socialism) in Takabatake, *Hihan Marukusu-shugi*, pp. 218–220.

150. Takabatake Motoyuki, "'Puroretaria kokka' no ronri-teki hatan" (The logical bankruptcy of the "proletarian state"), in Takabatake, *Hihan Marukusu-shugi*, pp. 86–92, 95; Takabatake, "Kokka shakai-shugi no hitsuzen-sei," pp. 194–198; and Takabatake Motoyuki, *Marukishizumu to kokka-shugi* (Marxism and statism; Tokyo: Kaizō-sha, 1930), pp. 165–166.

151. Ibid., pp. 109–110.

152. Hall, ed., *Kokutai no Hongi*, pp. 176, 93–94.

153. Sano Manabu, "Kenryoku to rōdō" (Authority and labor) in Sano, *Sano Manabu chosakushū*, II, 1001.

154. Sano Manabu, "Marukusu kokka-ron to sono hihan" (Marx's theory of the state and its critique) in Sano Manabu, *Sano Manabu chosakushū* (Collected writings of Sano Manabu), 5 vols. (Tokyo: Sano Manabu Chosakushū Kankōkai, 1959), I, 570–573; and Sano Manabu, *Gokuchū-ki* (Prison diary), in Nabeyama Sadachika and Sano Manabu, *Tenkō jūgo nen* (Fifteen years since *tenkō*; Tokyo: Rōdō Shuppan-bu, 1949), pp. 121–122.

155. Mizuno Shigeo, "Mizuno Shigeo shuki: Kansō (san)–dōshi M. K. atetaru keishiki nite" (Notes of Mizuno Shigeo: thoughts [3]–in a form addressed to Comrade M. K.), 26 March 1929, Tōkyō Chihō Saibansho Kenjikyoku Shisōbu sha, (Transcription of the Tokyo District Court Prosecutor's Office Thought Bureau), May 1929, pp. 2b, 3a, 8a–8b.

156. Ibid., pp. 10a, 15b–21b; and Mizuno Shigeo, "Nihon Kyōsantō dattai ni saishi tōin shokun ni" (To party members on seceding from the Japanese Communist Party), Tokyo Chihō Saibansho Kenjikyoku (Tokyo District Courts Prosecutor's Office) 3 June 1929, p. 1.

157. Takabatake, *Marukishizumu to kokka-shugi*, p. 161.

158. Totten, "National Socialism of Akamatsu," pp. 16–17; and Akamatsu, *Shin kokumin undō no kichō*, pp. 137–146.

159. Takabatake Motoyuki, *Kokka shakai-shugi taigi* (Outline of state socialism),

Nihon Shakai-shugi Kenkyūjo panfuretto tokushū (Japanese Socialist Institute Pamphlet, special issue; Tokyo: Nihon Shakai-shugi Kenkyūjo, 1932), p. 5.

160. Takabatake Motoyuki, quoted in Tanaka, "Takabatake Motoyuki ron," p. 50; Takabatake, *Kokka shakai-shugi taigi*, pp. 6–8.

161. Akamatsu, *Shin kokumin undō no kichō*, pp. 59, 70, 124; and Sano Manabu, "Bukkyō to shakai-shugi" (Buddhism and socialism), in Sano, *Sano Manabu chosakushū*, III, 735–736.

162. Takabatake Motoyuki, *Jiko o kataru* (Speaking about myself; Tokyo: Jinbunkai Shuppan-bu, 1926), pp. 73–75.

163. See Patricia Golden Steinhoff, "*Tenkō*: Ideology and Social Integration in Prewar Japan" (PhD dissertation, Harvard University, 1969), p. 159. Kobayashi Morito, comp. *Tenkōsha no shisō to seikatsu* (The thought and lives of *tenkōsha*; Tokyo: Daidō-sha, 1935), pp. 4–5; Nabeyama Sadachika, *Watakushi wa Kyōsantō o suteta: jiyū to sokoku o motomete* (I abandoned the Communist Party: Seeking freedom and the fatherland; Tokyo: Daitō Shuppan-sha, 1949), pp. 132–133; Nabeyama Sadachika, "Kokoro no sokuseki" (Footprints of my mind), in Nabeyama and Sano, *Tenkō jūgo-nen*, pp. 65, 66; and Arahata Kanson, *Sa no menmen: jinbutsu ron* (All of the left: Character sketches; Tokyo: Hayakawa Shobō, 1951), pp. 91–93. When he first was imprisoned, Mizuno recalled feeling as Jesus Christ must have felt at his trial; and this was the beginning of the spiritual struggle that culminated in his *tenkō*. See Mizuno, "Kaisō I: Dōshi K. ni atetaru keishiki ni oite" (Thoughts, Part I: In the form of addressing Comrade K.), Tōkyō Chihō Saibansho Kenjikyoku Shisōbu sha (Tokyo District Court Prosecutor's Office, Thought Bureau, Transcription), 27 June 1929, p. 1.

164. Kobayashi, "Tenkōsha," pp. 8–10; and Sano Manabu, "Waga gokuchū no shisō henreki" (The course of my thoughts while in prison), August 1944, marked confidential (N.p.: Shihōshō Keisei-kyoku), pp. 16–17, 20–21.

165. Takeda Kiyoko, "Kakumei shisō to tennō-sei—Takabatake Motoyuki no kokka shakai-shugi o chūshin ni" (Revolutionary thought and the emperor system: On the state socialism of Takabatake Motoyuki), in *Kindai Nihon seiji shisō shi* (II) (History of modern Japanese political thought), comp. Hashikawa Bunzō and Matsumoto Sannosuke, Kindai Nihon shisō shi taikei, no. 4 (Outline of modern Japanese thought; Tokyo: Yūhikaku, 1970), pp. 293–294.

166. Sano Manabu, *Minzoku to kaikyū* (Race and class), Minshu shiriizu no. 3 (Democracy series; Tokyo: Kinrō Jihō-sha, 1949), pp. 11–17; Sano *Gokuchū-ki*, pp. 113–118; and Sano Manabu, "Sei-Ou-teki sekai-kan to Tōyō-teki sekai-kan" (The West European world-view and the Eastern world-view), in Sano, *Sano Manabu chosakushū*, II, 941–949; and Sano Manabu, "Tōyō-teki sekai kan to shakai-shugi" (The oriental world view and socialism), in Sano, *Sano Manabu chosakushū*, II, 950–954.

167. Sano, "Waga gokuchū no shisō henreki," pp. 12–14. Cf. the references to the "formulaic intellectualism" and "abstract formulations" of orthodox Marxism-

Leninism in Mizuno Shigeo, "Jōshinsho: Nyūtō zengo yori 'san-ichi-go' ni itaru kikan ni okeru 'shisō no sui'i' ni tsuite" (Prison statement: From about the time [I] entered the party to [the] March 15[th Incident]), 28 January 1929.

168. Ibid., pp. 14–15.

169. Sano, "Bukkyō to shakai-shugi," III, 732.

170. Akamatsu Katsumaro, "Kaihō ka, gedatsu ka" (Liberation or deliverance?), *Tōyō hyōron* (Eastern review), September 1955, quoted in Totten, "Akamatsu Katsumaro," pp. 83–86.

171. Mizuno, "Jōshinsho," pp. 29, b5–b6; Mizuno, "Kansō," Pt. 3, pp. 29b, 30, 34; Mizuno Shigeo, "Kansō, Pt. 1," p. 11a.

172. *Die heilige Familië*, p. 186, in *Aus dem literarischen nachlass Marx-Engels*, 1902, Vol. II, quoted in Sidney Hook, *From Hegel to Marx: Studies in the Intellectual Development of Karl Marx* (New York: Humanities Press, 1950), p. 17.

173. See Miranda, *Marx and the Bible*; José Porfirio Miranda, *Marx against the Marxists: The Christian Humanism of Karl Marx*, tr. John Drury (Maryknoll: Orbis Books, 1980); José Miguez Bonino, *Christians and Marxists: The Mutual Challenge to Revolution* (Grand Rapids: William B. Eermans, 1976); Gutiérrez, *Theology of Liberation*; and the excellent overview of the historical context of Catholic social doctrine and the critique of it developed by liberation theologians in Latin America: Arthur F. McGovern, *Marxism: An American Christian Perspective* (Maryknoll: Orbis Books, 1980). For examples of Black theology, a counterpart of liberation theology developed by Blacks in South Africa, see Allan A. Boesak, *Black and Reformed* (Maryknoll: Orbis, 1984); Allan Aubrey Bocsak, *Black Theology Black Power* (Oxford: A. R. Mowbray, 1978); Allan A. Boesak, *Farewell to Innocence* (Maryknoll: Orbis, 1977); Allan Boesak and Charles Villa-Vicencio, *A Call for an End to Unjust Rule* (Edinburgh: Saint Andrew Press, 1986); and the essays collected in Itumeleng J. Mosala and Buti Tlhagale, ed., *The Unquestionable Right to be Free: Black Theology from South Africa* (Maryknoll: Orbis Books, 1986). A precursor to these efforts to produce a theology of liberation emerged in Weimar Germany in the work of Paul Tillich. See Paul Tillich, *The Socialist Decision*, tr. Franklin Sherman (New York: Harper & Row, 1977; originally published in 1933).

174. Simon Maimula, "Current Themes and Emphases in Black Theology," in *Unquestionable Right to be Free*, ed. Mosala and Tlhagale, p. 107.

175. See "The Condition of the Working Classes" (Encyclical letter *Rerum Novarum*, 15 May 1891), pp. 208–211, 218–224, and "Socialism, Communism, Nihilism" (Encyclical Letter *Quod Apostolici Muneris*, 28 December 1878), pp. 22–23, 30, both in Catholic Church, Pope, 1878–1903 (Leo XIII), *The Great Encyclical Letters of Pope Leo XIII* (New York, Cincinnati, and Chicago: Benziger Brothers, 1903); the excerpts from *Quadragesimo Anno* in Joseph N. Moody et al., eds., *Church and Society: Catholic Social and Political Thought and Movements 1789–1950* (New York: Arts, Inc., 1953), pp. 246–247 respectively; Pope John

XXIII, *Pacem in Terris* (1963), published as *Peace on Earth* (New York: Ridge Press and Golden Press, 1964), pp. 138; and Pope John Paul II's third encyclical letter entitled *Laborem Exercens*, published as *On Human Work*, pp. 15–19.

176. See, especially, the meticulous and cogent discussions in Miranda, *Marx and the Bible*, Miranda, *Marx against the Marxists*, and Bonino, *Christians and Marxists*, pp. 38–39.

177. One prominent scholar on Marx has observed that this "casual phrase of Marx's penned in 1843 when he was still a Feuerbachian . . . has itself acted like opium upon the minds of his followers, who have repeated it as if it constituted all that can be said on the subject." (Hook, *From Hegel to Marx*, p. 293.)

178. Karl Marx, "Contribution to the Critique of Hegel's *Philosophy of Right*: Introduction," in *Marx-Engels Reader*, ed. Tucker, p. 54.

179. Erazim Kohák, "Religion and Socialism'" *Dissent* 25.2:177 (Spring 1978) (emphasis in original). Cf. Bonino, *Christians and Marxists*, pp. 48ff.

180. *The Illusion of Progress* was a work published by Sorel in 1908. See Sorel, *Reflections on Violence*, p. 35; and E. E. Jacobitti, "Sorel and Croce: Myth and Faith," in *Revolutionary Humanism and Historicism in Modern Italy* (New Haven: Yale University Press, 1981), pp. 125–136.

181. See Alexis de Tocqueville, *Democracy in America*, ed. Phillips Bradley, 2 vols. (New York: Alfred A. Knopf and Random House, Vintage Books, 1945); and the sagacious analysis by George Armstrong Kelly, in "Faith, Freedom, and Disenchantment: Politics and the American Religious Consciousness," *Daedalus* 111.1 (Winter 1982): "Religion," pp. 132–133. Cf. Jan. M. Lochman, "Marxism, Liberalism, and Religion," in *Marxism and Radical Religion: Essays toward a Revolutionary Humanism*, ed. John Raines and Thomas Dean (Philadelphia: Temple University Press, 1970), pp. 20–21. Compare the sentiments voiced eloquently by the French writer Charles Péguy, who broke his official ties to the French socialist movement in 1900: "Le porche du mystère de la deuxième vertu," in Charles Péguy, *Oeuvres poétiques complètes* (Paris: Editions Gallimard, Bibliothèque de la Pléiade, 1957).

182. S. N. Eisenstadt, "Socialism and Tradition," in *Socialism and Tradition*, ed. S. N. Eisenstadt and Yael Azmon, The Van Leer Jerusalem Foundation Series (Atlantic Highlands, N.J.: Humanities Press, 1975), p. 13.

183. See Hook, *From Hegel to Marx*, pp. 52–53, 211.

184. Gordon S. Wood, "The Fundamentalists and the Constitution," *New York Review of Books* 35.2:34 (18 February 1988).

8. CONSTITUTIONAL ALTERNATIVES AND DEMOCRACY IN THE REVOLUTION OF 1911, BY DON C. PRICE

Research for this paper was conducted under an exchange with the Institute of Modern History, Chinese Academy of Social Sciences, on a grant from the Committee on Scholarly Communication with the People's Republic of China. Further research and preparation of early drafts were made possible by a grant from the Wang Institute of Graduate Studies. The present version has benefited from discussion at a colloquium at Columbia University in 1987, and at the U.S. Soviet Conference on China, 1900–1937, held under the auspices of the International Research and Exchanges Board at Princeton, 1988, from suggestions by the editors of the present volume, and criticisms from my colleague Norma Landau on questions of English history.

1. Not the least of the problems of such an undertaking is that of defining democracy. It is tempting for the purposes of this paper to follow John Plamenatz in using Schumpeter's definition, which requires open and organized political competition to insure the accountability of government to the governed. Such a definition does not explicitly address the problem of equal rights or the breadth of political participation. While such a definition ignores the modern Chinese achievement of a high degree of participation, it honors the continuing complaint that democracy has not thereby been achieved. The problem with such a definition is that it does not discriminate between types of disenfranchisement (for example, on grounds of wealth, race, gender, age) or the prevailing expectations that justify it, not to speak of the relation between the scope of the political arena and the issues on which the governed may be keenly interested to exercise a choice (e.g., social equality, personal liberties, control of economic power). For the purposes of this essay I am inclined to recognize a significant democratic movement in China at the time of the 1911 Revolution, when the desirability of full self-government in principle was recognized even as practical considerations seemed to dictate the postponement of majority franchise. For further discussion of these issues, see John Plamenatz, *Democracy and Illusion: An Examination of Certain Aspects of Modern Democratic Theory* (London: Longman, 1973), Andrew J. Nathan, *Chinese Democracy* (Berkeley: University of California Press, 1985), esp. pp. 226–228, and Samuel Bowles and Herbert Gintis, *Democracy and Capitalism: Property, Community, and the Contradictions of Modern Social Thought* (New York: Basic Books, 1986), esp. Chaps. 1 and 2.

2. For an analysis of one liberal's dilemma (and "irrelevance") in the face of the "disparity between [an optimistic] view of the potential of government and the possibility, in China, of exercising "effective and conscious methods of democratic control over it," see Jerome B. Grieder, *Hu Shih and the Chinese Renaissance: Liberalism in the Chinese Revolution, 1917–1937* (Cambridge: Harvard University Press, 1970), pp. 332–341.

3. Robert A Scalapino, *Democracy and the Party Movement in Prewar Japan: The Failure of the First Attempt* (Berkeley: University of California Press, 1953), Chap. 2 and pp. 397–398. Cf. Theodore H. von Laue, *The Global City: Freedom, Power and Necessity in the Age of World Revolutions* (Philadelphia: Lippincott, 1969), Chap. 8, esp. pp. 234–235. Barrington Moore, Jr.'s elaborate analysis of indigenous social, economic, and cultural factors in conjunction with the changing global contexts straddles the categories suggested here. He identifies the "crucial" Western feudal legacy as peculiarly favorable to the later development of democracy, stresses the particular interrelations between aristocracy, bourgeoisie, monarchy, and peasants/workers in any given case, and suggests that societies that enter "the modern world" late are at a disadvantage in developing democracy. While he seems to have underestimated the importance of foreign threats and was unable, for lack of adequate sources, to treat the 1911 Revolution seriously, his analytical framework is quite useful and finds echoes in some of the concluding ideas of this essay. See *Social Origins of Dictatorship and Democracy: Lord and Peasant in the Making of the Modern World* (Boston: Beacon Press, 1966), esp. Chap. 7.

4. *In Search of Wealth and Power: Yen Fu and the West* (Cambridge: Harvard University Press, 1964), p. 240.

5. Benjamin Schwartz, "Ch'en Tu-hsiu and the Acceptance of the Modern West," *Journal of the History of Ideas* 12.1:61–74 (January 1951). Lloyd Eastman, "Political Reformism in China before the Sino-Japanese War," *Journal of Asian Studies* 27.4:695–710 (August 1968).

6. Hao Chang, *Liang Ch'i-ch'ao and Intellectual Transition in Modern China* (Cambridge: Harvard University Press, 1971).

7. Lucien W. Pye, *The Spirit of Chinese Politics: A Psychocultural Study of the Authority Crisis in Political Development* (Cambridge: M.I.T. Press, 1968). Richard Solomon, *Mao's Revolution and the Chinese Political Culture* (Berkeley: University of California Press, 1971), esp. Chap. 9. Cf. Richard W. Wilson, *Learning to Be Chinese: The Political Socialization of Children in Taiwan* (Cambridge: M.I.T. Press, 1970).

8. Andrew J. Nathan, *Peking Politics, 1918–1923* (Berkeley: University of California Press, 1976), pp. 27–28, 44–55, 58.

9. John H. Fincher, *Chinese Democracy: The Self-Government Movement in Local, Provincial and National Politics, 1905–1914* (New York: St. Martin's Press, 1981), Chap. 1.

10. Ernest P. Young, *The Presidency of Yuan Shih-k'ai: Liberalism and Dictatorship in Early Republican China* (Ann Arbor: University of Michigan Press, 1977), p. 76.

11. Michael Gasster, *Chinese Intellectuals and the Revolution of 1911* (Seattle: University of Washington Press, 1969), pp. 125, 133n63.

12. The tension between monarchy and bureaucracy was cogently outlined by the Legalist philosopher Han Feizi (third century B.C.), and was a major component

of the political history of the former Han Dynasty (206 B.C.–A.D. 7). The system of "avoidance" (*huibi*) and the Qing institutions of governors-general, joint Han-Manchu board presidencies, the Grand Council and secret memorials were designed to preserve imperial control of a bureaucracy which had at times proven quite refractory.

13. Fincher, pp. 71–80.

14. Ibid., p. 173 n. 47, and Ming-Qing Archives, Palace Museum (Beijing), ed., *Qingmo choubei lixian dangan shiliao*, 2 vols. (Archival materials of the preparations for constitutional government at the end of the Qing dynasty; Beijing, 1979; hereafter *QMCBLX*), I, 547.

15. Fincher, pp. 173–175. *QMCBLX*, I, 558–565.

16. Mary Backus Rankin, *Elite Activism and Political Transformation in China: Zhejiang Province, 1865–1911* (Stanford: Stanford University Press, 1986), pp. 278–279, 295.

17. Fincher, p. 173.

18. Rankin, pp. 277–278.

19. "Lun jinri zhengfu zhi daoxing nishi" (On the perverse policy measures of the present government), *Minli bao* (hereafter *MLB*) 5–11 June, 1911; Chen Xulu ed., *Song Jiaoren ji* (Collected works of Song Jiaoren; Beijing, 1981; hereafter *Ji*), pp. 216–219. Song was, of course, well aware that the Meiji constitution made ministers responsible to the Emperor, but claimed that the Japanese cabinet system itself was incoherent.

20. Qiutong, "Lun qixing neige," *Diguo ribao* (hereafter *DGRB*) 20, 21, 22 May, 1911. Here Zhang echoed the general consensus regarding the Cabinet's unifying and policymaking function, reflected also in the Constitutional Commission's imperially endorsed plan of 8 May. See *QMCBLX*, I, 560. "The Freak Cabinet" was written before news of the 8 May cabinet reached him, but his subsequent criticisms of it reiterated this attack on its more unwieldy predecessor. All of Zhang's articles cited here are signed with the pen name Qiutong, which I omit in subsequent footnotes.

21. "Cabinet" is here used to translate the venerable term *neige*. The Qing dynasty institution of that name is generally referred to in English as the Grand Secretariat. Undergoing some changes, it survived until the inauguration of the new Cabinet in 1911.

22. "Wen hezhong zhengfu shi neng caozong yihui?" (What kind of government does it take to control parliament?), *DGRB*, 1 May 1911.

23. "Zhengdang zhengzhi guo shi yu jinri zhi Zhongguo hu?" (Is party government really suited to present-day China?), *DGRB*, 29 May 1911. Cf. "Russia and China," *Times*, 16 March 1911.

24. "Zhongguo ying ji zuzhi zhi zhengdang, qi xingzhi dang ruhe?" (What kind of political parties should be organized in China at present?), *DGRB*, 13 March 1911, and "Lun zizhengyuan yiyuan dang cai zhengdang bule zhi fa" (On the

way in which the National Assemblymen should divide themselves into parties), *DGRB*, 17 March 1911.

25. Albert Venn Dicey, *Introduction to the Study of the Law of the Constitution*, 7th ed. (London: MacMillan, 1908), pp. 400–405.

26. "Zhengdang neige guo you yu feizhengdang neige hu?" (Is party government really superior to non-party government?), *DGRB*, 20 August 1911.

27. Ibid., 18 August 1911.

28. This is not to say that all revolutionaries favored a constitutional republic; Zhang Taiyan was opposed to representative governments, and some revolutionaries were anarchists. But the Tongmeng Hui program envisioned a representative system, and most revolutionaries rallied behind a constitution that would insure such a system.

29. "Zhengdang zhengzhi guo shi yu jinri zhi Zhongguo hu?" 29 May, 1911.

30. "He wei bu chu daiyishi bu na zushui?" (What is no taxation without representation?), *DGRB*, 22, 23 October 1910.

31. "Yanlun ziyou yu baolü" (Freedom of speech and the journalism law), *DGRB*, 11 January 1911.

32. Ibid., 12 January. Zhang's concern was not unfounded, as Yan Xishan's later efforts to monitor his citizens' private affairs, even without the formality of licenses, was to show. Cf. Donald G. Gillin, *Warlord: Yen Hsi-shan in Shansi Province, 1911–1949* (Princeton: Princeton University Press, 1967), p. 35.

33. "Gao daibiao tuan" (To the [provincial] assemblymen's delegation), *DGRB*, 28 October 1911.

34. "Qing taihou zhi xianzheng tan" (The Qing empress dowager's discussion of constitutional government), *Xing shi* 1, in *Ji*, pp. 16–18. *Wo zhi lishi* (My history), in *ibid.*, pp. 687, 691.

35. Don C. Price, "Geming yu xianfa: Song Jiaoren zhengzhi celüe di fazhan" (Revolution and constitution: The development of Song Jiaoren's political strategy), in Zhonghua shuju ed., *Jinian xinhai geming qishi zhou nian xueshu taolun hui lunwen ji*, 3 vols. (Papers from the conference commemorating the 70th anniversary of the 1911 Revolution; Beijing, 1983), III, 2621–2622.

36. "Qinding xianfa wenti" (The problem of an imperially granted constitution) and "Riben neige gengdie gan yan" (Thoughts on the change of the Japanese cabinet), *MLB*, 11 February and 5 September, 1911; *Ji*, pp. 153, 305–307.

37. "Xianzheng meng ke xing yi" (Wake up from the dream of constitutional government), *MLB*, 25 March, 1911.

38. After graduating in political science from the Imperial University, Kobayashi worked in the Treasury and taught at Meiji University. He published *Hikaku zaiseigaku* (Comparative public finance) in 1905, won a Doctorate in Law at the Imperial University in 1907, and was in the same year made Chief of the Department of Finance in the Taiwan Colonial Administration, in which capacity he served until his retirement from the civil service in 1910. For some of the above

data I am indebted to Mr. Kubo Tōru, who drew my attention to "Chihō zaisei ron no meicho" (A classic in local finance theory), *Chihō jiji shokuin kenkyū* (Studies in local self-government personnel) 1981.9:82–84.

39. *Bijiao caizhengxue* (Tokyo, 1910; reprint Tokyo 1917), II, 436, 441, 443, 445, 447, 449, 463–468. I have not been able to find the Japanese original of this work.

40. See, for example, "*Minbao* yu *Xinmin congbao* bianbo zhi gangling" (Outlines of the debate between the *Minbao* and the *Xinmin congbao*), *Minbao* 3 supplement (*hao wai*; Beijing photographic reprint, 1957).

41. *Bijiao caizhengxue*, II, 302–307.

42. Ibid., II, 302–303, 308–323.

43. "Zai lun zhengfu jie Riben zhai shi zhao yuan" (More on the government's contracting a ten-million-*yuan* debt from Japan), *MLB*, 11 April 1911; *Ji*, p. 214; and "Riben neige gengdie gan yan."

44. *Bijiao caizhengxue*, II, 242, 306–308, 445, 465–466, 477, 495–500, 614–615.

45. Zhang Shizhao, "Yu Huang Keqiang xiang jiao shimo" (A complete account of my acquaintance with Huang Xing), *Xinhai geming huiyi lu* (Beijing, 1962), II, 142. It should be noted that Zhang Shizhao's articles were hardly Song's only source of information on English government, but in view of the attention Song paid to them, it seems likely that no other source had so prepared him to view England as a model. Kobayashi's treatment of England, in particular, did not discuss the advantages of the unity of executive and legislative, drew attention to Parliament's lack of regular annual review of the fixed budget (II, 245–246, 302–303), and suggested that legislative control of the purse represented a victory for the English nobility (II, 455). Such aspects of the English system would naturally have been severe drawbacks in the eyes of a democrat. In his article on the parliamentary reform of 1911, discussed below, Song himself summed up the popular image, which he shared, of England as a hitherto conservative and aristocratic country. It was the attention Zhang drew to the trend toward democratization in England that seems suddenly to have cast that country in an altogether new light, as a way out of the apparent contradiction between democracy and strength.

46. "Zhengdang neige guo you yu feizhengdang neige hu?", *DGRB*, 19 August, 1911. In casting parliament as defender of the taxpayer, Zhang's translation distorted Bagehot's position, but not seriously. See Bagehot's *The English Constitution* (Garden City: Doubleday, 1961), pp. 69, 73–74, 176–177.

47. "He wei bu chu daiyishi bu na shui" and "Gao daibiao tuan," *DGRB*, 22–23, 27–28 October 1910.

48. *Bijiao caizhengxue*, II, 296, 302–303.

49. "Guohui wanneng shuo" (The doctrine of the omnipotence of parliament) *DGRB*, 18, 19, 20 January 1911.

50. "Lun Zhongguo zhengdang zhengzhi dang yingshi fasheng" (It is time for party government to appear in China), *DGRB*, 26, 27 February 1911.

51. "Zhongguo ying ji zuzhi zhi zhengdang qi xingzhi dang ruhe?" "Lun zheng-dang zhi zuoyong ji qi jinxing zhi fa" (On the functions of political parties and how they should be carried out), and "Lun zizhengyuan yiyuan dang cai zheng-dang bule zhi fa," *DGRB*, 12–13, 17–18, 19–21 March 1911.

52. "He wei neige?" (What is a cabinet?), "He wei zhengdang neige" (What is a party cabinet?), "Zhengdang neige yu feizhengdang neige zhi bie" (The differ-ence between a party cabinet and a non-party cabinet), and "Zhengdang neige guo you yu feizhengdang neige hu?" *DGRB*, 11 June, 12–13 June, 15–17 August, 18–20 August 1911.

53. "Lun jinri zhengfu zhi daoxing nishi," p. 222.

54. While Zhang had urged the unification of parliament and executive for national strength in several articles in May 1911, especially "Zhengdang zhengzhi guo shi yu jinri zhi Zhongguo hu?" (29 May), his clearest exposition of the relations between parliament, party, cabinet, and finance in England and other countries began with the article "He wei neige" (11 June).

55. "Yingguo zhengzheng ji" (Account of the political struggle in England) ran intermittently through February in the *Imperial Daily*.

56. "Yingguo zhi guohui geming," *MLB*, 30–31 August 1911; *Ji*, pp. 298–303.

57. "Yingguo xin zongxuanju laodong dang zhi jinbu" (The gains of the Labor Party in England's new general elections) *Min bao* 3: *Shiping* 6–11. See Martin Bernal, *Chinese Socialism to 1907* (Ithaca: Cornell University Press, 1976), p. 120.

58. "Zhonghua minguo Yuezhou yuefa ji guanzhi caoan" (Draft provisional consti-tution and administrative regulations of Hubei, Republic of China), in *Ji*, pp. 350–364.

59. Matsumoto Hideki makes a very strong case that this provisional constitution was essentially Song's work and reflected Song's short-term political strategy, which envisioned the replacement of Li Yuanhong by Huang Xing as military governor. See his "Chūkaminkoku rinji yakuhō no seiritsu to Sō Kyōjin" (The establishment of the provisional constitution of the Republic of China and Song Jiaoren), *Ritsumeikan shigaku* (1981), II, 47–49.

60. Matsumoto, passim, and Zhang Guofu, "Guanyu 'Zhonghua minguo linshi yuefa' di qicao riqi he zhugao ren wenti" (On the question of dates of the draft-ing of the Provisional Constitution of the Republic of China and the identity of the drafter/s), *Beijing daxue xuebao* 1984.1:89–92. On the resentments and sus-picions that Song provoked in the course of his efforts to promote the cabinet system of government, see K. S. Liew, *Struggle for Democracy: Sung Chiao-jen and the 1911 Chinese Revolution* (Berkeley: University of California Press, 1971), pp. 130–141.

61. Sun's position can in part be explained by the fact that Yuan and the revolution-

aries remained at odds on the terms of the transfer of the presidency and that Sun felt he could secure the strongest position for the republican forces if he had a free hand in leading them. On the other hand, the subsequent history of his relations with Yuan suggests that he was inclined in principle to favor a strong presidency. See below.

62. Song's authorship of the Provisional Constitution of 8 March, long a matter of disagreement, has most recently been attacked by Zhang Guofu (see above, n 60). While Zhang demonstrates convincingly that Song's draft was initially rejected, and that he did not participate directly in the work of the committees that produced the later drafts, the essential provisions of the final product were in fact very close to those of Song's initial draft, and he appears to have been their most powerful advocate. See Matsumoto, p. 62–64, and Chen Ruxuan, *Zhongguo xianfa shi* (Chinese constitutional history; Taiwan reprint of 1947 rev. ed.), pp. 34–36. While a detailed comparison of Song's draft and the Provisional Constitution is beyond the scope of this paper, it must be pointed out that neither incorporated such integral features of the English system as the vote of no confidence or dissolution of parliament; and that, on the other hand, both provided for a strictly temporary system pending election within a year of a parliament empowered to adopt a regular constitution. See Chen Ruxuan, Appendix I, and Hunan sheng Taoyuan xian zhengxie weiyuanhui (Chinese People's Political Consultative Conference, Taoyuan, Hunan, County Committee) ed., *Song Jiaoren jinian zhuanji* (Commemorative collection on Song Jiaoren; Taoyuan, 1987), pp. 273–279.

63. Zhu Zongzhen and Yang Guanghui eds., *Minchu zhengzheng yu erci geming*, 2 vols., (Political struggles in the early republic and the second revolution; Shanghai, 1983), I, 54–55.

64. "Daicao Guomindang zhi da zhengjian" (Draft of major political positions for the Nationalist Party), pp. 3–5, in Ye Chucang ed., *Song Yufu* (Shanghai, 1913; Taiwan photographic reprint, 1963).

65. *The American Commonwealth*, 2 vols., 2nd ed., revised (London and New York: Macmillan, 1890), I, 110–111, 169.

66. Ibid., I, 224, 289–290.

67. *Zhongguo liguo da fangzhen shangjue shu* (Shanghai, 1912), p. 22.

68. Ibid., pp. 44–47.

69. Ibid., pp. 51–57.

70. Ibid., pp. 27–28, 41–43.

71. Wu Xiangxiang, *Song Jiaoren: Zhongguo minzhu xianzheng di xianqu* (Song Jiaoren: Pioneer for democratic constitutional government in China; Taibei, 1964), pp. 165–166.

72. *Zhongguo liguo da fangzhen shangjue shu*, pp. 77–78.

73. Don K. Price, *America's Unwritten Constitution* (Baton Rouge: Louisiana State University Press, 1983), pp. 6–7. Cf. Donald L. Robinson, ed., *Reforming Amer-*

ican Government: The Bicentennial Papers of the Committee on the Constitutional System (Boulder: Westview Press, 1985), esp. the Introduction to Part 3, "Reducing the Risk of Divided Government"; and Lloyd N. Cutler, "Modern European Constitutions and their Relevance in the American Context," pp. 127–130, 299–312.

74. Hu Shengwu and Jin Chongji, "Cong Nanjing linshi zhengfu dao erci geming (shang)" (From the Nanking provisional government to the second revolution [part 1]), *Lishi luncong* (Qilu shushe, 1983), III, 53, 66–70.

75. Lin Zengping, "Gemingpai, gailiangpai di lihe yu Qingmo minchu zhengju" (Estrangement and rapprochement between revolutionaries and reformers and the political scene at the end of the Qing and beginning of the Republic), *Lishi yanjiu* 1986.3 (181):76–89 (June 1986).

76. Although Sun Yat-sen had recommended Yuan's continuing in office, and the Guomindang governing committee endorsed this recommendation in January 1913, it was clear that a vote for the Guomindang was a vote to curb Yuan's power.

77. On the dangers of a large peasantry and a predominantly agrarian society to the development of democracy, see Moore, pp. 429–431, 437–438. For an interpretation of the 1911 Revolution according to which the elites were far less concerned with wielding power than with establishing a strong state which would protect them against the lower orders, see Joseph Esherick, *Reform and Revolution in China: The 1911 Revolution in Hunan and Hubei* (Berkeley: University of California Press, 1976).

78. Lin Zengping, "Qingmo minchu zhengju."

79. Nathan, *Chinese Democracy*, pp. 49–51, 111–112, 120–122, 127–129, 231–232.

80. Even the independence of the judiciary in England was the fruit of seventeenth-century battles, and rested on Parliament's recognition that its own sovereignty was secured by judicial independence. As Dicey observed, "Parliamentary care for judicial independence has ... stopped just at that point where on *a priori* grounds it might be expected to end. The judges are not in strictness irremovable; they can be removed from office on an address of the two Houses; they have been made by Parliament independent of every power in the State except the Houses of Parliament," p. 405; cf. pp. 152, 223–224.

81. For a sample of present-day American disillusionment with the high-handed English civil service see Marilynne Robinson, "Bad News from Britain," *Harper's* 270.1617:65–72 (February 1985). For current British and American commentary on freedom of speech and the press in England, and the differences between England and America in this regard, see Peter Jenkins, "Not-so Free Speech in Britain," *New York Review of Books* (8 December, 1988), pp. 17–23, and James Atlas, "Thatcher Puts a Lid On: Censorship in Britain," *The New York Times Magazine* (5 March, 1989), pp. 37–8, 97.

82. *Introduction*, p. civ.

83. Norman Gash, "Parliament and Democracy in Britain: The Three Nineteenth-Century Reform Acts," in *Pillars of Government and Other Essays in State and Society, c. 1770–c. 1880* (London: E. Arnold, 1986), p. 55.

84. Richard A. Cosgrove, *The Rule of Law: Albert Venn Dicey, Victorian Jurist* (Chapel Hill: University of North Carolina Press, 1980), p. 123.

85. Here I do not refer to John Stuart Mill, whom Yan Fu admired and misinterpreted. But even though Mill rejected traditional elitism, he remained a political elitist on rational grounds. See *Considerations on Representative Government* (New York: Liberal Arts Press, 1958), pp. 131–137. On the enormously complex relation between political democracy, utility, rights, and elitism among proponents of universal suffrage in England, see Elie Halévy, *The Growth of Philosophic Radicalism* tr. Mary Morris (Boston: Beacon Press, 1955), pp. 428, 506–507, and passim.

86. And especially that of a post-revolutionary China. Bagehot, pp. 59, 275–291. Apropos the uncertain performance of the French version, Bagehot observes "how difficult it is for inexperienced mankind to take to such a government," pp. 43–45.

87. Bagehot, pp. 181–182, 196–197; Dicey, *Introduction*, pp. c–ci; Cosgrove, p. 235.

88. Bagehot, pp. 252, 254.

89. Ibid., p. 305.

90. Ibid., p. 71.

91. Dicey, Chap. 5. Cosgrove, pp. 116, 123.

92. Bagehot, pp. 38–39, 84–85.

93. Ibid., pp. 195–196.

94. Dicey, *Introduction* (8th ed., 1915), pp. xli and (quoting Bagehot), civ.

95. Bagehot, pp. 184–185, 201, 106.

96. Ibid., pp. 201, 21, 13–14. For his comparison of the stratified English society with the more egalitarian and universally educated colonies and the United States, and the governments appropriate to each, see his Chap. 8.

97. This despite the fact that Dicey held that "the rules which in foreign countries naturally form part of a constitutional code are not the source but the consequence of the rights of individuals," for, as he went on to explain, the rights were defined by "the actions of the courts and Parliament." (pp. 202–203). For Dicey, the guarantee of freedom lay in the rule of law, which restricted discretionary government authority, and in the opinions of juries. See Cosgrove, pp. 78–82.

98. At this point it may occur to the reader (if it has not before) that such democracy as America enjoys also emerged out of a history of slavery, restricted white male suffrage, and the poll tax. Not only that, the early United States were not severally bound by the Bill of Rights, and as colonies had shared conceptions of the "rights of Englishmen" which did not rule out legal prohibitions against, and punishments for, failure to attend church, playing shuffleboard, or scolding

a husband. See Forrest McDonald, *Novus Ordo Seclorum: The Intellectual Origins of the Constitution* (Lawrence: Univerity of Kansas Press, 1985), pp. 20, 288. One difference with England, however, is that universal civil and political rights were enunciated in the American Revolution, and later invoked to justify the extension of freedom and democracy. More detailed comparisons of the English and American experience as they bear on the Chinese case will have to await further treatment elsewhere.

99. Bagehot, p. 304.

100. For a conservative monarchism which nevertheless rooted the king's position and powers in "the common agreement and original compact of the state . . . equally binding on king and people," see Edmund Burke, *Reflections on the French Revolution* (New York: Liberal Arts Press, 1955), p. 23. There is a profound difference between the withdrawal of the Mandate of Heaven, which for Mencius is reflected in a successful rebellion, and Parliament's legal manipulation of the royal succession as Burke understood it. For a recent Chinese effort to draw parallels between early Chinese and English views of the law's supremacy over the king, see Ma Keyao, "Zhong-Ying xianfashi shang di yige gongtong wenti" (A common question in the constitutional histories of China and England), *Lishi yanjiu* 1986.4(182):171–182 (August 1986). While Ma finds no more than a difference in degree and form between the authority of law in the early English and Chinese traditions, he does not find anything quite like the early English kings' dependency on a parliament for legislation, including taxation.

101. Bagehot, pp. 305–306.

102. Ibid., pp. 130–135, 302–303.

103. Chen Zhirang, "Hongxian dizhi di yixie wenti" (Some questions regarding the Hongxian reign), Institute of Modern History, Academia Sinica, ed., *Zhonghua minguo chuqi lishi yantao hui lunwen ji, 1912–1927*, 3 vols. (Taibei, 1984), I, 5–30.

9. Continuities between Modern and Premodern China: Some Neglected Methodological and Substantive Issues, by Thomas A. Metzger

1. Cited in Talcott Parsons et al., eds., *Theories of Society*, 2 vols. (New York: The Free Press of Glencoe, Inc., 1961), I, 214, 217.

2. On Weber's view of China, see Thomas A. Metzger, "Max Weber's Analysis of the Confucian Tradition: A Critique," *The American Asian Review* 2.1:28–70 (Spring 1984); also in Wolfgang Schluchter, ed., *Max Webers Studie über Konfuzianismus und Taoismus* (Frankfurt am Main: Suhrkamp, 1983), pp. 229–270.

3. Edwin A. Burtt, ed., *The English Philosophers from Bacon to Mill* (New York: The Modern Library, 1939), p. 949.

4. Ibid., pp. 993, 1005.

5. Benjamin I. Schwartz, *The World of Thought in Ancient China* (Cambridge: Harvard University Press, 1985), pp. 74, 68, 150. This summary of his position is also based on a paper (unpublished, so far as I know) which he kindly sent me in 1988, and which includes points replying to some in my review of his book above. The review is "The Definition of the Self, the Group, the Cosmos, and Knowledge in Chou Thought: Some Comments on Professor Schwartz's Study," *The American Asian Review* 4.2:68–116 (Summer 1986). I tried to reply in detail to Professor Schwartz's 1988 paper in my "Confucian Thought and the Modern Chinese Quest for Moral Autonomy," *Renwen ji shehui kexue jikan* 1.1:297–358 (November 1988).

6. Yang Guoshu, *Zhongguorende shuibian* (The metamorphosis of the Chinese; Taibei: Guiguan tushu gufen gongsi, 1988).

7. Tang Junyi, *Zhongguo wenhuazhi jingshen jiazhi* (The spiritual value of Chinese culture; Taibei: Zhengzhong shuju, 1972), pp. 153–154, preface, p. 2. An outline of this book's position is in Thomas A. Metzger, *Escape from Predicament* (New York: Columbia University Press, 1977), Chap. 2. Ying-shih Yü's book here referred to is *Cong jiazhi xitong kan Zhongguo wenhuade xiandai yiyi* (The modern relevance of Chinese culture: A discussion from the standpoint of the traditional value system; Taibei: Zhongguo shibao chuban shiye gongsi, 1984). On Feng Youlan, see the article by Liu Shuxian in *Dangdai* 35:54–64 (March 1989).

8. See my articles referred to in note 5 above.

9. This distinction is made in Uwe P. Gielen, Emily Miao, and Joseph Avellani, "Perceived Parental Behavior and the Development of Moral Reasoning in Students from Taiwan" (unpublished), p. 23. See also Metzger, *Escape*, pp. 42–45. See also Steven Lukes, *Individualism* (New York: Harper and Row, 1973). The remark by Weber is in Max Weber, *The Religion of China* tr. Hans. H. Gerth (Glencoe: The Free Press, 1951), p. 235.

10. Thomas A. Metzger, "Some Ancient Roots of Modern Chinese Thought: Thisworldliness, Epistemological Optimism, Doctrinality, and the Emergence of Reflexivity in the Eastern Chou," *Early China* 11–12:61–117 (1985–1987).

11. John Dunn, *Rethinking Modern Political Theory: Essays 1979–1983* (Cambridge: Cambridge University Press, 1985), pp. 140–141.

12. Yang Guoshu and Wen Chongyi, eds., *Shehui ji xingwei kexuede Zhongguohua* (The Sinification of research in the social and behavioral sciences; Taibei: Institute of Ethnology, Academia Sinica, Monograph Series B, No. 10, 1982).

13. Alasdair MacIntyre, *After Virtue* (Notre Dame: University of Notre Dame Press, 1981), p. 38. For the centrality of this knowledge problem and other work on it, see Dunn, pp. 141–142.

14. For a comparative analysis of the four leading contemporary Chinese ideological trends, see Thomas A. Metzger, "Developmental Criteria and Indigenously Conceptualized Options: A Normative Approach to China's Modernization in

Recent Times," _Issues & Studies_ 23:2:19–81 (February 1987). Also in Yu-ming Shaw, ed., _Changes and Continuities in Chinese Communism—Vol. 1—Ideology, Politics, and Foreign Policy_ (Boulder: Westview Press, 1988), pp. 36–85.

15. Yang Guoshu, _Shuibian_, p. 407. This sums up the first five of his categories. The last two are basic to his thinking as a whole, including his more political essays in collections such as his _Kaifangde duoyuan shehui_ (The open, pluralistic society; Taibei: Dongda tushu youxian gongsi, 1982).

16. See Yang Guoshu, _Shuibian_, pp. i–iv for Yang's vision of the current mission of Chinese intellectuals in clearing up the confused thinking of most Chinese at this current stage of their history.

17. Yang Guoshu, _Shuibian_, p. 228. For his argument in the opening part of _Kaifangde duoyuan shehui_ (e.g., p. 28) that increasing freedom in Taiwan is bound to enhance moral-political consensus throughout the society, see Mozike (Thomas A. Metzger), "Cong Yuehan Mier minzhu lilun kan Taiwan zhengzhi yanlun" (Political thought in Taiwan: A discussion from the standpoint of J. S. Mill's theory of democracy," _Dangdai_ 24:83–84 (1 April 1988).

18. See "Liang'an xuezhe tan Zhongguo wenhua (Scholars from both sides of the Straits discuss Chinese culture." A photographic copy of this article was generously sent me by Dr. Richard Wang. Originally printed in the leading Taibei periodical _Zhongguo luntan_ around late November, 1988.

19. Neo-Confucianism's preoccupation with conceptualizing and realizing certain key linkages in order to bring about the harmonious wholeness of all existence is discussed in my _Escape_, pp. 70–77.

20. Hu Qiuyuan, _Yibainianlai Zhongguo sixiangshigang_ (An outline history of Chinese thought during the last 130 years; Taibei: Xuesheng shuju, 1980), p. 217.

21. See article cited in note 18 above.

22. Li Zonggui, _Zhongguo wenhua gailun_ (An outline of Chinese culture; Canton: Zhongshan daxue chubanshe, 1988), prefaces, p. 7. Professor Tu's book was published in 1989 by Lianjing chupan shiye gongsi in Taibei.

23. Professor William Tay was kind enough to bring these three articles to my attention. They are all in the _Renjian fukan_ section of _Zhongguo shibao_, 14, 15, 16, July 1988. See also Lao Siguang, _Zhongguozhi luxiang_ (The direction of China's development; Hong Kong: Shangzhi chubanshe, 1981). Because of lack of space, I must here omit my attempt to describe and critique in detail Professor Lao's views about Chinese modernization.

24. Metzger, "Developmental Options," pp. 37–44.

25. Yang Guoshu, _Kaifangde duoyuan shehui_, p. 3.

26. On how much political thought in Taiwan has adopted extremely ambitious if not utopian criteria of successful modernization, see my article cited in note 17 above and my "Lun ziyi jingshen yu pinggu zhengzhide biaozhun" (On the spirit of self-doubt and the criteria of political success), _Dangdai_ 35:141–148 (1 March 1989). For a discussion of Chinese modernization explicitly using mod-

est criteria of successful modernization frequently used in Western and Chinese academic circles, see the three articles respectively by Alan P. L. Liu, Thomas A. Metzger, and Ramon H. Myers in "Chinese Modernization and the Methodology of Evaluation," a "special issue" of *Issues & Studies* 23.2 (February 1987).

27. John A. Hall, *Powers and Liberties: The Causes and Consequences of the Rise of the West* (Oxford: Basil Blackwell, 1985). The prevalence of the purely descriptive approach to culture in the West is illustrated by the refutation of it set forth by the psychologist Lawrence Kohlberg in his *The Philosophy of Moral Development* (New York: Harper & Row, 1981). More precisely, he attacks the theory of "the cultural relativity of ethics" to which this descriptive approach has widely led, adducing the belief of the American Anthropological Association around 1959 that "no technique of qualitatively evaluating cultures has been discovered." See ibid., pp. 105, 109. I am much indebted to Professor Uwe P. Gielen for guidance regarding these issues.

28. Tang Junyi, *Renwen Jingshenzhi chongjian* (The reconstruction of the humanistic spirit; Kowloon: Xinya yenjiousuo, 1955), pp. 269, 273.

29. See, e.g., Benjamin I. Schwartz, *In Search of Wealth and Power* (Cambridge: Harvard University Press, 1964); Hao Chang, *Liang Ch'i-ch'ao and Intellectual Transition in China, 1890–1907* (Cambridge: Harvard University Press, 1971); and Chu-yuan Cheng, ed., *Sun Yat-sen's Doctrine in the Modern World* (Boulder: Westview Press, 1989).

30. Li Zonggui, pp. 264, 217–272.

31. Professor Patricia Ebrey has argued that the Confucian classics, Neo-Confucianism, and the views of "classicists" like Sima Guang were out of accord with everyday Song attitudes legitimizing the efforts of families to increase their wealth by pursuing profits in the marketplace. Evidence that they were not out of accord with them was presented in a review article of mine and, in her reply, Professor Ebrey disputed neither my evidence nor my conclusion. For this debate, see *The American Asian Review* 4.1 (Spring 1986). Building on the magnificent articles of Fujii Hiroshi, Professor Ying-shih Yü has brilliantly shown how merchants in late imperial China used Confucian and Buddhist ideas to legitimize their commercial endeavors. See his "Rujia sixiang yu jingji fazhan: Zhongguo jinshi zongjiao lunli yu shangren jingshen" (Confucian thought and economic development: Religious ethics and the spirit of commerce in late Imperial China," *The Chinese Intellectual* 6:3–45 (Winter 1985). Complementing such merchant attitudes, a largely Confucian attitude prevalent in elite and bureaucratic circles approved of commerce, though ambivalently, according to the argument made in my "The State and Commerce in Imperial China," in *Asian and African Studies* (Annual of the Israel Oriental Society) 6:3–46 (1970). This argument is rather widely accepted today. See, e.g., Susan Mann, *Local Merchants and the Chinese Bureaucracy, 1750–1950* (Stanford: Stanford University Press, 1987), pp. 20, 220. The close fit between Confucian

culture and the ethics of free enterprise is emphasized by Professor John C. H. Fei, "The Chinese Market System in a Historical Perspective," in *The Second Conference on Modern Chinese Economic History,* 3 vols. (Taibei: The Institute of Economics, Academia Sinica, 1989), I, 31–57. Professor Fei, however, uses a normative concept of culture, viewing the "market system" as meeting basic societal needs, selecting out Chinese cultural traits according with the principles of the market, and ignoring as epiphenomenal those cultural traits out of accord with them.

32. Robert N. Bellah, Richard Madsen, William M. Sullivan, Ann Swidler, Steven M. Tipton, *Habits of the Heart* (Berkeley: University of California Press, 1985), p. 251.

33. See section on the Durkheimian Concern above.

34. On the structural significance of the PRC "line," see Ramon H. Myers, "Does the Chinese Communist Party Have a 'Line'?" *Issues & Studies* 23.12:120–138 (December 1987).

35. Ramon H. Myers, "Political Theory and Recent Political Developments in the Republic of China," *Asian Survey* 27.9:1003–1022.

36. Li Zonggui, p. 280.

37. For other reasons, see my articles cited in note 5 above.

38. Hao Chang, *Lieshi jingshen yu pipan yishi: Tan sitong sixiangde fenxi* (The spirit of heroism and radical criticism: An analysis of Tan Sitong's thought; Taibei: Lianjing chuban shiye gongsi, 1988). See also his *Chinese Intellectuals in Crisis* (Berkeley: University of California Press, 1987).

39. Wang Ermin, *Wan Qing zhengzhi sixiang shilun* (Historical essays on late-Qing political thought; Taibei: Huashi chubanshe, 1976), pp. 17–18.

40. For many of these points, see my *Early China* article cited in note 10 above.

41. Hao Chang, "You'an yishi yu minzhu chuantong (The democratic tradition and the consciousness of the dark side of life)," in Shao Yuming, ed., *Haineiwai zhishifenzi guoshi taolunji* (National affairs: A collection of writings and comments by intellectuals at home and abroad; Taibei: Published by Shao Yuming, 1983), pp. 417–436. Also in Hao Chang, *You'an yishi yu minzhu chuantong* (The democratic tradition and the consciousness of the dark side of life; Taibei: Liangjing chuban shiye gongsi, 1989), pp. 3–32. This important, now famous essay was first published in 1982 in *Zhongguo shibao.*

42. The rise of a new, very optimistic feeling about the imminence of great moral-political-economic progress in China occurred in the late nineteenth century, and this optimism has remained as a major characteristic of much Chinese political thought in the twentieth century. This point has been thoroughly documented now by various researchers coming upon it independently. The most substantial support for it is in Wang Ermin's seminal writings, *Wan Ching zhengzhi sixiang shilun* and *Zhongguo jindai sixiang shilun* (Historical studies on modern Chinese thought; Taibei: Huashi chubanshe, 1977). The same point is

strongly made also in Don C. Price, *Russia and the Roots of the Chinese Revolution, 1896–1911* (Cambridge: Harvard University Press, 1974) and in my *Escape*, Chap. 5, and it is supported by Wang Fansen, *Gushibian yundongde xingqi* (The rise of the movement to study the Chinese past critically; Taibei: Yunchen wenhua shiye gufen youxian gongsi, 1987). In his 1989 book cited in note 41 above, Professor Hao Chang sees a highly optimistic view of the polity as basic not only to contemporary Chinese thought (Marxist and non-Marxist) but also to the Confucian tradition. He does not raise the question of whether the modern optimism had any roots in the premodern. Yet he is not so far from my view that optimistic this-worldliness, like epistemological optimism and Professor Lin Yü-sheng's "intellectualism," were among the continuities bridging modern and premodern Chinese thought.

43. I have tried to discuss this question in "The Normative Way to Make Normative Statements: Some Reactions to Recent Kohlbergian Work on Chinese Moral Thinking," *The American Asian Review* (forthcoming).

44. For rich data on the Manichaean side of political conflict in the ROC, see Kuo Tai-chün and Ramon H. Myers, "The Great Transition: Political Change and the Prospects for Democracy in the Republic of China on Taiwan," *Asian Affairs* 15.3 (Fall 1988), esp. pp. 127–130. On the prevalent use in Taiwan of sublime criteria of political success, see my articles listed in notes 17 and 26 above.

45. Ying-shih Yü, *Cong jiazhi xitong*, p. 16.

46. The thesis in *Habits of the Heart* is partly outlined in my *Issues & Studies* article cited in note 14 above. For an attempt to sum up S. N. Eisenstadt's thesis of the axial age and his way of applying this thesis to the Chinese case, as well as bibliographical references, see my "Eisenstadt's Analysis of the Relations between Modernization and Tradition in China," *The American Asian Review* 2.2:1–87 (Summer 1984).

10. The Place of Values in Cross-Cultural Studies: The Example of Democracy and China, by Andrew J. Nathan

For comments on earlier drafts of this paper I am grateful to the editors of this volume, to participants in the Modern China Seminar and the Comparative Politics Group at Columbia University, and to Lisa Anderson, Linda Gail Arrigo, Douglas A. Chalmers, Michael Gasster, James C. Hsiung, Peter Juviler, Anthony Kane, Terrill E. Lautz, Steven I. Levine, Thomas A. Metzger, Don K. Price, James D. Seymour, James N. C. Tu, Ned Walker, John R. Watt, C. Martin Wilbur, Roxane Witke, and Kenton Worcester.

1. See, among others, Giovanni Sartori, "Philosophy, Theory and Science of Politics," *Political Theory* 2:2:133–162 (May 1974); Richard J. Bernstein, *The Restructuring of Social and Political Theory*, paperback ed. (Philadelphia: University of Pennsylvania Press, 1978) and *Beyond Objectivism and Relativism: Science, Her-*

meneutics, and Praxis, paperback ed. (Philadelphia: University of Pennsylvania Press, 1983); Abraham Edel, *Science, Ideology, and Value* (New Brunswick: Transaction Books, 1979), I, 276–332 and II, 339–363; Norma Haan, Robert N. Bellah, Paul Rabinow, and William M. Sullivan, eds., *Social Science as Moral Inquiry* (New York: Columbia University Press, 1983); Duncan MacRae, Jr., *The Social Function of Social Science* (New Haven: Yale University Press, 1976), Chaps. 3–4; Frank Fischer, *Politics, Values, and Public Policy: The Problem of Methodology* (Boulder: Westview Press, 1980).

2. I have in mind works like Thomas A. Metzger's *Escape from Predicament* (New York: Columbia University Press, 1977) and Wm. Theodore de Bary's *New Confucian Orthodoxy and the Learning of the Mind-and-Heart* (New York: Columbia University Press, 1981). Authors who undertake such a project may have a passionate value agenda of their own, and it may be quite clear from their work, yet the works in question are essentially descriptive rather than advocatory or judgmental.

3. See David Bidney, "Culture: Cultural Relativism," in David L. Sills, ed., *International Encyclopedia of the Social Sciences* (New York: Macmillan, 1968), III, 543–547.

4. For example, Peter Winch, "Understanding a Primitive Society," in *Ethics and Action* (London: Routledge and Kegan Paul, 1972), pp. 8–49; Paul Rabinow and William M. Sullivan, eds., *Interpretive Social Science: A Reader* (Berkeley: University of California Press, 1979); Martin Hollis and Steven Lukes, eds., *Rationality and Relativism* (Oxford: Basil Blackwell, 1982); Gerald James Larson and Eliot Deutsch, eds., *Interpreting Across Boundaries: New Essays in Comparative Philosophy* (Princeton: Princeton University Press, 1988). An extreme position is that of Edward Said, *Orientalism* (New York: Pantheon, 1978), who argues that the difficulty of cross-cultural understanding is so great as to bring into question "whether there can be true representations of anything" (p. 272).

5. See, among others, Charles Taylor, "Interpretation and the Sciences of Man," in Rabinow and Sullivan, *Interpretive Social Science*, pp. 25–71; Alasdair MacIntyre, "Is a Science of Comparative Politics Possible?" in his *Against the Self-Images of the Age: Essays on Ideology and Philosophy* (Notre Dame: University of Notre Dame Press, 1978), pp. 260–279. Howard J. Wiarda's "Is Latin America Democratic and Does It Want To Be?" in Wiarda, ed., *The Continuing Struggle for Democracy in Latin America* (Boulder: Westview, 1980), pp. 3–24, illustrates the danger of confusing these two questions. He discusses the conceptual distortions that arise when Western-based concepts are carelessly used in the *analysis* of Latin American politics, but then slides, in my view illogically, to the conclusion that Western values should not be used to *evaluate* Latin American politics.

6. See Paul Rabinow, "Humanism as Nihilism: The Bracketing of Truth and Seri-

ousness in American Cultural Anthropology," in Haan, Bellah, Rabinow, and Sullivan, eds., *Social Science as Moral Inquiry*, pp. 52–75.

7. John K. Fairbank, *China: The People's Middle Kingdom and the U.S.A.* (Cambridge: Harvard University Press, 1967), p. 142.

8. "Our Chances in China," *The Atlantic Monthly*, September 1946, reprinted in *China Perceived: Images and Policies in Chinese-American Relations* (New York: Knopf, 1974), pp. 7, 9.

9. *Chinabound: A Fifty-Year Memoir* (New York: Harper and Row, 1982), pp. 317–318.

10. Bruce Douglass and Ross Terrill, eds., *China and Ourselves: Explorations and Revisions by a New Generation* (Boston: Beacon Press, 1971), p. xv.

11. Ross Terrill, ed., *The China Difference: A Portrait of Life Today Inside the Country of One Billion* (New York: Harper and Row, 1979), pp. 7–9.

12. Paul Hollander, *Political Pilgrims* (New York: Oxford University Press, 1981), Chap. 7. For debate over the relationship between China studies and politics, see Edward Friedman, "In Defense of China Studies," *Pacific Affairs* 55.2:353–366 (Summer 1982); Friedman, "Maoism and the Liberation of the Poor," *World Politics* 39.3:408–428 (April 1987); Harry Harding, "From China, With Disdain: New Trends in the Study of China," *Issues and Studies* 18.7:12–39 (July 1982); Sheila K. Johnson, "To China, With Love," *Commentary* 56.6:37–45 (June 1973); and Robert Marks, "The State of the China Field Or, The China Field and the State," *Modern China* 11.4:461–509 (October 1985).

13. The following paragraphs and some material elsewhere in the essay draw from my article "Meiguo dui Zhongguo de taidu" (America's attitude toward China), *Zhishi fenzi* (*The Chinese intellectual*) 1.3:11–12 (March 1985).

14. See, for example, Richard Bernstein, *From the Center of the Earth* (Boston: Little, Brown, 1982) and Fox Butterfield, *Alive in the Bitter Sea* (New York: Times Books, 1982).

15. A good example was the scholarly discovery at about the time that it was beginning to disappear of the extremely important, pervasive, and unattractive, but hitherto unknown *chengfen* (class-status) system. See Richard Curt Kraus, *Class Conflict in Chinese Socialism* (New York: Columbia University Press, 1981).

16. *The New York Times*, 24 February 1987, p. A7.

17. An exception is Merle Goldman, "The Persecution of China's Intellectuals: Why Didn't Their Western Colleagues Speak Out?" *Radcliffe Quarterly* (September 1981), pp. 12–14.

18. Such articles in economics are too many to cite. In political science, they include Michel C. Oksenberg, "Evaluating the Chinese Political System," *Contemporary China* 3.2:102–111 (Summer 1979); Alan P. L. Liu, "How Can We Evaluate Communist China's Political System Performance?" *Issues and Studies* 23.2:82–121 (February 1987); and Stephen C. Thomas, "Social and Economic

Rights Performance in Developing Countries: The People's Republic of China in Comparative Perspective," *Policy Studies Journal* 15.1:84–96 (September 1986).

19. I have explored some of these differences in *Chinese Democracy* (New York: Knopf, 1985) and in my contribution to R. Randle Edwards, Louis Henkin, and Andrew J. Nathan, *Human Rights in Contemporary China* (New York: Columbia University Press, 1986).

20. See, for example, the remarks of Carole Pateman, *Participation and Democratic Theory*, paperback ed. (Cambridge: Cambridge University Press, 1970), pp. 1–17.

21. See *Chinese Democracy*, Chaps. 3–6.

22. *Mao's China and After: A History of the People's Republic*, rev. and exp., paperback ed. (New York: Free Press, 1986).

23. Thomas A. Metzger, "Developmental Criteria and Indigenously Conceptualized Options: A Normative Approach to China's Modernization in Recent Times," *Issues and Studies* 23.2:19–81 (February 1987), quotation from p. 26.

24. Said, *Orientalism*, cited earlier. Although a 1980 *Journal of Asian Studies* symposium (39.3:485–517) respectfully reviewed the application of this concept to East Asian studies, Said himself exempts post-1960s East Asian studies from his charges (p. 301).

25. An example of this process is found in Howard J. Wiarda, "The Struggle for Democracy and Human Rights in Latin America: Toward a New Conceptualization," in Wiarda, ed., *The Continuing Struggle*, pp. 231–254. Here he redefines human rights and democracy to fit the theories of Latin American military and authoritarian elites (whom he identifies with "Latin American culture"). This enables him to reach a far more favorable evaluation of Latin American democracy, but with the result that dialogue on important issues is evaded rather than advanced. For a similar exercise with respect to the concept of "development," see Wiarda, "Toward a Nonethnocentric Theory of Development: Alternative Conceptions from the Third World," in Wiarda, ed., *New Directions in Comparative Politics* (Boulder: Westview, 1985), pp. 127–150.

26. Gerald James Larson, "Introduction: The Age-Old Distinction Between the Same and the Other," in Larson and Deutsch, eds., *Interpreting Across Boundaries*, p. 17.

27. Bernard Williams, "An Inconsistent Form of Relativism," reprinted from his *Morality: An Introduction to Ethics* (New York: Harper and Row, 1972), in Jack W. Meiland and Michael Krausz, eds., *Relativism: Cognitive and Moral* (Notre Dame: University of Notre Dame Press, 1982), p. 171–174; and Geoffrey Harrison, "Relativism and Tolerance," in Meiland and Krausz, p. 239.

28. Although Hume argued that ethical standards are merely likes and dislikes, he went on to show that these likes and dislikes are far from arbitrary, and almost by definition no serious ethical philosopher denies that values can be reasoned about. For recent works, see, e.g., Frank Fischer, *Politics, Values, and Public Pol-*

icy, Duncan MacRae, *The Social Function of Social Science*, and David B. Wong, *Moral Relativity* (Berkeley: University of California Press, 1984).

29. Paul W. Taylor, *Normative Discourse* (Englewood Cliffs: Prentice Hall, 1961).

30. A similar point is made by I. C. Jarvie, "Rationality and Relativism," *The British Journal of Sociology* 34.1:44–60 (March 1983).

31. Paperback ed., New York: Signet, 1967, p. 22; orig. published by McGraw-Hill, 1966.

32. *Experience Without Precedent: Some Quaker Observations on China Today*, Report of an American Friends Service Committee Delegation's Visit to China, May 1972 (Philadelphia: AFSC, 1972), p. 7.

33. Williams, "An Inconsistent Form of Relativism," in Meiland and Krausz, eds., *Relativism*, p. 173.

34. Ken Ling, *The Revenge of Heaven* (New York: Putnam, 1972).

35. Richard M. Pfeffer, "Serving the People and Continuing the Revolution," *The China Quarterly* 52:650 (October/December 1972).

36. Stephen Andors, *China's Industrial Revolution: Politics, Planning, and Management, 1949 to the Present* (New York: Pantheon, 1977), p. 242.

37. *Experience Without Precedent*, p. 52.

38. Cf. C. Martin Wilbur, "China and the Skeptical Eye," *Journal of Asian Studies* 31.4:761–768 (August 1972).

39. The Universal Declaration is systematically applied to China in James D. Seymor, *China Rights Annals, 1: Human Rights Developments in the People's Republic of China from October 1983 through September 1984* (Armonk: M. E. Sharpe, 1985).

40. Third ed., paperback (New York: Harper and Row, 1962.)

41. E.g., Pateman, *Participation and Democratic Theory*; Robert A. Dahl, *Dilemmas of Pluralist Democracy: Autonomy vs. Control*, paperback ed. (New Haven: Yale University Press, 1982); Benjamin Barber, *Strong Democracy: Participatory Politics for a New Age* (Berkeley: University of California Press, 1984).

42. For useful recent surveys of this vast topic, see Graeme Duncan, ed., *Democratic Theory and Practice*, paperback ed. (Cambridge: Cambridge University Press, 1983), and David Held, *Models of Democracy* (Stanford: Stanford University Press, 1987).

43. The case for this is too familiar to need repeating here. For classic statements, see Robert A. Dahl, *A Preface to Democratic Theory*, paperback ed. (Chicago: University of Chicago Press, 1963) and John Plamenatz, *Democracy and Illusion: An Examination of Certain Aspects of Modern Democratic Theory*, paperback ed. (London: Longman, 1977).

44. Metzger, "A Normative Approach," p. 45, points out that these thinkers did not advocate full-scale "American democracy." But he would presumably concede that what they advocated encompassed the three minimal conditions of Schumpeterian pluralism.

45. See Benedict Stavis, *China's Political Reforms: An Interim Report* (New York: Praeger, 1987), pp. 129–145; and Andrew J. Nathan, "Politics: Reform at the Crossroad," in Anthony J. Kane, ed., *China Briefing, 1989* (Boulder: Westview, 1989), pp. 7–25.

46. Peng Zhen, "Zai bufen Yan'an shidai wenyi laozhanshi zuotanhuishang de jianghua" (Talk at a forum of old literary warriors of the Yan'an era), *Renmin ribao, haiwaiban,* 16 May 1987, p. 4.

47. AP report in N.Y. *Zhongbao,* 29 May 1987, p. 1.

48. Zhao Ziyang, "Advance Along the Road of Socialism with Chinese Characteristics," *Beijing Review,* North Amer. ed., 30.45:37 (9–15 November 1987).

49. J. Roland Pennock, *Democratic Political Theory,* paperback ed. (Princeton: Princeton University Press, 1979), pp. 239–253.

50. See, e.g., Wm. Theodore de Bary, *The Liberal Tradition in China* (Hong Kong: Chinese University Press, 1983); Metzger, *Escape from Predicament*; Metzger, "A Normative Approach"; Hao Chang, *Liang Ch'i-ch'ao and Intellectual Transition in China, 1890–1907* (Cambridge: Harvard University Press, 1971); Benjamin A. Elman, *From Philosophy to Philology: Intellectual Aspects of Change in Late Imperial China* (Cambridge: Council on East Asian Studies, Harvard University, 1984); Merle Goldman, "Human Rights in the People's Republic of China", *Daedalus* 112.4:111–138 (Fall 1983); Vitaly A. Rubin, *Individual and State in Ancient China: Essays on Four Chinese Philosophers,* tr. Steven I. Levine (New York: Columbia University Press, 1976); Edwards, Henkin, and Nathan, *Human Rights.*

51. "Di'erzhong zhongcheng" (The second kind of loyalty), originally published in *Kaituo,* no date given, reprinted in *Zhengming* 96:48–61 (1 October 1985). Some other cases are described in *Chinese Democracy,* pp. 25–26.

52. Wei Jingsheng offered the former argument, but received little support for it even among the democratic activists. The latter argument was offered by Hu Ping, in a mimeographed essay that formed the basis of his 1980 people's congress campaign at Beijing University and which in July 1986 was published in *Qingnian luntan* (Wuhan). In the Anti-Bourgeois Liberalization Campaign of 1987, *Qingnian luntan* was closed.

53. Leszek Kolakowski, *Main Currents of Marxism,* P. S. Falla, tr., paperback ed., 3 vols. (Oxford: Oxford University Press, 1981) II, 49 and throughout.

54. *Chinese Democracy,* pp. 98–100. For Wang's unrepentant later views, see *Wei rendaozhuyi bianhu* (In defense of humanism; Beijing: Sanlian shudian, 1986).

55. *Zhongguo zhi chun* 42:33–35 (December 1986); 45:11–33 (March 1987); and 46:61–74 (April 1987); partial translations in *China Spring Digest* 1.2:12–38 (March/April 1987).

56. Yangsun Chou and Andrew J. Nathan, "Democratizing Transition in Taiwan," *Asian Survey* 27.3:277–299 (March 1987).

57. Reprinted in *Political Man: The Social Bases of Politics,* expanded and updated

ed., paperback (Baltimore: The Johns Hopkins University Press, 1981), pp. 27–63.

58. *Contemporary Democracies: Participation, Stability, and Violence*, paperback ed. (Cambridge: Harvard University Press, 1982), pp. 34–41.

59. See, for example, "Meiyou gaige jiu meiyou Zhongguo tese de shehuizhuyi" (Without reform there can be no Chinese-style socialism), *Renmin ribao, haiwaiban*, 5 June 1987, p. 2.

60. I am using the 1972 figures reproduced in Powell, *Contemporary Democracies*, p. 36, and also, for the purposes of illustration here, his list of what were at that time democratic regimes. And I am using the World Bank's evaluation of China's GNP per capita as standing at $300 in 1980 and aiming at $800 (in 1980 dollars) in 2000 in *China: Long-Term Development Issues and Options*, paperback ed. (Baltimore: The Johns Hopkins University Press, 1985), p. 21.

61. For the concept of civic culture, see Gabriel A. Almond and Sidney Verba, *The Civic Culture: Political Attitudes and Democracy in Five Nations*, abridged, paperback ed. (Boston: Little, Brown, 1965).

62. For an analysis of the possibilities for a democratic transition, see Andrew J. Nathan, *China's Crisis: Dilemmas of Reform and Prospects for Democracy* (New York: Columbia University Press, 1990), Chap. 12.

63. Karl Popper, "The Myth of the Framework," in Eugene Freeman, ed., *The Abdication of Philosophy: Philosophy and the Public Good* (LaSalle, Illinois: Open Court Publishing Company, 1976), p. 38.

64. K. R. Popper, *The Open Society and Its Enemies* (Princeton: Princeton University Press, 1963), II, 375.

65. *The World of Thought in Ancient China* (Cambridge: Harvard University Press, 1985), p. 14.

Index

Harvard East Asian Monographs

114. Joshua A. Fogel, *Politics and Sinology: The Case of Naitō Konan (1866–1934)*

115. Jeffrey C. Kinkley, ed., *After Mao: Chinese Literature and Society, 1978–1981*

116. C. Andrew Gerstle, *Circles of Fantasy: Convention in the Plays of Chikamatsu*

117. Andrew Gordon, *The Evolution of Labor Relations in Japan: Heavy Industry, 1853–1955*

118. Daniel K. Gardner, *Chu Hsi and the* Ta Hsueh: *Neo-Confucian Reflection on the Confucian Canon*

119. Christine Guth Kanda, *Shinzō: Hachiman Imagery and its Development*

120. Robert Borgen, *Sugawara no Michizane and the Early Heian Court*

121. Chang-tai Hung, *Going to the People: Chinese Intellectual and Folk Literature, 1918–1937*

122. Michael A. Cusumano, *The Japanese Automobile Industry: Technology and Management at Nissan and Toyota*

124. Steven D. Carter, *The Road to Komatsubara: A Classical Reading of the Renga Hyakuin*

125. Katherine F. Bruner, John K. Fairbank, and Richard T. Smith, *Entering China's Service: Robert Hart's Journals, 1854–1863*

126. Bob Tadashi Wakabayashi, *Anti-Foreignism and Western Learning in Early Modern Japan: The New Theses of 1825*

127. Atsuko Hirai, *Individualism and Socialism: The Life and Thought of Kawai Eijirō (1891–1944)*

128. Ellen Widmer, *The Margins of Utopia:* Shui-hu hou-chuan *and the Literature of Ming Loyalism*

129. R. Kent Guy, *The Emperor's Four Treasuries: Scholars and the State in the Late Ch'ien-lung Era*

130. Peter C. Perdue, *Exhausting the Earth: State and Peasant in Hunan, 1500–1850*

131. Susan Chan Egan, *A Latterday Confucian: Reminiscences of William Hung (1893–1980)*

132. James T. C. Liu, *China Turning Inward: Intellectual-Political Changes in the Early Twelfth Century*

133. Paul A. Cohen, *Between Tradition and Modernity: Wang T'ao and Reform in Late Ch'ing China*

134. Kate Wildman Nakai, *Shogunal Politics: Arai Hakuseki and the Premises of Tokugawa Rule*

135. Hans Ulrich Vogel, *Chinese Central Monetary Policy and Yunnan Copper Mining in the Early Qing (1644–1800)*

136. Jon L. Saari, *Legacies of Childhood: Growing Up Chinese in a Time of Crisis, 1890–1920*

137. Susan Downing Videen, *Tales of Heichū*

138. Heinz Morioka and Miyoko Sasaki, *Rakugo: The Popular Narrative Art of Japan*

139. Joshua A. Fogel, *Nakai Ushikichi in China: The Mourning of Spirit*

140. Alexander Barton Woodside, *Vietnam and the Chinese Model: A Comparative Study of Vietnamese and Chinese Government in the First Half of the Nineteenth Century*

141. George Elison, *Deus Destroyed: The Image of Christianity in Early Modern Japan*

142. William D. Wray, ed., *Managing Industrial Enterprise: Cases from Japan's Prewar Experience*

143. T'ung-tsu Ch'ü, *Local Government in China under the Ch'ing*

144. Marie Anchordoguy, *Computers Inc.: Japan's Challenge to IBM*

145. Barbara Molony, *Technology and Investment: The Prewar Japanese Chemical Industry*

146. Mary Elizabeth Berry, *Hideyoshi*

147. Laura E. Hein, *Fueling Growth: The Energy Revolution and Economic Policy in Postwar Japan*

148. Wen-hsin Yeh, *The Alienated Academy: Culture and Politics in Republican China, 1919–1937*